Best of the Journals in Rhetoric and Composition

Best of the Journals in Rhetoric and Composition
Series Editors: Steve Parks, Jessica Pauszek, Kristi Girdharry, and Charles Lesh

The Best of the Journals in Rhetoric and Composition series represents an attempt to foster a nationwide conversation—beginning with journal editors, but expanding to teachers, scholars and workers across the discipline of Rhetoric and Composition—to select essays that showcase the innovative and transformative work now being published in the field's journals. Representing both print and digital journals in the field, the essays in each edition represent a snapshot of the traditional and emergent conversations occurring in our field—from classroom practice to writing in global and digital contexts, from border rhetorics to social justice research. Together, the essays provide readers with a rich understanding of the present and future direction of the field.

Essays included in the series undergo a rigorous review process. First, all essays must have already crossed the threshold to be published in an academic journal in the field. Then, out of all the essays published by a journal, the editor can only select two essays. Next, the series editors create reading groups across the country. These groups feature full-time faculty, adjunct faculty, and graduate students who teach in a range of institutions. In this way, all the nominated essays are assessed and ranked for how they speak to the interests of all those who work in our field—a review process that is unique to the series. The series editors, plus one guest editor, then assemble a final selection of essays that have the strongest support from the reading groups for inclusion in a particular volume.

In this way, the Best of the Journals in Rhetoric and Composition series includes the only publications in the field that can truly claim to represent the collective insight of students, teachers, and scholars into the pressing issues of the current moment. For this reason, authors selected for inclusion are celebrated at their home institutions and journals actively seek recognition for their work. The series provides the broadest conception of scholarship in our field and so each volume can find a home in introductory graduate courses and advanced undergraduate courses everywhere.

BEST OF THE JOURNALS IN RHETORIC AND COMPOSITION 2021

Edited by Kristi Girdharry, Charles Lesh, Jessica Pauszek, David Blakesley, and Steve Parks

Parlor Press
Anderson, South Carolina
www.parlorpress.com

Parlor Press LLC, Anderson, South Carolina, USA

© 2023 by Parlor Press. Individual essays in this book have been reprinted with permission of the respective copyright owners.
All rights reserved.
Printed in the United States of America

SAN: 254-8879

ISSN 2327-4778 (print)
ISSN 2327-4786 (online)

978-1-64317-329-0 (paperback)
(978-1-64317-330-6 (pdf)
(978-1-64317-331-3 (ePub)

1 2 3 4 5

Cover design by David Blakesley.
Printed on acid-free paper.

Parlor Press, LLC is an independent publisher of scholarly and trade titles in print and multimedia formats. This book is available in paper and digital formats from Parlor Press on the World Wide Web at http://www.parlorpress.com or through online and brick-and-mortar bookstores. For submission information or to find out about Parlor Press publications, write to Parlor Press, 3015 Brackenberry Drive, Anderson, South Carolina, 29621, or email editor@parlorpress.com.

Contents

Introduction   *vii*
  Genesis Barco Medina, Berte Reyes, and Brian McShane

CONSTELLATIONS
The Dirt Under My Mother's Fingernails: Queer Retellings and Migrant Sensualities   *3*
  Alejandra I. Ramírez and Ruben Zecena

WPA: WRITING PROGRAM ADMINISTRATION
The F-Word: Failure in WPA Work   *30*
  Heather Bastian

JOURNAL OF BASIC WRITING
"Let the People Rap": Cultural Rhetorics Pedagogy and Practices Under CUNY's Open Admissions, 1968–1978   *51*
  Tessa Brown

LITERACY IN COMPOSITION STUDIES
Independent Black Institutions and Rhetorical Literacy Education: A Unique Voice of Color   *90*
  Jamila M. Kareem

COMMUNITY LITERACY JOURNAL
"All I Need Is One Mic": A Black Feminist Community Meditation on the Work, the Job, and the Hustle (& Why So Many of Yall Confuse This Stuff)   *115*
  Carmen Kynard

THE JOURNAL OF MULTIMODAL RHETORICS
Dressed but Not Tryin' to Impress: Black Women Deconstructing "Professional" Dress   *138*
  Brittany Hull, Cecilia D. Shelton, and Temptaous Mckoy

WRITING CENTER JOURNAL
A Page from Our Book: Social Justice Lessons from the HBCU Writing Center   *159*
  Kendra L. Mitchell and Robert E. Randolph, Jr.

PEDAGOGY
Rhetorical and Pedagogical Interventions for Countering
    Microaggressions   *181*
    Rasha Diab and Beth Godbee

ENCULTURATION
Signs of Disability, Disclosing   *212*
    Stephanie L. Kerschbaum

COLLEGE COMPOSITION AND COMMUNICATION
Developing a Relational Scholarly Practice: Snakes, Dreams, and
    Grandmothers   *242*
    Andrea Riley Mukavetz

KAIROS
Arranging a Rhetorical Feminist Methodology: The Visualization of
    Anti-Gentrification Rhetoric on Twitter   *263*
    Desiree Dighton

RHETORIC OF HEALTH & MEDICINE
The Ostomy Multiple: Toward a Theory of Rhetorical
    Enactments   *271*
    Molly Margaret Kessler

Introduction

Genesis Barco Medina, Berte Reyes, and Brian McShane

The authors in the *Best of the Journals in Rhetoric and Composition 2021* invite readers to reflect on what sustains writers, teachers, learners, and thinkers of writing, rhetoric, literacy, and language learning and what best practices should be carried forward. The following readings engage in thinking, practices, and scholarship that broadly re-envision what is meant by sustainability.

Sustainability can be enacted by community groups or social movements, large institutions, or individual efforts. Given this past year's instability, many began to question operations that have long stood and ask if they are properly working to sustain the current climate. Many organized and implemented efforts of change and innovation across social institutions—particularly those working within the university. The pandemic opened a space to seriously consider sustainability as a balance between preservation and revision, innovation, change, critique, and transformation. This collection takes sustainability as a general premise to create a series of questions that broadly consider: Who has had a say in what is worth sustaining? Do the traditional structures and current practices continue to sustain us now? Or have they only been sustaining a part of us? Some of us? Certainly not *all* of us or all *within* us.

Individuals working towards sustainability start from general commonplaces and the following list is not exhaustive. First, sustainability focuses on the *environment*. Surveying the environment determines what organisms are surviving, which are perishing, what practices are helpful or harmful, and the severity of consequences that trickle down from the environment to the individual. In order to preserve the environment, a new type of environment must be imagined with new practices. Therefore, *changing practices* that have shown to produce unwanted, harmful results is an effort towards sustainability. Changes, small or large, are made with new kinds of practices that create a sustainable environment. Change is the engine of sustainability. Third, sustainability relies on a *common purpose*. To create meaningful change, the efforts of many are needed working towards a common value, belief, goal, or idea. And finally, sustainability is *future-oriented*. Although sustainability relies on present practices, they are practices to ensure success for future generations.

Writers in the collection approach questions and answers of sustainability from diverse angles. Alejandra Ramírez and Ruben Zecena's article, "'The Dirt Under My Mom's Fingernails': Queer Retellings and Migrant Sensualities," prioritizes the flesh as a means of knowledge derivation and production through what they call, "rhetorics of the flesh." Ramírez and Zecena recognize current places of knowledge production are not sustainable because they often exclude migrant women, their bodies, their work, and stories. In an effort to create a sustainable practice that includes migrant women's stories, both authors re-tell stories that prioritize their senses to understand their mother's migrant stories as rhetorical performances that rely on the body and piece together how rhetorics of the flesh operate intergenerationally.

Heather Bastian reflects on a personal journey of failure as a Writing Program Administrator (WPA) in "The F Word: Failure in WPA Work." Bastian engages with failure as means towards sustainability by reflecting and recycling failure as a place of learning rather than loss. WPA scholarship is often void of failure which has led to minimal conversation about how to approach, deal, and welcome failure in discourse about WPA work. Readers are left with a heuristic to examine how failure within WPA work can be reused and reclaimed as a transformative experience.

Tessa Brown's "'Let the People Rap': Cultural Rhetorics Pedagogy and Practices Under CUNY's Open Admissions, 1968-1978" discusses how academic institutions do not sustain Black and Brown instructors and their pedagogical practices for the writing classroom. Through archival work, Brown reveals the connection of hip-hop rhetorical practices from the Black Arts Movement that influenced the writing classroom during CUNY's Open Admissions. Brown finds that the pedagogical labor and practices of faculty members—faculty of color and particularly women of color—led not only to prominent pieces of writing and rhetorical thinking for students but also to consequences that mimic much of today's realities for BIPOC instructors and those who teach against traditional rhetorical and pedagogical practices.

Jamila M. Kareem's article "Independent Black Institutions and Rhetorical Literacy Education: A Unique Voice of Color" advocates that in order to have a more sustainable field of literacy where there are more conducive learning outcomes for students of diverse backgrounds, instructors must include more voices of color. Kareem highlights how a unique voice-of-color has always been present in independent Black institutions such as community centers, churches, citizenship schools, freedom schools, and Black Panther Liberation schools. Therefore, counterstorying from a voice-of-color is one way to work towards inclusivity within the predominantly white-informed scholarship on literacy. Alongside other Black literacy scholars, Kareem argues how Black literacy and rhetorical practices are prevalent and valid enough to sustain success within its own context without the authority of PWI/white scholarship.

Carmen Kynard's Black feminist approach to teaching composition has forced a reckoning with the power and prejudice of the university, including "linguistic oppression" (7). In advocating for a system that can overcome this oppression, Kynard mentions the recent work of Aja Martinez's *Counterstory: The Rhetoric and Writing of Critical Race Theory*. Kynard notes that "Education counterstories can thus reveal, in real talk, the everyday ways that whiteness and racism are remade and reaffirmed *in* schools and *via* schooling and the radical counter-narratives that make other worlds" (7). Brittany Hull, Cecilia D. Shelton, and Temptaous Mckoy's article, "Dressed but Not Tryin' to Impress," places the exclusion and white supremacy of conference and professional attire firmly in the crosshairs, asking all of us who read this article to wonder if our ideas of professional dress are rooted in the same kind of whiteness, maleness, and straightness that has excluded "historically marginalized communities, whose identities epistemologies, and even their very bodies are called into question" (Hull, Shelton, and Mckoy 7). Echoing threads of Kynard's article and Martinez's work, the authors of this article each tell the personal (counter)story of shedding the racist expectations of higher ed and conferences, academia largely, as a way to embrace their bodies and selves that the structures they move in are attempting to dress into silence.

Kendra L. Mitchell and Robert E. Randolph Jr. draw on their experiences at HBCUs to challenge another racist assumption in higher ed: the presumed inferiority of HBCU educational models. Pointing to the calls for social justice initiatives in writing center work, and conversations on active citizenship, the authors show that HBCU writing centers already do the work of social justice while being disregarded as legitimate sources of knowledge. The authors' experiences reveal a balancing act in HBCU instruction—empowering students by honoring their knowledge and engaging them on their own terms while also preparing those students for a world that will relegate them to second-class status. In this way, Mitchell and Randolph reveal that a foundational question for the future of the field is who is meant to be sustained by scholarly practices and policy. Creating a sustainable future for marginalized students means rejecting the assumed inferiority of "marginal" institutions and instead actively learning from them.

The question of who is meant to be sustained in institutions is also addressed by Rasha Diab, Beth Godbee, Cedric Burrows, and Thomas Ferrel in "Rhetorical and Pedagogical Interventions for Countering Microaggressions." The authors demonstrate the harm caused by microaggressions and detail the myriad spaces where microaggressions appear in academia—such as the presumed incompetence of scholars of color, textbook selections which relegate marginalized authors to limited subject matter, and closed-door departmental decision making. Calling for scholars to actively resist microaggressions in academia, Diab et al. show how sustainable futures for marginalized people require taking specific and intentional actions to challenge prevailing beliefs, where maintaining an institutional status quo comes at the expense of the people within it.

Stephanie L. Kerschbaum contends with a similar issue in "Signs of Disability, Disclosing." Kerschbaum examines reader interpretations of yellow diamond-shaped road signs announcing the presence of a person with disabilities (such as "Deaf Person in Area," "Blind Pedestrian Xing," etc.) and notes how the interactions between readers and signs can shape community perceptions of disability itself. Though the signs are framed as community safety efforts, Kerschbaum reveals that they perpetuate an assumption of disability as a lack of competency, a hazard for others to avoid, and an outside presence in a community. The yellow diamond-shaped road signs reflect the problems with thoughtless advocacy centering hegemonic interests as opposed to substantive changes in practice centering marginalized people.

Resolving that, however, demands active relationship building, which is at the heart of Andrea Riley Mukavetz's "Developing a Relational Scholarly Practice: Snakes, Dreams, and Grandmothers." In this piece, Riley Mukavetz proposes a scholarly practice which attends to the multitude of relationships that often go ignored in scholarly work such as one's relationship to the land they occupy, histories they are a part of, ancestral knowledge, dreams, animals, and their neighborhoods. Riley Mukavetz reflects experience to show how these often difficult relationships can inspire meaningful directions in scholarship and sustain writers in their work.

Universities and pedagogies are not the only systems that are opened up to questioning in this volume, and Molly Margaret Kessler takes aim at the rhetoric of health and medicine. By studying four groups of ostomy patients through the terms they use to describe their medical devices (parasite, companion, cyborg, and self), Kessler challenges a major assumption of the practice of talking about things like ostomy supplies: "We might ask: How do the practices that stage ostomy as parasite differ from those that stage the ostomy as self? If difference practices stage different ostomies, then changing practices (more so than attitudes) might better help patients" (317). We are no longer asking those who view themselves or their medical devices negatively and asking them to change, we are asking about the practices and outcomes that allowed others to view that same device as a benefit. By bringing the focus to the care patients are receiving, patients can be more likely to receive positive outcomes regardless of where they see the doctor.

Desiree Dighton offers a unique perspective in this collection, asking us to consider the ways in which big data can tell a story—a marginalized one at that. Focusing research on the social media journey of "gentrification," Dighton is expanding the feminist and Counterstory thread picked up by so many in this volume, showing how we can apply these methodologies to vast systems and draw a personal, traceable meaning—one humans have created and shaped.

The questions of what to change for the sake of sustainability are critical for the future of our field. The questions posed by the authors in the collection are not new. These questions and efforts are re-evaluations of problems that have been debated for decades. In a way, what has sustained the longest in many fields is caused by white supremacy, misogyny, homophobia, transphobia, ableism, classism, and other institutional forms of bigotry. Even this critique, that we're rehashing questions with no end in sight, is itself becoming old. We are tired of re-addressing the problems, and we are tired of re-addressing the re-addressing of the problems. But rather than fall into defeatism (another well-sustained cycle that's overstayed its welcome), the scholars of this collection challenge us to think of what has traditionally been disregarded as scholarship. If we mean to grow beyond the problems that we've faced for decades, then we cannot continue to privilege the same institutions, knowledges, and communities that we always have above others.

If we mean to.

After reading this collection, scholars should ask what we mean to sustain. The authors here each provide a variety of possibilities and means for change. We can do the work. We just need to be open to it.

A Note on the Selection Process

The articles selected for this volume represent important scholarship from journals in our field. Each selection was first nominated by the current editor(s) of the journal. From these nominations, graduate students and faculty of all ranks from a range of institutions read and ranked each article according to the following criteria:

- Article fosters a diverse and inclusive sense of the field.
- Article demonstrates a broad sense of the discipline, demonstrating the ability to explain how its specific focus in a sub-disciplinary area addresses broader concerns in the field.
- Article makes original contributions to the field, expanding or rearticulating central premises.
- Article is written in a style which, while based in the discipline, attempts to engage with a wider audience or concerns a wider audience.

Based on the recommendations from reading groups, the editors selected the final list of essays. We hope that this selection illustrates the richness and diversity of our field and the possibilities that emerge when we are given the chance to read across journals and publishing platforms.

We are very grateful to all of the associate editors who organized and participated in reading groups that helped choose the selected essays. We are also grateful to our assistant editors who took the time to diligently read and discuss the nominated articles and offer their insights. We proudly list them here:

Erin Costello Wecker, University of Montana (Associate Editor)
Patricia Portanova, Northern Essex Community College
Patty Wilde, Washington State University Tri-Cities

Hannah Taylor, Clemson University (Associate Editor)
Victoria Houser, Clemson University
Charlotte Lucke, Clemson University
Sarah Richardson, Clemson University
Haley Swartz, Clemson University

Michelle Niestepski, Lasell University (Associate Editor)
Gregory Cass, Lasell University
Alex Cronis, Lasell University
Sara Large, Lasell University
Annie Ou, Lasell University

Vincent Portillo, Boston College (Associate Editor)
Caleb Lee González, Ohio State University
Jordan Clarke Hayes, University of Pittsburgh
Katherine Highfill, University of Houston
Ellen Cecil-Lemkin, University of Wisconsin-Madison
Savannah Paige Murray, Appalachian State University
Andrew Appleton Pine, University of Michigan
Jacob D. Richter, Clemson University
Natalie Shellenberger, Texas Christian University
Kathryn Van Zanen, University of Michigan

Brent D. Chappelow, University of Southern California (Associate Editor)
Elizabeth Blomstedt, University of Southern California
Rochelle K. Gold, University of Southern California
Keasha R. Worthen, University of Southern California
Cory Elizabeth Nelson, University of Southern California
Alisa Catalina Sánchez, University of Southern California

Introduction xiii

Emily Kathryn Illingworth, Texas A&M University-Commerce
  (Associate Editor)
Charlotte Asmuth, University of Louisville
Sharmistha Basu, Texas A&M University - Commerce
Malcah Effron, Massachusetts Institute of Technology
Lucy Hoak, University of Virginia
Pritisha Shrestha, Syracuse University
Amanda Sladek, University of Nebraska at Kearney
Kelly L. Wheeler, University of Michigan, Ann Arbor
Anna Zeemont, City University of New York

Maria Novotny, University of Wisconsin-Milwaukee (Associate Editor)
Gitte Frandsen, University of Wisconsin-Milwaukee
Kristiana Perleberg, University of Wisconsin-Milwaukee
Danielle Koepke, University of Wisconsin-Milwaukee
Amanda Reavey, University of Wisconsin-Milwaukee

Rachel Huddleston, Texas A&M University-Commerce (Associate Editor)
Maddy Eglian, Boise State University
Genie Giaimo, Middlebury College
Christie Glebe, Texas A&M University-Commerce
Jeremy Levine, University of Massachusetts, Amherst
Ryan McCarty, University of Michigan
Megan Opperman, University of Northern Colorado-Extended Campus
Caitlin E. Ray, University of Louisville
Kristina Reard   on, College of the Holy Cross
Turnip Van Dyke, University of Texas at El Paso

David Riche, University of Denver (Associate Editor)
April Chapman-Ludwig, University of Denver
Richard Colby, University of Denver
Robert Gilmor, University of Denver
Lauren Picard, University of Denver
Pauline Reid, University of Denver
Daniel Singer, University of Denver

Kalyn Prince, University of Oklahoma (Associate Editor)
Rena Bradley, University of Houston
Alexander Champoux, University of Minnesota
Brooke Covington, Christopher Newport University
Eliza Gellis, Purdue University
Gabrielle Isabel Kelenyi, University of Wisconsin-Madison

Miranda Kuehmichel, Boise State University
Jannell McConnell Parsons, University of Kentucky
Susan Pagnac, Central College
Samuel Stinson, Minot State University

Brent Griffin, Northeastern University (Associate Editor)
Thomas Akbari, Northeastern University
Laura Beerits, Northeastern University
Lucy Bunning, Northeastern University
Crissy McMartin-Miller, Northeastern University
Matthew Noonan, Northeastern University

Luciana Herman, University of Texas at El Paso, (Associate Editor)
Colleen Coyne, Framingham State University
Megan Friess, Chapman University
Seven Kapica, Keuka College
Bess McCulloch, East Carolina University
Michelle Miller, Boise State University
Ruby Nancy, U of Minnesota Duluth
Courtney Patrick-Weber, Bay Path University

Rhiannon Scharnhorst, University of Cincinnati (Associate Editor)
Jay S. Arns, University of Cincinnati
Kevin Belknap, University of Cincinnati
Brooke Boling, University of Cincinnati
Chelsea Ensley, University of Cincinnati
Ben Hojem, University of Cincinnati
Aleashia Walton, University of Cincinnati

Melanie Davis-Sanchez, Texas A&M University-Commerce (Associate Editor)
Kelby Andrew, Boise State University
Kellie Cannon, Curry College
Kefaya Diab, Indiana University
Meg Mikovits, Moravian College
Bibhushana Poudyal, University of Texas at El Paso
Ulysses B. Texx, St. Cloud State University
Charles Woods, Texas A&M University - Commerce

Rose O'Connor, Boston College
We would like to thank Rose O'Connor for assistance on the design and layout of this publication

Best of the Journals
Rhetoric and Composition

CONSTELLATIONS

constellations is an online peer-reviewed publishing space focused on cultural rhetorics scholarship, teaching, and practice. The field of cultural rhetorics is anchored in the belief that all cultures are rhetorical and all rhetorics are cultural. This belief forms a set of constellating methodologies, theories, and practices that draw attention to the intricate ways meaning emerges in human practices.

constellations is on the web at https://constell8cr.com/

'The Dirt Under My Mom's Fingernails": Queer Retellings and Migrant Sensualities[1]

Alejandra I. Ramírez and Ruben Zecena travel through their own and their mothers' histories to create loving and profound portraits of what Latina migrant women offer to their families and to American culture. As Ramírez and Zecena explain, their mothers' stories are particularly vital at a time when our political and media cultures seem determined to paint Latinxs as threats. As they explain, "Through our discussion of the body as a story, we posit that a rhetorics of the flesh reveals traces of violence on the migrant body." Yet, as the essay shows, their mothers took that violence and turned it into love for their family. For me, it is that love that makes this such an impactful and important piece in today's combative global climate.

As the situation for Latinx immigrants and refugees attempting to enter the United States worsens under the Trump Administration's draconian policies against them, this article reminds us of the humanity of those who are hoping to make a better life for themselves and their families in the US. Because those who are writing the piece are children of women who came to the US to help their families thrive and the authors are now in academia, the essay tacitly makes the point that there is much of value that immigrants bring to this country. The personal stories and the love the authors feel for their mothers is also a vital, positive point to highlight as so many of us look for hope in the middle of the pandemic.

---

1. *Constellations*, no. 2, 2019, https://constell8cr.com/issue-2/the-dirt-under-my-moms-fingernails-queer-retellings-and-migrant-sensualities/. © 2019 by *Constellations*.

The Dirt Under My Mother's Fingernails: Queer Retellings and Migrant Sensualities

Alejandra I. Ramírez and Ruben Zecena

Rhetorics of the Flesh
...are the cracks at the edges of my lips
Que me mereci from holding smiles for too long,
The bite marks on the inner flesh of my cheeks
Trozos que me arranque out of fear from running
Away.
Rhetorics that I've silenced because callused hands have wrapped themselves around
My heart
My mouth
My
Mother.
They are the bodies of women that lie under wooden crosses, under mesquites, under oath
 Because they too often did
"The best they could."
Rhetorics
Unspoken
Because they are far too explicit to put into words.
Screams in the night that erupt when everything has been said
And we remain
Unheard.

El cuerpo sabe.

This co-written article proposes "rhetorics of the flesh" as an analytic framework and queer writing method that (re)tells stories about Latina migrant mothers within and against the violent, dominant, and forceful narratives of U.S. citizenship that criminalize their existence. Furthermore, our article serves as a place to build on the growing corpus in rhetorical studies that weaves together queer theory, embodiment, and intergenerational violences. Our theory of rhetorics of the flesh is a strategic writing act rooted in the assumption that el cuerpo sabe, the body knows, and it is through the senses and embodied knowledge wherein one remembers and can retell stories. Through a queer intellectual practice that arouses the senses and draws lines between small and large social issues and artifacts, we draw imaginary scribbles that connect the themes in our essay about intergenerational migrant trauma and pleasure:embodied knowledge, sensualities, and migration (Rodríguez 69).

Importantly, this article began over a coffee shop conversation about our migrant mothers. It began in graduate seminar classes, discussions on social justice movements, common readings on poetics, and conversations before and after class. In short, the project is an amalgamation of voices, thoughts, and feminist 'wonders' that imbricate us in a queer sociality (Ahmed, *Cultural Politics* 180-181). The conversation about the lived experiences of migrant mothers began when we were children. It began in the womb before we were even born. It began with the generations of subtle and explicit brutalities of institutional, colonial, and patriarchal violence, now sustained in the increased media depicting migrant women with children as "bad mothers" and "bad citizens." It also begins in the bodies of our mothers and in their mothers before them, extends to our bodies, and in one of our cases, to the bodies of my children. We wonder what it might take to imagine and to (re)tell the stories our mothers told us. We wonder about the historicity of what has been forgotten or untold—what we know and cannot know for certain (Ahmed, *Cultural Politics* 82; Purdue 8). In other words, we critically theorize, through an intergenerational and embodied analysis, the extent to which dominant ideologies and policies affect migrants, their children and their children's children.

We write our memories of our mothers at a moment when once again migrants, particularly Latina mothers, are represented as threatening to the nation-state. Our mothers became central to our conversation, and we continue to sit with tensions about the ethics of retelling their stories. We resist the benevolent or paternalistic researcher-position when writing about their experiences. Therefore, we draw upon queer women of color feminisms to provide a critical method of retelling that recognizes and honors our mothers' many labors and their complexities as women with dreams, desires, and pain.

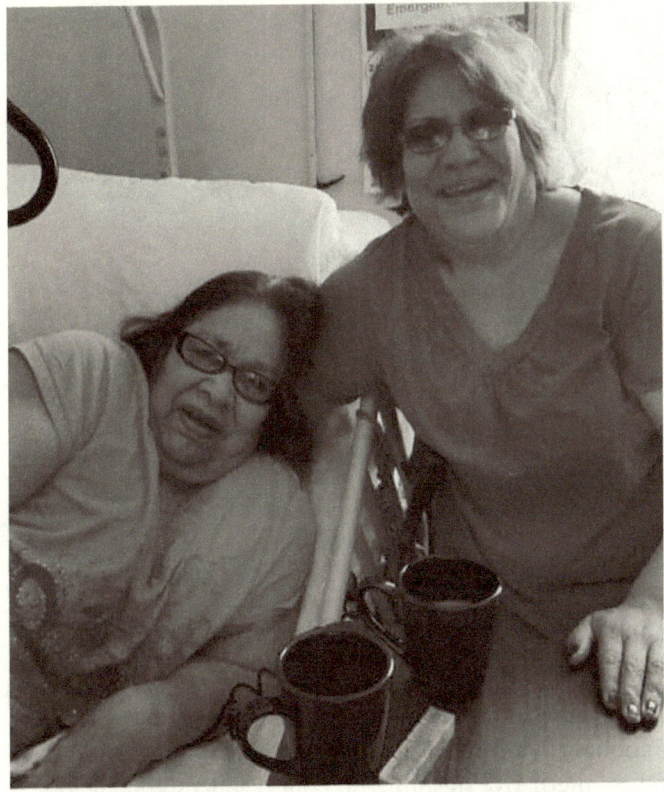

Figure 1. Tomasita Balderas-Hermosillo with her late mother, Irene Balderas-Leal. Carrizo Springs, Texas, 2015.

In our weaving of the narratives, discourses, and experiences that migrant mothers and their children have to endure in the U.S., we draw attention to the rhetoric that influences derogatory labels such as "welfare queens," "anchor babies," and the overall framing of migrant mothers as problem subjects in national media and U.S. politics. On a personal level, we also illustrate how our mom's stories and their working conditions have shaped us, their children.

By eliciting sensual, performative, and queer collaborative writing practices, this essay offers rhetorics of the flesh as a vital contribution and intervention within the study of rhetoric and the criminalization of Latina migrant mothers. Such analytic framework intervenes in the erasure of embodied knowledge as a valid means of knowing; furthermore, it recognizes the complexity of migrant mothers and acknowledges that they are sensual with shared desires, not only as laborers, migrants, and mothers, but also as complex human beings.

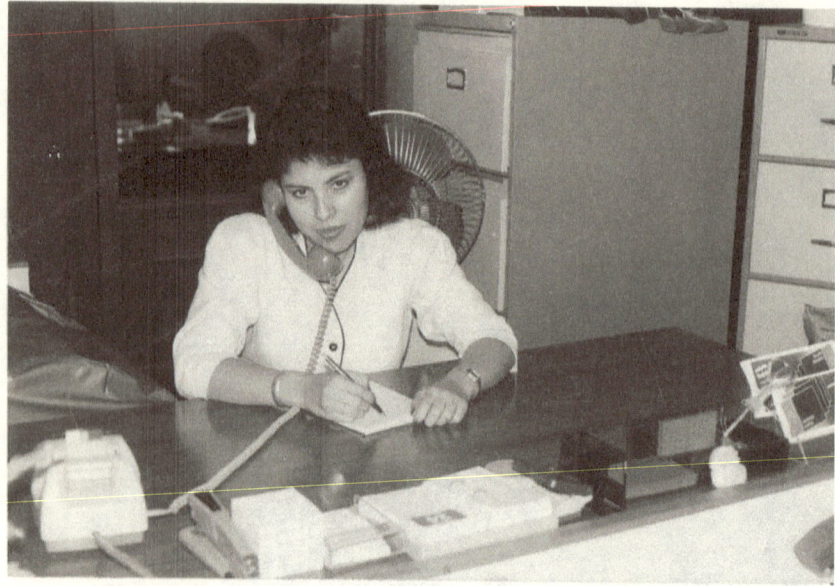

Figure 2. Image of Sandra Elizabeth Cartagena de Zecena working at Banco Agricola in San Salvador, El Salvador, 1983.

The purpose of this essay and rhetorics of the flesh is to situate the body, and the intergenerational embodied stories shared among migrants and their children, as central to alternative meaning-making practices and rhetorical imaginaries (Chávez 31). In the following section, we demonstrate how Cultural Rhetorics enables us to tell painful stories through embodied knowledge, and we propose the concept of a rhetorics of the flesh as our main intervention for retelling our migrant mothers' stories, a practice influenced by the work of Chicana and transnational feminists; a theory in/of the flesh (Moraga; Trujillo; Facio and Lara). This concept enables us to explore the importance of embodied knowledge and argues that an engagement with the body and the senses arouses critical reflections on migration. We therefore situate our essay within cultural rhetorics, informed by literature on gender and migration, as critical interlocutors for our methodological practice.

RHETORICS OF THE FLESH

Rhetorics of the flesh is a poiesis—a poetic and embodied way of knowing and being. It is a collision between poetry and rhetorics, and of bodies communicating in space. Our project builds on Theories of the Flesh, cultural rhetorics, and U.S. women of color feminism to conceptualize a rhetorical maneuver that does not speak for or about migrant mothers, but accounts for the complexities and contradictions of our experiences as queer children of migrant mothers (Cruz; Téllez). Rhetorics of the flesh helps us to think, feel, and write about the body's seemingly "silent" ability to narrate desire, trauma, violence, pleasure, dreams, and resilience in the lives of migrant mothers and their children.

Our project title, "The Dirt Under My Mom's Fingernails," is a reference to Cherríe Moraga's play, *Watsonville*. In this play, Moraga explores issues related to the cannery worker's strike in the mid-1980s in California coupled with environmental destruction and the appearance of the Virgen de Guadalupe on a tree in 1992. In Moraga's play, many of the leaders in the strike are Mexicana and Chicana activists whose voices play an important role in challenging labor exploitation, land degradation, and anti-immigrant rhetoric. We are drawn to a particular scene where Susana, a physician's assistant at the community clinic, asks Lucha, one of the cannery workers, if she is ever afraid to strike. Lucha responds by reminding Susana that if she had the courage to cross the U.S.-Mexico border, then she has the courage to strike until the cannery workers' demands are met. Later, Lucha asks Susana why she chooses to work in Watsonville when she says "[If I had gone to college] you wouldn't find me with the dirt under my uñas [nails]...I'd move to a big city" (37). She later speaks about her dreams for her children to obtain a college education and leave the town. Both women express ambivalence about their relationship to Watsonville, but Susana offers an important response that allows us to work through our own mothers' stories and the rhetorical forces that render their bodies deviant when she says: "Maybe [your children] won't be able to forget the dirt under your fingernails" (37). Towards the end of the play, Lucha confesses her love for Susana and asserts that she wants to be Susana's partner, a lesbiana, "un nombre sensual" [a sensual name] (104). The dirt under her fingernails, the traces of caring for the land, is the metaphor that guides our essay as we retell the memories we have of our migrant mothers, their care, their labor/s, and their fight, as well as the gendered criminalization of migrants in the U.S. We, like Susana, are invested in acknowledging the traumas of migration that are marked on our mothers' bodies and thus insist on remembering and retelling their stories. And just like Lucha, we do so queerly by insisting on the politics of desire, pleasure, and sensuality in our queer retellings.

Trying to articulate sentimientos y conocimentos that we have inherited, we opened a cherished and foundational text to our queer and feminist upbringings, *This Bridge Called My Back*. We did so quietly, hoping for some illumination as we recalled childhood memories of our mothers, their life stories, their struggles, their migrations. Max Valerio's essay, "It's In My Blood, My Face – My Mother's Voice, The Way I Sweat" helped to remind us of the purpose of our essay, asking how our bodies tell stories, how they shape stories and are shaped by them (36). The power of a mother's presence, her gaze, her posture, and all the in/visible traumas of migration, as well as the joys and pleasures, are part of their migrant histories. Our migrant histories. These painful and embodied rhetorics fuel our desire to situate our mothers' stories, and our queer retellings of their stories, as a form of liberatory praxis. Embodied political theory articulates experiences that transcend the written text. As Cindy Cruz elaborates, "our production of knowledge begins in the bodies of our mothers and grandmothers, in the acknowledgement of the critical practices of women of color before us" (658). Rhetorics of the flesh further delves into the layers of "flesh," below the surface, to theorize the body as a feeling and thinking site of knowledge production. A site of articulation and manifestation of politics—indeed, a place of meaning-making where narratives collide. Building on the work of Karma Chávez, we understand queerness as a "coalitional term, a term that always implies an intermeshed understanding of identity, subjectivity, power, and politics located in the dirt and concrete where people live, work, and play" (7). Queerness asks us to reach below the skin and down to the very soil in which we stand, the dirt from which this story begins.

Significantly, these rhetorics of the flesh are in critical dialogue with cultural rhetorics. The Cultural Rhetorics Theory Lab defines cultural rhetorics as the telling of stories about how the world works (Powell et al.); it is a methodological practice that challenges how academic disciples have traditionally conceptualized culture "*as* an object of inquiry" that is static and open to interpretation (Powell et al.). In other words, object-oriented approaches to "culture" erase, omit, and isolate the actual bodies within culture. Cultural studies scholar Stuart Hall defines culture as a "set of practices" where people make sense of the world, arguing that meaning-making practices have real effects on the social organization of everyday life (3). We situate rhetorics of the flesh in dialogue with cultural rhetorics because these theoretical and methodological practices argue that the traces of the body, like the dirt under our mothers' fingernails, have the capacity to re-story and reconfigure dominant narratives about migrants and mothers. Through a rhetoric of the flesh, we challenge a dominant culture that underestimates the power of story and the power of the migrant narrative. Our essay elucidates a queer methodological practice, which queer of color and performance theorist José Esteban Muñoz describes as the "remaking and rewriting of a dominant script" (23). In a similar vein, cultural rhetorics and rhetorics of the flesh tell a different story that challenges the rhetorics of the U.S. empire. As Daisy Levy proposes, cultural rhetorics pushes for transdisciplinarity as a methodological practice, positioning the body as a site of knowledge (8- 9).

Cognizant of the problems that Gayatri Spivak's essay "Can the Subaltern Speak?" poses for theories that attempt to speak for or let the subaltern speak, we insist on a rhetorics of the flesh that engages the body as a site of knowledge (78). Such rhetorics of the flesh enable us to analyze normative discourses about migrant mothers and disrupt anti-immigrant rhetoric that renders migrant mothers as always already criminal and abject. In positing the body as a site of knowledge, we ask: how can a rhetorics of the flesh *re-story* the criminalization of migrant mothers in the U.S.? (Driskill, *Asegi Stories*, 4) And what can this queer retelling reveal about the embodiment of migrant, intergenerational histories? Ultimately, rhetorics of the flesh enables us to see queer paths and queer pasts. It dislodges the heteronormative and racist rhetorical forces of anti-immigrant legislation and allows us to imagine an elsewhere within academia—expanding the intellectual space necessary to "make the world bigger" (Herrera y Lozano).

Structural Inequalities and the Criminalization of Latina Migrants

U.S. homonationalist rhetoric plays a central role in the creation of anti-immigrant legislation whereby mothers of color are blamed for social inequalities; and thus, those rhetorics create a cultural and political discourse that invisibilizes the role of the state in the creation of these structural conditions. Because this essay focuses on our queer retellings about our migrant mothers' labor, it is grounded in transnational feminist theory that equally informed our growing understanding of their (im)material conditions. Rhetorical forces, as we understand them, have material and violent effects on migrant mothers.

Gender and migration literature demonstrates how immigration and welfare reform policies of the 1990s worked to extract labor from poor migrant women while criminalizing their bodies. For example, Grace Chang identifies how cultural and political structures disproportionately target poor migrant women's mobility within the U.S. neoliberal imagination. As Chang argues in *Disposable Domestics,* immigrant women's reproduction is rhetorically imagined as a threat to the national body (4). In connection to the disproportionate criminalization of migrant women, Lynn Fujiwara sheds light on how the Personal Responsibility and Work Opportunity Reconciliation Act of 1996 (PRWORA) functioned to limit Asian and Latina migrant's access to citizenship, safe working conditions, and social services through nativist discourse (128-130). Neoliberal legislation such as PRWORA relies on the discourse of "personal responsibility" to privatize public resources away from those who most need them, namely migrant mothers and their children.

Martha D. Escobar goes on to describe the racialized policies of criminalization in the U.S. against Latina migrants and writes that Latina sexualities are "constructed as racialized national threats" (11). Furthermore, Escobar writes that migrant mothers' "irrecuperability is made viable because their origins are outside the US nation-state and their entrance is consigned to the realm of (il)legality since the dominant imagination equates the figure of the (im)migrant to that of the 'illegal'" (5). Such "irrecuperability" subjects migrant women to precarious working conditions and makes their access to citizenship impossible. In addition to the criminalization of migrant women, Tapia alerts us the rhetoric utilized in popular media, politics, and law to blame mothers for social inequalities; and thus, it creates a cultural and political discourse that invisibilizes the role of the state in the creation of these structural conditions (51).

In spite of migrant women's labor for the nation, their own bodies and sexualities have historically been regulated through eugenic rhetorics and policies where their labor, and reproductive capacities, are controlled by the state. The recent film *No Más Bebés* directed by Renee Tajima-Peña (2015) captures/documents the ways institutions of power control the bodies of Latinas. The film connects issues of gender with eugenics in the U.S. by providing testimonios from the mothers of the 1975 civil rights lawsuit against the University of Southern California Medical Center. This lawsuit brought visibility to the forced sterilization of Latinas in the 1960s and 70s. Overall, images, literature, and film on gender and migration provide historical and theoretical accounts of the ways U.S. anti-immigrant discourse "obscures the fact that the modern family—as an offspring of imperialism—was always an institution structured by and productive of inequalities based on gender, race, class" (Tapia 51). Such literature productively maps the effects of gendered U.S. racist rhetorics against migrant mothers and serves as a starting point for our own rhetorical engagement as we deconstruct our experiences as children of migrant mothers.

As a contribution to the literature on gender, sexuality, and international migration, a rhetorics of the flesh maps the memories of our mothers' stories and our eye-witness accounts of the "traces" of their working conditions on their bodies. Traces that include smells, scars, and pain, all of which speak to the title of our piece: the dirt under my mother's fingernails.

Queer Retellings and Textual Intimacies

"Learning happens through our bodies, through embodied practice, through doing."

—Qwo-Li Driskill ("Decolonial Skillshares" 57).

For our mothers, learning also happened through forced migrations, land dispossession, sexual violence, and inhumane labor conditions. Through our discussion of the body as a story, we posit that a rhetorics of the flesh reveals traces of violence on the migrant body. Thinking through rhetorics of the flesh is a queer decolonial practice that enables us to offer a *re-storying* of the colonized migrant body (Driskill, *Asegi Stories,* 4). A story that occurs both on the body and below the skin; a "happening" to the body. A body that sheds its skin. A body that knows from within—visceral knowledge. With the permission of our mothers, we discuss rhetorics of the flesh through their stories of migration, labor, and parenting, which offers an important contribution to academic discourses of queerness, heteronormativity, and cultural rhetorics.

Through centering the body, rhetorics of the flesh is a counterpoint to the criminalization of migrant mothers explicit in today's popular media, heteronormative anti-immigrant legislation, and what Nicholas De Genova calls *the deportation regime* (2010). These structural conditions and embodied realities necessitate a queer retelling, and contestation, of the material realities of Latina migrant mothers and their everyday experiences. In this next section, we offer our mothers' stories and our own reflections as the theory that we call rhetorics of the flesh: embodied practices of meaning-making that present opportunities for a nuanced analysis of migrant kinship structures, a critique of labor exploitation, and a turn to the senses as a means to remember and retell.

El Cuerpo es una Historia y Tiene Historias que Contar.

"For our bodies to be sites of theory, they must be honored as sites of desire."

—Lorenzo Herrera y Lozano ("What Courses Through My Veins").

Figure 3. Image of Sandra Elizabeth Cartagena de Zecena receiving an appreciation recognition award for her work at a Washington State Inspire Development center, Pasco, Washington, 2017.

Ruben: Where to begin? I could start with a story about the time when the big open-secret in my family was "revealed." Or the time when my mom told my dad that she would not leave El Salvador without both of her children. But instead, I want to start with a scene that I remember thoroughly and mainly through my senses. I was in middle school working on homework when my mom came home, and she was emphatically relieved to be out of work. She was a line worker whose job was to cut out the rotten parts of a potato, sort them, and do so under a quick pace. She sat at the kitchen table and told me that her supervisor threw a potato at her because she could not keep up with the speed of the line. And because she was undocumented, she did not report this incident out of fear that she would be fired, or much worse, reported to la migra. As I listened to her story, I looked and tended to her hands. They were usually swollen from long periods of cutting potatoes.

These are hands that have been marked by the experiences of migration and agricultural labor. It was these swollen hands that were always there to encourage me in my pursuit of higher education. My undocumented mom, her loving hands, were reduced to body parts at the factory that day, and all I was able to do was listen to her story.

I recount this story because I remember the touch of my mother's hands, the smell of potatoes on her hair, the sound of her voice, and the resilience that she continues to embody. Her story elucidates a non-normative and gendered critique of power that invokes the field of queer theory. In his articulation of "Quare" as a modality of knowing that differs from the term "queer," performance studies scholar E. Patrick Johnson asks: "what is the utility of queer theory on the front lines, in the trenches, on the street, or anyplace where the racialized and sexualized body is beaten, starved, fired, cursed—indeed, where the body is the site of trauma?" (5). Johnson challenges 'queer' due to its lack of intersectional analysis; thus, situating his piece within the broader field of queer of color critique. The title for his essay is indicative of queer of color material realities, and I thus reflect on his piece to make sense of my mother's story. As he notes, he learned about Quare, a queer of color analytic, from his grandma. And it is my mother who taught me that structural critiques of power can emerge from the body. In my retelling of her story, I am brief. I refuse to make my mom a spectacle of violence, and there are details that I keep to myself. However, this retelling, a queer retelling, shows that for my mom, the "American Dream" is defined in the moment that a factory supervisor threw a potato at her. Asking to extract more labor from her migrant body, this was a dehumanizing action aimed at reminding my mom of the precarious conditions that structure migrancy. And in particular, the gendered labor of undocumented Latina migrant mothers. While there are no easy answers to this story, I recognize that my mother's action, a lack of action, was a strategic act that allowed her to keep her job but also enabled a strong critique of the American Dream.

The rotten parts of the potato, lo desechable as Diana Taylor remarks, act as a metaphor in this story for Latina migrant mothers and their labor ("Performing Ruins" 22). So I ask: how can my mother's hands represent both violence and refusal? And more abruptly, how has the story about Latina migrants been confined to stories of criminality? In asking these questions I am wary of the "heroic" narrative that this story may present, as my mother is no longer undocumented and currently works as a family advocate for a migrant seasonal Head-Start program in Washington State. But my mother's story, and the story of her body, is complex and exists in the in-between spaces of the "good" and "bad" immigrant. Furthermore, in my use of memory through the senses, I posit a queer way of discussing and retelling my mother's story, one that refuses to reenact scenes of violence but also looks at the wounds that migration has inflicted. Refusing to heal and refusing to cause more violence, I reflect on this story because it challenges hegemonic framings of Latina migrants and allows me to think about ways of surviving that, in Johnson's language, quare our conceptions of migration.

Alejandra: I have to admit: I have mommy issues. I go back and forth with my feelings for her. She has healed me and hurt me. That being said, I know she did the best she could, and that's all you can do as a parent. Especially after my dad left, and abandoned my mom with six young children, I see my mom as the woman who fed us, clothed us, and saved us. Everything was for us. Sacrifice and duty were constant messages in our traditionalist family. The sacrificial mother who puts her children's desires, and her man's desires, before her own. This anti-feminist narrative in patriarchal and nationalist cultures is in part what makes the lives of women and mothers susceptible to domestic and labor abuse.

An odor triggers memories of my mom coming home in the early morning from working overnights at the turkey factory in central Minnesota. I can't get that smell out of my head. It was the smell of sterilized death, like attempting to purifying old blood, or something like a morgue. Sometimes it makes me sick to think about it. The white garments that she would wear for her job would be stained in pinks and reds. Her brown rubber boots always caused her feet and back aches.

The factories looked like some sort of airport hangar, and at night the lights would illuminate the nearby neighborhood of trailer homes in which many other migrant families lived.

I thought she was fierce and powerful with her knife sharpening tool, and I imagined her with large knives at work. Though I didn't want to think about what they were doing to the animals at the factory she worked at. My mom worked at two meat factories: one a turkey factory and the other a chicken factory.

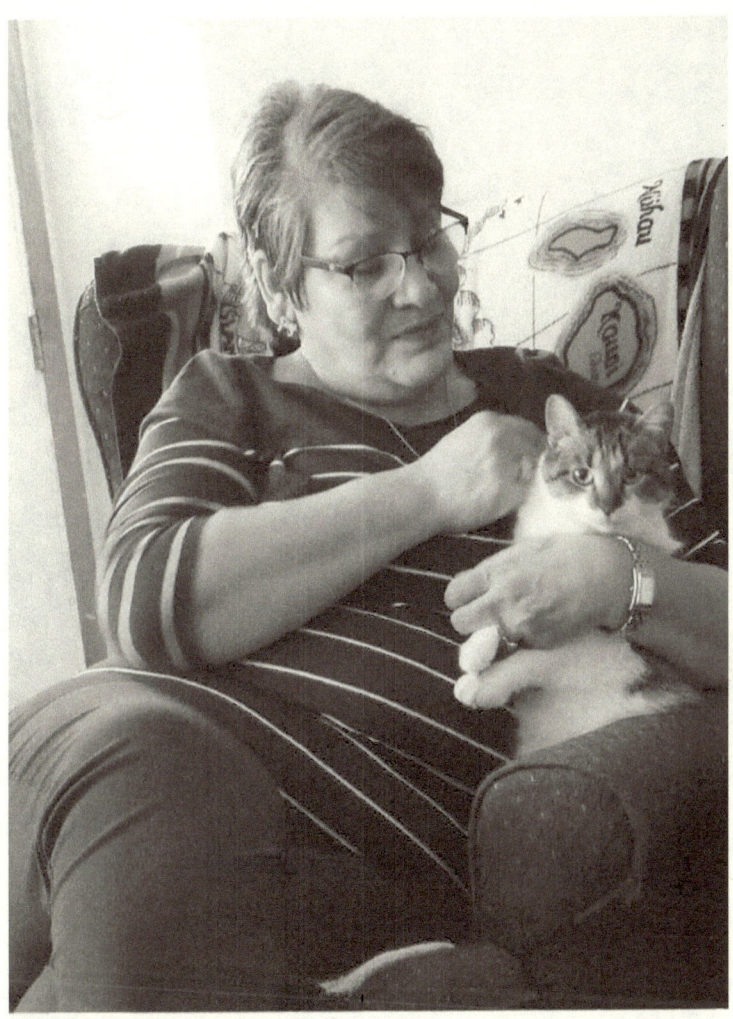

Figure 4. Tomasita Balderas-Hermosillo, with her cat, Lucille. Minneapolis, Minnesota, 2019.

Figure 5. Tomasita Balderas-Hermosillo with her children. Detroit Lakes, Minneapolis, 1990.

The turkey and chicken factories were, in many ways, an economic solution for a lot of the migrant families in the area. My mom and dad worked there; so did my older brother and older sister. Our family friends and conocidos also worked at the factory. It became a hub to socialize and central to the city. Our lives revolved around the factory.

I remind myself that the work I do in no way comes close to the degree of physical exhaustion and pain my mother endured in order to feed her family and pay the bills. She was on her feet all day for 8 hours, unless she worked overtime, which seemed like an ironic blessing to get to work 12+ hours at a job like this.

Her labor didn't just include factory work. It was her scratching my head and humming my favorite rancheras, it was cleaning hotel rooms, and it was making frijoles and tortillas de harina from scratch. Why can't her parenting, the masa under her fingernails, be celebrated as much as her ability to pay the bills? My mother is not just her labors or her ability to give birth; she's a sensuous woman first, with dreams and desires. I recall her love of bailes and after parties, and the times when she wiped the sweat from my brow after I'd given birth.

Sitting, typing this in an air conditioned library at a research one university seems so far away from those early mornings when I would see my mom come home from work, just in time to see us off when the school bus would pick us up in the mornings.

Amasando: Performing and Laboring Relational/Embodied Theory

Stories untold remain lodged in the throat, tightened
Always present, impatiently waiting to be undone
Spontaneous gestures of the body
Choking on tears because words refuse to come up.
To Surface.

Through gendered anti-immigrant discourse, the story that is told about Latina mothers is articulated as always already deviant, excessive, and burdensome on the nation. Those narratives are imprinted on the body. Yet, through a retelling and re-storying of our own mothers' migration narratives, we have bridged a gap between greco-roman centered rhetorics and corporeal realities (Juárez 13; Hinojosa 5). We do so with deep acknowledgement that our families and communities already have rhetorical practices that speak to our unique experiences. In this collaboration, we embody Anzaldúa's theory of amasamiento as "an act of kneading, of uniting and joining that not only has produced both a creature of darkness and a creature of light, but also a creature that questions the definitions of light and dark and gives them new meanings" (103).

This rhetorical practice of the amasamiento of re-storying is like the kneading of masa (103). It is tiresome, repetitive, and physically demanding, and it leaves the same physical and metaphorical traces. For example, working in the garden or in farm fields or labores causes direct contact with the soil, and the dirt lodges itself under your fingernails. It is this "dirt underneath my mother's fingernails" that we are invested in. Furthermore, amasando causes direct contact with all the organic materials. For example, the corn, manteca, salt, and boiling water: the masa, the dough. It stays under your fingernails and acts as another layer of knowledge and cultural memory. Amasando — working through embodied rhetorics as children of working class migrant mothers — hurts. In our case, this retelling process has been emotionally and intellectually exhausting. It is performative and methodological in the sense that amasando is a cultural practice with cultural memories (Taylor *The Archive*, 82).

We are invested in re-storying gendered labor, such as cooking tortillas and pupusas, to give visibility to migrant women's labor as a feminist rhetorical practice of survival that refuses to engage with the traditional canon of rhetoric. It was, after all, our migrant mothers who taught us how to teach rhetoric not as static, but as relational and embodied.

A Queer Turn, Indeed: On Performing a Rhetorics of the Flesh at NACCS 2018

In the following and final section, we turn to our experiences presenting this working essay, "rhetorics of the flesh," at an academic conference to analyze the possibilities, difficulties, and limits of sharing embodied knowledge. A "rhetorics of the flesh" is a scholarly and academic thinking/feeling process; therefore, it makes sense to include the academic conference presentation as part of this intellectual/emotional process. Here we engage our collaborative writing as a queer retelling full of world-building possibilities.

Figure 6. NACCS Panel titled "Encuentros in Translation: Sharing Queer Knowledges accross Borders y Lenguas". Sandibel Borges, Sebastian Ferrada, Ruben Zecena, and Alejandra I. Ramírez. Minneapolis, Minnesota, 2018

For the 2018 National Association for Chicana and Chicano Studies (NACCS) conference in Minneapolis, Minnesota, the theme was "The Queer Turn." For us, this theme implies a movement that constitutes the work of feminist "wondering" (Ahmed, *Cultural Politics of Emotion* 180-181). It weaves in and out and together; we wondered/wandered around the rooms of the conference hotel, the indigenous lands of Minnesota and the Dakota peoples, and even with the table at which we sat and presented. We were "moved" by the theme and purposefully decided to include a performative element to our paper presentation. In the spirit of the "queer turn" and feminist wonderings, like a dance, we decided to maneuver through our essay and to read a paragraph each, and that we would go back and forth, exchanging voices, in a kind of literary dance. A queer reading or performance of our collaborative writing process that is modeled after the cultural rhetorics "storying" tradition (Powell, Levy, et al.). We had first performed this paper in a small group setting on our campus. At the presentation white students were our main audience, with the exception of one queer Chicana professor. When it came to the part about retelling our mothers' stories, we both cried. We cried for one another, and we each cried for our mothers. The tears came as a surprise, but were a deshaogo and cleansing cry.

Figure 7. Image of Alejandra Irene Ramírez and Ruben Zecena, "before the tears," presenting this paper at the University of Arizona, Tucson, Arizona, 2018.

At NACCS, we performed this paper as part of the panel: "Encuentros in Translation: Sharing Queer Knowledges Across Borders y Lenguas," which invoked queer couplings and queer affinity forms: the meeting together of bodies, closeness of proximity, friendship, and intimacy in scholarship. We practiced right before and told ourselves that this time we wouldn't cry. *¡No llores!* We joked. Prior to the conference, we discussed how the university has taught us not to cry. Patriarchy has taught us not to cry. *Femme-phobia* has taught us not to cry. Visible emotion challenges the objectivist tradition, within which subjectivism and embodiment are not acknowledged as valid epistemologies or ways of knowing. The body that cries is feminine—not "civil" or "respectable" or "logical"—because it wonders and wanders too much. It feels too much.

And so we took deep breaths. And our voices sounded strong and bold. Our mothers would be proud. The larger group made up of our friends, colleagues, and esteemed professors and mentors was comforting. It also challenged us to be vulnerable, as the piece hailed us to embrace the powers and politics of emotion. The atmosphere in the room was heavy, almost palpable. The immateriality of emotion in a way created an affective bond. The audience was in sync as we performed. Some were teary eyed, the room was silent with occasional sniffs from audience members. Bodies were leaning forward, listening. We opened the panel by asking for permission to be open.

Though we had promised ourselves that we wouldn't cry, when it came to telling their stories, again, our voices cracked. Our speech slowed. We had to pause, inhale and exhale. Tears burst, so heavy that they dropped onto the printed essay. Se nos salieron hasta los mocos! We were ugly crying! But we pushed and pushed through the nudos en la garganta, until we finally finished. To our surprise, the performance continued with engagement from the audience, hugs, pictures, and a sense of affirmation post Q&A. Afterwards, audience members approached us. A group of high school students came up to us and told us that our performance reminded them of their mothers coming home after work. The performance continues as we write, months later.

We realize we quite literally poured our hearts onto the writing. We could not have come to this conclusion without having performed this collaboration, and thus performing a rhetoric of the flesh. Still, we ask: What do/can we make of our tears and our corporeal responses?

Queremos Bailar: Dando Vueltas, Back to the Body

Queer-inclusive scholarship should set amygdalas on fire as you resist the push, the tug, the prodding of the boundaries of your imagination. Queer-inclusive scholarship should hurt a little, it should be hard, because making the world larger is hard. And what is the point of scholarship if not to make the world larger?"

—Lorenzo Herrera y Lozano
"What Courses Through My Veins"

Due to homophobic violence in the public sphere, for many queer subjects the academic conference does not end at the last panel; it continues on the dance floor at the nearest queer club. In a sense, our bodies are oriented or gravitate toward similar spaces. As Ahmed contends, "Sexuality itself can be considered a spatial formation not only in the sense that bodies inhabit sexual spaces...but also in the sense that bodies are sexualized through how they inhabit space" (*Queer Phenomenology* 67). The ambiente, the environment, is palpable at the queer club because it is a space of celebration that permits us to be ourselves.

There is no need to "straighten up," as Justin Torres reminds us in his poetic rendering of the Pulse shooting ("In praise of Latin Night"), or professionalize our bodies in order to feel liberated—this is the "how" of what Sara Ahmed calls a queer phenomenology. It is through rhetorics of the flesh that we understand such inhabitation of space as venue for embodied knowledge and collaborative meaning-making. This liberating and scholarly dance for us is about how bodies are oriented toward each other, how they come together in motion, in tempo with one another in liberatory ways. We remembered to avoid over-simplifying or romanticizing "dancing," and honor the threats against queer joy. The Pulse Nightclub shooting reminds us that for the ideologies of homonationalism there is something that is threatening about queer of color joy coming together in celebration of queerness, liberation, and pleasure.

Similarly, we danced through our writing, thinking, remembering— back and forth, in circles, like cumbias, spinning, and returning. Even after our NACCS panel presentation, audience members noticed the dance and asked questions or approached us to comment on our back & forth presentation style and collaborative writing. A queer intellectual and embodied dance on paper, a textual intimacy, and a remembering or recalling moments of exuberance, pain, and resilience.

An act of e/motion, (e)motion.

We remember in our bodies and through our senses, the sweat from jotería night after NACCS conferences, just as we remember the smells and sights of the lives and labors of our migrant mothers. In the process of writing the essay, we shared queer affinities and difficulties but also stories of possibility. We realized that in the performance of co-creating meaning, there is a space for generative growth and new understandings. Our moms, whose seemingly impossible location within the immigrant rights movement (as demonstrated through immigration reform that continues to exclude them), make possible our refusal to be victimized and criminalized. Like the scene in the film *Selena*, where her mom teaches her to do the "washing machine," our mothers teach us to make beauty out of seemingly impossible situations. Accordingly, we dance, write, and celebrate together as a liberatory praxis. The retelling of what we previously perceived as bad memories prompted us to conceive of our paper as a dance, one in which we share public space and hold hands with like-minded people. Through dancing we are able to learn from one another and continue writing, thinking, and remembering. We maintain a strong commitment to queer women of color feminisms, wherein intersectionality is central to making sense of how systems of oppression intersect in varying moments at the conference, the coffee shop, and the dance floor.

This is not a conclusion, but a joining of bodies with sentimientos and conocimientos. A continuation.

Aqui volvemos a empezar.

Figure 8. Alejandra Irene Ramírez and Ruben Zecena at Lucce Coffee Shop, Tucson, Arizona, 2016.

Works Cited

Ahmed, Sara. *The Cultural Politics of Emotion.* Routledge, 2004.
—. *Queer Phenomenology: Orientations, Objects, Others.* Duke University Press, 2006.
Anzaldúa, Gloria E. *Borderlands/La Frontera: The New Mestiza.* 4th ed., Aunt Lute Books, 2012. Blackwell, Maylei. *Chicana Power:Contested Histories of Feminism in the Chicano Movement.* University of Texas Press, 2011.
Chang, Grace. *Disposable Domestics: Immigrant Women Workers in the Global Economy.* 2nd ed., Haymarket Books, 2016.
Chávez, Karma. *Queer Migration Politics: Activist Rhetoric and Coalitional Possibilities.* University of Illinois Press, 2013.
Cruz, Cindy. "Toward an Epistemology of the Brown Body." *Qualitative Studies in Education,* vol. 14, no. 5, 2001, pp. 657-669.
De Genova, Nicholas. "The Deportation Regime: Sovereignty, Space, and the Freedom of Movement." *The Deportation Regime: Sovereignty, Space, and the Freedom of Movement,* edited by Nichola De Genoval and Nathalie Peutz, Duke University Press, 2010, pp. 33-65.
Driskill, Qwo-Li. *Asegi Stories: Cherokee Queer and Two-Spirit Memory.* University of Arizona Press, 2016.
—. "Doubleweaving Two-Spirit Critiques: Building Alliances between Native and Queer Studies." *GLQ: A Journal of Lesbian and Gay Studies,* vol. 16, no. 1-2, 2010, pp. 69-92.
Escobar, Martha D. *Captivity Beyond Prisons: Criminalization Experiences of Latina (Im)migrants.* University of Texas Press, 2016.
Facio, Elisa and Irene Lara. editors. *Fleshing the Spirit: Spirituality and Activism in Chicana,Latina, and Indigenous Women's Lives.* University of Arizona Press, 2014.
Levy, Daisy E. *This book called my body: An embodied rhetoric.* 2002. Michigan State University, PhD dissertation.
Hall, Stuart. "Introduction." *Representation: Cultural Representations and Signifying Practices,* edited by Stuart Hall, Sage Publications & Open University, 1997, pp. 1-12.
Herrera y Lozano, Lorenzo. "What Courses Through My Veins: Forging and Forcing Space for Queer Brown Desire and Memory." *Facebook,* 5 Apr. 2018,
Hinojosa Jr., Yndalecio Isaac. *Cuerpo, or a Spatial-Material Rhetoric: Embodied Approaches Using Chicana Third Space Feminism for Understanding and Teaching Literacy on the Border.* 2015. University of San Antonio, PhD dissertation.
Johnson, E. Patrick. "'Quare' studies, or (almost) everything I know about queer studies I learned from my grandmother." *Text & Performance,* vol. 21, no. 1, 2010, pp.1-25.
Juárez, Marisa Marie. *Bodily Force and Rhetorical Function in the Afro-Brazilian Art Form of Capoeira.* 2012. University of Arizona, PhD Dissertation.
Moraga, Cherríe. *Watsonville: Some Place Not Here and Circle in the Dirt: El Pueblo de East Palo Alto.* West End Press, 2002.
Nava, Gregory, director. *Selena.* Q-Productions, 1997.

Perdue, Theda. *Cherokee Women: Gender and Culture Change, 1700-1835 (Indians of the Southeast)*. University of Nebraska Press, 1998.

Powell, Malea, Daisy Levy, Andrea Riley-Mukavetz, Marilee Brooks-Gillies, Maria Novotny, and Jennifer Fisch-Ferguson. "Our Story Begins Here: Constellating Cultural Rhetorics." *Enculturation*, no. 18, 2014, http://www.enculturation.net/our-story-begins-here.

Rodriguez, Juana Maria. *Sexual Futures, Queer Gestures, and other Latina Longings*. New York University Press, 2014.

Tajima-Peña, Renee, director. *No Mas Bebes*. Moon Canyon Films and the Independent Television Service, 2015.

Tapia, Ruby C. *American Pietàs: Visions of Race, Death, and the Maternal*. University of Minnesota Press, 2011.

Taylor, Diana. *The Archive and the Repertoire: Performing Cultural Memory in the Americas*. Duke University Press, 2003.

——"Performing Ruins." *Telling Ruins in Latin America*, edited by Michael J. Lazzara and Vicky Unruh, Palgrave MacMillan, 2009, pp. 13-26.

Téllez, Michelle. "Lectures, Evaluations, and Diapers: Navigating the Terrains of Chicana Single Motherhood in the Academy." *Feminist Formations*, vol. 25, no.3, 2013, pp. 79-97.

Torres, Justin. "In praise of Latin Night at the Queer Club." *The Washington Post*, 13 June 2016, https://www.washingtonpost.com/opinions/in-praise-of-latin-night-at-the-queer-club/2016/06/13/e841867e-317b-11e6-95c0-_2a6873031302_story.html?noredirect=on&utm_term=.bc2ed3e2e8fb

Spivak, Gayatri. "Can the Subaltern Speak?" *Colonial Discourse and Post-Colonial Theory: A Reader*, edited by Patrick Williams and Laura Chrisman, Columbia University Press, 1993, pp. 66-111.

Valerio, Max. "It's In My Blood, My Face--My Mother's Voice, The Way I Sweat." *This Bridge Called my Back: Writings by Radical Women of Color*, edited by Cherríe Moraga and Gloria Anzaldúa, 4th ed., SUNY Press, 2015, pp. 36-40.

Ruben Zecena is a PhD Candidate in the Department of Gender & Women's Studies at the University of Arizona. He is a queer migrations scholar whose scholarship focuses on the cultural practices of LGBT migrants as an important avenues for imagining the world differently. His work appears or is forthcoming in *WSQ: Women's Studies Quarterly*, *Border-Lines*, and the edited collection *Queer and Trans Migrations*.

Alejandra I. Ramírez is a PhD Candidate in the Rhetoric, Composition, and Teaching of English (RCTE) Program at the University of Arizona. Alejandra is an award winning artist and global humanities scholar, and proud parent. Her research on the intersections of rhetoric and social justice have been published in *Understanding & Dismantling Privilege*, *El Mundo Zurdo 6*, and *Present Tense*. She has forthcoming work in *Xchanges*--an interdisciplinary Technical Communication, Writing/Rhetoric, and Writing Across the Curriculum journal, and in anthologies through NCTE Press, Ohio State UP, and the University of Washington Press.

About The Mentor

Kate Vieira is associate professor and the Susan J. Cellmer Distinguished Chair in Literacy in the School of Education at the University of Wisconsin, Madison. She is the author of *American by Paper: How Documents Matter in Immigrant Literacy* (University of Minnesota Press, 2016; Honorable Mention CCCC Outstanding Book Award, 2017) and *Writing for Love and Money: How Migration Drives Literacy Learning in Transnational Families* (Oxford University Press, 2019). She is a recipient of a Fulbright Scholar Award (2018-2019), a Spencer/National Academy of Education Postdoctoral Fellowship (2015-2016), a CCCC Chair's Research Initiative Grant (2017), and the Donald Murray Prize for Creative Nonfiction (2018).

Production Credits

Copyeditor(s): Jessica Gibbons, Sophie Schmidt
Editorial Assistant(s): Lauren Brentnell, Catheryn Jennings
Reviewer (s): Ann-Marie Lopez-Esquivel, Kate Vieira

Supplemental Material

"The Dirt Under My Mom's Fingernails": Queer Retellings and Migrant Sensualities
Alejandra I. Ramírez and Ruben Zecena

Part I: Reflection on the Origins of the Article

When having a conversation about the origins of this piece, we struggled to pinpoint one origin as we ambivalently recognize that our piece maps multiple traces of violence on the body and in the stories of migration; these are the origins of our piece. Origins that we retell and write against. Amidst so much violence, the body speaks, thinks, and feels–offering a new vantage point from which to view the world. Thus, by turning attention to the rhetorical practice of embodied knowledge, *rhetorics of the flesh*, we are able to articulate these origins, stories, and relations of power. While the origins of this piece speak to the intersectional and intergenerational effects of nation-state violence, the means through which we make sense of these violences manifest in shared moments of pleasure, pain, joy, dancing, story-telling, and memory. The piece materialized when we recognized shared memories of our mothers, particularly remembering the scents and sights of seeing our moms come home after long hours of industrial labor (at chicken factories and cutting potatoes). Our stories, identities, subject positions, and histories are different--and yet, these differences offer the opportunity to write about shared struggles and possibilities.

We thought about our own bodies in relation to our mothers, how our stories were part of their migration stories, and how migration was not only a painful or traumatic experience. Their recollections were also full of pleasurable moments with friends, family, and even romantic encounters. These sensual intimacies, their expressions of joy and their hopes for the future, for us, their children, are what we wanted to highlight throughout the piece. As our piece evolved, we presented different iterations of it at a conference and roundtable. We cried with the audience, shared common experiences and memories with them. These experiences, our tears, the audience feedback, also formed part of the foundation of the final piece. In a way, there is no origin, as even when returning to discuss writing this reflection, our piece evolves and continues to inform others.

Part II: Description of Research Methods, Findings, and/or Pedagogical Impact

We are both interdisciplinary scholars who traverse the fields of cultural rhetorics, women of color feminism, queer of color critique, border studies, amongst many. Writing this piece meant holding ourselves accountable to our mothers and doing justice to their stories. While we hold uneasy relationships with academia, we also understand that we must speak up because, as Audre Lorde teaches us, "even at the risk of having [speech] bruised or misunderstood" it must be shared publicly and put into words. Our words must be spoken.

Three important aspects that were important for our queer writing methods include the following:

A Queer Writing Practice

We scheduled flexible writing times where we worked on a google document at the same time and maintained vulnerability and trust in what we wrote. Escribimos en/con confianza. We always began with chisme sessions, jokes, and thus constantly created a space where our stories could be heard on their own terms. These stories did not always make it onto the page but nevertheless were an important aspect of co-authorship. Because we wanted to play with form and queerly veer off the straight lines of academic writing, sometimes we decided to write poetry and embed the poetry within the writing. Poetry helped to center our writing on embodied knowledge and experiences. It allowed us to compose along the margins and embrace the queer potentials of not holding ourselves up to the normative standards of academic writing. These are practices we encourage students to follow in our classrooms as they engage their own writing; to liberate themselves from rigid writing expectations, similar to the queer dance Anzaldúa performs in her own work.

Community Performances

Presenting the piece, at its different stages, in a public conference and roundtable, helped us get feedback, but more than anything, we wanted to share our mothers' stories and speak out about the violences migrant women often endure. We have, jokingly, ugly cried in front of audiences who cried with us. Hearing their pain made the story of this piece, and our mothers' stories, and the audiences' stories, more dignified and worthy of recognition. High school students came to us after one presentation and told us they shared experiences that aligned with our story, and thanked us for putting it out into the world. They told us they fundraised to get to the conference on their own. It was an honor for us that they decided to attend our panel. As a methodological practice, we write alongside multiple communities who share embodied knowledge.

Emotions

Writing is an emotional experience for us. We mention several times how we cried writing and presenting this piece. We joke that a copy still has mascara-stained tears on it. It is also scary to write, to put our mothers' experiences on paper and send to publication. While we encourage students to write what they know and feel, we warn them about the possibility of their stories being tokenized, or worse yet, become a tool by which to further discriminate against their identities. To write is an act of vulnerability and reciprocity. We share our emotions with the world in hopes that they move you, the reader, into action and hopefully encourage meaningful reflection on embodied knowledge.

Part III: Discussion Questions

1. What are our commitments to writing and publishing when we write with, about, and near others?

2. What stories do you carry within your body, underneath your skin?

3. How does queerness work as a method and writing practice?

WPA: WRITING PROGRAM ADMINISTRATION

WPA: Writing Program Administration is on the web at https://wpacouncil.org/aws/CWPA/pt/sp/journal

For forty years, *WPA: Writing Program Administration* has published practical, empirical, and theoretical research on issues in writing program administration. As the flagship journal of the Council of Writing Program Administrators, WPA publishes a wide range of research that not only serves administrators of writing programs in a variety of institutional contexts, but also advocates for the broader discipline of rhetoric and composition.

The F-Word: Failure in WPA Work[1]

We admired Heather Bastian's honest, introspective, and at times personal work analyzing "WPA scholarship to expose how WPAs often struggle to accept and make sense of failure in their work." Bastian weaves together a compelling overview of WPA scholarship with her own experiences of failure as a new program administrator to develop what the board believes is a workable "heuristic for failure in WPA work" that can help administrators come to terms with and move on from their own failures. Her process involves acknowledging the ways in which "(1) failure exists outside of success, (2) failure is an important term, (3) failure causes negative yet worthwhile emotions, and (4) failure is valuable."

---

1. *WPA: Writing Program Administration*, vol. 43, no. 1, 2019. © 2019 by the Council of Writing Program Administrators.

The F-Word: Failure in WPA Work

Heather Bastian

> *This essay addresses failure in WPA work, specifically what happens when WPAs experience failure. I analyze WPA scholarship to expose how WPAs often struggle to accept and make sense of failure in their work. I then draw from recent efforts in writing studies to engage failure within the context of teaching to develop a heuristic for failure in WPA work.*

WPAs are described as many things in scholarship: agents of change and activists (McLeod; Adler-Kassner); researchers engaged in reflective practice (Rose and Weiser; Brown, Enos, and Chaput); kitchen cooks, plate twirlers, and troubadours (George); theorists (Rose and Weiser); and managers (Bousquet). Rarely, if ever, are WPAs described as failures; yet four years into a tenure-track position, I was a failed WPA.

A brief history. In fall 2010, I started a tenure-track position as the only rhetoric and composition specialist at a small, private, comprehensive, regional college. I was to teach the standard 3/3 with the additional expectation that I would "work with adjuncts, the Director of the Writing Center, and other faculty to promote writing," as outlined in the job description. Essentially, I was the *de facto* WPA with no existing program and no reassignment time. By fall 2011, I negotiated a one-course reassignment on a semester-to-semester basis to develop a writing program focused on faculty development. To fulfill the job description, my idea was to support English department adjuncts while facilitating WAC/WID outreach through one-on-one meetings and workshops with departments and faculty across the disciplines. In spring 2012, I expanded my efforts to pilot a writing enriched curriculum (WEC) initiative (inspired by the WEC model out of the University of Minnesota) with the Department of Graduate Nursing while I continued WAC/WID outreach. This work continued through fall 2012 and spring 2013, and faculty demand was so great that I could not meet it. During this time, the vice president of academic affairs convened a writing task force composed of faculty and staff. The task force recommended continuation of the faculty and curricular development work that I was doing with even more financial support. In fall 2013, I began a WEC project with the MBA program.

By spring 2014, my one-course reassignment was revoked due to budget concerns. The cut occurred with no consultation, no warning, and no fanfare. The program just ended, and I was no longer a WPA. Larger budget cuts occurred just one semester later. The Center for Teaching Excellence, the only other institutional outlet for faculty development, was eliminated. The Writing Center experienced a budget cut that forced them to reduce their staff. Overall, fifteen faculty and staff positions were eliminated. I may have lost a course reassignment and with it a program, but I retained my position.

Despite its short existence, the WAC program that I worked to develop experienced several successes according to conventional metrics. Faculty support and demand for the program was strong, and the task force recommended its continuation with more funding—no small feat. The curriculum in the graduate nursing program was transformed, and both the faculty and students were experiencing positive results. Additionally, this work led to three publications, two co-authored with nursing faculty, and one conference presentation with nursing faculty. Still, at the end of four years, neither these successes nor I could save the program, and I felt like a failed WPA.

Before proceeding, let me clarify. This article is not a rant against university administration nor is it a cautionary tale about jWPA work. I was promoted and tenured at that institution with no setbacks and am now happily a full-time, nonfaculty WPA at another institution by choice. It also is not a description or defense of my actions or decisions. I could have made other decisions, perhaps better ones that would have saved the program or maybe even worse ones that would have put a swifter end to it. I also want to acknowledge at the outset that my story ultimately is one of personal success, but this does not preclude my story also being one of failure. Success and failure do not have to be either/or experiences that exist in opposition to each other but rather can be both/and experiences that exist simultaneously and independently. My previous institution no longer has a WAC program, and I was part of this failure. My experience and the program at that moment in time will forever remain a failure and, with it, I a failed WPA, but this does not mean that I am not also a successful WPA.

In this article, I explore the complexities of failure in WPA work. I analyze WPA scholarship to examine what happens when WPAs, especially those new to the position, experience failure, large and small. As I hope to demonstrate, WPAs often struggle to accept and make sense of failure in their work. I then draw from recent efforts in writing studies to engage failure within the context of teaching to develop a heuristic for failure in WPA work. Failure may be an inevitable part of WPA work, but it does not have to be nor should it be an aspect that WPAs internalize, hide, or fear.

The F-Word

Within the last decade, popular culture, the business world, and Silicon Valley have championed failure as a pathway for success. Popular self-help books with titles like *How to Fail at Almost Everything and Still Win Big* (Scott Adams); *Adapt: Why Success Always Starts with Failure* (Harford); and *Failing Forward: Turning Mistakes into Stepping Stones for Success* (Maxwell) encourage readers to channel their failures into successes. Similarly, popular business magazines including the *Harvard Business Review*, *Forbes*, and *Entrepreneur* regularly feature articles like "Strategies for Learning from Failure" (Edmondson), "5 Ways Fear of Failure Can Ruin your Business" (R. L. Adams); and "8 Ways Smart People Use Failure to Their Advantage" (Bradberry) that tout failure as essential to business success and provide strategies to make failure work for, not against, you.

Despite this newfound (if not faddish) appreciation for failure outside the walls of the academy, academic culture has a complicated relationship with failure. While some universities and colleges have developed student-focused programs that foreground the role of failure in learning (see Bennett), success remains the primary metric for evaluating and valuing faculty and staff whether that be in research, teaching, assessment, or administration. The 2016 viral phenomena of Johannes Haushofer's "CV of Failures" nicely demonstrates this tension. Taking up Melanie Stefan's suggestion to compile an "alternative CV of failures," Haushofer, an assistant professor of Psychology at Princeton, published his "CV of Failures" that lists rejections he received as well as awards, recognitions, and funding he did not get. Haushofer and his CV quickly gained fame as it was picked up by several national and international news organizations. The widespread admiration and recognition his "CV of Failures" garnered—as he writes, "This darn CV of Failures has received way more attention than my entire body of academic work"—suggests just how unusual it is for an academic to admit their own failures, let alone share them publicly and in writing. Faculty may tell students that failure is okay and even necessary for learning, but faculty rarely demonstrate or admit failure in their own work.

Failure occupies a precarious position in academic culture because academe relies on, as Judy Z. Segal calls it, "a professional discourse of success" (175) in which scholars generally write and talk about their successes rather than their failures. In other words, success primarily drives and underlies academic work and scholarship. Segal points out that this discourse of success poses problems because "when we do not write about failure, we write in the *context* of a rhetoric of success, not associating one response to failure with any other" (175). Segal is particularly interested in failure when one attempts to "decenter" the writing classroom, but her words here highlight the limitation a discourse of success poses to the larger academic culture. Without attention to failure in academic professional discourse, failures are understood as isolated incidents that deviate from the context of success rather than connected experiences that constitute their own context and from which one can learn.

This discourse of success underlies much WPA scholarship with monographs and edited collections providing WPAs with guidance for how to be successful in their positions. Edward M. White's *Developing Successful Writing Programs* outlines theoretical and practical issues for WPAs to consider in order to make "decisions that are appropriate to individual campus situations" (xviii). Linda Myers-Breslin in *Administrative Problem-Solving for Writing Programs and Writing Centers Scenarios in Effective Program Management* brings together contributors who work through different scenarios to demonstrate WPA decision-making skills; as she writes, "each contributor provides a description of a problematic situation, as well as enough information about the institution and program to resolve the situation" (xv). Irene Ward and William J. Carpenter's *Allyn and Bacon Sourcebook for Writing Program Administrators* includes 23 essays to serve as "a resource for finding the right solution for a particular program or institution" (xi). Most recently, Bryna Siegel Finer and Jamie White-Farnham's *Writing Program Architecture: Thirty Cases for Reference and Research* asks contributors to outline the architecture or the "material, logistical, and rhetorical elements" (4) of their programs to provide "models and case studies of how writing programs of all types are structured and sustained" (23).

WPAs specifically interested in WAC programs (as I am) can turn to edited collections and articles to help make their WAC work a success. Susan McLeod and Margot Soven's edited collection *Writing Across the Curriculum: A Guide to Developing Programs* serves as a resource for WPAs to initiate or expand WAC programs and, in the words of Elaine P. Maimon in the preface, "defines terms, presents helpful suggestions, even provides models for useful documents (everything from workshop evaluation forms to contracts for visiting consultants), and in short, makes everyone's work easier" (vii). McLeod's later edited collection *Strengthening Programs for Writing Across the Curriculum* addresses how "second-stage" WAC programs (programs that have been in existence for three or more years) can overcome common challenges, including Keith A. Tandy's piece on how to redesign a program when funding and support are reduced or run out. *WPA: Writing Program Administration* too features articles like Susan H. McLeod and Margot Soven's "What Do You Need to Start—and Sustain—a Writing-Across-the-Curriculum Program?", Jay Carson's "Ways to Connect WAC Programs to their Context," and Martha A. Townsend, Martha D. Patton, and Jo Ann Vogt's "Uncommon Conversations: How Nearly Three Decades of Paying Attention Allows One WAC/WID Program to Thrive" that provide WAC directors with concrete strategies and recommendations for success.

The discourse of success also pervades WPA narratives. As others have pointed out, scholarship frequently explores WPA work in terms of storytelling or personal narratives (e.g. Enos and Borrowman; George; Stolley). These stories tend to "paint us as the romantic hero who defends the program against administrative whims or the tragic martyr who sacrifices herself for the good of the program or her own ethical principles" (Stolley 22). Edward M. White's "Use it or Lose It: Power and the WPA" is a classic example in which White saves the WAC program from budget cuts by moving the program out of the School of Humanities and into the Office of Undergraduate Studies. Of course, not all narratives follow this storyline, but as Thomas P. Miller suggests, "our scholarship still includes more self-effacing narratives about how canny administrators managed adversity to make the best of a bad situation" (81). WPAs don't fail; they overcome.

To point out that a discourse of success underlies much WPA scholarship is not to say that WPAs do not seriously engage with challenges and problems that they face. In all of the examples cited above, scholars engage with challenging aspects of writing program work or directly address common problems that WPAs encounter. WPA scholarship certainly does not simplify or minimize challenges and problems, and no one would accuse WPAs of presenting a rose-colored view of their work.

Additionally, I am not suggesting that past WPA scholarship is not important, valuable, and needed. Without the guidance of seasoned WPAs, I, like many others, would certainly have been lost in my first position and the outcome could have been far worse. WPAs are fortunate to have such a robust body of scholarship. In fact, it is precisely because of this scholarship and my graduate school preparation that I felt at least somewhat prepared to tackle the many challenges and problems that awaited me as a new jWPA even though I was well aware of the many cautions against non-tenured WPA work (see, for example, Debra Frank Dew and Alice Horning's *Untenured Faculty as Writing Program Administrators* or Theresa Enos and Shane Borrowman's *Promises and Perils of Writing Program Administration*). This is also perhaps why when I was faced with what seemed like a significant failure of losing a program that I was hired to create, I felt especially lost and ashamed.

Scholars already have explored limits of narratives in WPA scholarship, arguing for the inclusion of voices and stories from nonfaculty WPAs (Duffey), early career WPAs (Stolley; Rose), and liminal WPAs (Phillips, Shovlin, and Titus). The need for alternative narratives of WPA work is nicely articulated and demonstrated by Amy Ferdinandt Stolley in her recent *WPA* article in which she examines how WPA narratives "are more restrictive and disciplining than we might imagine" (19). She observes that:

narratives and collective experiential knowledge can align neatly with certain aspects of our professional identities, but significant truth claims repeated in WPA narratives do not always match the experiences of some WPAs and can be at odds with the values and choices WPAs make. (20)

Stolley is interested in how the mantra of "Don't take an administrative position before tenure" emotionally affects early career WPAs who choose to follow this career path and seeks to open a space for narratives that explore this experience (20).

Extending Stolley's work and her focus on narratives, I am interested here in how the discourse of success that underlies much WPA scholarship and the lack of attention to failure emotionally affects WPAs, especially early career WPAs. The potential emotional impact of failing to address failure in scholarship has been observed by others. Thomas Newkirk, for example, finds that teaching of writing scholarship tends to focus on "upbeat success stories" that reflect ideal situations and circumstances (3). This poses problems, however, because "these ideals, to the extent that they are unrealistic, inflict psychological damage; they induce guilt, envy, and a sense of inadequacy" (Newkirk 3). Similarly, on reflecting on her CV, conference presentations, and scholarship, Melanie Stefan notes that "as scientists we construct a narrative of success that renders our setbacks invisible both to ourselves and to others . . . therefore, whenever we experience an individual failure, we feel alone and dejected." Both Newkirk and Stefan argue for making failure visible, with Newkirk suggesting writing teachers "create forums for telling failure stories" (6) and with Stefan suggesting scientists compose alternative CVs of failure, so that the negative emotional impact of failure is reduced. Without this visibility, negative feelings can flourish.

Recent attention to emotion in WPA work also speaks to the need to address failure in scholarship although it does so less directly than Newkirk and Stefan. Laura R. Micciche adopts Sarah Ahmed's concept of "stickiness" to explore how objects, like narratives, "amass affective associations" that in turn stick to and influence those who read them (27). In terms of WPA scholarship, Micciche examines how disappointment has come to characterize WPA work. She analyzes two WPA narratives to uncover how disappointment is inextricably linked to WPA working conditions, conditions in which WPAs may seem to hold power only to find out that they often have very little. While working conditions certainly contribute to WPA feelings of disappointment, another related source of disappointment might stem from WPA scholarship. In other words, WPA scholarship may contribute to feelings of disappointment by directly addressing them (as Micciche suggests) but also by emphasizing success or overcoming adversity. Disappointment may stick to WPAs as they read scholarship, but, I would argue, so too does success. Micciche argues that WPAs must consider more carefully "how disappointment is woven into the fabric of our work lives and how we can combat destructive disaffection by improving our working conditions" so that WPAs do not simply become accustomed to disappointment (90). I would add that WPAs also need to directly address failure in their work as another way to engage disappointment and combat disaffection.

One can find glimpses of the emotional impact that the lack of attention to failure creates in WPA scholarship. Finer and White-Farnham begin their recent collection *Writing Program Architecture* with an email from Shevaun Watson regarding her chapter revision. She expresses concern about including her chapter in the collection because the changes to the first-year writing program that she discusses in her chapter will most likely be undone by budget cuts and she has since accepted a WPA position at a different institution. After communicating this news, she writes:

> So revising this [chapter] has entailed a very heavy heart. I think there is valuable information in what I was able to accomplish here, but it was fleeting and will go out as quick as it came in. Surely, that cannot be the "lesson" here, which is why I don't know if I want this included in the final publication. (3)

For Finer and White-Farnham, Watson's email highlights the importance of attending to a writing program's architecture—its "material, logistical, and rhetorical elements"—in order to "disentangle [the WPA] role from the program itself" and "to strengthen [WPA] positions in times of turmoil or in the face of dismantling" (4). While Finer and White-Farnham's reading of Watson's email is certainly valid and important, I read something additional in her email, a hesitation (and even concern) to share a change that most likely will fail. As Finer and White-Farnham point out, the fault of the failure wasn't necessarily with Watson herself but rather the result of decisions outside of her control. Still, Watson's search to find a lesson in her experience beyond its fleeting nature and her questioning of whether that alone is a valuable and viable lesson speaks to the limits of the discourse of success. Paul Cook in "Notes from the Margins: WAC, WID, and the Politics of Place(ment)" finds himself in a different situation as a jWPA at a small, rural liberal arts college but with a similar outcome. As he reflects on his experience, he recalls what drew him to the position: "I saw an opportunity to have a lasting, positive impact on an institution, a chance to leave my mark." What he finds, however, is that "ongoing material, pedagogical, and institutional challenges" are too much to overcome so he accepted a position elsewhere as a non-WPA. He sums up this decision as such: "In short, I felt as though *I* had failed" (emphasis added). What strikes me about Cook's rendering of his experience is the impulse I think many WPAs feel, a chance to leave a mark, to affect positive change, and I identify with Cook's subsequent feelings of personal failure when that does not come to fruition. Cook examines his experience to reveal "larger concerns about WAC/WID's vulnerability in rural SLACs, [small liberal arts colleges]" but, importantly, he ultimately seems to understand and position the failure to effect change in that context as his alone.

What Watson's and Cook's words highlight, for me, are the ways in which WPAs struggle to accept and make sense of failure in their work as well as their tendency to internalize failure (and to fear that others will associate it with them). I too struggled to understand my experience and felt uncomfortable and hesitant to share it with others. I worried what the loss of a writing program would say to others about me as a WPA and even as an educator and scholar. When WPAs do not experience success, do not overcome adversity, or do not make the best of a bad situation, where can they turn to help make sense of these experiences?

A Heuristic for Failure

Writing studies scholars have recently turned their attention to failure within the context of teaching writing (Alvarez; Carr; Gross and Alexander; Inoue; Segal). Noting the relative dearth of attention to failure within the field, these scholars argue that failure is valuable for teaching and learning and, as such, warrants a place within the classroom but also within scholarship. While these scholars focus on failure as a pedagogical strategy, their work provides a basis from which to develop a heuristic for failure in writing program administration.

Failure seems to be useful for at least two reasons: it opens a space for reflection and for critique of structures and norms. John Dewey in *How We Think* argues for the role of failure in reflective thought. For Dewey, reflective thought is an important educational aim, and in his five stage process, he addresses the value of failure in the fifth stage, testing the hypothesis by action. He writes:

> but a great advantage of possession of the habit of reflective activity is that failure is not *mere* failure. It is instructive . . . [failure] either brings to light a new problem or helps to define and clarify the problem on which he has been engaged. (114)

Dewey argues that failure should be part of the educational process, allowing for further reflection in which a person seeks to understand the failure and then make use of this knowledge. While Dewey's emphasis on the role of reflective thought in learning and his rendering of failure within it are certainly valuable, they rely on an understanding of education as "a forward-moving, product-oriented march toward some mark of achievement" (Carr). Within this formulation, failure is positioned as a step or movement toward success, toward resolution, rather than embraced in its own right.

Embracing failure in its own right provides for a different kind of reflective space, as Allison Carr explores in "In Support of Failure." When people allow themselves to dwell in failure and experience it in its own terms rather than in relation to success, failure, Carr argues, can be a "*deeply felt,* transformative process." She highlights the value of this understanding of failure and her proposed "pedagogy of failure" by drawing from her own experience of failing to complete a written assignment as a Ph.D. student. In positioning herself as a failure in the weeks following this experience, Carr was able to slow down, to notice, to pay attention, and "to let myself feel the pain of failure and to find a way to make that work for me." It is important to distinguish here that Carr makes failure work for her as a person rather than for the situation. Failure "works" for Carr not as a way to succeed in a specific situation or project but instead as a way to see herself as a person. As a result, Carr embraces and advocates for the transformative power of failure, finding ways to "*do it better,* to stay there longer, to take it on as an epistemological choice" because it allows her to "ask myself how I got to where I am, where I am trying to go, and if there is maybe somewhere else I should be instead. I ask myself how I am feeling and why I am feeling that way." These self-reflective questions differ from the kind of reflection that Dewey encourages as the impetus and goal are not on outward progress but rather on inward feelings of the moment, questioning where they come from, why did they come from there, and do I even want to be here?

Other scholars find that failure allows insight into structural power dynamics. Daniel M. Gross and Jonathan Alexander advocate for frameworks for failure in their critique of the *Framework for Success in Postsecondary Writing*. Like Carr, Gross and Alexander encourage educators to consider the value of failure on its own terms rather than placing it in relation to (and lesser than) success. Tracing the roots of the *Framework* to positive psychology, they find the success-oriented nature of the document to be problematic in that by focusing on success in the classroom and the positive emotions associated with it, the *Framework* leaves little room for failure and the negative emotions that often come with it. However, failure and negative emotions, they argue, can and should play a crucial role in education. They draw from queer theory's engagement with failure and negative emotion, especially Judith Halberstam's *The Queer Art of Failure*, to argue that "unhappiness, dissatisfaction and even failure might serve as entry points to critique the power structures and normalizing discourses" (288). As they further explain:

> The cost of forgetting negative emotion, even the experience of failure, is high. Success feels good but it does not reorient us against unjust norms. Success, as it trumps personal failure, can also numb us to failures that are structural. (290)

For Gross and Alexander, failure provides a critical lens, shifting the locus of failure (and success) from the individual to the structures and norms in which he or she operates.

Building on Carr and Gross and Alexander's work, I propose here a heuristic to help WPAs make sense of failure. It incorporates the following elements: (1) failure exists outside of success, (2) failure is an important term, (3) failure causes negative yet worthwhile emotions, and (4) failure is valuable. While I address these four elements separately below, I see them as working together as a process and not necessarily experienced in a particular order. I draw on my own firsthand experience to illustrate the value of the heuristic for WPAs, but I believe other WPAs whose experiences of failure or circumstances differ slightly or significantly from my own still will find this heuristic to be valuable. Failure in my case was primarily the result of institutional decisions that were outside of my control rather than decisions that I made regarding the program, and my job security and professional reputation were not on the line and no one was calling into question my personal fitness for my position. My personal circumstances at the time also allowed for much flexibility in terms of career paths and geographical location. This was, in many ways, an ideal failure situation. The heuristic, however, is intended to be dynamic and responsive, enabling a WPA to make sense of their own experiences of failure within their individualized professional and personal circumstances. Even WPAs who have a similar experience of failure as my own may not respond to the heuristic in the same ways that I did. WPAs will have different responses to the heuristic that will lead them to different places but all who adopt it would take failure as their focal point to find a way to make failure work for them.

One element of the heuristic is that WPAs situate their understanding of failure outside of success. Both Carr and Gross and Alexander stress the importance of understanding failure in its own terms rather than positioning it as a pit stop to success or in opposition to success. As Gross and Alexander remind us, success is not contextless—it is defined in accordance with existing structures and norms, and, as such, success may have positive implications for the individual but may have negative consequences for others. In other words, success is not all good all the time nor is failure all bad all the time. Additionally, success does not have to be the all-consuming goal or resolution for every experience, as failure offers another valid and valuable experience.

Allowing the failure of the writing program to exist outside of the context of success was hard for me and took time. The only future I had imagined was one with a successful program, perhaps not as successful as I would have liked but certainly not a failure. So when I first received news about my course reassignment being revoked, my first thoughts were "what did I do wrong" and "how did I let this happen?" I was searching for what I did that kept the program from being a success. It was not until the next semester when the other larger budget cuts occurred that I began to consider that a successful writing program may not have been possible regardless of what I did. At the same time, I knew that the program still did a lot of good for faculty and students even as a failure. Reconciling these two seemingly opposed thoughts challenged me to complicate my understanding of failure as bad and success as good. It also allowed me to use and even embrace the word failure to describe the program without the internal judgement that I was a bad WPA despite the fact that I failed to save it.

Another element of the heuristic is that WPAs need to use the term failure. Instead of recasting failure as a challenge, opportunity, or even a problem or disappointment, WPAs, at times, need to resist this impulse and just let experiences or projects be failures and they need to call them that at least internally (they need not always or ever do so privately or publicly with others). While positioning failure outside of success was hard for me, resisting the urge to recast my experience in more optimistic terms was relatively easy. As I mention above, my course reassignment was revoked suddenly and without warning. I, quite frankly, was caught off guard because from my perspective, the program was going strong: faculty supported it and the task force endorsed it. The extreme disconnects between my understanding of the situation and the budgetary reality coupled with the resulting feelings of anger and hurt allowed me to more easily cast the program as a failure than if I was more prepared for the budget cut or if faculty support was wavering or inconsistent. It also was relatively safe for me to name the program a failure since my own personal qualifications for the job were not under attack.

I found immense power in naming my own experience a failure. Hearing myself say "failure" either with others in private or in my own self talk allowed me to slow down, like Carr describes, and resist the impulse to keep moving forward with this particular program. To be clear, using the term failure did not mean that I was leaving WPA work and my experience entirely behind me but rather that I was letting go of this version of the program at this institution at this point in time. Failure allows for (but does not dictate) a finality that challenge, opportunity, problem, and disappointment do not, and in some situations, a sense of finality can be incredibly freeing. For me, failure gave me permission to discontinue all WPA-related work as I returned to a full teaching load when I lost funding instead of doing more or the same amount of work with less. When faculty contacted me for assistance (and they continued to do so), my message was simple and straightforward: "I'd really like to help you, but the College has discontinued support for my work with faculty." While this was a potentially risky message as a pre-tenure faculty member, it allowed me to retain some power over my workload in a situation where I had very little power otherwise.

Another element of the heuristic is that WPAs need to acknowledge and grapple with the emotions that accompany failure. Both Carr and Gross and Alexander encourage readers to dwell in the negative emotions of failure as those emotions can provide insight—for Carr that insight is into self and for Gross and Alexander that insight is into structures and norms. Negative emotions might not feel good, but they should not be ignored or rushed past as simply unpleasant interruptions. Allowing oneself to feel negative emotions prompts self-reflection and ideological critique that can be used in worthwhile ways.

In my case, losing the program hit me incredibly hard. I was profoundly sad, hurt, and angry and continued to be so for well over a year (and maybe even still a little to this day). While I did not openly express these emotions to colleagues, I felt them deeply every day and especially when faculty would contact me for assistance. Staying with these emotions while unpleasant and difficult allowed me to start asking after a few months, "why do I still feel *so* terrible?" rather than "what did I do wrong?" or "what mistakes did I make?" Focusing on my feelings instead of my actions prompted introspection on my own commitments, goals, and values. I discovered that my career and academic interests were shifting from first-year writing to WAC work. When I began this position, much of my WPA work was focused on first-year writing and working with adjuncts in this course, but over time, first-year writing needed little attention because the English department was hiring fewer adjuncts due to declining enrollments and WAC work needed much more attention because disciplinary faculty were requesting more assistance. In my WAC work, I deeply valued the connections I made with faculty and simply enjoyed experiencing other disciplinary ways of knowing, teaching, and communicating. WAC work allowed me to flex my own disciplinary and pedagogical knowledge in new and exciting ways that had the potential for a much wider impact than first-year writing and my own teaching. With these realizations, my commitments to faculty and curricular development across the disciplines rather than solely in first-year writing came into a clear focus for the first time.

This reflective look inward was paired with a critical look outward at the "power structures and normalizing discourses" in which I was working (Gross and Alexander, 288). Despite my best efforts and at that point in time, the program's "architecture," in Siegel and White-Farnham's words, could not support or sustain the kind of work I was doing and wanted to do. The institution had other priorities that did not align with my own commitments, and I did not see those priorities aligning with my own in the near future. This understanding allowed me to shift the failure from one that I "owned" as mine alone to one that was the result of the confluence of complex factors, both personal and contextual. It also brought me to a personal decision—stay at an institution whose values and priorities did not currently match my own but may in the future or find another institution whose priorities and values were more closely aligned with my own in the present.

My critical gaze outward extended beyond the physical institution to the larger academic context in which I worked. The lure of tenure required me to split my time between teaching, research, administration, and service yet perform in each area at levels in ways that were simply unsustainable for me, and I resented the "the grin and bear it" pre-tenure attitude I adopted out of fear of reprisal. I began to question what success and failure looks like and requires of people in tenure positions especially those that also carry administrative duties. This questioning continued as I looked for positions in other institutions. I was drawn to non-tenure track, full-time administrative positions in WAC programs, as they aligned most clearly with my commitments and allowed me to exit a tenure system that I was beginning to question and in which I no longer wanted to participate. While I am still working through many of the issues I raise here and do not pretend to have the answers to what I see as larger systemic concerns, embracing the emotions of failure provided me with a clarity of purpose and focus that I had not yet experienced at that point in my career.

The final element of the heuristic is that WPAs need to value failure. Admittedly, valuing failure is difficult and even feels counterintuitive given larger cultural and academic emphases on success, but, as I hope to have demonstrated above, failure can be a "*deeply felt*, transformative process" (Carr) that exists outside the context of success. By embracing failure as a process, I came to see its value not only for me as a person and WPA but also for a program. Failure allowed me as a person to clarify my own values, commitments, and goals and identify the ways in which they were or were not aligned with the program, its institutional context, and the larger academic contexts. Failure allowed me as a WPA to resist internalizing failure and seeing it as solely bad by providing me with another lens through which to analyze and understand the contexts in which I work and writing programs operate. And failure allowed the program to stop existing and to stop trying to get by with less. Failure, just as much as success, allows WPAs to prioritize and make decisions about a program, which, at times, means not taking on more, cutting back instead of adding, failing instead of succeeding. Failure in this light is not just an inevitable aspect of WPA work but also a necessary one.

I recount my experience above not to dictate how others should use the heuristic or how others should respond to failure but rather to illustrate how the heuristic worked for me in my particular situation. I encourage other WPAs to adopt this heuristic for private use in their own individual practice to help them make sense of their own experiences with failure. A WPA who is faced with a failure similar to my own but does not have the option or flexibility to leave the institution or position can still benefit from the heuristic as it allows insight into how they want to move forward within the current constraints. Or a WPA in a situation similar to mine may experience and respond to the emotions of failure differently than me to discover a deep commitment to the institution or community and work toward incremental change. Or a WPA who is facing criticisms because of professional decisions they made can benefit from slowing down and engaging with the emotions of failure, as Carr does, to explore how they got there, where they want to go, and where they do not want to go. By adopting failure as an important and valuable term, allowing failure to exist outside the context of success, and dwelling in the emotions of failure, WPAs can make failure work for them regardless of why the failure occurred or the circumstances surrounding it.

I also encourage WPAs to adopt more public uses of this heuristic in scholarship. In doing so, I recognize that not all (and perhaps not most) WPAs can openly and publicly admit failure without facing significant consequences, including denial of tenure and loss of employment or other career opportunities. But when those who have less to risk make failure public, they are helping to break its stigma and normalize it so that WPAs do not inwardly suffer when success does not await them. This is, in part, why I am sharing my story of failure and proposing a heuristic for failure for WPAs. I now am in a full-time nonfaculty administrative position where I am evaluated based on my work at this institution, not my past work at another institution. This position is situated within an office in academic affairs, not a department, where I work with other administrators engaged in similar tasks. I may experience some professional consequences for sharing my story of failure, but the risk is relatively small because, as I acknowledge above, my story is also one of success. I hope others who can share their stories of failure will do so too; but if not, I hope my story of failure and this heuristic can provide other WPAs, especially those who are new to the position, nonfaculty, or pre-tenure, with some comfort and guidance when they encounter failure. The failure in my story was significant, but WPAs encounter little failures (and successes) every day. In many ways, WPAs are masters of failure, and they should embrace this role.

Works Cited

Adams, R. L. "5 Ways Fear of Failure Can Ruin your Business." *Entrepreneur*, 19 Sept. 2017, entrepreneur.com/article/299403.

Adams, Scott. *How to Fail at Almost Everything and Still Win Big: Kind of the Story of my Life*. Penguin, 2013.

Adler-Kassner, Linda. *The Activist WPA: Changing Stories about Writing and Writers*. Utah State UP, 2008.

Alvarez, Deborah. "Why Students Fail." *Journal of Teaching Writing*, vol. 19, nos. 1–2, 2001, pp. 76–93.

Bennett, Jennifer. "On Campus, Failure is on the Syllabus." *New York Times*, 24 June, 2017, nytimes.com/2017/06/24/fashion/fear-of-failure.html.

Bousquet, Marc. "Composition as Management Science: Toward a University with a WPA." *JAC*, vol. 22, no. 3, 2002, pp. 493–526.

Bradberry, Travis. "8 Ways Smart People Use Failure to their Advantage." *Forbes*, 12 Apr. 2016, forbes.com/sites/travisbradberry/2016/04/12/8-ways-smart-people-use-failure-to-their-advantage/#32756d694489.

Brown, Stuart C., Theresa Enos, and Catherine Chaput, editors. *The Writing Program Administrator's Resource: A Guide to Reflective Institutional Practice*. Lawrence Erlbaum, 2002.

Carr, Allison. "In Support of Failure." *Composition Forum*, vol. 27, 2013, compositionforum.com/issue/27/failure.php.

Carson, Jay. "Ways to Connect WAC Programs to their Context." *WPA: Writing Program Administration*, vol. 22, no. 7, 1994, pp. 35–48.

Cook, Paul. "Notes from the Margins: WAC, WID, and the Politics of Place(ment)." *Across the Disciplines*, vol. 11, no. 3, 2014, wac.colostate.edu/docs/atd/rural/cook.pdf.

Dew, Debra Frank, and Alice Horning, editors. *Untenured Faculty as Writing Program Administrators: Institutional Practices and Politics*, Parlor P, 2007.

Dewey, John. *How We Think: A Restatement of the Relation of Reflective Thinking to the Educative Process*. D. C. Heath, 1933.

Duffey, Suellynn. "Skeletons in the Closet, Ghosts, and Other Invisible Creatures." *The Promise and Perils of Writing Program Administration*, edited by Theresa Enos and Shane Borrowman, Parlor P, 2008, pp. 139–45.

Edmondson, Amy C. "Strategies for Learning from Failure." *Harvard Business Review*, Apr. 2011, hbr.org/2011/04/strategies-for-learning-from-failure.

Enos, Theresa, and Shane Borrowman, editors. *The Promise and Perils of Writing Program Administration*, Parlor P, 2008.

Finer, Bryna Siegal, and Jamie White-Farnham, editors. *Writing Program Architecture: Thirty Cases for Reference and Research*, Utah State UP, 2017.

George, Diana, editor. *Kitchen Cooks, Plate Twirlers, and Troubadours: Writing Program Administrators Tell Their Stories*. Boynton/Cook, 1999.

Gross, Daniel M., and Jonathan Alexander. "Frameworks for Failure." *Pedagogy: Critical Approaches to Teaching Literature, Language, Composition and Culture*, vol. 16, no. 2, 2016, pp. 273–95.

Halberstam, Judith. *The Queer Art of Failure*. Duke UP, 2011.

Haushofer, Johannes. "CV of Failures." princeton.edu/~joha/Johannes_Haushofer_CV_of_Failures.pdf.

Harford, Tim. *Adapt: Why Success Always Starts with Failure*. Picador, 2012.

Inoue, Asao B. "Theorizing Failure in US Writing Assessments." *Research in the Teaching of English*, vol. 48, no. 3, 2014, pp. 330–52.

Maimon, Elaine P. "Preface." McLeod and Soven, pp. vii–x.

Maxwell, John C. *Failing Forward: Turning Mistakes into Stepping Stones for Success*. Thomas Nelson Publishers, 2007.

McLeod, Susan H. "The Foreigner: WAC Directors as Agents of Change." *Resituating Writing: Constructing and Administering Writing Programs*, edited by Joseph Janangelo and Kristine Hansen, Heinemann-Boynton/Cook, 1995, pp. 108–16.

McLeod, Susan H., editor. *Strengthening Programs for Writing Across the Curriculum*, Jossey-Bass, 2002.

McLeod, Susan H., and Margot Soven. "What Do You Need to Start—and Sustain—a Writing-Across-the-Curriculum Program?" *WPA: Writing Program Administration*, vol. 15, nos. 1–2, 1991, pp. 25–33.

McLeod, Susan H., and Margot Soven, editors. *Writing Across the Curriculum: A Guide to Developing Programs*. 1992. WAC Clearinghouse, 2000, wac.colostate.edu/books/landmarks/mcleod-soven.

Micciche, Laura R. *Doing Emotion: Rhetoric, Writing, Teaching*. Boynton/Cook, 2007.

Miller, Thomas P., Chris Anson, and Jeanne Gunner. "Portraits of a Field." *The Promise and Perils of Writing Program Administration*, edited by Theresa Enos and Shane Borrowman, Parlor P, 2008, pp. 79–91.

Myers-Breslin, Linda, editor. *Administrative Problem-Solving for Writing Programs and Writing Centers: Scenarios in Effective Program Management*. NCTE, 1999.

Newkirk, Thomas. "Silences in Our Teaching Stories: What Do We Leave Out and Why?" *What to Expect When You're Expected to Teach: The Anxious Craft of Teaching Composition*. Boynton/Cook, 2002.

Phillips, Talinn, Paul Shovlin, and Megan Titus. "Thinking Liminally: Exploring the (com)Promising Position of the Liminal WPA." *WPA: Writing Program Administration*, vol. 38, no. 1, 2014, pp. 42–63.

Rose, Jeanne Marie. "Coming of Age as a WPA: From Personal to Personnel." *WPA: Writing Program Administration*, vol. 28, no. 3, 2005, pp. 73–87.

Rose, Shirley K, and Irwin Weiser, editors. *The Writing Program Administrator as Researcher: Inquiry in Action and Reflection.* Heinemann, 1999.

—. *The Writing Program Administrator as Theorist*, Boynton/Cook, 2002.

Segal, Judy Z. "Pedagogies of Decentering and a Discourse of Failure." *Rhetoric Review*, vol. 15, no. 1, pp. 174–91.

Stefan, Melanie. "A CV of Failures." *Nature*, 17 Nov. 2010, nature.com/naturejobs/science/articles/10.1038/nj7322-467a.

Stolley, Amy Ferdinandt. "Narratives, Administrative Identity, and the Early Career WPA." *WPA: Writing Program Administration*, vol. 39, no. 1, 2015, pp. 18–31.

Tandy, Keith A. "Continuing Funding, Coping with Less." McLeod, pp. 55–60.

Townsend, Martha A., Martha D. Patton, and Jo Ann Vogt. "Uncommon Conversations: How Nearly Three Decades of Paying Attention Allows One WAC/WID Program to Thrive." *WPA: Writing Program Administration*, vol. 35, no. 2, 2012, pp. 127–59.

Ward, Irene, and William J. Carpenter, editors. *The Allyn and Bacon Sourcebook for Writing Program Administrators.* Longman, 2002.

White, Edward M. *Developing Successful Writing Programs.* Jossey-Bass, 1989.

—. "Use It or Lose It: Power and the WPA." *WPA: Writing Program Administration*, vol. 15, nos. 1–2, 1991, pp. 3–12.

Heather Bastian is associate director of the Communication Across the Curriculum (CxC) program at the University of North Carolina at Charlotte. Her research interests include composition pedagogy, WAC/WID, and writing program administration. Her work has appeared in *College Composition and Communication, Composition Studies, Composition Forum, Across the Disciplines,* and *Reader.*

Supplemental Material

The F-Word: Failure in WPA Work
Heather Bastian

PART I: REFLECTION ON THE ORIGINS OF THE ARTICLE

When I learned nearly seven years ago that the writing program I had worked to build would no longer be funded, it was the first time I experienced a large-scale and public academic failure. I had received paper, conference, grant, and job rejections, but these were private failures that only affected me. Losing a program, however, was a public failure that affected not just me but other people too. My emotional reaction caught me off guard: I was surprised, confused, angry, and ashamed. I blamed myself and struggled to address practical issues that result from losing a program.

Internalizing this failure and muddling through it easily could have been the end of my story, but prior to losing funding, I joined a *CCCC* proposal where I was slated to talk about my "promising WPA work." The panel brought together contributors from a special issue of *Across the Disciplines* on WAC/WID Program Administration at Rural, Regional, and Satellite Campuses to provide "snapshots of WPAs charged with innovative program development at regional/branch campuses plagued by identity and retention crises." I faced a decision: proceed as planned and briefly acknowledge the loss or fess up and focus on the loss. I took a risk and went with the latter. Using Laura Micciche's work on emotions as my foundation, I described how I negotiated the practical issues and emotional fallout of losing a program. While I talked publicly about failure and even used it to describe the program and myself in this presentation, I still was internalizing it as mine alone.

This one fleeting public admission also could have been the end of my story if not for the post-presentation lunch with my fellow panelists. As another panelist and I talked, he commented that I seemed very zen about my experience. I was horrified that I was creating this impression. I absolutely was not zen about it, but I did not feel comfortable openly and honestly talking about failure. I realized that I needed to rethink my own relationship with failure and success.

It took another six years, a new position, a lot of reading, and plenty of soul searching before I felt compelled to write about failure and my experience with it. By that point, this piece was one of the easiest for me to compose because I had a clear idea of what I wanted to say and why I needed to say it, but it also was one of the hardest because it meant revealing a deeply personal and emotional journey. My decision to submit came from a place of care and concern for those doing WPA work but also for others in the field and academia more broadly. I stand strongly by other scholars' and my own critiques of larger institutional and cultural structures and norms within this piece and the damage they can cause. This piece aims to work against that damage.

PART II: DESCRIPTION OF RESEARCH METHODS, FINDINGS, AND/OR PEDAGOGICAL IMPACT

Developing a heuristic for failure had a profound impact on my career trajectory and professional identity and on my mental health as well. Grappling with failure forced me to slow down for the first time in a long time. Throughout graduate school, I fully internalized the academic culture of busyness and overwork as well as its "professional discourse of success" (Segal). I was "good" at it. Not even receiving significant mental health diagnoses slowed me down (and to be clear, it should have). I maintained a nonstop pace in my faculty position, always pushing, always looking for the next project, the next presentation, the next publication, the next committee, the next grant, with little attention to my mental health and actual needs, wants, and desires or to how this mentality might impact others. I was operating to produce with no end in sight because institutional and academic systems always want more.

Forcing myself to slow down and truly feel failure made me realize that losing the program felt bad, but additionally, that nearly every academic success I had experienced up to that point never really felt good. Academic success is narrowly defined and not celebrated but expected continuously, more bullets for institutional promotional materials and the C.V. Moreover, not all academic success is reflective of what I value and want but, rather, what others value and want. I see now that I applied a mostly uncritical lens to this aspect of academic culture as well as to my participation in it and I acknowledge that my relative position of privilege allowed me to do so, but, at the time, these were major revelations for me. I began to seriously question what success and failure look like in academia, what success requires of people (faculty, students, staff, and administration), and who experiences success and, more importantly, who does not. I also began to question my participation in the system, whether or how I wanted to continue participating in it, and what I wanted myself and others to get out of my participation.

What I realized from other scholars' important work on failure and my own personal journey is the profound, damaging, and lasting effect the overarching academic narrative of success can have on WPAs because WPA work, perhaps more than other academic work, will fail and often fail publicly. This is a reality, and it should be acknowledged, accepted, and addressed especially because the academic system may demand success but it also requires failure. Academic structures and institutions are not built to support the success of all its participants or disciplines but rather a select few. Internalizing failure kept me from critiquing and challenging a culture of overwork and academic inequities because I identified myself as the problem. Working to understand failure cast a more critical light on the success driven contexts in which I worked as a WPA, teacher, and scholar and challenged me to reimagine my role in them.

PART III: DISCUSSION QUESTIONS

1. The author observes that in many WPA narratives, "WPAs don't fail; they overcome" (98). Where else have you seen this message play out? And what are the implications of this message?

2. How is failure "not just an inevitable aspect of WPA work but also a necessary one" (107)?

3. The author focuses in this article on the emotional impact the academic discourse of success has on WPAs. Who else is impacted by it and what are those impacts?

4. In what ways does the heuristic for failure challenge conventional metrics of academic success?

5. How has this article influenced or reinforced your own understanding of success and failure in academic and non-academic contexts?

6. How might you apply this heuristic of failure to your own administrative work, scholarship, or teaching? And what do you anticipate gaining from it?

JOURNAL OF BASIC WRITING

The *Journal of Basic Writing* is on the Web at http://wac.colostate.edu/jbw/index.cfm

Journal of Basic Writing is a refereed print journal founded in 1975 by Mina Shaughnessy and is published twice a year with support from the Office of Academic Affairs of the City University of New York. Basic Writing, a contested term, refers to the field concerned with teaching writing to students not yet deemed ready for first-year composition. Originally, these students were part of the wave of Open Admissions students who poured into universities as a result of the social unrest and demand for equal access of the 1960s and the resulting reforms. As scholars and educators continue to debate the gains and harms of Basic Writing programs, "basic writer" as a category of college writer persists. *JBW* is dedicated to ensuring the visibility of students for whom the typical supports for college writing are insufficient, whether or not these supports exist inside of so-called Basic Writing programs. Articles that explore the social, political, and pedagogical questions related to educational access and equity, especially as these concern students new to college writing, are the core of *JBW*'s history and mission.

"Let the People Rap": Cultural Rhetorics Pedagogy and Practices Under CUNY's Open Admissions, 1968–1978[1]

At a cultural and political moment when many communities are now searching for and demanding the overhaul of systems for equal access, Tessa Brown's provides a model—the CUNY SEEK program—inside a rich contemporary context. This article spotlights the cultural, linguistic, and artistic literacies that grew the intersections between the Black Arts Movement and CUNY's Open Admissions in the late 1960s. Brown reveals the concurrence of this Movement and the demand for educational access effectively mapping multi-directional routes of influence—individuals and communities, equipped with a cultural rhetorics praxis, shaping the impetus toward equal education. Brown emphasizes the principal roles played by SEEK instructors such as June Jordan, Adrienne Rich, Toni Cade Bambara, Addison Gayle, and Audre Lorde, artists and writers who took students' Black and Puerto Rican urban cultures as key pedagogical resources. The burgeoning of hiphop culture serves as the backdrop, driver, and encapsulator of the potential for equal access in education that characterized this too-brief era in CUNY's history.

---

1. *Journal of Basic Writing*, vol. 38, no. 2, 2019, DOI: 10.37514/JBW-J.2019.38.2.05. © 2019 by the *Journal of Basic Writing*.

"Let the People Rap": Cultural Rhetorics Pedagogy and Practices Under CUNY's Open Admissions, 1968-1978

Tessa Brown

This article writes the histories of CUNY Open Admissions and hiphop toward each other, illuminating both. Bringing Open Admissions to bear on hiphop history helps us see that, while historians locate the birth of hiphop culture in a 1970s New York gutted by divestment and displacement, in fact the decade before hiphop's birth was characterized by a flourishing Black and Puerto Rican arts scene in New York and the radical education of tens of thousands of students of color in the CUNY system. Revisiting the archives of Open Admissions with a hiphop lens draws attention to the cultural rhetorics education being taught in remedial writing classrooms by adjunct lecturers like June Jordan, Adrienne Rich, and others, who drew students' attention and inquiry to their own communities and language practices. Looking at a selection of documents chosen for their use of the term "rappin," including teachers' reflective writing, administrative documents, and community writing, this article argues that, as bureaucratic language evolved to disguise racism in the 1960s and 1970s, a resistive, identity-based language of rappin evolved in response. Ultimately, hiphop language only entered the commodity market at the end of the 1970s when CUNY instituted tuition for the first time in its history, pushing out many of the students Open Admissions had been designed to welcome in.

KEYWORDS: Adrienne Rich; Basic Writing; Black Arts Movement; cultural rhetorics; hiphop; June Jordan; Open Admissions

Histories and hagiographies locate the birth of hiphop culture at a Back to School party thrown by Clive Owens and his sister Cindy Campbell in the Bronx, New York, during the summer of 1973. A Jamaican immigrant, Owens arrived to New York with knowledge of Jamaican DJ culture, lessons he continued learning from his father (Chang 79). Known as DJ Kool Herc, Owens is credited with looping the first break beats, using duplicates of records spun back by hand, his technical and rhetorical innovation making the dancers go wild. That night in '73, when he became the first MC to rap over the break beat, hiphop was born.

But why Owens and Campbell were excited to go back to school, historians don't know. By the early 1970s, massive deindustrialization had gutted New York's labor market, and intrusive city planning projects led by Robert Moses had been uprooting these increasingly unemployed communities. Jeff Chang and Tricia Rose both open their hiphop histories with the construction of Moses's Cross-Bronx Expressway, which displaced 170,000 Black, brown, and ethnic white residents of the borough, recreating the city in the interests of white commuters and the financial industry they sped to past the neighborhoods of the city's increasingly desperate working poor. Literary theorist and CCNY professor Marshall Berman recalled that during his childhood in the Bronx, "through the late 1950s and 1960s, the center of the Bronx was pounded and blasted and smashed," creating a "deafening noise" (293-94) that may well have inspired hiphop's powerful early sounds. While Berman's Jewish family moved to the suburbs, Black and Puerto Rican families like Owens' were increasingly pushed into housing projects being built in the South Bronx. By 1970, Daniel Moynihan would famously suggest that these communities be handled with "benign neglect" as federal policy (qtd. in Chang 14).

Despite this dominant framing, scholars know that hiphop did not emerge *sui generis* from Black and brown youths' survivalist response to structural devastation; hiphop culture's five elements of rapping—DJing, graffiti writing, breakdancing, and "dropping knowledge"— also drew on generations of African-American and African practices of storytelling, sound organization, and dance. Less consideration has been paid to hiphop's immediate cultural precedent in the African American artistic community in New York, the Black Arts Movement (BAM) although Marvin Gladney has argued that hiphop's rage, Black capitalism, and Black aesthetic emerged directly out of BAM, an argument taken up by Gwendolyn Pough when she charted connections between hiphop and the Black Power Movement. And no one to my knowledge has interrogated the relationship between hiphop culture and the Open Admissions years at the City University of New York system, a shift in admissions standards that brought hundreds of thousands of additional students into the multi-campus college system, including its flagship campus, the City College of New York (CCNY). Located on the north side of Manhattan, between Harlem and Washington Heights and just south and west of the South Bronx, the CCNY campus was "a major site of protests and uprisings for Black and Puerto Rican students" in the late 1960s (Kynard 160). These protests, taken up by New York legislators of color, led the state to found the Search for Education, Elevation, and Knowledge (SEEK) Program in 1966 with a small class of students of color who would be traditionally excluded from the CUNY system. Compositionist Carmen Kynard carefully recounts how "it would be the SEEK students who [then] led the way for campus inclusion policies" (161). In 1969, students led a sit-in at CCNY with one of five key demands being that the racial makeup of the CUNY system reflect the racial composition of New York's public high schools (Arenson).

After 1970, the year Open Admissions was fully implemented, the freshman class across all CUNY campuses ballooned from 17,645 to over 34,000 (Lavin and Hyllegard). Racially, the numbers of white students rose to about 26,000 from 15,000, while the numbers of students of color rose to over 8,000 freshmen annually from about 1,600 in 1969. With these numbers, which admitted an increase of over 50,000 students of color between 1970 to 1978, CUNY reached its goal of matching its demographics to New York's public high schools (Arenson). David Lavin and David Hyllegard's important study of the impacts of Open Admissions show that 50% of students admitted to community colleges ultimately transferred to four-year colleges (48), a number made easier by the Open Admissions policy allowing automatic transfer between CUNY's community and four-year colleges. They also show that, although degree attainment by students of color was lower than that of their white peers, Open Admissions tripled the number of Bachelor's and Associate's degrees going to Black students and significantly multiplied those for Hispanic students as well (67).

Beyond merely admitting students to college, the SEEK program offered counseling, stipends, tickets to cultural events, and free textbooks ("The CUNY Center Seek Program 1969-1970 Catalogue" 7). Thus, during the decade that hiphop culture germinated as a local culture and launched into a major musical and culture industry that has overtaken global fashion, music, and dance trends, tens of thousands of New Yorkers of color, predominantly Black and Puerto Rican students (including AfroLatinx Puerto Ricans), as well as immigrants and ethnic whites, streamed through often POC-led classrooms at CUNY where before had been underfunded and undervalued, functionally segregated K-12 public education. The energy of the Black Arts Movement rushed into the schools as community educators, artists, and organizers became university professors—often off the tenure track, as adjuncts.

Figure 1. Photos of WBCC Radio operators from: Bronx Community College Yearbook 1975. Archives, Bronx Community College, Bronx, NY. Accessed 4 August 2016.

In *Vernacular Insurrections,* a book inflected with hiphop but not about hiphop's origins, Kynard shows that, in New York and nationwide, the Black Arts Movement was deeply intertwined with the Black freedom struggle, a fusion that profoundly shaped late 20th century American literacies. Rewriting the Black Arts Movement into the history of postsecondary writing instruction, Kynard argues that the new literacies of Black and Puerto Rican student protestors, embedded in chants, signs, demands, leaflets, course proposals, and other extracurricular writings (Kynard 125), "redefined what it means to be successful and literate" (65). While compositionists have long studied the history of the Open Admissions period at CUNY with a focus on Mina Shaughnessy, the white woman administrator of the CCNY Basic Writing program, Kynard re-roots that history in artistic Black activism, identifying compositionist, sociolinguist and Black woman Geneva Smitherman as a more appropriate avatar for the period. While Kynard clarifies the contributions of BAM and the Black liberation struggle to composition studies, these twin cultural and activist movements have not been adequately theorized for hiphop's history.

In this study, I return to CUNY's archives to interrogate the coincidence, in both time and space, of the birth of hiphop culture with the Open Admissions period at CUNY. My attention to what Amy Devitt calls the "origin of genres"—in this case, hiphop genres of rap, graffiti pieces, DJ compositions, and break dances—shapes a study of rhetoric pedagogy and production at CUNY under Open Admission that extends beyond the disciplinary limits of writing and speech classrooms. In my archival visits—to institutional archives at CCNY, Hunter College, Medgar Evers, Bronx Community College, and Queens College, to Radcliffe to look at Adrienne Rich's and June Jordan's papers, both writing instructors in SEEK at CCNY, as well to Spelman to look at the papers of Toni Cade Bambara (from CCNY) and Audre Lorde (from John Jay)—I used my knowledge of hiphop's roots in musical, poetic, technological, and protest traditions to guide the materials I studied. Beyond looking at institutional documents relating to SEEK, Open Admission, and Basic Writing on multiple campuses, I also looked at yearbooks, student publications, and in course catalogs at departments of English; Ethnic, Black, and Puerto Rican studies; Music; Speech; Visual Arts; and Engineering. This purview allows me to expand on the work of composition scholars like Steve Lamos and Mary Soliday whose focus has been restricted to writing classrooms. This widened scope for rhetorical research allows me to recognize the wide-ranging and overlapping studies in rhetoric, critical ethnic studies, and artistic and technological production undertaken by tens of thousands of poor and working-class New York college students during the decade of 1968-1978 at CUNY, an enormous educational movement that has not been previously theorized as part of the history of hiphop.

Building on Kynard's attention to Black teachers and specifically Geneva Smitherman as a foil to Shaughnessy, as well as Sean Molloy's attention to the lecturers teaching in the SEEK program at CUNY, in this article, I repopulate our historical memory of the Open Admissions years across multiple CUNY campuses, focusing on the teacher-artist-activists Shaughnessy managed—Toni Cade Bambara, Barbara Christian, Addison Gayle, and in particular June Jordan and Adrienne Rich. Claimed by women's and Black studies, these individuals, active in the Black Arts Movement and the women's movements, all taught in Shaughnessy's Basic Writing program at CCNY yet their presences and pedagogies have not been studied by compositionists. I conclude with attention to course offerings and writing in student newspapers and yearbooks during the same time frame, looking at materials from Hunter College, Queens College, and Medgar Evers to better understand the rhetorical culture of CUNY students during Open Admission, in the years immediately preceding and coinciding with hiphop's rise. Ultimately, I argue that a resistive literacy of rappin was growing and cultivated within the CUNY system during this decade, developing dialogically with an emerging bureaucratic language of standards developed in response to the Civil Rights gains of the late 1960s.

The intellectual, cultural, and political clashes between progressives and reactionaries from 1968 to 1978 in New York City are important sites for understanding the current ideological moment, and its genesis over the last fifty years. In the decade after 1968, when Black people protested the unmet promises of the Civil Rights movement across the nation's major cities, state power moved to reconstruct racism as what Ferguson has called an "increasingly illegible phenomenon" (58), developing new colorblind or what Kynard has termed "race-evasive" (166) discourses to reinscribe white power using unraced language. In the papers of CUNY's teachers and students, unspooling across a decade of investment in and then divestment from equitable public access, we can see the development of resistive rap discourses that use the language of personal identity and experience to counter the dehumanizing language of the white bureaucracy. These language practices are developed in the context of bureaucratic processes around funding and hiring, defunding and firing, that disproportionately affected students and teachers of color, but never using the language of race. While hiphop scholars root the culture's history in destitution, it was only after the CUNY retrenchment took hold with the institution of tuition for the first time in the school's history, in 1976, that hiphop transcended its roots as a community art form to enter the commodity market. By the 1982, when Grandmaster Flash and the Furious Five released "The Message," with its snarling chorus—"It's like a jungle sometimes it makes me wonder/ how I keep from going under"—hiphop's critical thesis of bureaucratic abandonment, urban decay, and racial capitalism had solidified in an idiom borne, I argue, out of a decade of critical and open access education.

LINER NOTES: TOWARD A HIPHOP FEMINIST COMPOSITION HISTORIOGRAPHY

If this article were a hiphop track, Carmen Kynard's *Vernacular Insurrections* would be the bassline, Roderick Ferguson's *The Reorder of Things* would be the snare, and Sean Molloy's research, some for this journal, the hi-hat. Looped as the chorus would be Shaughnessy's *Errors and Expectations,* pitched up, sped up, and reversed. Rapping over this track are all the Black, Puerto Rican, and queer students and adjunct teachers of Open Admissions, theorizing their world in their own words, many quoted here. June Jordan sings the hook; Dean Ted Gross mutters in the cut. The riddim is a faint sample of Jeff Chang's "dub history," a hiphop history from below.

But if this article were an article, it would continue like this:

Hiphop, an increasingly important exigence in the study of student writing practices, is what originally drew me to the archives. Hiphop culture, now a dominant feature of the U.S. cultural landscape, has been prompting compositionists, rhetoricians, and literacy researchers to account for the rich composing processes that occur in hiphop's multimodal culture of five elements: MCing (writing and delivering raps); DJing (producing or spinning beats); drawing, spray/painting, or "writing" graffiti art; breakdancing; and philosophizing or "dropping science" (see Alim, Banks, Craig, Green, Kirkland, Milu, Pough, Richardson). Across multiple disciplines, hiphop feminists draw attention to the contributions and negotiations of Black and brown women, girls, queer people and femmes within hiphop culture (Lindsey). Emerging from a vernacular artistic culture, hiphop's continued resistive politic is in tension with its contemporary shape as a source of mass-marketed commodities. Using a hiphop lens to study rhetorical production foregrounds multimodality and cross-genre composing, because hiphop's intrinsic multimodality reflects African American cultural priorities that resist Western taxonomies that separate communicative modes like speech, language, music, and dance.

Studying cultural rhetorics like hiphop redirects our attention to the rhetorical production and theorizing of marginalized groups, while also defamiliarizing the Euro-American discourses we regularly accept as normative (Powell et al.). Cultural rhetorics provides a useful framework for understanding the ways that SEEK's Basic Writing lecturers, themselves active in local ethnic and gender liberation movements in New York City, theorized out of their own locations and explicitly invited students to do the same. Their pedagogies were "culturally relevant," defined by Gloria Ladson-Billings as pedagogies which "empower[ ] students intellectually, socially, emotionally, and politically by using cultural referents to impart knowledge, skills, and attitudes" (16-17). In the U.S. context of composition and rhetorical studies, cultural rhetorics approaches have enriched studies of and with indigenous peoples, Latinx communities, African-Americans, Asian-Americans, white-identified groups, queer people, disabled people, digital media users, and rhetorical relations between and among them (see Banks; Bratta and Powell; Gubele, King, and Anderson; Haas; Hitt and Garrett; Mao and Young; Powell; Pough; Pritchard; Royster; Ruiz and Sanchez). As a critical scholar of white femininity (Brown), I recognize how cultural rhetorical studies can help us critique dominant rhetorical frameworks like those ultimately embraced by Shaughnessy (Molloy) while also reminding us to decenter whiteness and center the work of rhetors of color, as I do here.

Culturally relevant pedagogies that directed students to their communities' rhetorical practices were embraced by CCNY SEEK lecturers, including June Jordan and Adrienne Rich. Yet the story of Jordan and Rich must be understood intersectionally, because the differences in how they were treated by Shaughnessy's Basic Writing program, and the white English Department professors she reported to, highlights how systems of power intersect to create different experiences of privilege and oppression for groups and individuals with different identities (Crenshaw). Although Mina Shaughnessy was a powerful woman administrator, her experiences as a white woman gave her considerable advantage over her female colleagues. None of the adjunct women instructors I consider here—Adrienne Rich, June Jordan, Barbara Christian, Toni Cade Bambara—had the same normative female identity as Shaughnessy, a cisgendered heterosexual white woman, who was, by many accounts, considered very pretty by other white people. Shaughnessy's identity gave her an advantage vis-a-vis the white power structure, run by straight white men like English Department chair Theodore "Ted" Gross, over queer white women like Rich and queer Black women like Jordan.

Intersectionality is also a rejoinder to remember Puerto Rican faculty who do not appear in this study but who are present in the archives as pedagogical innovators and objects of discrimination. While my study focuses on Black students and teachers, their studies, and their language practices, Puerto Rican students and teachers fought for and participated in Open Admissions, and the archives are full of their presence and their languaging. Indeed, even thinking of these groups separately obscures the identities of Afro-Boricuas in New York and surely present in Open Admissions classrooms.

Recognizing the tension between administrators like Shaughnessy and Ted Gross and radical lecturers like June Jordan is a recognition that the forces that would undo Open Admissions were present from its beginning. Derrick Bell's critical race theory of interest convergence holds that "the interest of blacks in achieving racial equality will be accommodated only when it converges with the interest of whites" and not when it diverges with whites' interests (23). This notion is crucial for understanding the wave of investment and divestment that swept CUNY and communities of color nationwide from 1968 to 1978. Interest convergence is engaged by multiple historians of Basic Writing, including Kynard and Steve Lamos, as well as literary and higher education theorist Roderick Ferguson, to explain how the impetuses that made Basic Writing and Open Admissions possible seemed so quickly, a decade later, to disappear. The mass anti-racism protests of the late 1960s (including uprisings in Philadelphia, Watts, Newark, Chicago and Pittsburgh as well as student protests across the country) coupled with the U.S.'s international Cold War persona as the land of liberty against Soviet autocracy, put it in the white power structure's interests to make concessions to the demands of marginalized groups—for example, the higher-ed investments advised by Nixon's 1970 President's Commission on Campus Unrest (Kynard 120, Lamos 23-24). Compared with a narrative of racial progress, interest convergence and divergence better explain how between 1968 and 1969, 700 higher-education institutions added "ethnic studies courses, programs, or departments" (Ferguson 33) and by 1971 600 Predominantly White Institutions had created remediation programs for newly admitted poor students and students of color (Kynard 166), yet, by changing admissions tuitions requirements, the presence of people of color in higher education collapsed from the mid-1970s into the 1980s. Kynard recognizes this austerity move as part of a "united front in social policy" (Kynard 230) that starved communities of color, while independent scholar Alexis Pauline Gumbs theorizes Open Admissions alongside the expansion of prisons in New York as "two sides of the coin of population control" for New Yorkers of color (241).

"On location" (Kirsch) in the archives, I found that moving through the materials was an emotional experience. The early documents from SEEK at CCNY are suffused with positive affect: teacher and student enthusiasm, a sense of a changing and opening world, the joys of learning and teaching. Course catalogs are full of revolutionary curricula, and student newspapers and yearbooks are full of vibrant student voices. Yet even in the files from the 1960s, I could feel the coming retrenchment like a tide, like when you can feel the undertow pulling away at your ankles even as the water is still rushing in at your waist. The pressure is there, but no single drop is to blame. Drawing on interest convergence, Ferguson theorizes the institutional discourses that developed to reinstate white rule against desegregationist civil-rights era policy, positioning "excellence" as a discursive caveat to policies that opened the doors of white colleges and universities in the 60s and 70s. Looking specifically at Open Admissions CUNY, and closely engaging June Jordan's writings from her time at CCNY, Ferguson argues that the advance of standards-based arguments was a way for schools to present *de jure* desegregation while maintaining "standards" that functionally locked out people of color. In my study, I match a rhetorical attention to bureaucratic and identity-based discourses with an intersectional, materialist attention to racialized and gendered labor relationships. I follow contemporary scholars of

Writing Program Administration like Stacy Perriman-Clark, Collin Craig, and Asao Inoue in seeking to racialize discussions of workplace management in writing programs across hiring, curriculum design, pedagogy and assessment practices.

Gesa Kirsch and Jacqueline Jones Royster's notion of "critical imagination" as feminist rhetorical research practice grounds my inquiry into previously untheorized intersections of hiphop and Open Admissions, and grants me the gumption to challenge the near-ossified narratives of hiphop's birth. Writing separately, Kirsch with Joy Richie also enjoin me as a white feminist researcher to recognize how "whiteness structure[s my] thinking" (10), and with Royster reminds me to demonstrate "respect for the communities [I] study" (226). As a white Jewish woman, a queer teaching off the tenure track, I come to this history in solidarity with my sisters of color and with an intersectional recognition that the unjust systems I navigate are magnified for my colleagues of color.

The remainder of this article is constructed around a selection of documents from teachers and students loosely chosen for their engagement with "rap," a word with long roots in Black American speech (Campbell 36). When Wonder Mike of the Sugarhill Gang intoned incredulously in 1979, "Now what you hear is not a test, I'm rappin to the beat," he was acknowledging the transference of the verbal art of rappin onto and into a four-beat musical line in the first-ever recorded hiphop song. In studying these instances of "rap" under Open Admissions, I see the cultural rhetorics of rappin being sharpened in dialogic opposition to neoliberal discourses of standards and excellence. I theorize the "rap literacies" of Black and Puerto Rican New Yorkers as reveling in the opposite of whatever it is that "standards" measure—the richness of identity, experience, and language, the opposite of administrative doublespeak that only Jordan (and recently, Kynard) had the nerve to call racist. In the documents I sample from the archives, rappin refers to making connections the man doesn't want you to make, using language he doesn't want you to use, in genres he doesn't know how to standardize. The language of rap offers one through-line between the cultural rhetorics of Black and Puerto Rican New Yorkers in the late sixties, CUNY classrooms, and the emerging hiphop culture of the 1970s. In the sections that follow, I focus on a 1968 NEA report in which several lecturers reflect on their summer writing workshops; pedagogical materials by as well as institutional documentation about June Jordan and Adrienne Rich, and writing by students and staff for campus papers in the context of on- and off-campus Black poetic culture. These texts demonstrate a sense of reflexive, critical rap literacies as a discursive tool marginalized teachers and students, all scholar-artists, used to self-define and self-defend against encroaching bureaucratic abjection.

"The Square People Versus the Globular People": Rap and Resistance in a 1968 SEEK Summer Session

A coauthored SEEK report from an NEA-funded summer seminar in 1968 offers compelling evidence that Black teachers rooted in the Black Arts Movement pioneered rap pedagogies at SEEK centered around the cultural rhetorics of Black and Puerto Rican New Yorkers and their ancestors, pedagogies that were not fully appreciated by Shaughnessy and were never taught to scale. While Molloy shows that Shaughnessy moved CCNY's writing instruction from a more rhetorical model towards grammar-focused test prep ("A Convenient" 8), my research suggests that, at least for a time and at least in individual classrooms, lecturers of color were teaching a deeply rhetorical curriculum focused on the rhetorics of modernity, the African diaspora, the postcolonial world, New York City's communities of color, and students' own experiences of these spaces and heritages. In the typescript report on the 1968 summer seminar, prepared to document their work for the NEA, instructors Mina Shaughnessy, Fred Byron, Toni Cade (later Cade Bambara, and referred to such throughout the following), Barbara Christian, David Henderson, and Addison Gayle were each tasked with describing and reflecting on their assignments' successes after being given significant freedom to design their own courses. In the instructors' descriptions of and reflections on their courses, we can see how, although all the teachers were deeply invested in their students' successes, the white teachers tended to teach toward school literacies, forwarding the discourses of lack that plagued the students, while teachers of color and creative writing teachers were more driven by introducing students to the unseen richness of their home cultures. Paradoxically, the existence of the report itself both attests to a culture of reflexivity within the teaching ranks of SEEK Basic English even as it demonstrates how the program's reliance on grants for funding, under Shaughnessy's leadership, immediately imbued it with a research agenda that had been deprioritized only a year earlier as reported in other records.

Comparing Gayle, Christian, and Cade Bambara's pedagogical reflections with Byron and Shaughnessy's dramatically illustrates the differences between culturally relevant, cultural rhetorics pedagogies that move across multiple rhetorical modalities, and pedagogies oriented toward institutional whiteness. Addison Gayle's class centered on storytelling culture from African and African American history, and worked to root students' writing and storytelling in a grand literary culture. He reflected that

> we also made the point that many of the successful black writers have also excelled as orators, in the cases of Ralph Ellison, James

> Baldwin, Eldridge Cleaver, Malcolm X, and Lester. And that as orators they were aware of the way words sounded to the ear and of the order in which a talk is organized. This knowledge, we maintained, was an essential element in the discovery of one's own voice. (26)

Gayle's reflection showcases an integrated understanding of written and spoken rhetoric rooted in the Black literary tradition. In his section of the course, students focused on two main texts: *Look Out Whitey, Black Power's Gonna Get Your Mama* by Julius Lester, and *Tales from the Arabian Nights*, by Richard Burton. Gayle built up student confidence not by directing students to school culture but by turning them away from it to reconsider the home cultures and heritages they could draw upon in their own rhetorical production across writing and speech. He wrote:

> we held a lot of discussions. We had the students relate anecdotes, write them down and then compare them... We talked a great deal about the oral tradition in Africa. Of how African people were used to hearing news and stories instead of reading them. We read *The Arabian Nights* and talked a great deal about the literary devices employed in the rendering of these tales by Shahrazad... We also had the running assignment of interviewing our older relatives, our grandmothers and grandfathers, grand aunts and the like, soas to give us clues to the ways of our clan. We discussed at length the fantastic Odyssey of Alex Haley, the editor and compiler of the *Autobiography of Malcolm X*, in discovering and tracing his ancestors back to a small town in Africa. In general, we attempted to provide our aspiring writers with a base from which to work. And to buttress them with historical fact and tradition. (26-27)

Connecting students' "grandmothers and grandfathers" to Shahrazad and Malcom X, Gayle's pedagogy is an example of the culturally situated Black Arts pedagogies that were present at CUNY in the years before hiphop's emergence as a dynamic Black rhetorical culture.

In another reflection, Barbara Christian noted that she specifically asked students for input and recommendations, then built "a course that they would like." Student suggestions led to a "focus on Black literature, contemporary preoccupations, techniques of argument" (10), using texts like Fanon's *Wretched of the Earth*, Eldridge Cleaver's *Soul on Ice*, and LeRoi Jones's *Home* to study "Colonialism, Neo-Colonialism, and Liberation." Beyond recommending newspapers to them, she wrote, "good libraries and bookstores were suggested to the students" (1). That the students recommended these texts speaks to our need to re-contextualize this curricular moment in the broader New York City cultural moment, in which Black bookstores were thriving and seeing city and state investment, and students descended from the overlapping African and Caribbean diasporas were taking a broad-minded interest in third-world solidarity and the transition out of the colonial era. Looking beyond the SEEK archives, we can see that by 1969 the SEEK program already had curricular offerings in ethnic studies, so that students learning about the rhetorics of Black and Puerto Rican communities in their Basic English courses were also learning these cultures' histories, philosophies, and literatures elsewhere across the curriculum.

Kynard's argument that literacies from the Black Arts Movement anticipated a range of later composition trends is borne out by Christian's suggestion, in line with later pedagogies like literacy narratives or Writing About Writing, that students' research begin with themselves. She writes:

> The students suffer from a lack of awareness of the importance and relevance of their own lives. The most frequent complaint in just about any beginning course is "I don't have anything to write about." And particularly for our students, who are mostly black and Puerto Rican and who therefore have seen little resembling their own lives in a written form, the problem is compounded. The books that I chose to work with in this course, then, were crucial. (17)

Like Gayle, Christian saw students as unaware of their own cultural context as resources for their own writing. Christian continued on to discuss her section's focus on integrated discussions of literature and music:

> I had intended *Blues People* to be a counterpoint to *Invisible Man* since it is primarily a book-length essay rather than a novel. But the students saw a tie-up between Ellison's constant use of the blues in his novel and Jones' analysis of them. We got into the music much more than we did into the essay form. They all knew this music, some of them were ashamed of it, some proud but they were all surprised to see that it could be analyzed, discussed and related to a cultural history of a people. Along with the reading of the book, I brought records to class, dating back from Work Songs, Early Primitive Blues all the way to Contemporary Rhythm n blues and New Jazz. It is particularly noteworthy that most of the students were not aware of Contemporary Jazz and had not even heard of such classic names as Charlie Parker or John Coltrane... I left the summer session with a feeling that we had just gotten started, that the jump to more rigorous writing could be made in a few weeks, that some

> though not all of the students had begun to overcome their fear of writing. (18)

Despite Christian's in-class focus on music, she sees her students quickly becoming more advanced writers as well, and develops her own improvisational ethic in course design and her attention to the integration of different modes of cultural production in Afrodiasporic cultures. Thus, in Gayle and Christian's reflections we can see the similarities between their pedagogical strategies and the work of cultural rhetorics, as they drew students' attention to the rhetorical practices they had already, perhaps unknowingly, learned from their home cultures, or could root in their cultures' historical and current practices.

Meanwhile, Cade Bambara's reflection on her course included an extended discourse by one of her students which we might view as a self-assessment given and received in a culturally relevant pedagogical context. What better way for a student to synthesize course concepts, than to rap? In any case, Cade Bambara saw fit to reproduce this extensive account of her student's speechifying, and I follow her in doing so. She writes:

> At least one hour was given over to students... The last meeting, for example, ran two hours over the usual end because one student needed "uninterrupted time to rap." He delivered non-stop machine gun style interrupting his interrupters on the third or fourth syllable a two and a half hour dissertation on at least 80% of themes we had touched on in the last two and a half month time and hit upon related ideas which cemented the themes together: the irrationality of logic, the impossibility of objectivity, the stultifyling [sic] effects of the English language, the masking role of reason which makes mental gymnastics pass for reality, the defects in Black Nationalism, the holes in Fanon, the criminality of education, the paternalism of the Seek Program, the stupidity of students who kept raising their hands to challenge him as he spoke ("Do you think Paul McCartney and John Lennon ran all the way up to the mountains to bug the guru with 'hey Mahareeshi, you wrong baby'? No, they sat and listened.") point omega in one's consciousness, the square people versus the globular people, the evolution of the Black man, the foolishness of "things are getting better," the limited role of regular teachers as opposed to real mentors. After his treatise on the freedom and limits of learning, he offhandedly congratulated the instructor as the only one who had sense enough to listen and urged the others to realize that had they been sure of who they were, they would have felt no compulsion to argue audibly but would simply have checked him

out and separated the brass from the gold quietly, privately, within their own "globe." Quite a wind-up. (11)

In this excerpt we see rap as a space for verbal play, for making connections, for critique. In quoting this passage at length, Cade Bambara valorizes this student's speech as knowledge-making of value to the academy. Its description as a "dissertation" and a "treatise," connecting and "cementing" the themes of the course, suggests a view of assessment on Cade Bambara's part that is far distant from standardized language exams and is rather rooted in the student's own culturally-situated ways of making meaning and discourse, that is, by rapping. In this extended student speech we can see the outcome of a pedagogy that invites students to compose from their own personal and cultural locations—that is, to rap about what they learned.

In the report, the pedagogical approaches of Gayle, Christian, and Cade Bambara, which rooted instruction and assessment in students' home cultures, differed from those of their colleagues Fred Byron and Mina Shaughnessy, who taught toward school literacies and seemed more attuned to what students lacked than to the cultural resources they already held. For example, Shaughnessy's reflection relays that "I have often noticed... that students usually 'talk' a better-organized paper than they write" (30), but doesn't make any note of the value placed on oral communication in Black cultures. And Fred Byron, teaching an all-male, almost all-European syllabus of Chekhov, Sartre, Akutagawa, Stevenson and plays from Aeschylus, Sophocles, Euripides, and Shakespeare, wrote that "My particular aim in the scope of this summer course was... to provide these students with a broad (liberal arts), classical foundation or background of knowledge." He continued:

> I am sure that I am not alone in having been told by students as they have sat in my English classes that they are sorely "lacking" or "deficient" or "weak" in background reading, especially the "classics," and so they are pitifully unable to make the necessary cross-references or to understand the allusions which continually barrage them in their English and Social Science/Humanities courses. Hence, my two summer seminar courses (which I trust will be readily replicable) were, in a sense, attempts to supply this much-needed background material to students who feel inadequate. (6)

To his credit, Byron goes on to describe some very successful lessons, noting that students "began to radiate with confident knowledge and rewarding self-achievement" (6) after delving deeply into the character of Iago. But his focus on student deficit regarding European classics—his characterization of students as "pitiful[ ]," "barraged," and "inadequate" in their attempted acculturation to white liberal arts study—is a different approach than that of some of his Black colleagues, Cade Bambara, Christian, and Gayle, all of whom were writers active in the Black Arts Movement.

Taken together, these reflections show a program of writing teachers working collaboratively and reflectively to support experimental pedagogy that engaged students' hearts as the way to their minds. All the teachers were deeply motivated by igniting student pleasure in learning—Shaughnessy concluded her reflection by remarking that, "I can only say that we seemed often to be talking about writing in a way that made sense to the students and a way that they seemed to enjoy" (34). But when we think back to the innovations and student successes under SEEK Basic English, it behooves us to remember and foreground the major pedagogical contributions—in what today we'd call multimodality, translingualism, remix theory, and cultural rhetorics—of teacher-practitioners active in the Black Arts Movement and foundational to Black Studies like Toni Cade Bambara, Barbara Christian, and Addison Gayle, those teachers granting their students time and space to rap.

"Alas": An Intersectional Comparison of Adrienne Rich and June Jordan's Working Conditions

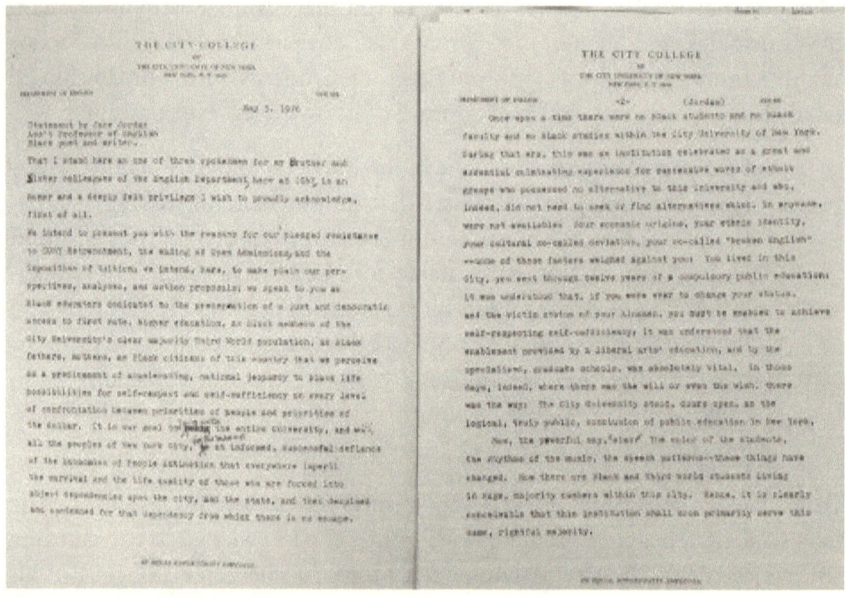

Figure 2. Manuscript pages from: "Statement by June Jordan/Ass't Professor of English/Black poet and writer." TS. Box 76, Folder 14. 5 May 1976. June Jordan Papers, Radcliffe Institute for Advanced Study at Harvard University, Cambridge, MA. 8 August 2016.

An "integrationist narrative" (Kynard 150) of Shaughnessy's work at CUNY casts her as the hero who made change for students of color. However, the archives attest to the rich poetic culture of Black New York in the 1960s, a culture that Open Admissions did not create but simply allowed onto campus. Audre Lorde's collection of ephemera from her years at John Jay includes references to numerous grassroots organizations for Black poets in the city, including the Harlem Writers' Guild, Black Poets Reading, the Black Academy of Arts and Letters, and the Langston Hughes Community Library and Cultural Center. Her papers hold a clipping from a 1972 copy of the new publication *Essence* Magazine on "The Explosion of Black Poetry" which highlights the role of identity and self-definition to the new Black poetry. The article quotes June Jordan as well as Lorde herself on this subject, with Jordan stating that "Poetry is the way I think and the way I remember and the way I understand or the way I express my confusion, bitterness and love," and Lorde adding, "I am Black, Woman, and Poet—in fact and outside the realm of choice. I can choose only to be or not to be, and in various combinations of myself... The shortest statement of philosophy I have is my living, or the word 'I'" (66). In 1977, Columbia and the Frederick Douglass Creative Arts Center on 104th Street co-hosted a Cultural Festival in which Black poets were featured prominently. Organizer Quincy Troupe told the *New York Times* that

> black poetry was "entering a new phase, evolving." "It is drawing more on personal experience," he explained, "becoming more personal and relating back to the African-American folk roots, especially in its use of idiomatic speech, colloquialisms and the vernacular. It is also drawing on the rhythms of jazz and blues... [It] has located itself in black American culture and, like a tree, it is branching out to communicate internationally with cultures around the world... We are being listened to now... The speech and language of the African-American has had an impact. (Fraser)

With Open Admissions, this blossoming poetic culture was welcomed onto campus especially through the staff and non-tenure-track faculty who were hired to teach the newly admitted students. Beyond this reflexive poetry's presence in classrooms, SEEK provided curricular and extracurricular support—through theater tickets, movie screenings, and course offerings—for newly admitted CUNY students to embrace off-campus culture and bring those cultural happenings back onto campus as well.

Before I visited the archives, my inkling that rap might have been present at CUNY during Open Admissions was first confirmed by Adrienne Rich in her essay, "Teaching Language in Open Admissions." Rich recalls:

> Some of the most rudimentary questions we confronted were: how do you make standard English verb endings available to a dialect-speaker? how do you teach English prepositional forms to a Spanish-language student? where are the arguments for and against "Black English"? the English of academic papers and theses? Is standard English simply a weapon of colonization? Many of our students wrote in the vernacular with force and wit; others were unable to say what they wanted on paper in or out of the vernacular. We were dealing not simply with dialect and syntax but with the imagery of lives, the anger and flare of urban youth—how could this be used, strengthened, without the lies of artificial polish? How does one teach order, coherency, the structure of ideas while respecting the student's experience of his thinking and perceiving? Some students who could barely sweat out a paragraph delivered (and sometimes conned us with) dazzling raps in the classroom: how could we help this oral gift transfer itself onto paper? (261)

This quotation is remarkable, first of all, for how many of these questions composition teachers are still grappling with, now often under the labels of translingualism, code-meshing, and contact-zones. It resonates, too, with Kynard's critique of Shaughnessy's *Errors and Expectations* as valorizing revisions of student writing that elevate "artificial polish" over the "anger and flare" of earlier drafts (Kynard 205-209). Yet in the workplace of SEEK at CCNY, Rich was Shaughnessy's ally, not her critic. To understand the racialization of workplace dynamics in the context of innovative student-centered pedagogies, it is instructive to compare the records of Adrienne Rich with June Jordan's. Even as defunding already threatened Open Admissions from its earliest days, individual teachers like June Jordan and Adrienne Rich worked to theorize and teach writing as a practice that would allow students to intervene in worlds that sought to control and limit their fates. Jordan and Rich both used and developed the intellectual practices of reflexivity that were being strategically engaged in the rhetorics of the 1960s liberation movements to theorize from their own experiences and identities, and teach their students to do the same. Their pedagogies built on the Black poetic tradition—writing from the word "I"—that emerged in Lorde's archives.

In her Basic English syllabi, Rich stressed the value of theorizing the world from personal experience, and from a willingness to engage with the real world—what Kynard theorized as anticipating our field's "social turn" (33). In a 1969 syllabus, Rich wrote:

> I am concerned with the student's response to literature as a part of his life, rather than as a preparation for scholarship in an English

Ph. D. program; and with his discovery that one writes because one needs to say things to others, that he himself has much to say, and that when writing effectively one is addressing a potential reader, not simply fulfilling an academic requirement. (2)

Rich's socially-situated pedagogies root rhetorical production in the world, which is to say, in culture and in identity. Her theorizing continues in a 1971 syllabus, which began:

> This class will start from the idea that language—the way we put words together—is a way of acting on reality and eventually gaining more control of one's life. The people in the class and their experiences will be the basic material of the course, about which we will be talking and writing. In writing, we will be trying to define the actual experiences we ourselves are having, and to make others more aware of our reality as we perceive it. The reading will consist of writings in which the authors or their characters have tried to understand and criticize their situations, and to change or move beyond them.

Although Rich was a white Jewish woman, her archives reveal a significant effort to engage with Black and Puerto Rican students' home cultures and to encourage them to do the same, for example by visiting local bookstores listed on a handout titled "Books to buy, beg, borrow, steal, or read standing up in the bookstore."

> While Rich's attention to students' home rhetorics are admirable, an intersectional comparison with Jordan's materials show how Jordan's pedagogy, own writing, and experiences of institutional discrimination were shaped by her Black identity. In a handwritten journal from 1969, we can see Jordan theorizing writing for her pedagogy and for her essay "Black Studies: Bringing Back the Person," which Ferguson engages extensively in his book. In one undated entry, Jordan wrote, "Now language is our medium of community... For these reasons and for other reasons, reasons I hope our course of studies will articulate and analyze, language is always political. Always political... As a Black person and poet, I entertain an excruciating sense of language as political" (12-13). On another page, perhaps addressing her students, she writes, "I call upon you to self-consciously abandon the passive voice, in your writings + also watch the verbs you choose so that you don't combine 3 verbs where one would serve more forcefully" (65-66, formatting in original). A few

pages later, a strange note appears in hard blue ink, forceful against the pencil on the rest of the page:

obe | is | ant

written description of course

AND Reconsider curriculum (76, formatting in original)

This entry in particular suggests that even as Jordan was theorizing writing for her students in ways that would have a national and historical impact, she was receiving pushback from administrators—presumably Shaughnessy—for her curriculum. In 1970, Jordan penned an extended letter to Shaughnessy highlighting her students' work investigating issues in their communities in papers with titles like "Inferior Education in the Williamsburg Community"; "Self-Concept As A Determining Factor in Choice of Occupation: The Black Male Hustler"; "Inadequacy of Acceptable Food and Inadequate Systems of Food Supply in Harlem"; and "Drug Addiction in the South Bronx" (1). In this letter, Jordan inveighed against the testing regime Shaughnessy implemented for the English Department. Jordan wrote:

> I object to the value placed upon writings accomplished under stress… If you want to know what a student thinks, how a student can synthesize different ideas and aspects of material given to him, then so-called leniency should be the rule. Leniency: Extra time granted, as requested, consultation of books, as desired, and so forth… [C]onsider what our literary heritage would be, if writers were forced to submit their manuscripts, ready or not, on the day of the contracted deadline. I guess I am saying that the problem papers, for example, reveal more important data about a student, when the student is working hard, and trying for excellence, than any contrived examination-essay. (2)

In this passionate statement, Jordan draws on her own expertise as a professional writer to fundamentally challenge the validity of timed, standardized tests. With its plea for "leniency," this statement challenges the validity of the "standards" students at CUNY were held to, arguing that such standards are arbitrary, "stress[ful]," and invalid measures of students' thinking and writing skills which bear no resemblance to the demands of real-world writing situations. This letter resonates with Ferguson's analysis of Jordan's 1969 essay, in which he argues that "One of the ways Jordan summarized the 'deadly' and 'neutral' aspect of excellence was by demonstrating how it rendered black and Puerto Rican students as the antithesis of standards and achievement" (86-87). In the letter above, we can see Jordan longing for a view of assessment that makes space for rapping, like Toni Cade Bambara did in 1968.

By 1976, as the defunding of Open Admissions deepened into crisis and full reversal, Jordan spoke more holistically about the role of standards and testing in the oppression of Black and brown students. In May 1976, she wrote:

> We intend to present you with the reasons for our pledged resistance to CUNY Retrenchment, the ending of Open Admissions, and the imposition of tuition... we speak to you as Black educators... Now, the powerful say, 'alas:' The color of the students, the rhythms of the music, the speech patterns—these things have changed... Now, the powerful say, 'alas:' CUNY is no longer 'a great university;' it has become a 'jungle', a 'carnival', 'an unmanageable problem.' What do they mean?... We say that the judgement, the aim, and the consequences of this changed attitude towards the City University, we say that the Kibbee Plan, Marshak's Retrenchment Proposals, we say that the impending end of Open Admissions, the impending establishment of tuition requirements are, one and all, racist events that we cannot countenance, nor in any wise [sic] accept. If you do not agree with this analysis then how can you explain the elimination of The Hostos and Medgar Evers Colleges as fully operating, distinct schools serving predominantly Black and Hispanic students?... How can you explain official estimates that the proposed transformation of the City University will result in a 65% decline in Black enrollment, come September, 1976: Sixty-five percent! [Yet this is] the City of New York that can spend more than two hundred million dollars on Yankee Stadium... ("Statement by June Jordan" 1-4)

This statement has commonalities with Jordan's 1969 essay "Black Studies—Bringing Back the Person." According to Ferguson, Jordan's careful efforts to clarify the racist effects of race-evasive funding decisions occurred in response to the move by state powers in the post-Civil Rights era to "construct racism as an increasingly illegible phenomenon" (58). By calling for "Black studies as life studies" (Jordan qtd. in Ferguson 109), Jordan works to rhetorically analyze the race-evasive discourses of standardized assessment and dispassionate financial policy decisions that profess equal access to all while materially damaging the possibilities for Black and brown lives.

The quoted statement above was written in May 1976. In August of that year, Jordan received a dismissal notice from the college which noted that "The College's budget for fiscal 1976-1977 compels us to discontinue the services of persons currently holding appointments. The reason your services are being discontinued is that all employees in the rank of Assistant Professor with less than four years of continuous full-time service are being discontinued" (Marshak). Jordan was then rehired in 1977, but lost her seniority (Malkoff). Meanwhile, in 1975 Adrienne Rich was granted a "Special Leave of Absence" through January 1976 with no loss of seniority (Marshak). These disparities between the institutional treatment of Rich and Jordan are reflective of the ways that funding cuts disproportionately affected women of color instructors, especially vulnerable because they were often adjunct instructors, off the tenure track, who had been recently hired. For example, in 1970 the *New York Times* covered ten SEEK lecturers' claim that they were "purged" from the SEEK program at CCNY for being disruptive, that is, for protesting with students (Farber). And a letter from the Black and Puerto Rican Faculty at John Jay College from 1972 informed the Personnel Review Committee that three-fourths of the adjunct faculty not rehired were women of color.

In the spirit of critical imagining (Kirsch and Royster 21), it is worthwhile to consider these firings and layoffs juxtaposed with the extremely rapid promotion of Mina Shaughnessy, a process carefully reconstructed by Sean Molloy, who finds that "in the spring of 1967, Shaughnessy was hired as an untenured lecturer" in City College's new SEEK program; "before she even started work in September, Shaughnessy was promoted to be SEEK's English Coordinator" (106). Molloy continues:

> As a City College lecturer with no PhD and almost no academic publications, Shaughnessy normally would have had little hope for a tenure track appointment. But in the chaos of open admissions, normal faculty politics were temporarily suspended. In December of 1969, Shaughnessy was promoted to assistant professor... The new English Chair Ted Gross noted that Shaughnessy's abilities had already "won her recognition, unusual for one of lecturer rank, throughout the college" (1969 3). Even for a promotion endorsement, Gross's personal admiration was remarkable: "A woman of rare and keen intelligence, poetic sensibilities, and humane warmth, she is an extraordinary teacher and a fine human being who has won the unstinting admiration of her students, her Seek staff, and her colleagues in this Department" (1969 2)... Gross named Shaughnessy as "an Assistant Chairman in charge of all composition work in the English Department" (Gross 1970). Shaughnessy now administered all City College composition courses and all writing placement tests for incoming students (Shaughnessy 1970). She quickly expanded her program and asserted her authority over it. (114-15)

Shaughnessy was not the most qualified lecturer employed by the new SEEK program in 1967. While she may have possessed a "poetic sensibility," her colleagues—later her charges—were poets. June Jordan, also an untenured lecturer in the program, by the time of her employment by CUNY was a published writer and had already successfully run writing workshops for teens of color. It is important to consider Shaughnessy's rise in the context of other forces at work at CUNY, not all of which supported the equalizing mission of Open Admissions. That Shaughnessy's rise was supported by Theodore "Ted" Gross is also noteworthy. In many ways, Gross—who left his position in the English department to become a Dean—was responsible for turning the public against Open Admissions. In 1978, the *Saturday Review* published a salacious excerpt of his forthcoming memoir, with the article titled "How to Kill A College: The Private Papers of a Campus Dean." The article, in which Gross pays lip service to Open Admissions' mission but insists it led to a lowering of standards and student quality, led to public outcry from students and a public repudiation by City College president Robert Marshak. To Gross's description of "black, Puerto Rican, Asian, and varieties of ethnic white [students] playing radios, simulating sex, languidly moving back and forth to classes, dancing and singing, eating and studying and sleeping and drinking from soda cans or from beer bottles wrapped in brown paper bags" (Gross "How to" 78), Marshak wrote in a public letter:

I find it hard to believe that the Dean of Humanities would publish an article so deeply offensive to our students and faculty and so devoid of understanding of the progress made in the past few years at City College... I also question the tone, style, and insensitivity of your article. Your use of code words and stereotyping language about women and minorities constitutes a dangerous appeal to the forces of unreason and bigotry in our society. ("Open Letter")

As we reconsider writing pedagogies under SEEK, we must remember how the forces of white supremacy still constrained the teaching and promotion opportunities for writers and teachers of color on the faculty, limiting their implementation of meaningful cultural rhetorics pedagogies.

"Who We Intend to Be: Ourselves": Developing the Rap Idiom While Being Pushed Out of School

In the late 1960s and early 1970s, ethnic studies offerings expanded rapidly throughout the CUNY system. Black, Latino, and Caribbean literatures were included in the SEEK curriculum at CCNY as early as 1969, with separate SEEK courses in Black Literature and Latin American Literature and Romance Languages courses in Puerto Rican Literature, Contemporary Spanish, and Spanish American Literature ("The City University of New York University Center Seek Program 1969-1970 Catalog"). Meanwhile, students in the Music Department could take a course called "History and Literature of Jazz" offering a "return to personalized expression in rediscovery of origins leading to 'soul', rock, etc. and experimentation and development of new techniques" ("Spring 1970 Course Descriptions"). During the early years of SEEK, these offerings were also supplemented with film screenings and theater workshops that similarly blended white institutional boundaries between literature, music, and visual art ("SEEK Alamac Cinemateque"). Hunter College's Department of Black and Puerto Rican Studies also offered significant coursework in nonwhite literatures. In 1972-1973, the department's courses included "African Literature," "African-American Literature," "Puerto Rican Literature" (Hunter College Bulletin 72-73), and by 1975, offerings had expanded to include "Puerto Rican Folklore" and "The Image of the Puerto Rican National Identity in Its Literature." Courses were also offered in Afro-American Humanism, African Literature, Afro-Caribbean Literature, Puerto Rican Literature, Spanish Language in Puerto Rico, and Autobiography As a Special Theme in Black Literature ("The Hunter College Bulletin 75/76"). Medgar Evers College, founded in 1971 to serve Brooklyn's populations of color, offered courses like these and more, with Economics courses on "Economics of Poverty and Racism" and "Economic Development of the Inner City" (MEC 117 Bulletin 1973/74). In the Speech Department, the course descriptions promised analysis of speeches by only Black orators—mostly male, though students could alternatively register for "The Black Woman Speaks." All these courses were part of the context of students' educations in their writing classrooms, especially in classrooms like Cade Bambara's, where student input directly shaped curriculum.

Access to school resources gave students opportunities to develop the literacies of their home communities, and learn new modes of communication. Yearbooks from these years are full of pictures of desegregating academic departments and clubs, including new clubs based around ethnic identities and the desegregation of older extracurriculars like campus radio stations and the Institute of Electrical and Electronics Engineers (*Genesis* 1967). In a 1969 speech contest at City College, "two of the eight finalists were in the SEEK Program, and a freshman SEEK student took second place" (Berger "University Programs"). In 1978, Medgar Evers College students placed second in the New York Reggae Festival Song Competition, singing an original song about Jamaican women's role building the modern state of Jamaica ("Everites Place 2nd in Reggae Contest").

> The Editorial Board of THE LAST WORD has an obligation to print the feelings and ideas of all Brothers and Sisters in the College Community whether they agree with our personal Ideologies or not. KEEPING THIS IN MIND, WE SAY LET:
>
> # THE PEOPLE RAP
>
> ## DEMOCRACY AND OPPRESSION
>
> Greetings and salutations to you in this new school year of '72-'73. I am Jerry Harris, your representative head of student government, and dedicated servant. It is for you that United Third World Front exists and it is to you that it is responsible.
>
> In a democracy, government is of the people, for the people, and by the people. Through the power and justice found in
>
> The brother's name was Earl Walker. Earl was a member of the United Third World Front and a SEEK student. When I found out that he had been shot, I immediately got in contact with the U.T.W.F. and assisted them in the arduous task of making preparations for the funeral and distributing the information to the various media so that the community could be informed of the event.
>
> Brother Earl was just preparing for a trip to the Motherland when he was cut down in the prime of his life. After the funeral I picketed the store where he was

Figure 3. Detail from: "Letter from the Editor." *The Last Word* 1.1. 29 September 1972. Box 1. Open Admissions Collection 1969-1978, Queens College Archives, Queens, NY. 3 August 2016.

Against the ebb and flow of investment and retrenchment at CUNY, with the help of non-tenure-track instructors of color, students engaged what they themselves described as rap literacies to theorize themselves and their worlds in student publications. The three student papers I studied, from Hunter, Queens College, and Medgar Evers, all used the language of "rap" to describe speech that was purposive and productive, whether describing letters to the editor, exchanges with faculty, or conversations between friends. *The Last Word*, the SEEK paper at Queens College, proclaimed at the top of its letters to the editor page: "WE SAY LET: THE PEOPLE RAP!" ("Letter from the Editor.") These publications also demonstrated a tremendous interest in poetry among youth of color in New York, and specifically articulated a BAM-aligned orientation to poetry that was about self-definition, community uplift, and political action, with all three papers, not to mention several yearbooks from these years, devoting significant space to student poetry. In fact, *The Last Word* devoted two pages in every issue to student poetry, and in one issue from 1970 the editors remarked:

> So far we have received a great deal of poetic material. Because of the tremendous interest in poetry, we think that it would be a good

idea if the COMMUNICATOR sponsored and invited some well-known poets of the Third World to Hunter College... The over-all purpose of such a meeting would be to discuss methods and ways to improve, and, moreover, create more effective poetry, and thus better poets. ("Editor's Note")

This wasn't an idle hope, since the papers from both Hunter and Queens described campus visits by BAM poets Amiri Baraka and Nikki Giovanni.

The *SEEK Communicator*, the SEEK paper at Hunter College, showcases how newly hired SEEK staff members from the community—not all as famous as June Jordan—helped shape student literacies. In an issue from October 1970, a staff member, a self-identified Black woman named Yvonne Stafford, penned an extended history of SEEK which rooted the program in the rise of Black Power, the rhetoric of Malcolm X and Stokely Carmichael, the English translation of Fanon's *Wretched of the Earth*, the rise of Black Art as defined by LeRoi Jones, the music of James Brown, Aretha Franklin, Coltrane and others, and Black dance like the Jerk and the Boogaloo ("The Idea of Student Action in the SEEK Program"). As in Barbara Christian's class discussions, Stafford's intellectual history of SEEK at Hunter collapses categorizations between the poetry, music, dance, and theory of this activist, artistic, decolonial moment. As a SEEK counselor, she writes, "the object as I saw it was not destruction, but construction. I had to lend my help in getting students through in such a way that they would not be jammed by the traditional European educational rap." With this goal in mind, Stafford helped set up the theater workshop students had been asking for by starting as a poetry group with the theme "Black is (a definition of Blackness)" (Stafford "The Idea"). This genesis is expanded upon in another *Communicator* article. Information Officer Joel Washington penned a "Philosophy and History— What We Are About— What We Intend to Be: Ourselves." He wrote, "seizing the opportunity to introduce ourselves, we have decided to rap a little about definition. We are about meaningful expression... We are about being a workshop... We are about culture" (7). In the explicit language of "definition," we can see the context of an audience that was not listening to how these young people defined themselves, despite allowing their presence in the CUNY system. The explicitness of Stafford's institutional history stands in stark contrast to a poem she wrote in another issue which asked, rhetorically, "If we wrote them a revolutionary poem/ Would they read it?" ("IF").

Yet as Ferguson has theorized, demands for disciplinarity are contradictory and ironic: creating new departments insulates the old ones. Curricular spaces remained hostile to Black and Puerto Rican students' cultural rhetorics, and the opening of new spaces often insulated legacy institutions from change. While in 1972-72 Hunter's Department of Black and Puerto Rican Studies offered extensive coursework in Afrodiasporic and Caribbean literatures, in the 75-76 course catalog, only one writer of color, Ralph Ellison, was mentioned in any of the English Department's class descriptions ("The Hunter College Bulletin 75/76"). And at CCNY, one essay topic on a 1972 Proficiency Exam, which determined whether students could graduate, went like this: "The world that college graduates will be entering requires writing and reading skills of a high order. I refer not to the 'gift of gab' but to those forms of communication that have been developed for the academic, political, and scientific professions. They [future workers] will have to carry on the counseling, conferring, interviewing, proposing, reporting, reading, interpreting, and writing that most jobs are already requiring." ("Essay Topic").

Despite this resistance, throughout the '70s, student newspapers helmed by students of color contained creative writing, institutional histories, reviews of popular cultural events, and opinion and reporting on issues like international third world politics, socialism, campus administrative policies, and local and state education policy. In the Medgar Evers *ADAFI*, student writers chronicled the decay of school funding and morale as policy priorities shifted. In 1974, amidst the joy at receiving teacher certification capabilities, the paper noted that faculty were already leaving due to "apathy... because of gradual deterioration in school services and subjective administrative policies" ("Why are M.E.C. Faculty Leaving?"). Amidst coverage of underfunding and the state's plan to begin charging tuition for the first time in CUNY's history, the paper reprinted students' protest cries as headlines: "Don't let them kill free tuition" and "Medgar Evers must not die twice." Amid a 20% overall drop in applications to CUNY for the 1976-1977 school year, the paper published a special issue to be distributed within Brooklyn, countering the rumor that the school had closed and informing community members about new federal grant programs. But the paper's archives abruptly end after 1978, suggesting the end of the story students had fought so hard to keep alive.

Further research is needed to see whether individual CUNY students, admitted through the Open Admissions policy, were active in the New York hiphop scene that became a serious presence in the mid-to-late 1970s. We do know, however, that students admitted through Open Admissions were sources of rhetorical excellence. The tens of thousands of Black and Caribbean students who flooded into CUNY during these years—and then were pushed back out with the onset of tuition in 1976—have not been taken into accounts of hiphop history. And the historical record is clear: hiphop did not emerge as a commodity product—that is, hiphop was not pressed onto wax and labelled "For Sale"—until 1979, in the years immediately after the retrenchment took hold at CUNY. Perhaps the story of hiphop's early history is not of a culture rising from the ashes, but a culture negotiating with a stark economic reality: when the door of funded public education closes, the window of individualist pursuit of capital stays open, beckoning.

Outro: Reflexin, Or, Why Pedagogy Is a Labor Issue

As a white Jewish woman I have a queer relationship to the histories I promote here. I am white like Shaughnessy, part of a history of white women literacy educators in a colonial U.S. education system. I am also a white Ashkenazi queer like Adrienne Rich—who, though a radical educator and thinker, was politically aligned with whiteness in the CCNY Basic Writing program, a friend and ally of Shaughnessy's while working alongside the specifically Black brilliance of June Jordan, Toni Cade Bambara, and Barbara Christian. Throughout the archives, though I do not dwell on it in this paper, I noticed how Jewish community groups appeared in tension with the prerogatives of Open Admissions: Jewish alumni fought Open Admissions at City College; Jewish students charged the Queens College SEEK paper *The Last Word* with anti-Semitism. Yet a mere thirty years earlier, Jewish students had been those newly admitted minorities whom conservative faculty wanted cleansed of their accents and identities. The later alignment of Jewish communities with white supremacist priorities suggests the ways that white power pitches its own interests to other minoritized groups in the service of anti-Blackness. As we continue to enrich our understandings of the diverse rhetorical production during the Open Admissions years, the earliest years of hiphop culture, we must stay attuned to the complex interplay of "interests and opportunities" (Lamos) that opened, closed, and guarded avenues toward equity, advancement, and autonomy, and be willing to reflex on our own place in these historical movements.

In my case, I notice that my research for this article was funded by the continued support of a Mellon Mays fellowship I received as an undergraduate, meant to diversify the ranks of university faculty. Yet the open-ended language under whose guidelines I was awarded the fellowship—"This goal [of a diversified faculty] can be achieved both by increasing the number of students from underrepresented minority groups (URM) who pursue PhDs and by supporting the pursuit of PhDs by students who may not come from traditional minority groups but have otherwise demonstrated a commitment to the goals of MMUF" ("Mission")—was developed in response to a call from the second Bush Administration's Office of Civil Rights for "colleges and universities to change or drop race-and ethnic-specific academic enrichment and scholarship programs" (Roach). Despite NAACP complaints, this anti-affirmative action direction from the Bush Administration opened the way for white and structurally privileged students like me to take advantage of programs and funds meant for structurally disadvantaged students of color. Perhaps as much as anything in the archives, this element of my own story clarifies how, as Ferguson says, neoliberal discourses emerged "as a way of preempting redistribution," (191). By acknowledging how I, a white woman, profited from race-blind discourses, I hope to demonstrate even further how reflexive narratives, a discursive tool developed by Black poets like June Jordan in the 1960s and 70s, have transformational power to disrupt such processes. The tensions and play of privilege between June Jordan and Adrienne Rich continue to question how a minoritized white woman can stand in solidarity with her sisters of color.

Twenty years ago, Ira Shor insisted that "if we are serious" about good teaching and learning, "then we need a Labor policy on the one hand and a curricular policy against tracking, testing, and skills-based instruction on the other" (100). This paper's archival findings suggest that protecting vulnerable faculty and promoting valid, culturally relevant assessment practices are not two tasks, but one, and that providing innovative, culturally relevant pedagogies to diversifying student bodies is primarily a labor issue, a question of hiring, retaining, promoting, and following the lead of faculty whose identities resemble in some ways those of their students. Put another way—as woke as I may be or become, I just can't teach Black discourses like that. With their knowledge, their language, and their pedagogies rooted in their identities and their experiences, Black queer women poets like Audre Lorde and June Jordan remind us that supporting minoritized pedagogies is not separable from supporting minoritized teachers.

When we think of hiphop's emergence in mid-to-late 1970s New York, we must remember the decade beforehand when tens of thousands of students were formally educated in the rhetorical practices of their home communities by members of those communities; free books and theater tickets were distributed by SEEK; the academy directed newly admitted students to their home bookstores and theater workshops; a large network of community literacy and poetry organizations received city, state, and national funding and attention; students received education in media production in TV, radio, and sound engineering; and wide swaths of students at the college and high school level brought the lessons of the Black Arts Movement into their lives, using first-person poetry, fiction, and essays to define themselves in the context of their cultures, their communities, and their plans to change the world. As hiphop embraced the commodity market at the beginning of the 1980s and took the world by storm with its third world consciousness, griot poetics, and Caribbean beats, it emerged not merely out of destruction but out of the destruction of a funded public education system deeply oriented to cultural rhetorics, taught and theorized by untenured faculty of color inviting students *to rap*.

WORKS CITED

Ahmed, Sara. *Living a Feminist Life*. Duke UP, 2017.

Alim, H. Samy. "Creating 'An Empire Within an Empire': Critical Hip Hop Language Pedagogies and the Role of Sociolinguistics." *Global Linguistic Flows: Hip Hop Cultures, Youth Identities, and the Politics of Language*, edited by H. Samy Alim, Awad Ibrahim, and Alastair Pennycook. Routledge, 2009: pp. 213-30.

Arenson, Karen W. "Study Details CUNY Successes From Open-Admissions Policy." 7 May 1996. *The New York Times:* A00001.

Banks, Adam. *Digital Griots: African American Rhetoric in a Multimedia Age*. Southern Illinois UP, 2011.

"Baraka Opens Black Symposium." *The Last Word 14*. 22 March 1973. Box 1. Open Admissions Collection 1969-1978, Queens College Archives, Queens, NY. 3 August 2016.

Bell, Derrick. "*Brown v. Board of Education* and the Interest Convergence Dilemma." *Critical Race Theory: The Key Writings That Formed The Movement*, edited by Kimberlé Crenshaw, Neil Gotanda, Gary Peller, and Kendall Thomas. The New Press, 1995, pp. 20-28.

Berger, Leslie. "University Programs for Urban Black and Puerto Rican Youth." Educational Record 49.4 (Fall 1969). Box 1. SEEK Collection, Queens College Archives, Queens, NY. 3 August 2016.

Black and Puerto Rican Faculty at John Jay College. Letter to Personnel Review Committee. 20 March 1972. Box 9, Folder 1.2.048. Audre Lorde Papers, Spelman College, Atlanta, GA. 10 August 2016.

Bratta, Phil, and Malea Powell, eds. *Cultural Rhetorics,* special issue of *Enculturation*, issue 21. 20 April 2016. Web. 2 January 2018.

Brown, Tessa. "Constellating White Women's Cultural Rhetorics: The Association of Southern Women for the Prevention of Lynching and Its Contemporary Scholars." *Peitho*, vol. 20, no. 2, 2018, pp. 233-60.

Campbell, Kermit E. *Gettin' Our Groove On: Rhetoric, Language, and Literacy for the Hip Hop Generation*. Wayne State UP, 2005.

Chang, Jeff. *Can't Stop Won't Stop: A History of the Hip-Hop Generation*. Picador, 2005.

Christian, Barbara. "The Pre-Baccalaureate Program – Chapter 1." TS. Box 4. City University of New York, City College, Department of Special Programs/SEEK Program Records, 1968 - ongoing. City University of New York. City College, Library, Archives. 1 August 2016.

"The City University of New York University Center Seek Program 1969-1970 Catalogue." Box 1. City University of New York, City College, Department of Special Programs/SEEK Program Records, 1968 - ongoing. City University of New York. City College, Library, Archives. Accessed 1 August 2016.

Craig, Collin Lamont, and Staci Maree Perryman-Clark. "Troubling the Boundaries: (De)Constructing WPA Identities at the Intersections of Race and Gender." *WPA: Writing Program Administration* vol. 34, no. 2, 2011, pp. 37-58.

Craig, Todd. "'Jackin' for Beats': DJing for Citation Critique." *Radical Teacher,* vol. 97, 2013, pp. 21- 29.

Crenshaw, Kimberlé Williams. "Mapping the Margins: Intersectionality, Identity Politics, and Violence Against Women of Color." *Critical Race Theory: The Key Writings That Formed The Movement,* edited by Kimberlé Crenshaw, Neil Gotanda, Gary Peller, and Kendall Thomas. The New Press, 1995, pp. 357-83.

Devitt, Amy J. "Generalizing about Genre: New Conceptions of an Old Concept." *Relations, Locations, Positions: Composition Theory for Writing Teachers,* edited by Peter Vandenberg, Sue Hum, and Jennifer Clary-Lemon. NCTE, 2006.

"Editors Note." *The SEEK Communicator 1.2,* October 1970. Folder 11. Hunter College Student Clubs, Organizations, and Publications Collection, Hunter College, New York, NY. 2 August 2016.

"Essay Topic." December 1972. Box 2. City University of New York, City College, Mina Shaughnessy Papers. City University of New York. City College, Library, Archives. 1 August 2016.

"Everites Place 2nd in Reggae Contest." *ADAFI 4-6.* 9 August 1978. College Archives, Medgar Evers College, Brooklyn, NY. 4 August 2016.

Farber, M.A. "Bowker Changes Stand on 7 SEEK Lecturers." 3 September 1970. *The New York Times.* Box 1, Folder 9. Academic Skills/Seek Department, Hunter College Archives, New York, NY. 2 August 2016.

Ferguson, Roderick A. *The Reorder of Things: The University and Its Pedagogies of Minority Difference.* U of Minnesota P, 2012.

Fraser, Gerald. "Black Poets Read Their Work in Cultural Festival at Columbia." p. C23. 28 October 1977. *The New York Times.* Box 45, Folder 3.366. Audre Lorde Papers, Spelman College, Atlanta, GA. 10 August 2016.

Genesis 1967. Bronx Community College Yearbook. Archives, Bronx Community College, Bronx, NY. 4 August 2016.

Gladney, Marvin J. "The Black Arts Movement and Hip-Hop." *African American Review* vol. 29, no. 2, 1995, pp. 291-301.

Grandmaster Melle Mel, Edward G. Fletcher, Sylvia Robinson, Clifton "Jiggs" Chase. "The Message." Performance by Grandmaster Flash and the Furious Five. Sugar Hill, 1982.

Green, Jr., David F. *It's Deeper Than Rap: A Study of Hip Hop Music and Composition Pedagogy.* Dissertation, Pennsylvania State University, 2011. UMI, 2015.

Gross, Theodore L. "How to Kill a College: the Private Papers of a Campus Dean." *Saturday Review*, 4 February 1978, pp. 12-20.

Gubele, Rose, Lisa King, and Joyce Rain Anderson, eds. *Survivance, Sovereignty, and Story: Teaching American Indian Rhetorics*. Utah State UP, 2015.

Gumbs, Alexis Pauline. "Nobody Mean More: Black Feminist Pedagogy and Solidarity." *Imperial University: Academic Repression and Scholarly Dissent*, edited by Piya Chatterjee and Sunaina Maira. U of Minnesota P, 2014, pp. 237-60.

Gunner, Jeanne. "Iconic Discourse: The Troubling Legacy of Mina Shaughnessy." *Journal of Basic Writing*, vol. 17, no. 2, 1998, pp. 25-42.

Haas, Angela M. "Wampum as Hypertext: An American Indian Intellectual Tradition of Multimedia Theory and Practice." *Studies in American Indian Literatures* vol. 19, no. 4, 2007, pp. 77-100.

Hitt, Allison, and Bre Garrett, eds. *Engaging the Possibilities of Disability Studies*, special issue of *Reflections*, vol. 14, no. 1, 2014. Web. 2 January 2018.

Hudson, Theodore R. "Activism and Criticism During the Black Arts Movement. *Connections: Essays on Black Literatures*, edited by Emmanuel Sampath Nelson. Aboriginal Studies Press, 1998, pp. 89-99.

Hunter College Bulletin 72-73. 1973. Box 22. Hunter College Publications Collection, Hunter College, New York, NY. 2 August 2016.

The Hunter College Bulletin 75/76. Box 22, Folder 4. Hunter College Publications Collection, Hunter College, New York, NY. 2 August 2016.

Inoue, Asao B. *Antiracist Writing Assessment Ecologies: Teaching and Assessing Writing for a Socially Just Future*. WAC Clearinghouse, 2015.

Jordan, June. "Africa/Harlem on My Mind—Met Museum Centennial." 21 November 1969. Box 55, Folder 5. June Jordan Papers, Radcliffe Institute for Advanced Study at Harvard University, Cambridge, MA. 8 August 2016.

—. Handwritten journal. 1969. Folder 1, Box 8. June Jordan Papers, Radcliffe Institute for Advanced Study at Harvard University, Cambridge, MA. 8 August 2016.

—. Letter to Mina Shaughnessy. 1 November 1970. Folder 13, Box 76. June Jordan Papers, Radcliffe Institute for Advanced Study at Harvard University, Cambridge, MA. 8 August 2016.

—. "Statement by June Jordan/ Ass't Professor of English/ Black poet and writer." TS. Box 76, Folder 14. 5 May 1976. June Jordan Papers, Radcliffe Institute for Advanced Study at Harvard University, Cambridge, MA. 8 August 2016.

Kirkland, David E. *A Search Past Silence: The Literacy of Young Black Men*. Teachers' College Press, 2013.

Kirsch, Gesa E., "Being On Location: Serendipity, Place, and Archival Research." *Beyond the Archives: Research As a Lived Process,* edited by Liz Rohan and Gesa E. Kirsch. Southern Illinois UP, 2008, pp. 20-27

Kirsch, Gesa E., and Joy S. Ritchie. "Theorizing a Politics of Location in Composition Studies." *College Composition and Communication,* vol. 46, no. 1, 1995, pp. 7-29.

Kynard, Carmen. *Vernacular Insurrections: Race, Black Protest, and the New Century in Composition- Literacies Studies.* State U of New York P, 2013.

Ladson-Billings, Gloria. *The Dreamkeepers: Successful Teachers of African American Children.* Jossey-Bass, 1994.

Lamos, Steve. *Interests and Opportunities: Race, Racism, and University Writing Instruction in the Post-Civil Rights Era.* U of Pittsburgh P, 2011.

Lavin, David E., and Davi Hyllegard. *Changing the Odds: Open Admissions and the Life Chances of the Disadvantaged.* Yale UP, 1996.

"Letter from the Editor." *The Last Word 1.1.* 29 September 1972. Box 1. Open Admissions Collection 1969-1978, Queens College Archives, Queens, NY. 3 August 2016.

Lindsay, Treva. "Let Me Blow Your Mind: Hip Hop Feminist Futures in Theory and Praxis," *Urban Education* vol. 50, no. 1, 2015, pp. 52-77.

Malkoff, Karl. Letter to June Jordan. 17 January 1989 [79?]. Box 76, Folder 14. June Jordan Papers, Radcliffe Institute for Advanced Study at Harvard University, Cambridge, MA. 8 August 2016.

Mao, Luming, and Morris Young, eds. *Representations: Doing Asian American Rhetoric.* Utah State UP, 2008.

Marshak, Robert. Letter to Adrienne Rich. 5 March 1975. Box 5, Folder 389. Adrienne Rich Papers, Radcliffe Institute for Advanced Study at Harvard University, Cambridge, MA. 8 August 2016.

—. Letter to June Jordan. 15 July 1976. Folder 14, Box 76. June Jordan Papers, Radcliffe Institute for Advanced Study at Harvard University, Cambridge, MA. 8 August 2016.

—. "Open Letter to Dean Gross." 21 February 1978. Box 4. City University of New York, City College, Department of Special Programs/SEEK Program Records, 1968—ongoing. City University of New York. City College, Library, Archives. 1 August 2016.

Medgar Evers College City University of New York Bulletin 1971-1972 1.1. College Archives, Medgar Evers College, Brooklyn, NY. 4 August 2016.

Medgar Evers College City University of New York Bulletin 1973/74 1.2. College Archives, Medgar Evers College, Brooklyn, NY. 4 August 2016.

Medgar Evers College City University of New York Bulletin '74-'75. College Archives, Medgar Evers College, Brooklyn, NY. 4 August 2016.

Milu, Esther. "Translingual Practices in Kenyan Hiphop: Pedagogical Implications." *Literacy as Translingual Practice: Between Communities and Classrooms,* edited by A. Suresh Canagarajah. Routledge, 2013, pp. 104-112.

Molloy, Sean. "Diving In or Guarding the Tower: Mina Shaughnessy's Resistance and Capitulation to High-Stakes Writing Tests at City College." *Journal of*

Basic Writing, vol. 31, no. 2, 2012, pp. 103-41.

"Nikki Giovanni." Advertisement. *The Last Word 4.5.* 18 December 1974. Box 1. Open Admissions Collection 1969-1978, Queens College Archives, Queens, NY. 3 August 2016.

"Poetry Readings by Florence Cronin and Oscar Rubin." Event Announcement. *ADAFI* 2.1. 23 December 1975. College Archives, Medgar Evers College, Brooklyn, NY. 4 August 2016.

Pough, Gwendolyn D. *Check It While I Wreck It: Black Womanhood, Hip-Hop Culture, and the Public Sphere.* Northeastern UP, 2004.

—. "Seeds and Legacies: Tapping the Potential in Hip-Hop." *That's the Joint: The Hip-hop Studies Reader*, edited by Murray Forman and Mark Anthony Neal. Routledge, 2004, pp.283-89.

Powell, Malea. "Stories Take Place: A Performance in One Act." 2012 CCCC Chair's Address. *College Composition and Communication* vol. 64, no. 2, December 2012, pp. 383-406.

Powell, Malea, Daisy Levy, Andrea Riley-Mukavetz, Marilee Brooks-Gillies, Maria Novotny, Jennifer Fisch-Ferguson, The Cultural Rhetorics Theory Lab. "Our Story Begins Here: Constellating Cultural Rhetorics." *Enculturation*, vol. 18, 2014. Web. 22 March 2019.

Pritchard, Eric Darnell. *Fashioning Lives: Black Queers and the Politics of Literacy.* Southern Illinois UP, 2017.

Rich, Adrienne. "Books to buy, beg, borrow, steal, or read standing-up in the bookstore." Box 5, Folder 390. Adrienne Rich Papers, Radcliffe Institute for Advanced Study at Harvard University, Cambridge, MA. 8 August 2016.

—. "Eulogy for Mina Shaughnessy." 8 December 1978. Box 5, Folder 354. Adrienne Rich Papers, Radcliffe Institute for Advanced Study at Harvard University, Cambridge, MA. 8 August 2016.

—. "Pre-Baccalaureate Program City College – Report on the Summer Seminar July 1- August 30, 1968." 1968. Box 5, Folder 385. Adrienne Rich Papers, Radcliffe Institute for Advanced Study at Harvard University, Cambridge, MA. 8 August 2016.

—. "[Syllabus] English 1-H Fall term 1971." 1971. Box 5, Folder 388. Adrienne Rich Papers, Radcliffe Institute for Advanced Study at Harvard University, Cambridge, MA. 8 August 2016.

—. "[Syllabus] SEEK English 1.8 G." April 1969. Box 5, Folder 388. Adrienne Rich Papers, Radcliffe Institute for Advanced Study at Harvard University, Cambridge, MA. 8 August 2016.

—. "Teaching Language in Open Admissions." *On Lies, Secrets, and Silence: Selected Prose, 1966-1978.* W. W. Norton & Company, 1979, pp. 51-68

Richardson, Elaine. *Hiphop Literacies.* Routledge, 2006.

Rose, Tricia. *Black Nose: Rap Music and Black Culture in Contemporary America.*

Wesleyan UP, 1994.

Royster, Jacqueline Jones. *Traces of a Stream: Literacy and Social Change Among African American Women*. U of Pittsburgh P, 2000.

Royster, Jacqueline Jones, and Gesa Kirsch. *Feminist Rhetorical Practices: New Horizons for Rhetoric, Composition, and Literacy Studies*. Southern Illinois UP, 2012.

Ruiz, Iris. D., and Raúl Sánchez, eds. *Decolonizing Rhetoric and Composition Studies: New Latinx Keywords for Theory and Pedagogy*. Palgrave Macmillan, 2016.

"SEEK Alamac Cinemateque." Box 2. City University of New York, City College, Department of Special Programs/SEEK Program Records, 1968— ongoing. City University of New York. City College, Library, Archives. 1 August 2016.

Shor, Ira. "Our Apartheid: Writing Instruction & Inequality." *Journal of Basic Writing*, vol. 16, no. 1, 1997, pp. 91-104.

Soliday, Mary. *The Politics of Remediation: Institutional and Student Needs in Higher Education*. U of Pittsburgh P, 2002.

"Spring 1970 Course Descriptions." 1970. Box 2. City University of New York, City College, Department of Special Programs/SEEK Program Records, 1968—ongoing. City University of New York. City College, Library, Archives. 1 August 2016.

Stafford, Yvonne (Adiv). "The Idea of Student Action in the SEEK Program– A History." p. 8. *The SEEK Communicator 1.2*, October 1970. Folder 11. Hunter College Student Clubs, Organizations, and Publications Collection, Hunter College, New York, NY. 2 August 2016.

[Stafford], Yvonne Adiv. "IF." *The SEEK Communicator 1.1*, June 1970. Folder 11. Hunter College Student Clubs, Organizations, and Publications Collection, Hunter College, New York, NY. 2 August 2016.

The Sugarhill Gang, Sylvia Robinson, Nile Rodgers, Bernard Edwards, Grandmaster Caz. "Rapper's Delight." Sugar Hill, 1979.

Washington, Joel. "Philosophy and History—What we Are About- What We Intend to Be: Ourselves." p. 7. *The SEEK Communicator 1.1*, June 1970. Folder 11. Hunter College Student Clubs, Organizations, and Publications Collection, Hunter College, New York, NY. 2 August 2016.

"Why Are M.E.C. Faculty Leaving?" Medgar Evers *ADAFI* 1.2. 1 May 1974, p.7. College Archives, Medgar Evers College, Brooklyn, NY. 4 August 2016.

Supplemental Material

"Let the People Rap"

Tessa Brown

Part I: Reflection on the Origins of the Article

If you read Jeff Chang's *Can't Stop Won't Stop* or Tricia Rose's *Black Noise* — and you *should* read them—you'll learn that hiphop began in 1973 when Bronx teen DJ Kool Herc, a recent immigrant from Jamaica, spun two copies of the same record together, manually mixing the break beat. When he rapped over it, talking smoothly over the track, hiphop was born.

When I was a doctoral student studying literacy, rhetoric, and college writing education at Syracuse University, my professors didn't talk much about this moment. But they did talk about New York in the 1970s, specifically in regard to the Open Admissions movement at the City University of New York (CUNY), during which waves of student protests led to state legislators of color desegregating CUNY by changing their admissions requirements. The new requirements stated that admission to one of the system's 2 or 4 year colleges would now be guaranteed to anyone who graduated from New York City's public schools, no matter their grades. Although the city's K-12 schools were still intensely segregated, with Black and Puerto Rican students receiving vastly inferior educations to those in predominantly white schools, this new "open admissions" policy significantly expanded access to college for all NYC students.

As someone who was studying hiphop history and teaching hiphop in my writing classes, I became interested in this moment in the 1970s when hiphop history and composition history collided. Hiphop historians like Chang and Rose rooted hiphop's birth in the burning Bronx, where graffiti and break beats rose up out of a broken-down community whose only resource was a centuries old poetic and musical tradition. But the story of Open Admissions suggested that, before the Bronx burned, it was blossoming. This led me to wonder whether hiphop culture might be a product not of devastation but, incredibly, of investment in public schools. This question pushed me to the archives. Across two weeks in the summer of 2016, I visited six CUNY archives in four New York City boroughs (sorry, Staten Island), then headed to Boston to study Adrienne Rich and June Jordan's papers at Radcliffe, and finally shot down to Atlanta where Audre Lorde and Toni Cade Bambara's papers were housed at Spelman. As I discuss in the piece, I used my knowledge of hiphop's multimodal culture of rapping, DJing, graffiti and breakdance to push my research beyond the archives of Basic Writing so that I could understand more holistically what was being taught and learned under CUNY Open Admissions. Ultimately, my findings bring together histories of hiphop, writing pedagogy, adjunct academic labor, and students' multiliteracies to refocus our attention on the underremembered New Yorkers who made Open Admissions and hiphop history what they are.

PART II: DESCRIPTION OF RESEARCH METHODS, FINDINGS, AND/OR PEDAGOGICAL IMPACT

One of the first documents I looked at when beginning this historical research was an essay by Adrienne Rich, the lesbian Jewish poet and essayist who, like several other radical and famous writers, chose to teach in the newly created remedial writing programs at CUNY in the late 1960s and early 1970s. My archival research would later show that, as a white woman, Rich's experience as a CUNY employee was significantly different than that of her equally noteworthy Black colleagues, including Toni Cade Bambara, Audre Lorde, and, especially and most intimately, June Jordan. Before I followed hiphop to CUNY's archives, I read this in Rich's essay "Teaching Language in Open Admissions":

> Many of our students wrote in the vernacular with force and wit; others were unable to say what they wanted on paper in or out of the vernacular. We were dealing not simply with dialect and syntax but with the imagery of lives, the anger and flare of urban youth—how could this be used, strengthened, without the lies of artificial polish? How does one teach order, coherency, the structure of ideas while respecting the student's experience of his thinking and perceiving? Some students who could barely sweat out a paragraph delivered (and sometimes conned us with) dazzling raps in the classroom: how could we help this oral gift transfer itself onto paper?

With her mention of "dazzling raps," I knew I was onto something.

What I found was complex, and beautiful–the ephemera of little-known history with implications for how we understand both hiphop culture and funded public education. Open Admissions led to a massive expansion of CUNY with new programs and departments, all radical, funded, and inclusive. But the forces who were against this evolution evolved themselves, too, and quickly, learning to use the language of austerity to institute tuition in

1978 for the first time in CUNY's history—thus pushing out the same students the school system had just welcomed in.

In the article, I revise our understanding of hiphop's history, arguing that hiphop didn't just emerge from devastation—it emerged from investment in, and *then* divestment from, Black and Brown New Yorkers. Under CUNY's open admission policy, marginalized New Yorkers were suddenly offered a world-class, radical education for a single, glimmering decade, before tuition was instituted for the first time in the system's history in 1978, pushing many of these students back out. Following theorist Roderick Ferguson, in my article I show how the re-segregation of CUNY in the late 70s is a case study in the development of a bureaucratic language of austerity and meritocracy, which re-created the pre-civil rights caste system without using the explicitly racist categorization of Jim Crow. Furthermore, my study of primary documents allowed me to argue that the identity-centered language of modern rap was pioneered by queer Black women poets and emerged specifically to counter this depersonalized, bureaucratic language. Finally, speaking directly to my colleagues in rhetoric and composition, I push back on our focus on white woman administrator Mina Shaughnessy and instead center the radical poets like Jordan, Rich, Bambara and Lorde whose culturally relevant pedagogies became part of the DNA of early hiphop culture even as these women were never promoted and have barely even been remembered by the discipline where they chose to work. This work solidified and substantiated many of my core beliefs about teaching and learning: that public investment in education unearths tremendous brilliance, and that radical and radically successful pedagogies start with diverse and supported workforces.

Part III: Discussion Questions

1. This piece uses extensive quoted materials from the archive to highlight the creative rhetorical production of the students and teachers it studies. Which was your favorite quotation or detail from the archives and why?
2. The piece significantly expands both hiphop history and CUNY Open Admissions history. How did you respond to these expansions? Are there parts of this revised history that you resist, that you embrace? Why?
3. Brown's argues "that a resistive literacy of rappin was growing and cultivated within the CUNY system during this decade, developing dialogically with an emerging bureaucratic language of standards developed in response to the Civil Rights gains of the late 1960s." How do you make sense of this claim? Do you see the persistent tension between bureaucratic and personal discourses in your own communities or workplaces? How so?

LITERACY IN COMPOSITION STUDIES

Literacy in Composition Studies is on the web at http://licsjournal.org

Literacy in Composition Studies (LiCS) is a refereed open access online journal that sponsors activity at the nexus of literacy and composition studies. We publish long-form scholarly articles and short-form pieces including book reviews, interviews, symposium essays, and work in new and emerging genres. Given its ideological nature, *literacy* is a particularly fluid and contextual term. It can name a range of activities from fundamental knowledge about how to decode text to interpretive and communicative acts. The term *composition studies* points to the range of writing courses at the college level, including FYC, WAC/WID, writing studies, and professional writing, even as it signals the institutional, disciplinary, and historically problematic nature of the field.

Independent Black Institutions and Rhetorical Literacy Education: A Unique Voice of Color[1]

Jamila M. Kareem offers a corrective to current histories and constructions in composition/rhetoric by describing the significance of these vastly understudied yet influential educational institutions. Borrowing the framework of a "unique voice of color" from Delgado and Stefancic, Kareem speaks to this current historical moment by considering the influence of four Black-American-built forms of institutionalized education: Citizenship Schools and education programs, Freedom Schools, Black Panther Liberation Schools, and pre-college independent Black institutions. Kareem specifically examines the curricular, pedagogical, and instructional practices of these institutions and offers "counter-stories" to the historical narratives about Black Americans typically gentrified by White and European-American perspectives. By highlighting these institutions—and the Black voices that created them—Kareem argues that these models and the critical race theories on which they are based should be integrated into today's college literacy and writing education programs to help reduce ignorance of systemic racism.

---

1. *Literacy in Composition Studies,* vol. 8, no. 1, 2020, DOI: https://doi.org/10.21623/1.8.1.2 © 2020 Jamila M. Kareem.

Independent Black Institutions and Rhetorical Literacy Education: A Unique Voice of Color

Jamila M. Kareem

Keywords: literacy education; critical race theory; rhetorical education; counter-story; race-conscious; community literacy; African American literacy

"There is a cultural price-tag to literacy."

—Carl F. Kaestle, *The History of Literacy and the History of Readers*

The tales of my people's literacy education history have been gentrified. The truth about the valiant fore-teachers and students wading against the political, economic, physical, and rhetorical barricades to their learning objectives is removed from the collective consciousness of American history. Historians assessed the agency earned by Black-built practices and traditions developed by Black communities, Black-owned rhetorics, discourses, and literacies and determined that agency worthy of being traded out for literacy histories owned and operated by sanctioned middle-class White patriarchal sociocultural constructions. And so, our true literacy history is relegated to the margins of cultural knowledge about the needs and goals of education for Black Americans, historically and contemporarily. Save for the work of a small collective of composition and literacy scholars, the history of rhetorical literacy education in and for American Black communities has been reduced to "romantic adaptations" (Lathan xxvi) that appease "majoritarian stories" (Solórzano and Yosso) about the place of Black people and blackness in American culture. Rhetorical literacy education constitutes instruction in social and civic-based literacy practices for the purposes of rhetorical participation in society and culture. I employ this term rather than rhetorical education because I intend to emphasize the rhetoricity—the rhetorical force and influence—of literacy practices taught in these divergent education sites rather than to emphasize the persuasive purposes of formal education.

For Black folks, like me and my kin, descendants of American slavery, literacy education has always been rhetorical (Royster, *Traces*; Logan, *Liberating*; Kynard, "Writing"; Lathan; Karega; Richardson). Both the pursuit of literacy and its uses have been wielded to strengthen our social and political stations and resist assimilationist practices. In this essay, I apply the critical race theory "voice-of-color" tenet (Delgado and Stefancic) to establish a counter-story about the rhetoricity of literacy education for Black Americans by analyzing the literacy instruction of independent Black institutions, a style of education developed outside of majoritarian Eurocentric voice. Our literacy education has often occurred in community sites outside of formal schooling. By adopting central features of these Afrocentric literacy education programs, college composition programs and faculty can create race- and community-conscious writing curriculum, pedagogy, and instructional practices.

I detail critical race theory's unique voice of color principle and how, as a lens for framing cultural narratives, it reshapes historical and perpetual narrative constructs of American literacy education. The unique voice of color suggests that individuals outside of racial-cultural norms can best speak to experiences of those outside of racial-cultural norms. This principle focuses on narratives that counter accepted social myths, as "because of their different histories and experiences with oppression, black, American Indian, Asian, and Latino/a writers and thinkers may be able to communicate to their white counterparts" better than Whites can to each other (Delgado and Stefancic 4). Eurocentric literacy instruction persists as a central tactic for the dominant culture to rob students of color of the opportunity to use academic discourses as one of many ways to respond to their social, cultural, and political positions (Delpit). This pattern, however, results in part from the divide between the public community and the college or university that has historically prevailed within Eurocentric educational models, models that have been challenged and reimagined by composition-literacies (Kynard, *Vernacular*) recently. In venerating school literacies for the singular purpose of being academic, "such efforts mistake the official purposes assigned to academic knowledge and academic discursive and institutional forms for the full range of uses to which these can and have been put" (Horner 169). The unique voice of color will aid me in presenting a counter-story to the dominant academy tale about the rhetorical of literacy education for Black Americans. This unique voice of color reveals the objectives of rhetorical literacy education for Black Americans as *instruction in the social actions, civic practices, and language performances for the purposes of rhetorical participation in society and culture in advancement of Black communities, locally and globally*. The following pages first outline attributes of the predominant Euro-American voice about literacy education for Blacks in America and then outline the implications of a unique voice of color for speaking against that dominant voice. In discussing some critical practices of independent Black institutions, I exemplify a unique voice of color counter-story to the prevailing perspective about rhetorical literacy education for Black Americans. This Afrocentric education model is grounded in truthfully representing and advancing Black American and African-centered cultures. I end with a discussion of implications for composition-literacy approaches that support the education of Black American students.

Black Rhetorical Literacy Education from the Majoritarian White Voice

Majoritarian historical and contemporary accounts of Black Americans' place in American higher education literacy instruction are those that dismiss the legacy of educational endeavors initiated out of Black American communities. These endeavors often privilege Afrocentric ways of knowing, and because majoritarian stories often "generate from a legacy of racial privilege" (Solórzano and Yosso 28), those about literacy education "distor[t] and silenc[e] the experiences of people of color" (29). The majoritarian White voice speaking to the subject of Blacks in American higher education literacy generally imposes the narrative of the White savior. Yes, these tales say, Blacks had their own community-developed education outlets, but none were sufficient as systemic forms of academic learning. It was only when the mainstream White education system *allowed* Black Americans into predominantly White colleges that our rhetorical literacy education became adequate and relevant to American society.

This majoritarian historical and contemporary account of Black Americans' place in literacy education is constructed from a whiteness-valued Eurocentric epistemological perspective. I draw this term from Black feminist intellectual activist Patricia Hill Collins, who defines the Eurocentric epistemological perspective as knowledge validation practices that honor or privilege Eurocentric cultural ways of being (253). Jacqueline Jones Royster and Jean C. Williams describe the consequences of excluding selected perspectives from the history of a discipline like composition studies. The Eurocentric narrative about Black Americans' literacy instruction in higher education proclaims that, except for in a few anomalous cases, our curricular options were subpar until we were allowed to enter White-majority education sites in the 1960s (Brereton; Brubacher and Rudy; Miller; Thelin). Even though select Blacks accessed and succeeded in mainstream White American colleges and universities, most of the rhetorical purposes of literacy education were aimed at assimilating into mainstream, White-dominated society and culture.

John Seiler Brubacher and Willis Rudy imply that Black Americans, indigenous Americans, and Latinxs received vast changes to their higher educational opportunities with the implementation of affirmative action admissions policies in 1964 and open admissions in 1970 (78-79, 401). The authors deduce that the "threats to withhold federal funds … [to] institutions which were held to be too slow in implementing" affirmative action guidelines resulted in findings by the Carnegie Commission on Higher Education that "many colleges and universities were being forced to lower their academic standards and to undermine the quality of their faculties because of the demands flowing from Affirmative Action programs" (79). In noting that Black Americans and other racial formation groups underrepresented in colleges and universities fell behind those of Asian descent in accessing higher education (401), the historical account fails to note that this gap existed within predominantly White institutions. John R. Thelin, by contrast, does include a partial history of historically Black American institutions of higher education. Although, in the discussion of predominantly White institutions, the inclusion of experiences of color remains in step with the majority of historical texts on the subject. Thelin's approach of considering "key historical episodes that have enduring implications for colleges and universities" (Introduction) ignores, for instance, the inaugural graduation of Black American Richard Henry Green from Yale College in 1857 (JBHE Research Department). Nor does the historical record chronicle the impact of approximately forty Black students graduating from universities and colleges in the North or Lucy Ann Stanton's certificate in literature from Oberlin College, the first Black American woman to receive such an honor (JBHE Research Department). These events are but a few that create a racial perspectives gap in how researchers historicize American higher education. I share them to show that the majoritarian White voice in historicizing rhetorical literacy education is but a product of a larger cultural phenomenon in college-level education.

Turning to literacy and composition histories in higher education institutions, the discipline has not fared much better in eliminating an absent presence of race (Prendergast) from how it historicizes the discipline in higher education. In the introduction of *The Origins of Composition Studies in the American College, 1875–1925*, John Brereton notes that "the 1865 founding of Cornell University, a school which promised that anyone could learn anything there, was a sign that a determined philanthropist with enough money could influence the course of education" (8). This change led to the 1869 ascension of Charles W. Eliot as Harvard's president and to the rise of modern English composition literacy instruction and practices. The year 1869 also marks the year that Massachusetts's first Black American judge, George Lewis Ruffin, graduated from Harvard Law School. Brereton does not examine the role that admitting and educating Black Americans had in executing the new installation of composition.

Brereton's goal for this collection is to "supply ... all those interested in the history of English composition with some of the most significant documents in readily accessible form" (xii) by connecting theory to practice (xiv) through the central documents that compositionists of the time sourced (xv). Brereton acknowledges the limitations of focusing on the public record, because "a great deal of what we would now regard as postsecondary writing was done by ... men and women . . . at historically black institutions," and even as these marginalized institutions may have borrowed pedagogical and curricular methods and outcomes from majority White schools, "some students and some teachers asserted themselves in new and important ways" (xv-xvi). Although, the Introduction does remark that "[Black American] writers were forging a distinctive voice (or series of voices) in nineteenth-century America," it additionally notes that Black students and faculty were still expected to perform discourses of whiteness (Inoue) in their writing practices (Brereton 21). In *The Evolution of College English: Literacy Studies from the Puritans to the Postmoderns*, Thomas P. Miller narrates a history of college English studies, broader than composition studies but including composition and literacy studies. This historical record does make a few strides in acknowledging the presence of Black Americans in literacy instruction and its development in the American education system through the centuries. Similarly to the accounts reviewed thus far, Miller includes the cases of Black Americans in the development of English and literacy studies within the purview of Euro-American histories. These acknowledgements are significant, but their limitations represent yet another erasure of lived experiences from Black American students with literacy in the education system.

These tales about the arrival of Black Americans at historically White sites of higher education ignores the history of Black American-centric education in Black communities, constructing Eurocentric education as the ultimate key to social mobility for Black Americans. The result of these perspectives is that they construct histories that have "social, political, and cultural *consequences*" (Royster and Williams 563). The account of the Black American presence in composition studies that Royster and Williams present counters or revises the conventional Eurocentric epistemological perspectives of this presence. Drawing inspiration from the ways that Royster and Williams "counter mythologies about African American presence" in the history of composition studies (579), I aim to wield a unique voice of color to counter perspectives that emulate the "majoritarian racial privilege" within American rhetorical literacy education.

COUNTER-STORY OF THE UNIQUE VOICE OF COLOR

Critical race theory can help explicate this racialized construction of literacy education. Critical race theory hypothesizes that people of color have a unique voice that can provide vital counter-stories to accepted knowledge about racialized experiences. In other words, in a society ordered in part by racial identifications, racialized experiences may allow writers and intellectuals of marginalized races to communicate issues to the dominant White racial culture that Whites do not have the language to communicate to each other (Delgado and Stefancic 4). According to this tenet, racial counter-narratives are essential to providing a complete historical perspective of American social institutions. Aja Y. Martinez proposes that critical race theory, and particularly counter-story, can act as a testimonial method of narrative methodology to bring to light persistent racism in the field of composition studies and the academy itself (34). Martinez notes that such narrative forms are necessary as the field faces a "demographic shift" in the students it serves (34).

Counter-story has been used as a research methodology that allows researchers to challenge the de-humanizing expectations of "empirical data" (Martinez 37) that propagate deficit narratives about people of color (Solórzano and Yosso 4) and the privilege of the dominant cultural ways of knowing (Solórzano and Yosso 33). Literacy research in composition studies has alluded to the need for such ways of knowing (Kynard, *Vernacular*; Lathan;). In *Freedom Writing: African American Civil Rights Literacy Activism*, Rhea Estelle Lathan pushes back against the notion that "literacy *belongs* to white people" (28) by performing cognitive mapping of Jim Crow and composition studies (30) as they relate to the teaching and learning practices of Citizenship Schools. This mapping, or "spatial diagram or distribution of both" (Lathan 30) cultural productions, distorts cultural ideologies about literacy education and literacy activism, therefore providing a space to interject theoretical counter-stories. In another look at the possible ways of knowing in contrast to those advocated by dominant racial epistemologies, Carmen Kynard explores the ways that the Black Arts Movement, Black Studies, and the Black Power Movement could craft an "alternative social world" when connected to language arts and composition pedagogy (*Vernacular* 111). Cognitive mapping of historical and disciplinary narratives and imaginings of unconventional social worlds can help create a unique voice of color that acts as a critical race counter-story to prevailing narratives and imaginings.

Critical race researchers see "counter-story [as] also a tool for exposing, analyzing, and challenging the majoritarian stories of racial privilege" (Solórzano and Yosso 32). The voice of color is essential to this process as it calls for inquiries into the impaired judgement of the singular Eurocentric epistemological voice. The voice-of-color thesis has its complications, including that it risks essentializing racialized experiences. In theorizing that a unique voice of color exists for speaking to systemic racist practices, critical race theory complicates the principle that races are constructed through thought and social relation (Delgado and Stefancic 8). I apply the voice-of-color thesis here as a theoretical frame to analyze one case of rhetorical literacy education for Black American students through non-Eurocentric perspectives. Instead of essentializing the Black American literacy education experience through the unique voice of color, I hold it as protection against epistemological gentrification around this education.

Counter-stories to American Rhetorical Literacy Education

Two critical works in composition-literacies studies have detailed the rhetorical purposes of postsecondary education for Black Americans. *Traces of a Stream: Literacy and Social Change Among African American Women* by Jacqueline Jones Royster and *Liberating Language: Sites of Rhetorical Education in Nineteenth-Century Black America* by Shirley Wilson Logan provide counter-stories, revisionist narratives, or an alternative social world to dominant conceptions of what rhetorical literacy education has looked like for Black Americans, one of several groups typically marginalized in education histories. For a long time, White America crafted the official accounts of Black Americans' acquisition of literacy and rhetorical education through formal higher education. Yet as far back as 1903, *The Souls of Black Folk* by W.E.B. Du Bois offered a counter-story about the formal education of Black Americans. In "On the Wings of Atalanta," Du Bois distinguishes Atlanta University's exceptionality from other distinguished universities:

> Not at Oxford or at Leipsic, not at Yale or Columbia, is there an air of higher resolve or more unfettered striving; the determination to realize for men, both black and white, the broadest possibilities of life, to seek the better and the best, to spread with their own hands the Gospel of Sacrifice, — all this is the burden of their talk and dream.

Du Bois sees Atlanta University as "the organ of that fine adjustment between real life and the growing knowledge of life." Contradicting the principal narrative of Black Americans and higher education, this period-based description of an HBCU conveys an opportunistic perspective.

If one central goal of higher education is liberation through assimilation into culturally dominant ways of knowing and being, then writing in literacy education, as it is most generally accepted, is central to this goal. Revisionist narratives through counter-stories have been central to Black communities owning their identities and creating meaning. The Literacy Narratives of Black Columbus Project, developed out of The Ohio State University with community partners, presents a unique voice of color from stories that complicate the dominant narratives about Columbus, Ohio, and its history.1 Studying the rhetorical literacy education practices of Black Americans prior to inclusion in Eurocentric sites of education may have proven complicated, since much of the education happened in non-academic settings (Kates; Logan "Liberating"; Royster). This exclusionary rationale might be just a poor excuse to omit Black Americans from the narrative, however, because plenty of our instruction in literacy education happened in what would be considered formal institutions today. Yet because of the second-class status during particular historical moments, it takes the efforts of dedicated researchers to locate the records of these institutions. Along with accounts of informal instruction in literacy education, details of rhetorical literacy education through formal Afrocentric curricular applications crafts counter-stories to the dominant narrative about the history of rhetorical literacy education in America.

Rhetorical Education in America (Glenn, Lyday, and Sharer) provides a broad scope of approaches to defining and applying rhetorical education in American classrooms. The contributors inquire into the institutional policies around rhetorical education meant to uphold the status quo but also propose rhetorical education practices that empower traditionally subjugated groups wishing to overturn the status quo (Glenn, Lyday, and Sharer). My research into the unique voice of color of IBI literacy education speaks to the latter of these approaches. Kynard's *Vernacular Insurrections: Race, Black Protest, and the New Century in Composition-Literacies Studies* expounds on the ways that Black American students have brandished composition-literacies for rhetorical, political, and social action across twentieth century decades. While many composition studies and literacy studies scholars have examined various aspects of literacy education for Black Americans, most have not considered what this unique voice of color productively adds to examine the role of literacy education histories in their influence on contemporary rhetorical literacy education practices. Further, no scholar has addressed explicitly the literacy education in the instance of Afrocentric education outlined here, independent Black institutions (IBIs). Overall, writing studies focuses little on the rhetorical literacy education of Black Americans during these eras and within these sites; the majority of information stems from interdisciplinary literature. Two key texts, *Teach Freedom: Education for Liberation in the African-American Tradition* and *Education as Freedom: African American Educational Thought and Activism*, provide grounding for this exploration.

The collection *Teach Freedom* provides essays and primary texts related to the educational institutions discussed in this article. From historical analysis of Afrocentric education just around the Civil Rights Movement to proposals and firsthand accounts from those who were there, this book supplies crucial perspectives on the dissemination of education to Black Americans. *Education as Freedom* complements *Teach Freedom* by illustrating how oppression and liberation have constituted two sides of the same coin for Black American education throughout history. The collection brings together authors who exemplify the objectives around social progression of Civil-Rights-era rhetorical education for Black Americans as well as perspectives on alternatives to the mainstream instruction provided by Afrocentric education. These works are vital to situating the revisionist, counter-story, and alternative social world narratives that create a unique voice of color from Afrocentric frames for rhetorical literacy education at the college level. In the next section, I will closely consider the curricular and extracurricular approaches of these types of education and their potential for adoption in composition-literacies curriculum.

ADDING A UNIQUE VOICE OF COLOR TO AMERICAN RHETORICAL LITERACY EDUCATION

Several embodiments of formal education for Black Americans have sprung from community education models. These formal education forays succeeded in granting Black students access to pre-college and higher education for transformative purposes. Afrocentric models from the 1960s and 1970s succeeded in transforming the ways of thinking about social status for Black community members and that rhetorically educated a wide range of Black community members. Contemporary education programs for Black American students have a number of predecessors.

Particularly for Black American students, rhetorical literacy education often occurred in community sites outside of formal schooling (Enoch). Black communities have a history of utilizing rhetorical education as a tool of civic engagement and civic responsibility. After all, "[l]ooking to the past for models and uses of rhetorical education ... [g]iven that rhetorical action is initiated in response to mediated exigencies, few Americans have had a greater need to respond than have African Americans nor a greater desire to respond effectively" (Logan "'To Get an Education,'" 37). For many Black

Americans, even today, our introduction to the practices of language and power as a tool of social action is through the church or community centers. Mainstream school forms of literacy education often undermine rhetorical literacies conferred by our communities.

Readers will be familiar with Black-built institutions of higher education such as Fisk University, Tuskegee Institute, and Atlanta University, all of which serve as forerunners to the programs of education highlighted in this unique voice of color. Among the schools produced by goals of community-building literacy education was Mary McLeod Bethune's Daytona Educational and Industrial School for Negro Girls—transformed currently into Bethune-Cookman University, established in 1904 with a mission to promote racial uplift for young Black girls through education, in order to help them "earn a living" (Bowie qtd in McCluskey 67). The curriculum put students in a position where they could use education to transform their lives by applying their learned knowledge and skills to gainful employment in service to themselves and their local communities. Normal schools for teacher training are a significant example of the rhetoricity of literacy education, because they carried out the specific purpose of serving the Black American community through educating future teachers as a resource for social change. Any of the remaining normal schools started by and for formerly enslaved Blacks during Reconstruction and post-Reconstruction are now historically Black colleges or universities (HBCUs).

Teacher education held a significant role in growing Black communities, as long-established debates questioned whether students were better taught by Black teachers or White teachers, southern teachers or northern teachers (Du Bois; Morris). This educational progress aimed to produce politically and socially conscious teachers. In *The Mis-Education of the Negro*, Carter G. Woodson argues that vocational training, like teacher training, should help teach Black students how to make a living (38-40)—not just a living for the students themselves, but to make a living for the community. Independent Black institutions embody these goals and outcomes. In the US, these homeschooling institutions for Black students came out of the spirit of Civil-Rights-era Citizenship Schools, Freedom Schools, and Black Panther Party liberation schools, as outlined in the next section. Just as "the 'legal storytelling' movement urges black and brown writers to … apply their own unique perspectives to assess law's master narratives" (Delgado and Stefancic 11), the voice-of-color perspectives presented about these instructional sites provide an assessment of narratives about mainstream rhetorical literacy education.

The Unique Voice of Color from Independent Black Institutions

Independent Black institutions arose as a way for parents and community members to counter the hidden curriculum of White supremacy offered in traditional schools. Unlike these homeschool collectives and online sites of community learning, Citizenship Schools, Freedom Schools, and Black Panther Liberation Schools constituted more official sites of general education and literacy education for Black communities. Each offered its own counter-story to dominant narratives of literacy education histories. Lathan proclaims Citizenship Schools as "a chapter in the continuing struggle against the overwhelming justification for relegating black people to subhuman positions: the belief that they were, by and large, illiterate" (xiii). The literacy and political education of older community members became central to Civil-Rights-era Black American communities in the South and prompted the creation of Citizenship Schools in 1957 Tennessee. These counter-stories also provide a Black American perspective of the range of uses for rhetorical literacy education in community affairs. Along with Freedom Schools, Citizenship Schools developed within the Black communities and taught formal writing education to enhance citizenship practices as well as service to the community. Citizenship Schools created a unique voice of color to the White American education perspective "that Black students were capable of little learning" and in doing so developed a participatory student body where such an opportunity did not exist for these students before (Levine 37). A key goal of both Citizenship Schools and Freedom Schools was to create more Black voters, particularly in the South in order to bring Black American interests and concerns to government representation.

Freedom Schools developed as a derivative of the civil rights goals established during Freedom Summer, 1964. The schools aligned with the overall Freedom Summer objective "[t]o create a truly representative political party [from] the vast majority of disempowered African Americans" by "develop[ing] the self confidence [sic] and organizational skills required of active citizens" (Emery, Braselmann, and Gold 5). Freedom Summer activists aimed to change the perception that registering to vote was something only White people did, believing their "main challenge was getting Black people to challenge themselves" (Cobb 70). The Freedom School model of education produced formal literacy education as a resource for preparing students for social action of multiple kinds, for example, to teach others and organize boycotts. The everyday reality of Black students that Freedom Schools aimed to upset included "[n]ew brick school buildings built to give the illusion of 'separate but equal' [but] contained virtually bookless libraries and science labs with no equipment" (Cobb 71) and teachers removing Black students from class for questioning about voting and organized freedom rides (67). Thus, one concern of Freedom Schools was to inspire students to brave their public-school classrooms to ask critical questions of their teachers (Cobb 67). Carmen Kynard suggests that this inspiration derived from the very racial oppression in the education system that created critically conscious and educated citizens to challenge that system (*Vernacular* 25). Part of the rhetorical literacy education of Freedom Schools included preparing students for participation within the mainstream education programs.

The Black Panther Party's Liberation Schools built upon and enhanced the previously discussed models with a resolute political approach to the education of young Black Americans. Liberation Schools reflected a distinct connection between politics and pedagogy, an approach that counters the formative, universalist Eurocentric epistemological perspectives to keep politics out of the classroom. Like the Black Panther Party that developed the education program, these schools aimed to "chang[e] the way Black people were viewed in the public sphere, and in the process [they] changed the way Black people looked at themselves" (Pough 71). Its vision for creating young revolutionaries addresses Shirley Wilson Logan's central question in "'To Get an Education and Teach My People': Rhetoric for Social Change," which is "Rhetorical education for what?" (36) The rhetorical literacy education at Liberation Schools taught students the history of socio-political conventions including "racism, capitalism, fascism, cultural nationalism, and socialism" (Perlstein 262). Rather than teaching reading, writing, and other literacies as disconnected from social contexts, teachers urged students to confront and question the entire gamut of school-related practices (Perlstein 264), including the "Pledge of Allegiance." Not unlike Freedom Schools, the educational system itself became a topic of study within Liberation Schools.

Citizenship, Freedom, and Liberation Schools' educational models stem from critical moments in American history, where the literacy education of Black Americans was a source of either oppression or progression. Independent Black institutions are modern-day constructions of Afrocentric rhetorical literacy education representing a unique voice of color. With modern versions first established in the early 1970s, IBIs have gained increasing popularity over the last thirty years. These schools use an Afrocentric program of education to teach relevant curriculum and values to preschool through high school-aged students (Lomotey 455). They come in the form of "home-school collectives" and "African-centered schools" (Changa)—or *Afrikan*-centered, as many practitioners prefer to spell the term, where they hold a more encompassing view of success than do mainstream schools (Lomotey 456). IBIs' unique voice of color about the most effective curriculum to help

Black Americans prepare for active community life can inform approaches for theorizing and teaching literacy in composition studies.

This counter-narrative to traditional rhetorical education practices responds to Kynard's argument that "when we have talked about understanding the social contexts of literacy, language, and discourse, ... we have not done so from the perspectives of interrogating deep political and ideological shifts that have left structured inequalities and violence firmly in place, especially in reference to, but not solely based on, race" ("Literacy/Literacies," 64) and Logan's question "[r]hetorical education for what?" ("'To Get an Education,'" 36). It takes on Jacqueline Jones Royster and Jean C. Williams's call for *"a systematic commitment to resist the primacy of 'officialized' narratives"* (582) about literacy education. They are able to uphold these approaches in part because "moneyto support IBIs comes directly from African American communities" (Bush 392). Such a financial model permits these institutions to "refrain from depending on outside financial support to prevent unwanted control and influence" (Bush 392).

Lawson Bush, Edward C. Bush. and Tonia Causey-Bush trace IBIs through a 10,000-year historical evolution through ancient African systematic apprenticeship education. These roots can be detected in modern iterations of IBIs, which include as part of student success "attitudes toward school and the nature of the relationships between school personnel, students, and families" (Lomotey 456). Community relations is a central aspect of IBIs. This community connection is embedded within the Afrocentric institutional philosophies. These philosophies originate from various principles based in African diasporic epistemological perspectives. IBIs privilege Afrocentric narratives of history and culture, which may be one of the reasons that their institutional histories, like those of their HBCU cousins, are absent from mainstream narratives about literacy education in America. These collectives of homeschool, virtual, and community-based education teach through an African-centered worldview, a perspective that conflicts with the perpetuation of Eurocentric ways of being of dominant rhetorical literacy education. Similar to indigenous American tribal community schools (Lee and McCarty), this unique voice of color rejects the notion that students are best rhetorically prepared for society when they learn and adopt Euro-Western rhetorical traditions and literacy practices.

For example, some IBIs are based in the concept of "nommo," the notion that "all magic is word magic, and that the generation and transformation of sounds contribute to a [rhetor's] power" (Asante 60). Some are based in "Ma'at" or "ancient African principles of ethical character development" (Lee 166).2 Others share values with the seven Kwanzaa traditions of Umoja (unity), Kujichagulia (self-determination), Ujima (collective work and responsibility), Ujamaa (cooperative economics), Kuumba (creativity), Nia (purpose), and Imani (faith) (Lee; Lomotey). According to a Facebook post citing Kalonji Jama Changa on the page for the Council of Independent Black Institutions, these institutions are "growing everyday [sic], not as an alternative to public school, but as our own paradigm for academic excellence, cultural awareness, and the quintessential foundation for Black self-sufficiency and sovereignty for African people" (Council of Independent Black Institutions). Their community-based approaches to curriculum, pedagogy, and administration exhibit an emphasis on rhetorical action. By grounding their curricular and pedagogical approaches in Nguzo Saba, or "Seven Principles of Blackness," IBIs deliver literacy education that "develops in students a communal and civic identity" (Enoch 7) relevant to who they are and their social positions by teaching Black American students "to look at the world through an African-centered set of lenses that ... has a wider periphery and more depth" (Lomotey 456). Further, as Kynard suggests, it helps Black American literacies mobilize beyond systemic stifling that never positions these literacies or their participants as equal (*Vernacular* 26).

Taking the definition of rhetorical education for Black American students proposed earlier, these schools aim to develop communicative and behavioral practices based on the students' cultural and community histories. The pedagogy underscores *social action* and *civic practices* relevant to Black people. Among the eight goals for Afrocentric pedagogy within these schools, four center on the progress of community life (Lomotey 465-66). These include a goal for teachers to amplify support for serving students' multiple local, cultural, and world communities as well as to champion the belief that individuals and communities are producers instead of simply consumers of knowledge (Lomotey 466). The other goals for pedagogy build on an Afrocentric consciousness, including consciousness of language performance which "[e]xtend[s] and build[s] upon the indigenous language" (Lomotey 465). Kofi Lomotey does not elaborate on what "the indigenous language" is, but I take it to mean the student's "mother tongue." The intention is for teachers to expose students to both the progress of community life and Afrocentric critical consciousness as early as possible. In doing so, IBI educators help ensure that these values and ways of knowing influence students' overall engagement with education.

In terms of literacy instruction at IBIs, let's consult two examples of IBIs for middle and high school students. The Fawohodie Sua Pan-Afrikan Educational Online Co-op and Maroon Life Learning online course collection provide examples of teaching and learning practices that challenge the majoritarian White voice about the rhetoricity of Black-centric literacy education. Eurocentric epistemological perspectives of literacy education promote the literacy practices of Euro-Western cultures as the race-less, decontextualized norm (Barnett; Kincheloe). However, these two IBIs, along with others, interrupt this majoritarian voice that suppresses or outright denies literacy practices meant to create and sustain sovereignty of African diasporic cultures, including those in the US. Fawohodie's Word Power course offered the 2020 winter quarter teaches students "scholarly analysis and critique of the values, virtues and culture transmitted through Afrikan folktales and lore, and their evolution and propagation in the diaspora" ("Fawohodie Sua"). Instead of speaking against Eurocentric epistemological perspectives, this outcome of literacy instruction sustains Afrocentric literacy practices and literacies. Django Paris and H. Samy Alim explain that sustaining cultural practices in education requires not only honoring them but also critiquing and problematizing their context and use, in the same ways that this approach has become reflexive in our treatment of traditional reading, writing, speech and research practices.

Through its outcomes, this course also inspires students to "explore Afrikan traditional folkways and culture that 'appear' in Afrikan life in America, via the spoken words, lore and literature that was and continues to be a part of black life in America" ("Fawohodie Sua"). This approach to literary analysis reflects some of the concepts of African American rhetorics (Richardson and Jackson), such as "a view of culture, as influenced by African ancestral traditions, as an appropriate factor in analyzing performance" (Royster, "Foreword" x). If one aim of Eurocentric epistemological perspectives is to sustain absent-present, acontextual knowledge-making conventions of White supremacy through institutionalized literacy curriculum (Ladson-Billings; Ladson-Billings and Tate; Collins; Richardson; Barnett; Keating; Leonardo; Villanueva, "Maybe"; Villanueva "On"), this learning objective collides with such an aim. To maintain a majoritarian voice and dominance in culture, instruction based in Eurocentric epistemologies cannot truly "explore, honor, extend ... [or] problematize" (Paris and Alim 3) the lore and literature representing *Afrikan* folkways and culture. Furthering the cultural sustenance goals of IBI literacy education, the Word Power course expects students to "discover the Afrikan retentions in their own family traditions and evaluate their benefits" as well ("Fawohodie Sua"). This aim of the course also opposes the goal of propagating Eurocentric worldview, which detaches knowledge development from social and cultural contexts (Kincheloe).

Even in their application of an Afrocentric worldview, not all IBIs are the same, as not all mainstream education institutions are the same. Take the Maroon Life Learning (MLL) online course collection. Their website states, "The main objective of our programs is to show youth and all people of African descent their own personal potential by introducing them to their history and to the achievements of Africans through the Ages [sic]." The courses are similar to most IBIs in that they strive to "connect the student to [the] awareness that Africans have had a long history, perhaps the longest of any other people on [E]arth" (MaroonLifeLearning). In contrast to Fawohodie aims, MLL's pedagogical methods for literacy include "decipher[ing] the world in which they live and to continue to find ways to not just survive but to thrive spiritually, mentally and materially" and "us[ing] primary sources of information ... to connect to the past through the lives and views of people from the past ... [and] then move from concrete observations and facts to questioning and making inferences about the materials" (MaroonLifeLearning "Pedagogy"). While we teachers in traditional college literacy education can connect with some of the goals identified here, the recognition of the history and to the achievements of Africans through the ages, as well as the link to lives and views of ancestors, exhibits the unique voice of color missing from our literacy education practices.

Faculty in mainstream sites of education who want to sustain all students' racial cultural language practices as a teaching tool can turn to this objective and the previously discussed IBI objectives for inclusive literacy instruction. For example, the commonplace practice of conducting scholarly analysis of texts and textual practices of writers and intellectuals of color still approaches these materials from dominant cultural theoretical perspectives about literacy. Taking direction from the Fawohodie and MLL course objectives, composition teachers would invite students to study these texts under the lens of Afrocentric values, virtues, culture, traditional folkways, and other ways of being or knowing, in conjunction with Eurocentric traditions of literacy, language, and discourse. Studies by several composition and literacy studies scholars examine an array of pedagogical approaches that loosely apply Afrocentric cultural perspectives to composition curriculum (see: Gilyard and Richardson; Kynard "Writing"; Perryman-Clark). Where the White supremacist cultural script of mainstream education literacy curriculum (Ladson-Billings; Richardson) teachers discourses of whiteness as the universal truth, IBIs teach these discourses as one of many ways of being and thinking. Because their contemporary methods are influenced by literacy histories detached from the Eurocentric narratives, IBIs illustrate a true unique voice of color in literacy education.

IBIs continue to steadily prosper today, even with limited financial support. However, they are built on the tradition of Citizenship Schools, Freedom Schools, and Liberation Schools, and they use rhetorical education as a means for community engagement. Each of the schools detailed here operates on the premise that all children deserve to receive a curriculum relevant to their worldview and therefore the lives they face. Rather than inculcating Eurocentric ways of knowing and acting through rhetorical education, these educational models demonstrate how academic knowledge can serve purposes outside the academic setting. This kind of knowledge allowed the students of these schools to take accountability for the advancement of their communities, or it gave them the tools for civic responsibility. To conclude, I reinforce the need for the unique voice of color that IBIs offer to college-level literacy education and histories in America so that we, as composition-literacies teacher-scholars, may shape rhetorical literacy education experiences that consciously sustain raciolinguistically marginalized students' literacy cultural traditions.

THE NEED FOR UNIQUE VOICE OF COLOR COUNTER-NARRATIVES IN RHETORICAL LITERACY EDUCATION INCLUSIVE CURRICULUM DESIGN

The counter-story to Black students' engagement with literacy education in America that I have provided shows a missing link in the ways education histories frame the social-rhetorical purposes of this education, as well as the rhetoricity of its outcomes for a portion of socially subjugated students. While traditional approaches to literacy education have centered on acquisition of literacy practices to serve the dominant culture, my definition of rhetorical literacy education for Black Americans expands on the approach recommended by Logan, "a rhetoric of social change" ("'To Get an Education,'" 39). The counter-story provided by the unique voice of color represented in IBIs postulates that educators must consider, in addition to rhetorical literacy education for what, literacy education in service of whom.

Long before present-day IBIs, educational psychologist Inez B. Prosser studied the effects of non-academic social and psychological factors on Black American schoolchildren. The study compared the experiences of these children at segregated and integrated schools. Prosser concluded that that "the teacher-pupil relationships in the mixed schools are not as satisfactory as those in the segregated schools" (178). Still, even among teachers in segregated schools, Prosser suggests that they "strive to rid pupils of definite personal inferiority feelings unless such feelings are warranted" and recommends "teacher re-education in newer aspects of mental hygiene" (186). Using Prosser's research into "certain attitudes and interests, the emotional stability, and the personality adjustment of two groups of Negro pupils ... in the two types of schools commonly called mixed and segregated" (1), pedagogues of literacy education might better serve their Black student populations by understanding the non-academic variables that influence them inside the classroom. One of these nonacademic factors might be the psychological undertow that Black students feel that they "live and work in a world built up largely by and for someone else" (Prosser 30), because typical Eurocentric-privileged literacy education experiences reinforce this perception.

Since "counterstory [sic] functions as a method for marginalized people to intervene in research methods that would form master narratives based on ignorance and on assumptions about minoritized peoples" (Martinez 33), countering White savior narratives about Black students in literacy education can help reduce systemic ignorance about the purposes of this education, particularly within composition theory. The counter-story of IBIs, supported by Citizenship Schools, Freedom Schools, and Black Panther Liberation Schools, gives authority to marginalized perspectives in the history of literacy education. The rhetorical action promoted by the targeted literacy instruction of the Afrocentric educational approach demonstrates how the ways that we frame our teaching of literacy practices, such as writing, can impact the rhetoricity of those practices in social and civic contexts. Rather than focusing on using rhetorical behaviors for sole engagement with dominant society, this unique voice of color emphasizes how Black Americans applied the literacy education they gained from school to respond to the needs of their subordinated racial community.

For example, *reciprocity* is an African principle expected of IBI teachers and one that they instill in students. This African principle long precedes mainstream, predominantly White universities' community-based work and writing studies community literacy research. It puts forth the idea that the teachers are symbolically connected to the success of the students, and the students are symbolically connected to the success of their communities, and therefore, communities are symbolically connected to the success of both the teachers and students (Lee 165, 168); however, such a postulation is foreign to Eurocentric epistemological perspectives of mainstream college-level education. As Carmen Kynard notes, the tradition of "action/activism-based class alliances" is embedded within the tradition of Afrocentric American education, even at mainstream institutions where students often ally across class and across racially subjugated communities on and off campus (*Vernacular* 58).

This goal of serving Black communities stands in contrast to what many see as the central goal of institutional literacy education for this demographic. That goal has been to assimilate Black American students out of the "black ghetto" (Smitherman 202) by "inculcating the values of the dominant society and eliminating the cultural distinctiveness of Black America" (203). That rhetorical impetus of literacy education for Black Americans is the accepted gentrified narrative. It is happily accepted by mainstream higher education. By presenting these unique voices of color, I hope to join the tradition of literacy in composition studies scholars who have begun to reject these whitewashed assimilationist stories and reclaim historical and contemporary truths about the racialized ideologies of rhetorical literacy education. Privileging this narrative for Black Americans reframes the purposes of institutionalized literacy education in order to better serve the lives of more of our students.

Notes

1. For further details about The Literacy Narratives of Black Columbus Project, please see http://blackcolumbus.osu.edu/theProject/default.

2. Ma'at is a concept described in what most Westerners know as *The Egyptian Book of the Dead* but which title actually translates as *The Book of Coming Forth by Day*.

Works Cited

Asante, Molefi Kete. *The Afrocentric Idea*. Temple UP, 1998.

Barnett, Timothy. "Reading 'Whiteness' in English Studies." *College English*, vol. 63, no. 1, 2000, pp 9-37.

Brereton, John C. *The Origins of Composition Studies in the American College, 1875–1925: A Documentary History*. U of Pittsburgh P, 1995.

Brubacher, John Seiler, and Willis Rudy. *Higher Education in Transition: A History of American Colleges and Universities*. 4th ed., Taylor & Francis, 1997.

Bush V, Lawson. "Access, School Choice, and Independent Black Institutions: A Historical Perspective." *Journal of Black Studies*, vol. 34, no. 3, 2004, pp. 386-401, http://dx.doi.org/10.1177/0021934703258761.

Bush V, Lawson, Edward C. Bush, and Tonia Causey-Bush. "The Collective Unconscious: An Opportunity for New Thoughts on the Existence of Independent Black Institutions and Black Achievement Theories." *The Journal of Pan African Studies*, vol. 1, no. 6, 2006, pp. 48-66, www.jpanafrican.org/docs/vol1no6/TheCollectiveUnconscious_vol1no6.pdf/.

Changa, Kalonji Jama (on Council of Independent Black Institutions). "There's a growing (long overdue) national wave of support." *Facebook*, 18 May 2016, 9:54 p.m.

Cobb, Charles E. Jr. "Organizing Freedom Schools." *Teach Freedom: Education for Liberation in the African-American Tradition*, edited by Charles M. Payne and Carol Sills Strickland. Teachers College P, 2008, pp. 69-74.

Collins, Patricia Hill. *Black Feminist Thought: Knowledge, Consciousness, and the Politics of Empowerment*. Routledge, 1991.

Council of Independent Black Institutions. Home. *Facebook: Council of Independent Black Institutions*

– *CIBI. Facebook*, 18 May 2016, 9:54 p.m.
Delgado, Richard, and Jean Stefancic. *Critical Race Theory: An Introduction*. New York UP, 2006. Delpit, Lisa. *Other People's Children: Cultural Conflict in the Classroom*. The New Press, 1995.
Du Bois, W. E. B. *The Souls of Black Folk*. Bartleby.com, 1999, www.bartleby.com/114/
Emery, Kathy, Sylvia Braselmann, and Linda Gold. *Freedom School Curriculum: Mississippi Freedom Summer, 1964*. 2004. PDF File.
Enoch, Jessica. *Refiguring Rhetorical Education: Women Teaching African American, Native American, and Chicano/a Students, 1865-1911*. Southern Illinois UP, 2008.
"Fawohodie Sua Pan-Afrikan Educational Online Co-op Classes." *Fawohodie Sua*, www.fawohodiesua. com/. Accessed 18 Mar. 2020.
Gilyard, Keith, and Elaine Richardson. "Students' Right to Possibility: Basic Writing and African American Rhetoric." *Insurrections: Approaches to Resistance in Composition Studies*, edited by Andrea Greenbaum. SUNY P, 2001, pp. 37-53.
Glenn, Cheryl, Margaret Lyday, and Wendy B. Sharer, editors. *Rhetorical Education in America*. U of Alabama P, 2004.
Horner, Bruce. "Resisting Academics." *Insurrections: Approaches to Resistance in Composition Studies*, edited by Andrea Greenbaum. SUNY P, 2001, pp. 169-84.
JBHE Research Department. "Key Events in Black Higher Education: JBHE Chronology of Major Landmarks in the Progress of African Americans in Higher Education." *Journal of Blacks in Higher Education*, www.jbhe.com/chronology/. Accessed 28 March 2020.
Kaestle, Carl F. "The History of Literacy and the History of Readers." *Review of Research in Education*, vol. 12, 1985, pp. 11–53. JSTOR, www.jstor.org/stable/1167145.
Karega, Joy. "Beyond Basic Reading and Writing: The People's House and the Political Literacy Education of the Student-Activists of the Black Liberation Front International, 1968-1975." *Literacy in Composition Studies*, vol. 4, no. 1, 2016, pp. 24-49, http://dx.doi. org/10.21623%2F1.4.1.3.
Kates, Susan. *Activist Rhetorics and American Higher Education, 1885-1937*. Southern Illinois UP, 2001.
Keating, AnnLouise. "Interrogating 'Whiteness,' (De)Constructing 'Race.'" *College English*, vol. 57, no. 8, 1995, pp. 901-918.
Kincheloe, Joe L. *Knowledge and Critical Pedagogy: An Introduction*. Springer, 2008.
Kynard, Carmen. "Literacy/Literacies Studies and the Still-Dominant White Center." *Literacy in Composition Studies*, vol. 1, no. 1, 2013, pp. 63-65, http://dx.doi.org/10.21623%2F1.1.1.16.
—. *Vernacular Insurrections: Race, Black Protest, and the New Century in Composition-Literacy Studies*. SUNY P, 2013.
—. "Writing while Black: The Colour Line, Black Discourses and Assessment in the Institutionalization of Writing Instruction." *English Teaching: Practice and Critique*, vol. 7, no. 2, 2008, pp. 4-34.

Ladson-Billings, Gloria. "Just What is Critical Race Theory and What's it Doing in a Nice Field Like Education?" *Qualitative Studies in Education*, vol. 11, no. 1, 1998, pp. 7-30.

Ladson-Billings, Gloria, and William F. Tate IV. "Toward a Critical Race Theory of Education." *Teachers College Record*, vol. 97, no. 1, 1995, pp. 47–68.

Lathan, Rhea Estelle. *Freedom Writing: African Civil Rights Literacy Activism, 1955-1967.* NCTE, 2015.

Lee, Carol D. "Profile of an Independent Black Institution: African-Centered Education at Work." *African Americans and Independent Schools: Status, Attainment, and Issues.* special issue of *The Journal of Negro Education*, vol. 61, no. 2, 1992, pp. 160-77.

Lee, Tiffany S., and Teresa L. McCarty. "Upholding Indigenous Education Sovereignty Through Critical Culturally Sustaining/Revitalizing Pedagogy." *Culturally Sustaining Pedagogies: Teaching and Learning for Justice in a Changing World*, edited by Django Paris and H. Samy Alim. Teachers College P, 2017, pp. 61-82.

Levine, David. "The Birth of Citizenship Schools: Entwining the Struggles for Literacy and Freedom." *Teach Freedom: Education for Liberation in the African-American Tradition*, edited by Charles M. Payne and Carol Sills Strickland. Teachers College P, 2008, pp. 25-41.

Logan, Shirley Wilson. *Liberating Language: Sites of Rhetorical Education in Nineteenth-Century Black America.* Southern Illinois UP, 2008.

—. "'To Get an Education and Teach My People': Rhetoric for Social Change." *Rhetorical Education in America*, edited by Cheryl Glenn, Margaret Lyday, and Wendy B. Sharer. U of Alabama P, 2004, pp. 36-52.

Lomotey, Kofi. "Independent Black Institutions: African-Centered Education Models." *The Journal of Negro Education*, vol. 61, no. 4, 1992, pp. 455-62.

MaroonLifeLearning. "Pedagogy." *Maroon Life Learning*, https://maroonlifelearning.com/pedagogy/. Accessed 5 April 2020.

Martinez, Aja Y. "A Plea for Critical Race Theory Counterstory: Stock Story vs. Counterstory Dialogues Concerning Alejandra's 'Fit' in the Academy." *Composition Studies*, vol. 42, no. 2, 2014, pp. 33-55.

McCluskey, Audrey Thomas. "Educational Leadership: 'The Unfolding Soul' (1902-1942)." Mary McLeod Bethune: Building a Better World, Essays and Selected Documents, edited by Audrey Thomas McCluskey and Elaine M. Smith. Indiana UP, 1999, pp. 67-130.

Miller, Thomas P. *The Evolution of College English: Literacy Studies from the Puritans to the Postmoderns.* U of Pittsburgh P, 2010.

Paris, Django, and H. Samy Alim, editors. *Culturally Sustaining Pedagogies: Teaching and Learning for Justice in a Changing World.* Teachers College P, 2017.

Perlstein, Daniel. "Live the Truth: Politics and Pedagogy in the African American Movement for Freedom and Liberation." *Education as Freedom: African American Educational Thought and Activism*, edited by Noel S. Anderson and Haroon Kharem. Lexington Books, 2009, pp. 137-62.

Perryman-Clark, Staci. "Africanized Patterns of Expression: A Case Study of African American Students' Expository Writing Patterns across Written Contexts." *Pedagogy*, vol. 12, no. 2, 2012, pp. 253-80.

Pough, Gwendolyn D. "Rhetoric That Should Have Moved the People: Rethinking the Black Panther Party." *African American Rhetoric(s): Interdisciplinary Perspectives*, edited by Elaine B. Richardson and Ronald L. Jackson II. Southern Illinois UP, 2004, pp. 59-72.

Prendergast, Catherine. "Race: The Absent Presence in Composition Studies." *College Composition and Communication*, vol. 50, no. 1, 1998, pp. 36-53.

Prosser, Inez Beverly. "Non-Academic Development of Negro Children in Mixed and Segregated Schools." PhD Dissertation. University of Cincinnati, 1933. Ann Arbor: *ProQuest*. Web. 20 June 2020.

Richardson, Elaine B. "Coming from the Heart: African American Students, Literacy Stories, and Rhetorical Education." *African American Rhetoric(s): Interdisciplinary Perspectives*, edited by Elaine Richardson and Ronald L. Jackson II. Southern Illinois UP, 2004, pp. 155-69.

Royster, Jacqueline Jones. "Foreword." *African American Rhetoric(s): Interdisciplinary Perspectives*, edited by Elaine Richardson and Ronald L. Jackson II. Southern Illinois UP, 2004, pp. ix-xi.

—. *Traces of a Stream: Literacy and Social Change Among African American Women*. U of Pittsburgh P, 2000.

Royster, Jacqueline Jones, and Jean C. Williams. "History in the Spaces Left: African American Presence and Narratives of Composition Studies." *College Composition and Communication*, vol. 50, no. 4, 1999, pp. 563-84.

Smitherman, Geneva. *Talkin and Testifyin: The Language of Black America*. Wayne State UP, 1977.

Solórzano, Daniel G., and Tara J. Yosso. "Critical Race Methodology: Counter-Storytelling as an Analytical Framework for Education Research." *Qualitative Inquiry*, vol. 8, no. 1, 2002, pp. 23-44.

Thelin, John R. *A History of American Higher Education*. Kindle ed, John Hopkins UP, 2019.

Villanueva, Victor. "Maybe a Colony: And Still Another Critique of the Comp Community." *Race, Class, Writing*, special issue of *JAC*, vol. 17, no. 2, 1997, pp. 183-90.

—. "On the Rhetoric and Precedents of Racism." *College Composition and Communication*, vol. 50, no. 4, A Usable Past: CCC at 50: Part 2, 1999, pp. 645-61.

Wei, Debbie. "The Black Panther Party Legacy and Lessons for the Future." *Civil Rights Teaching*, 2004, https://static1.squarespace.com/static/5948733cf5e23161d7d8bf60/t/5bc63650104c7bc3ec11b0f7/1539716688798/BPPhandout.pdf. Accessed 24 May 2016.

Woodson, Carter G. *Mis-Education of the Negro*. Associated Publishers, 1933.

Supplemental Material

Independent Black Institutions and Rhetorical Literacy Education: A Unique Voice of Color

Jamila M. Kareem

Part I: Reflection on the Origins of the Article

This article originated as part of my dissertation, which argued for including civic responsibility in the high-school-to-college transition curriculum made to be especially inclusive for Black and Black American students. My goal, I think, was to illustrate the already-in-practice versions of the curricular aspects I was arguing for. I really wanted to show how, as a field focused on the classroom, career, and community, one of the most marginalized, socially disenfranchised groups has a history of doing the kinds of work we are just beginning to theorize in our discipline.

Part II: Description of Research Methods, Findings, and/or Pedagogical Impact

My research methods involved primarily secondary research and archival research of current Independent Black Institutions' pedagogical methods. To apply the unique voice of color methodology, it was important to research a range of applications of the basic principles of IBIs to demonstrate the limitations of the majoritarian voice about Black Americans and the presence of our culturally-grown literacy education practices. I wanted to show readers multiple ways that IBIs have applied their core teaching and learning principles. Presenting these as counter-stories to the conventional mainstream knowledge about Black people's engagement with literacy education situates the approaches within the cultural traditions that they honor. When I teach, I work to decenter Eurocentric or Euro-American perspectives on literacy and writing and try to give students a chance to examine different understandings of what it means to be literate, which I think the article encourages.

Part III: Discussion Questions

1. What is meant by "rhetorical literacy education" in the article, and how does it connect to civic and social action in participants?

2. What approaches to rhetorical education have succeeded in granting Black students access to using higher education for transformative purposes (transforming self or community)?

3. What contributes to the majoritarian White voice about the rhetoricity of Black American literacy education?

4. How could you apply the unique voice of color methodological approach to your writing course design?

5. Why should you consider the cultural implications of literacy education when assessing its purposes, outcomes, or efficacy?

COMMUNITY LITERACY JOURNAL

Community Literacy Journal is on the Web at http://www.communityliteracy.org/

The *Community Literacy Journal* is an interdisciplinary journal that publishes both scholarly work that contributes to theories, methodologies, and research agendas and work by literacy workers, practitioners, and community literacy program staff. We are especially committed to presenting work done in collaboration between academics and community members, organizers, activists, teachers, and artists. We understand "community literacy" as including multiple domains for literacy work extending beyond mainstream educational and work institutions. For us, literacy is defined as the realm where attention is paid not just to content or to knowledge but to the symbolic means by which it is represented and used.

"All I Need Is One Mic": A Black Feminist Community Meditation on the Work, the Job, and the Hustle (& Why So Many of Yall Confuse This Stuff)[1]

In her powerful essay, Carmen Kynard argues that a Black feminist imaginative is essential for dismantling white supremacy in our classrooms. Since Kynard's Conference on Community Writing keynote in October 2019, which addressed Atatiana Jefferson's life and murder, many, many more Black people have been murdered by police, in the streets and in their homes. The antiracism protests happening daily in cities across the country only heighten the urgency of Kynard's question: how, in everything we do, are we addressing white supremacy and the unrelenting violence against Black and Brown lives? Through a series of meditations and counterstories, Kynard navigates her own and imagined classrooms to investigate why she has "been sent" to do the work she does. Her advisor, Suzanne Carothers, urged Kynard, "do not confuse the WORK with the JOB." Ultimately, Kynard finds a violence in universities that we must counter through radical and disruptive antiracist work, which we must do often in spite of job requirements or the professionalization obligations Kynard calls "the hustle."

---

1. *Community Literacy Journal*, vol. 14, no. 2, 2020. © 2020 by *Community Literacy Journal,*.

"All I Need Is One Mic": A Black Feminist Community Meditation on the Work, the Job, and the Hustle (& Why So Many of Yall Confuse This Stuff)

Carmen Kynard

At the heart of this essay[1] is a series of narratives about classrooms and teaching in both undergraduate and graduate spaces. Classrooms represent geographies of Black Feminisms for me because, above all else, a critical/ intersectional/ anti-racist pedagogy in classrooms is the practice of a Black Feminist imaginative. I am not referencing "creativity," multimodalities, or some other tenet of liberal/progressive education, however, when I think about the imaginative. I am also not looking to John Dewey canons, open access policies, writing process theory, or tomes of progressive pedagogy that have abstractly centered benevolent whiteness for schools and classrooms and missed the concretization of Black feminist practices. Instead, the Black feminist imaginative as I see it here means something completely different because only the most radical imaginations can conjure up alternative learning spaces that work towards new visions of a world that could be but has yet to be (Ohito). Teaching for and with the kind of freedom that upends white supremacy simply can't look like most of the paths that appear before us (Alexander).

As I write this, Breonna Taylor's murder is still ignored despite national headlines and protest. Close to home for me here in Texas, there has been no justice for Atatiana Jefferson or the five Black women suing my university for the blatant discrimination and neglect they faced, with very few noting the connections between the police murder of Black women "off-campus" and the spirit murders of Black women "on campus" (Love). This non-seeing is the space in which theories and practices of composition-rhetoric, language, and literacies are currently being shaped on my campus and everywhere else.

Meanwhile, the Coronavirus wreaks havoc on Black and Latinx communities across the United States as I watch and listen to campus conversa-

---

1. I want to especially thank Veronica House, the founder of the Conference on Community Writing, for her friendship and support of this essay.

tions about attendance, absence, and lateness polices in new online, remote learning environments, as if revising the old rules will somehow offer new experiences of humanity in our classrooms. The obligatory land acknowledgement on our syllabi is now followed by online-learning versions of western, white settler rules of managing bodies, time, and deadlines (Patel). We now acknowledge the lands that we newly re-settle as the digital/syllabus practice of COVID-related online learning (Benjamin). I am not suggesting that land acknowledgements are negative. However, as Leonardo argues, we can do deep intellectual work in anti-intellectual times and still realize that more than concepts are at stake. A land acknowledgement has to commit to decolonization as action, not just metaphor and line on the common syllabus (Tuck and Yang).

Black folx and Black language run social media/digital communication right now; yet I have seen and heard nothing of a digital classroom approach that matches the current, public Black digital pedagogies that we are all living in. I am sure that this is what Marvin Gaye had in mind when he sang: *make me wanna holla way they do my life*. Only the imaginative can think up new possibilities for classrooms and communities right now. To that end, I am opting for a Black feminist narrative-meditation towards such imaginative work.

Movements towards a Narrative-Meditative Essay

This essay circles multiple narrative-meditations in relation to the various communities in which I work that link specifically with Black feminist ways of knowing and doing. As a series of meditations rather than a presentation of research-driven answers and findings, I want to ask explicit questions for renewed focus and presence. My inspiration for narrative-meditative writing comes from Alexis Pauline Gumbs's "*17th Floor*: A Pedagogical Oracle from/with Audre Lorde," where Gumbs offers what she calls a poetic oracle as she uses and is used by Audre Lorde to travel us back to Lorde's 1974 poem, "Blackstudies." In this "freeform dream villanelle," Lorde meditates on her teaching+life as a Black lesbian feminist in English departments at the City University of New York during the radical protests of Black and Puerto Rican youth of New York City. Lorde's poem takes us to the seventeenth floor of her CUNY building that she repurposes with new dreamscapes. Gumbs, in turn, takes us back to this 17th Floor as a "poetic oracle" that can guide us in the ongoing work of "Blackstudies" and, therefore, the Black freedom dreams as imagined/ lived by Brown and Black youth. In her poetic oracle, Gumbs offers us a new methodology--or rather a counter-methodology—as its own praxis where Black and Brown youth demands for new university spaces are historically rooted and thereby ancestrally sanctioned processes.

Gumbs's focus on Lorde is especially important. As Tina Campt reminds us, these connections between fugitive imaginations, refusal of the status quo, and Black radical thought have always had their roots in Black feminist study. The imaginative, as I see it here, is thus a practice of refusal where, as Campt urges us, we reject the current status quo as something that is livable for us and work instead towards the deep possibilities and generative creativity that are always open to us even "in the face of negation" (Campt 25). Yanira Rodríguez, in chronicling her own teaching, further shows us what a pedagogy of refusal for composition and literacy teachers might mean and do and what its imaginative capacities hold for us. The imaginative refuses as it generates (Hartman, Sharpe).

Gumbs moves us away from white, traditionalist research paradigms that are far too commonplace where a list of pedagogical and/or research resolutions are offered as grand finale. Instead, Gumbs creates new openings and cyclical loops rather than false endings. In that spirit, I am also rejecting final resolutions and instead attempt to offer imaginations, questions, mantras, and meditations where the ongoing work of teaching for Black freedom is an infinite yet life-affirming loop. To quote Ruha Benjamin: "the facts, alone, will not save us... we are drowning in the facts of inequality and injustice" (2). We have done the studies showing the sophistication of the languages and epistemologies that Brown and Black youth bring to their classrooms and communities (Paris and Alim) and so many now have developed curricula and events that raise awareness about injustice. We have, at least in some corners but not nearly enough, invested in research paradigms and publications about young Brown and Black people. Yet all this research has not halted schools and societies from still pursuing oppression, including linguistic oppression (Lewis). Like April Baker-Bell insists we come to terms with: no acquiescence to white (communicative) norms has halted Black deaths. As Benjamin argues, we have maintained "an underdeveloped investment in social transformation" that refuses to imagine we can alter schools and corrupt the idea that even universal access to college is enough. Ruth Wilson Gilmore has continually reminded us that the prison industrial complex, alongside the destruction of the global environment and greater white wealth hoarded by the 1%, have happened alongside the largest numbers of college-educated people in U.S. history.

White universalist calls for a progressive education are simply not good enough (i.e., civic education, global good, etc.). Abstract, distant, formal social science research reports just won't do right now either. What we need now is counterstory like the work Aja Martinez does in her book, *Counterstory: The Rhetoric and Writing of Critical Race Theory*. Counterstory, as Martinez theorizes+practices it, shows us the everyday materiality of race as a process of "race-making" (Knowles). Race-making helps us understand that anti-black racism is reproduced actively and daily in how people move, look at, and interact with one another. Race thus has its own "grammars" that are taught, learned, and shared by people in real time and space (Carbado). I have in mind here the white, activist undergraduate students in my African American rhetoric class in spring of 2020 who argued that their traditionally-framed college courses on race taught them how to argue with statistics, a stance that ultimately did not alter people's views or even their own spirit. In contrast, African American rhetoric taught them to talk and think and live alternatively. Educational counterstories can thus reveal, in real talk, the everyday ways that whiteness and racism are remade and reaffirmed *in* schools and *via* schooling and the radical counternarratives that make other worlds.

Figure 1. Cover for Syllabus Zine of My Undergraduate Course: "Word is Bond: Introduction to African American Rhetoric" (go to funkdafied.org for syllabus and more)

Story and narrative are always choices and theoretical interventions (Brayboy). In my case here, it is a choice to reject the white rationality that organizes writing styles, essay formulas/subsections for social science research reports, and obtuse/anti-praxis humanities critique (Boggs, Meyerhoff, Mitchell, and Schwartz-Weinstein). I intend to disturb and unsettle the authority of white research's discursive and, thereby, ontological approach. Instead, I turn to a Black feminist imaginative narrative.

Narrative-Meditation on the Teaching of First Year Writing

I want to start this narrative-meditation in what I see as the place of origins for the college classroom: First Year Composition. Perhaps, an opening to the re-imagination of that space is a think-back on the actual first day of class in the very first year in college. With the words of soul-singer-sista-extraordinaire, Betty Wright (R.I.P.), I will add some emphasis for this backtrack:

> I want you to do this for me if you will, EV'RYBODY! Think back—to your—veeeery— first— time. (Pause) Now I'll give you a little while longer, cuz I know some of you have to think back a little bit furrrrther than others. Come on now, I want you to play catch up, cuz I don't want you waiting until I get to the end of my [meditation] saying: oh yeah, now I remember.... Now whether it was good (aside: oh you just smiling, it was good) or on other hand, if it was not so good, *here's my story* [emphasis, mine].

Mine was not good at all. I see a lecture on the novel that we were assigned that week. I no longer remember the novel, just that it was something white and dull. I see a discussion guided by the questions of a white professor. More whiteness and dullness. I remember being assigned an essay on the novel which was really just a vacuous, bourgeois written performance of literary theory that I had no use for. I remember the sensations and tasks and the name of one person in the class who didn't talk in that schoolish-literary-speak. I never knew why they called it a composition class. Such a course is still normative for many college students in first year writing, though not as prevalent as when I was an undergraduate student. I knew that I would never teach this way.

On the first day of my own classes, I ask students to do something that is still pretty rare in many college classrooms: I ask them talk to each other. I write out 2-3 questions, ask students to write their responses, and then I move them into pairs to partner with someone in the room who they do not know. When they get in pairs, they must add their own question to the mix and interview their partner. After the paired discussions, we go around the circle and each person introduces their partner and I do this whether I have 27 students in the room or 40. I follow that with an opening icebreaker for the next few days of class that requires students to know each person's correctly-pronounced name and pronoun in class. I have done this for many years now and somehow it is still a novel expectation for students to actually know the names of their classmates. Ask them to also know the pronunciations and pronouns and you have a revolution up in there.

In the spring semester of 2019, despite the fact that I had done this activity for many years, as in decades, I really messed up one of the prompts. I was proud that I had asked students to write this first assignment with some fire, especially their opening lines. I even asked them to give it some Sam Cooke style like those classic, first two lines that have come to signify African American freedom struggles in just 20 words: *"I was born by the river in a little tent and just like the river, I've been running ever since..."* I knew that these predominantly Black and/or Latinx college students and their families had been to hell and back to get to college. I wanted their writing to bring the same kind of fire that they bring to their lives each and every day.

Figure 2. Cover for Syllabus Zine of My First Year Writing Course: "Digital Justice/Digital Rhetorics" (go to digirhetorics.org for syllabus and more)

Maybe I was exhausted or something, I'm not sure, but once I read one of my prompts aloud to the students, I tracked all the way back on it. Here was the prompt:

What, if anything, are you leaving behind in 2018 and why?

As soon as I read-said it aloud, I was hella annoyed with myself and sighed. The question leaves too much room for those typical study-skills-sessions that are entirely problematic for the students who I was teaching at the time: working Brown and Black students in part-time or full-time jobs, mostly in the service industrial complex, who are parents and caretakers and paying the most for college today, both psychically and financially (Lang and Hamer). I have little tolerance for the never-ending programs, workshops, and offices with paid employees who spend their time talking to these students about things like time-management and planning. The single mothers and families in my classes who are barely making it are not struggling because they do not know how to use a calendar, day planner, or time-management app. This is the logic of fast capitalism that suggests they are not running their bodies into the ground efficiently enough mixed in with the residue of racist educational/behavioral sciences that mark these students' lack of time as an individualized phenomenon of their own choosing. And it is also simultaneously the logic of racialized capitalism (Melamed) that is now killing them in larger numbers than the rest of the U.S. population due to COVID-19 (Oppel Jr. et al). I abhor these kinds of approaches to capitalist time-ownership and here I was, standing in front of young Black and Brown people asking these dumb questions that could very much be construed within the terms of neoliberalist body management (Ferguson). So I said as much to the students.

I couldn't come up with a revised question on the spot so I just asked students NOT to give ridiculous answers like with those typical time-management questions written by people who have never had to juggle all of the limitations and barriers that they have confronted. My suggestion to students is to let them know that, when in doubt, keep it real, and attack the question if you need to. There was silence... and then one, lone voice: "Aiiiight, bet"! They started laughing and then they got to writing. After the writing, students went into their pairs.

It didn't take long for the pairs to start moving chairs from the designated pairs and into four-somes and six-hoods. I somewhat eavesdrop in these moments, but I'm mostly gauging the noise level in the room. Without fail, if this activity is loud, that space is about to be a turnt-up group of students who may say or do anything in the course of the semester. If it's quiet, these are some dull folk who will require a whole lot of support in unthinking their ideas of school, bourgeois decorum, individualism, and white affect (#goals that they may never fully achieve). Based on the noise level, my guess was that this class was gonna be lit all semester long, with even a bit of foolishness coming into the mix.

I was right.

Ten minutes into the paired discussions and it was on. For pair after pair, in a go-around in the room, there was ONE recurring answer to the dumb question that I asked about what students were leaving behind in 2018. What was the one, common answer? KANYE WEST. By the time we made it around the entire room of 28 students, I was laughing so hard I was in tears. They had not seen the syllabus, did not know one another, had never seen me in their lives and they were just going in. Kanye ain't have a chance up in there. No one in that room would be surprised by what we are seeing today and no one in that room was conflating Ye's current misogynoir (Bailey and Trudy) with his mental health issues (Howard). While Ye might have the latter, that does not cause the former.

> In this first narrative-meditation, I remind myself, as a life-mantra if you will, to know, feel, and focus on the ways that Black language, life, and literacies flow from alternative histories of making meaning in the world that exceed what we think we are doing in "best practices." Even seemingly microscopic moments, like in my story where I intuitively knew to discard a neoliberalist utterance and give it over to Black and Brown youth, deep histories and legacies are in place. Even in those first thirty moments of class on the very first day of first year composition in the very first year of college, multiple pedagogical and literate histories are possible. Black and Brown people are NOT what Alex Weheliye calls "merely the ethnographic localities" at the side of the field of study or theoretical practice— we are the whole history. How does that history show up in the daily work that we do? When do we allow for its presence? How and why do we obstruct it?

HISTORYING THE BLACK FEMINIST IMAGINATIVE

I jumpstarted this narrative by traveling back to First Year Composition. But I want to travel way back more to perhaps a fictional context. I am talking about the moment when teaching first year writing wasn't seen as punishment for teachers or as the dead-end for the prestige-and-visibility-seeking researchers of our field. I imagine a time when first year writing laid the groundwork for composition-rhetoric as the space where Black and Brown college students composed Brown and Black lives with Black Feminist teachers that tripped and left open the closed white circuits of knowledge in the western university. Audre Lorde (Atkin and Brown), June Jordan (Reed and Shalev), and Toni Cade

Bambara (Lavan and Reed) probably came closest to this at the City University of New York, but what if this was how we wrote and narrated our roots writ large in this field?

I write and talk about critical moments in Black communities and classrooms to remind myself of who I am, where I come from, why I been sent, and the work I am here to do. I'm not talking here about some kind of warm, feel-good notion of student-centered, progressive pedagogy, collaborative learning, or student-led discussions. That's all certainly part of what is happening in my classrooms, but all of that still misses the whole point. I am interested in the moments like the one I described with my first-day prompt when the white, neoliberalist, racial-affect-sanitized ethos of the western academy and its epistemological violence were disrupted. That's the point of the work. That's the only work that is worthwhile in the academy; everything else—including the disbelief of the university as violent—is just the set of white maintenance labors of a system designed to exclude. ... *and Lawd only knows there are plenty of folk in rhet-comp about that life.*

Part of the work here also, especially when we are in communities, is to accurately locate the radicalization of the young people who, as just one example, overturned my problematic and potentially violent first-day writing prompt into a political, cultural, contemporary conversation that could be of some actual intellectual value. On the best day, I am a conduit for the higher calling of community knowledges, ancestral life-forces, and radical protest histories. Those are the days that I am a compositionist and a community literacy organizer. *I love this work, but I hate this field.* A Black feminist imaginative always allows me to distinguish the two and work the in-betweens (Cohen, Bey).

Now Loop All the Way Back to Black

The classroom narrative that I have offered here represents a lens to see the history of Black youth, especially college student activism. We still give too little credit to the major transformations of college learning that Black students, especially Black students at HBCUs, have designed and that's all the more reason we gotta understand this history and feel it with every fiber of our being. If young Black people get lit in our classrooms and community programs, IT AIN'T US and the wonders of our work. It's the histories that they belong to; to not deeply center these histories belongs to a kind of white paternalism where we diminish the power of Black and Brown youth activism and protest histories by allowing a white-hero-narrative that always positions Brown and Black people in need of a pied-piper.

We have to come to terms with that fact that the western academy never intended for college learning to look like, sound like, or be like the students who

I have described here in my opening narrative. Like Sylvia Wynter has always insisted of her generation, I too, as Black faculty, am here because Black youth demanded it (Kynard). No other space or place in the history of higher education has so continuously insisted that Black teachers have a unique perspective and should be paid equally. It was never even a given when HBCUs were first created in the 1800s that Black people would teach there. That was a battle that had to be fought and is still being fought on PWI colleges across the country. It has continually been Black students who have made the argument and shut down buildings until they got heard. This is the legacy that Black college students carried forward from the dawn of emancipation; this was LITERALLY THE DREAM of our enslaved ancestors and we've carried it past centuries now (Kynard, Rogers, Williamson). Young Black people got us here, not 4Cs (and other such professional organizations), not our individual mentors, not our book publishers.

The rather everyday conversation among my students about leaving Kanye behind is also part of the legacy of Black student knowledge systems. The class talked at length about the intersections between white supremacy, popular culture, current iterations of racism, all with an unrelenting disgust of Black accommodation of white racial violence as called up in the figure of Kanye West. The western academy and all of higher education was NOT designed to talk about, theorize, or support this kind of thinking. This very idea that college students and college spaces could and should address contemporary social problems, especially around race, begins with young Black people. It might seem rather commonplace to young Black people, especially at HBCUs, to have these kinds of conversations, to read these kinds of things, and to do assignments on these kinds of things, but that's only because they invented the very concept.

This very idea that contemporary culture is worthy of inclusion in college discussions is also rooted in the experiences of Black college students and made further possible by Black feminist icons like bell hooks. That Kanye West is a proxy for discussions about music, popular culture, and white supremacy might seem obvious now. But once again, this is because Black students designed the concept of talking about their here and now as relevant and critical to intellectual inquiry. Think tanks around race and racism begin with the HBCUs and the Black faculty who Black students demanded be there to teach them. When you see universities with research institutes today that look at issues of Blackness and race, know that the very concept came from them. It was UNTHINKABLE in the academy before they got here.

The simultaneous identity of student and activist—the very idea of the student-activist—is also an invention. The very idea that you go to college AND protest and speak up against the racial injustices that you see all around you and in your classrooms begins at the HBCUs and with Black students. The western academy was not designed around the notion that a racially subjugated college student would see their activism against their condition as part of their very identity and time on campus. Not only was it inconceivable, it was also always unwanted and, in many ways, still is.

I remain stunned by the graduate faculty who argue that graduate students should not be criticizing the racism of their graduate programs because that's not what students are there to do. It's like they aren't even speaking the same language as Black students. Black students have been calling out the racism of their administrators, curriculum, and campus life since at least the 1890s, given their multiple letters and demands that are archived at Tuskegee. When Black graduate students feel like they are speaking a different language to their faculty, as has been the case in all of the graduate programs where I have worked, the truth of the matter is that it is a distinct language and identity that might take folks another one hundred years to catch up to.

In many ways, graduate education sits at the epitome of the university's whiteness as its property (Harris). Of course, I am referencing Harris's still crucial work in critical race theory alongside the reminder that slave labor quite literally built and maintained college campuses on stolen lands with a white research faculty at the helm who were simultaneously "researching" and "arguing" for the "evidence" of their own white superiority (Wilder, Anderson and Span, Tallbear). The barriers that universities thus manifest are not fictional or subtle, especially as they are now often major purveyors of the gentrification of Black and Brown neighborhoods in poor, urban city centers across the country. Settler colonialism is quite literally the context of college campuses (la paperson, Patel). Ahmed has taught us to see these longstanding colonial rituals and histories of the university as an affective whiteness where white power has accumulated to such a degree that the embeddedness of whiteness seems to permeate the very air that we breathe there.

Graduate education is a pinnacle of colonial expression as this is the space that really mines the next generation of researchers and knowledge makers, a fact that no graduate program in the field of composition-rhetoric has ruptured. It should come as no surprise that so much of the enterprise rests on grooming graduate students as the parrots and proprietary goods of their advisors. More bodies of color, even if a larger number make it out of the program, are not enough to unsettle graduate education and the affective whiteness of our universities' colonial legacies (Leonardo and Zembylas).

Brown and Black graduate students who refuse the academy's affective whiteness in content, form, language, style, and intellectual purposes are especially rendered as illegible and unintelligible. It's blatant too. In my own experience at a recent, required graduate faculty meeting, one professor rather forthrightly asserted that her longstanding experience with the graduate students in that setting was evidence of the fact that the students who were "complaining" the most were simply people who did not do their work. Their very intelligence and literacy were called publicly into question. Critical race theorists of education like David Gillborn have noted that such seemingly banal talk solidifies, remakes, and re-affirms whiteness as a routine process. Though no students' names were used, the program is small enough that we all knew who was being referenced. It didn't stop there though. As another example, a professor described a graduate student with significant medical bills and named the hitherto-anonymous white professor in the room who paid $1,000.00 (anonymously) from their own pocket towards this student's bills. Though I was the latest member of the faculty, even I knew which student was spotlighted, a queer disabled student, further cementing the process where the faculty and deans publicly mark all "complaining" graduate students as Ungrateful Extraordinaire for all that the white, liberal faculty has done for them. In the least, such open, public, and hostile conversation about a disabled, queer graduate student struggling to pay medical bills constitutes all kinds of legally-actionable stuff. Since the formerly-anonymously-bankrolling professor was neither shocked nor upset that her identity was publicly revealed in this way, it was clear to me that this public exchange was pre-meditated, as much of the discourse, down to the turn-taking, in white academic departments is pre-arranged. No one in the room said a word to counter these offensively racist and ableist descriptions of graduate students. The total negation of the most marginalized and race-conscious graduate students in the program came naturally. The most that white empathy ever offered in that space for these graduate students who supposedly do not know that they have to do their homework was a call to give students more years and courses so that they can "catch up." We moved seamlessly from the grist of an outright lawsuit to an outright argument for cultural deficit. We would do well to remember that cultural deprivation theory was an educational invention hurled at Black children that coincided with school integration (Valencia). It has since been upgraded to cultural deficit theory, but both are systems of logic with its very roots in the plantation economy (McKittrick) and white superiority research of the founders of the very universities who profited from slave labor. The Brown/ Black/ Queer/ Disabled graduate students who survive the "emotional geography" of this "forcefield of whiteness" (Zembylas) while also rejecting the logic of white settler colonialism should be at the center of how we imagine the future of our field. What would unsettling graduate education mean for our work in composition and community literacies studies? What are the consequences if we don't?

Public Pedagogies, Black Feminisms, and the Life of Atatiana Jefferson

In the semester that I began writing this piece, I was teaching a graduate course in Fort Worth, Texas, called #BlackGirlMagic: @The Intersections of Literacies, Public Pedagogies, and Black Feminisms. In the days before, we had started this subtheme on Black Girls' Literacies (Muhammad and Haddix). Then, Atatiana Jefferson was murdered in her home, about ten minutes away from our college, by a Fort Worth police officer who shot through the window of her home imagining her to be an intruder while her 8-year old nephew watched her die. In fact, I was attending the Conference on Community Writing[2] while the public wake and funeral for Atatiana were taking place. The meditations of this part of my texts were inspired by Atatiana's life and represent part of my class's teach-in strategy and are applicable beyond that:

> What in the institution's existing curriculum (the one you are required to teach or the one you are required to take as a student) contextualizes the life and murder of Atatiana Jefferson? Be specific—name the texts and teaching methods. List it all here. If there is very little connection, diagnose AS EXPLICITLY as you can this deliberate erasure. *Read it for filth.* List it all here.

While these questions were very specific to my fall 2019 course, they apply to all of us in our work. What have we all assigned to others or to ourselves that illuminates both the social death and murder of Black women like Atatiana and also the complexity and beauty of their lives? What have we peer-reviewed recently that illuminates both the social death and murder of Black women like Atatiana and also the complexity and beauty of their lives? What have we seen published recently in the journals that we read/ in the journals that are most coveted in our fields that illuminate both the social death and murder of Black women like Atatiana and also the complexity and beauty of their lives? What you have heard at the professional meetings that illuminates both the social death and murder of Black women like Atatiana and also the complexity of their lives? There are other specific examples of things we can ask ourselves: How do our understandings of community literacies, for instance, contextualize Atatiana's care-taking roles where Black women like her are caring for elderly parents at a rate that exceeds every other group in this country? How does that show up in our methodologies, in our curriculum, in our instruction? How does the public nature of Atatiana's execution shape the counter-publics that we build now—with and in our communities? While the questions that I have here, the meditations, are ongoing, I

---

2. For the slides for this presentation, go to: http://bit.ly/kynard-ccw

want to place the ONTOLOGICAL ABSENCE—both real and symbolic—of Atatiana in our theoretical work as representative of the material site of violence which justified, in her white murderer's eyes, her murder. #BlackSpring2020 and its formidable protests against ongoing, anti-Black racism should be central to how we shape new #BlackFallCurriculum2020.

Figure 3. Cover for Syllabus Zine of My Graduate Course: "#BlackGirlMagic: @The Intersections of Literacies, Public Pedagogies, and Black Feminisms" (go to blackfeministpedagogies.com for syllabus and more)

Such intellectual queries around curriculum, instruction, schooling, and theory have deep roots in radical Black intellectual traditions, from Carter G. Woodson's reminder in *The Miseducation of the Negro* that the ideological justificatory system for lynching had its roots in the classroom to Sylvia Wynter's reminder in "No Humans Involved" that the policies and theories that academics develop hold within them the explanatory models that justified the police beatings of Rodney King and the subsequent acquittal in 1992. When I asked my graduate students to READ FOR FILTH every ontological absence of Black women in their curriculum, I meant that quite literally and I meant something bigger than the neoliberalist strategy of including a Black woman author on a document. Ontological absence is not altered by inclusion.

There are more questions that further guided my graduate classroom but apply beyond just those walls: What does it mean to be a graduate student— right here and right now (not just the dissertation or the articles you will publish later)? We could all ask ourselves the same questions here: What does it mean to be a community scholar/teacher/activist right here and right now? What do our research and scholarship—RIGHT NOW—challenge and remake? What do our institutional practices—RIGHT NOW—challenge and remake? Whether we are in high schools, colleges, or the non-profit industrial complex, we work in institutions. What institutional practices are we interrupting? And perhaps, this is the harder, more inward question: What institutional practices and actors are we sustaining? And at whose detriment?

The Work, the Job, and the Hustle

My advisor from graduate school, Suzanne Carothers, always stressed knowing the difference between the work and the job and also knowing and feeling when the job is interfering with the work. As a mentor, she offered a vision for an alternative to making white liberal concessions as the price of the ticket. I add to these two distinctions between the work and the job one other component: the hustle. Here I am referencing the ability to understand and navigate the arbitrary neoliberalist structures of the job market, publishing, tenure, and the grind of academia in a way that pushes beyond our race/class-neutralized language of "professionalism" and "professionalization." This newest vocabulary is merely a screen for white assimilation and really obscures the racial biopolitics of the processes we are witnessing in higher education.

I was lucky to have Suzanne Carothers as mentor because she imagined our lives in ways much richer than what the research literature on mentoring suggests. Mentoring of young Black faculty (and graduate students) who work at colleges across the country usually hinges on teaching young Black professors the rules of college life as it pertains to tenure and promotion. You can find all kinds of empirical research on the best strategies for mentoring young Black faculty so that they secure that golden fleece of tenure in the end. This research is also really clear about the importance of Black mentors for these early career professionals. But there's always been something missing from these discussions for me. It's not just about teaching young Black faculty the rules of the academy. It's about centering Black thought and Black life in people's lives *at the academy.*

When I have become obsessed with yet another dysfunctional episode at the colleges where I have worked, the words of Suzanne Carothers always ring in my head: *do not confuse the WORK with the JOB.* Those words have kept me sane and grounded and those words have helped me move onwards and higher when the limited horizons of other folk have attempted to confine me. I locate this mantra—and its many offshoots—squarely within Black culture and Black language.

The reality is that many professors base their entire scholarly and professional identity within the college where they work—but that's the job, not the work. The conflation of the job and the work, however, is only possible for those groups sanctioned within the terms of a default white norm and privilege. *It is easy to see the job as your work when the people and the culture around you are YOU.* The fact of the matter is that Black folk cannot readily find themselves in most university spaces (outside of the HBCUs) and non-profit funding cultures so they have to understand rather quickly where the institution ends, where their own lives and minds begin, and not expect a centering unless by way of tokenism. This is an important praxis for leading intellectual and activist lives at institutions today because neoliberalism does not love anyone, not even its white citizenry. Some people have been learning that lesson in deep ways and things will only get thicker post-COVID: tenure and promotion denials after years of dedicated service, entire departments and fields obliterated because of a corporate "bottom-line" and takeover (sometimes called austerity), decimation of tenure track lines in favor of multiple, exploited lecturer lines. The list goes on. Black faculty, especially those with Black content, know the university doesn't want us, hasn't ever humanized us, and only allowed us entry because of Black student protest. While I am definitely borrowing from the work of critical university studies and neo-marxist managerial critiques in composition-rhetoric studies, even that work is still too white (Boggs, et al) and cannot imagine a Black feminist epistemology at the American university as a center force of social gravity.

In addition to knowing the difference between the work and the job, there is also the hustle. Here I am referencing what many refer to as "professionalization." I do not use this language because it functions as a white-masking discourse. So, alternatively, by the hustle, I mean the arbitrary rules and processes you chase down to get your paper/ to make that money/ to get tenure and promotion, rules like: journal article rankings, university press rankings, CV lines, job market trends, hiring committees, salary negotiations, job applications, interviews, and other submissions of all kinds. The list goes on. Winning at these games is part of the hustle, but it ain't the work, but some of us can get so caught up in the visibility and fleeting status of what all that means that we lose sight of the work. And because we call all of this "professionalism" or "professionalization," especially for early career folk, rather than a hustle, it is easy to neutralize these neoliberalist regimes and forget that this hustle has nothing to do with helping communities of color. By calling it a hustle, yes as in, "Everyday I'm hustlin," yes, like what me and my peers in the '80s and '90s called the underground economy of crack dealing, I distance myself from any false imagination that our "professionalism" is somehow more ethical or is somehow making a positive difference somewhere. It's not. I say this especially to graduate students and community organizers whose precarity can be exploited in such a way as to make you think that all you need to do is gather networks or CV lines without ever having something to say and without ever moving towards the work that you have been called to do. The work is not in the job and it is not in the hustle. The mentoring offered by Black culture and Black language can teach us and remind us of these differences.

Though rapper Rick Ross and his greatest fan, comedian Katt Williams, re-popularized the words "the hustle" in 2006, they were certainly not the originators. Hip Hop re-coined and re-circulated "the hustle" many decades before. Well before that, my parents would tell you that the word and its use belong to their generation. The generation before them would make the same argument. It could go on and on. My point is that Black culture has centered this expression with everyone non-Black, as usual, merely appropriating it. The critique of white cultural appropriation of Black language applies here (Baker-Bell) and the violence of such theft leaves the political origins of "the hustle" muted. Black culture and Black language are doing more than offering popular terminologies here; Black culture and Black language are defining experiences through the specific terrain of Black life that could not be achieved otherwise. Black bodies have their own humanizing language in a system that has extracted labor for centuries without recognition or pause. Everybody else is just borrowing a language that could never come from or represent them. My use here of the hustle to articulate the labor of Black bodies in the academy is therefore quite intentional as it signals the university as just another common site for the routine, exploited labor and violence against Black bodies struggling to just live.

The coercion towards unnamed and uncompensated labor in the academy, especially for Black women, is insidious. In fact, I would argue that far too many of us perform the vocabularies of maroonage, flight, fugitivity, and refusal today like it is a script straight from the *Undercommons* handbook (Moten and Harney). Performing these definitions in white university spaces, white academic language, and white academic publications is not the same, however, as living a Black fugitive life. Ongoing concessions to white liberalism belie any full achievement of a Black undercommons by far too many of its proponents right now: the ad nauseum search for white colleagues/allies in professional organizations and on our campuses who will offer so-called "support" while ignoring the harms and offenses that they have caused to Black peoples; accepting multiple committee assignments where the connection to real-time, real-life transformation for large numbers of Brown and Black students and communities is obscure and long far-away at best; teaching all of the entry-level diversity classes that become the punching bag for white animosity that then cement simplistic political processes; working at the snail's pace of white progress and comfort again on every collective that comes your way; dedicating one's energy to teaching/moving white students and faculty towards anti-racism rather than the always more radical work of centering Blackness (Pritchard). It's pretty simple actually: fugitivity is about running *away* from the university's stamp on your time, mind, and political directions and self-determinations; if you find yourself going *to* the university all of the time to do its work instead of physically and ideologically *away* from it, then you are moving in the *wrong direction*. As Campt argues, Black feminist study embraces Black fugitivity in ways that are more complex and grounded than grand, institutional masculinist and binaristic notions of power vs. resistance for Black peoples. Black feminist life lodges fugitivity in the "microlabors of Black struggle" and the "everyday struggles" that grand narratives often dismiss as ineffectual or take for granted (Bey). It is within these microlabors, however, that Black feminism positions its stare-down with Black precarity without compromise.

"All I Need Is One Mic": Resting Mediations and Meditations

I close with my own sort of appropriation. I'm traveling back to 2002, back to Nas's haunting lyrics in "One Mic." For me, Nas's lyrics here deconstruct every aspect of the consumerism that he faced as an artist in Hip Hop's most lucrative appropriation phase, although he never fully achieved what I might consider a heightened awareness, especially as it relates to Black women. I am appropriating Nas's words here as a Black feminist to achieve the effect, affect, and political possibility that the lyrics bring forth in the world.

> All you ever need is one mic.
> Not white approval.
> Not disciplinary accolades.
> Not celebrity visibility.
> Not departmental support.

Not academic fame and status.
Just one mic.
One beat.
One stage.
Your "own voice ... to the whole world."

We are not without precedents, without ancestors, or without a history that shapes alternative ways of knowing and doing, even when they try to erase our presence, even when they gun us down.

I close with these final meditations: What are our healing and regenerative practices when the job tries to undermine our work? What do we do/say/chant/read/write to remind ourselves that our jobs are not the work? How do we self-check on our own consciousness when we get so deep into the hustle that we forget who we are and what we came here for? What do we need to do within ourselves/within our spirits/within our minds for that one mic to center real and dynamic transformation?

Works Cited

Ahmed, Sara. "The Phenomenon of Whiteness." *Feminist Theory*, vol. 8, no. 2, 2007, pp. 149-168.

Alexander, M. Jacqui. *Pedagogies of Crossing: Meditations on Feminism, Sexual Politics, Memory, and the Sacred*. Duke University Press, 2005.

Anderson, James, and Christopher Span. "History of Education in the News: The Legacy of Slavery, Racism, and Contemporary Black Activism on Campus." *History of Education Quarterly*, vol. 56, no. 4, 2016, pp. 646-656.

Atkin, Miriam, and Iemanjá Brown, eds. *Audre Lorde: "I teach myself in outline," Notes, Journals, Syllabi, & an Excerpt from Deotha*. Center for the Humanities, the Graduate Center, The City University of New York, 2017.

Bailey, Moya and Trudy. "On Misogynoir: Citation, Erasure, and Plagiarism." *Feminist Media Studies*, 2018, pp. 1-7.

Baker-Bell, April. *Linguistic Justice: Black Language, Literacy, Identity, and Pedagogy*. Routledge: 2020.

Baker-Bell, April. "Dismantling Anti-Black Linguistic Racism in English Language Arts Classrooms: Toward an Anti-Racist Black Language Pedagogy." *Theory Into Practice*, vol. 59 no. 1, 2020, pp. 8-21.

Benjamin, Ruha. "Racial Fictions, Biological Facts: Expanding the Sociological Imagination through Speculative Methods." *Catalyst: Feminism, Theory, Technoscience*, vol. 2, no. 1, 2016, pp. 1-28.

Bey, Marquis. *Them Goon Rules: Fugitive Essays radical Black Feminism*. University of Arizona Press, 2019.

Boggs, Abigail, Eli Meyerhoff, Nick Mitchell, and Zach Schwartz-Weinstein. Abolitionist University Studies: An Invitation. https://abolition.university/invitation/

Brayboy, Bryan. "Toward a Tribal Critical Race Theory in Education." *Urban Review*, vol. 37, no. 5, 2005, pp. 425-446.

Campt, Tina. "The Visual Frequency of Black Life." *Social Text 140*, vol. 37, no. 3, 2019, pp. 25-46.

Carbado, Devon. "Afterword: (E)racing Education." *Equity and Excellence in Education*, vol. 35, no. 2, 2002, pp. 181-194.

Cohen, Cathy and Sarah Jackson. "Ask a Feminist: A Conversation with Cathy Cohen on Black Lives Matter, Feminism, and Contemporary Activism." *Signs*. http://signsjournal.org/ask-a-feminist-cohen-jackson/ Accessed October 2019.

Ferguson, Roderick. *The Reorder of Things: The University and Its Pedagogies of Minority Difference*. University of Minnesota Press, 2012.

Gillborn, David. *Racism and Education: Coincidence or Conspiracy?* Abingdon, UK: Routledge, 2008.

Gilmore, Ruth Wilson. *Golden Gulag: Prisons, Surplus, Crisis, and Opposition in Globalizing California*. University of California Press, 2006.

Gumbs, Alexis Pauline. "17th Floor: A Pedagogical Oracle from/with Audre Lorde." *Journal of Lesbian Studies*, vol. 21, no. 4, 2017, pp. 375-390.

Harney, Stefano, and Fred Moten. *The Undercommons: Fugitive Planning and Black Study*. Minor Compositions, 2013.

Harris, Cheryl. "Whiteness as Property." *Harvard Law Review*, vol. 106, no. 8, 1993, pp. 1707-1791.

Hartman, Saidiya. "The Belly of the World: A Note on Black Women's Labors." *Souls: A Critical Journal of Black Politics, Culture, and Society*, vol. 18, no. 1, 2016, pp. 166-176.

Howard, Kirsten. "We Let Kanye Get Away with Being Kanye For Too Long." *Black Youth Project*. http://blackyouthproject.com/we-let-kanye-get-away-with-being-kanye-for-too-long/ Accessed October 1, 2019.

Knowles, Caroline. *Race and Social Analysis*. London: Sage, 2003.

Kynard, Carmen. *Vernacular Insurrections: Race, Black Protest, and the New Century in Composition-Literacy Studies*. SUNY Press, 2013.

Kynard, Carmen. "Black as Gravitas: Reflections of a Black Composition Studies." *Spark: A 4C4Equality Journal*. https://sparkactivism.com/volume-2-call/vol-2-intro/black-as-gravitas/

Lang, Jennifer and Clarence Hamer. "Race, Structural Violence, and the Neoliberal University: The Challenges of Inhabitation." *Critical Sociology*, vol. 41, no. 6, 2015, pp. 897–912.

la paperson. *A Third University Is Possible*. University of Minnesota Press, 2017.

Lavan, Makeba, and Conor Tomás Reed. *Toni Cade Bambara: "Realizing the Dream of a Black University," & Other Writings*. Center for the Humanities, the Graduate Center, The City University of New York, 2017.

Leonardo, Zeus, and Michalinos Zembylas. "Whiteness as a Technology of Affect: Implications for Educational Praxis." *Equity and Excellence in Education*, vol. 46, no. 1, 2013, pp. 150-165.

Leonardo, Zeus. *Race Frameworks: A Multidimensional Theory of Racism and Education*. Teachers College Press, 2014.

Leonardo, Zeus. *Race, Whiteness, and Education.* Routledge, 2009.

Lewis, Mark. "A Critique of the Principle of Error Correction as a Theory of Social Change. *Language in Society*, vol. 47, 2018, pp. 325–384.

Love, Bettina. "Anti-Black State Violence, Classroom Edition: The Spirit Murdering of Black Children." *Journal of Curriculum and Pedagogy*, vol. 13, no. 1, 2016, pp. 22-25.

Love, Bettina. "'I See Trayvon Martin: What Teachers Can Learn from the Tragic Death of a Young Black Male." *The Urban Review*, vol. 45, no. 3, 2013, pp. 1–15.

Martinez, Aja. *Counterstory: The Rhetoric and Writing of Critical Race Theory.* National Council of Teachers of English, 2020.

McKittrick, Katherine. "Plantatuon Futures." *Small Axe*, vol. 17, Number 3, 2013, pp. 1-15.

Melamed, Jodi. "Racial Capitalism." *Critical Ethnic Studies*, vol. 1, no. 1, Spring 2015, pp. 76-85.

Muhammad, Gholnescar and Marcelle Haddix. "Centering Black Girls' Literacies: A Review of Literature on the Multiple Ways of Knowing of Black Girls." *English Education*, vol. 48, no. 4, 2016, pp. 299-336.

Nas. "One Mic." Ill Will Columbia, 2002.

Ohito, Esther. "Some of Us Die: a Black Feminist Researcher's Survival Method for Creatively Refusing Death and Decay in the Neoliberal Academy." *International Journal of Qualitative Studies in Education*, vol. 33, no. 8, 2020.

Oppel, Richard, Robert Gebeloff, K.K. Rebecca Lai, Will Wright, and Mitch Smith. "The Fullest Look Yet at the Racial Inequity of Coronavirus." *The New York Times*, July 5, 2020.

Paris, Django, and H. Samy Alim. "What Are We Seeking to Sustain Through Culturally Sustaining Pedagogy? A Loving Critique Forward." *Harvard Educational Review*, vol. 84, no. 1, 2014, pp. 85-100.

Patel, Leigh. *Decolonizing Educational Research: From Ownership to Answerability.* Routledge, 2015.

Pritchard, Eric. "'When You Know Better, Do Better': Honoring Intellectual and Emotional Labor Through Diligent Accountability Practices." http://carmenkynard.org/featured-scholar-eric-darnell-pritchard-when-you-know-better-do-better-honoring-intellectual-and-emotional-labor-through-diligent-accountability-practices/

Reed, Conor Tomás, and Talia Shalev. *June Jordan "Life Studies": 1966-1976.* Center for the Humanities, the Graduate Center, The City University of New York, 2017.

Rodríguez, Yanira. "Pedagogies of Refusal: What It Means to (Un)teach a Student Like Me." *Radical Teacher*, vol. 115, 2019, pp. 5-12.

Rogers, Ibram. *The Black Campus Movement: Black Students and the Racial Reconstitution of Higher Education, 1965-1972.* Palgrave Macmillan, 2012.

Sharpe, Christina. *In the Wake: On Blackness and Being.* Duke University Press, 2016.

Tallbear, Kim. *Native American DNA: Tribal Belonging and the False Promise of Genetic Science.* University of Minnesota Press, 2013.

Tuck, Eve, and K. Wayne Yang. "Decolonization is Not a Metaphor." *Decolonization: Indigeneity, Education & Society*, vol. 1, no. 1, 2012, pp. 1-40.

Valencia, Richard, ed. *The Evolution of Deficit Thinking: Educational Thought and Practice*. Falmer Press, 1997.

Weheliye, Alex. *Habeas Viscus: Racializing Assemblages, Biopolitics, Black Feminist Theories of the Human*. Duke University Press, 2014.

Wilder, Craig. *Ebony and Ivory: Race, Slavery, and the Troubled History of America's Universities*. Bloomsbury Publishing, 2014.

Williamson, Joy Ann. *Black Power on Campus: The University of Illinois, 1965-75*. University of Illinois Press, 2003.

Williamson, Joy Ann. *Radicalizing the Ebony Tower: Black Colleges and the Black Freedom Struggles in Mississippi*. Teachers College Press, 2008.

Woodson, Carter G. *The Education of the Negro Prior to 1861*. Associated Publishers, 1919.

Wynter, Sylvia. *'Do Not Call Us Negros:' How Multicultural Textbooks Perpetuate Racism*. Aspire Books, 1990.

Wynter, Sylvia. "'No Humans Involved': An Open Letter to My Colleagues." *Forum N.H.I.: Knowledge for the 21st Century*, vol. 1, no. 1, 1994, pp. 42-72.

Wright, Bette. "Tonight is the Night." T. K. Disco, 1979.

Zembylas, Michalinos. "Investigating the Emotional Geographies of Exclusion at a Multicultural School." *Emotion, Space and Society*, vol. 4, no. 3, 2011, pp. 151-159.

Carmen Kynard is the Lillian Radford Chair in Rhetoric and Composition and Professor of English at Texas Christian University. She interrogates race, Black feminisms, AfroDigital/African American cultures and languages, and the politics of schooling with an emphasis on composition and literacies studies. Carmen has published in *Harvard Educational Review, Changing English, College Composition and Communication, College English, Computers and Composition, Reading Research Quarterly, Literacy and Composition Studies* and more. Her award-winning book, *Vernacular Insurrections: Race, Black Protest, and the New Century in Composition-Literacy Studies*, makes Black Freedom a 21st century literacy movement. Her current projects focus on young Black women in college, Black Feminist/Afrofuturist digital vernaculars, and AfroDigital Humanities learning. Carmen traces her research and teaching at her website, "Education, Liberation, and Black Radical Traditions" (http://carmenkynard.org) which has garnered over 1.8 million hits since its 2012 inception..

THE JOURNAL OF MULTIMODAL RHETORICS

The *Journal of Multimodal Rhetorics* is on the web at http://journalofmultimodalrhetorics.com/

The *Journal of Multimodal Rhetorics*, or JOMR, is a completely online, open-access journal featuring essays and other items that examine multimodality in all of its cultural, material, temporal, and pedagogical manifestations. While we do welcome work that focuses on the digital, we stress that multimodality does not automatically refer to digital tools or the use of specific (new) media. We are especially interested in perspectives that complicate typical views of multimodality and that highlight those traditional multimodal practices and praxes that sustain our cultures and everyday lives. We welcome compositions that draw attention to the political dimensions of under/privileged modes and the ways that media perpetuate or contest dominant attitudes and hegemonic norms.

Dressed but Not Tryin' to Impress[1]

Brittany Hull, Cecilia D. Shelton, and Temptaous Mckoy critique racialized norms as they emerge in professional dress codes. Using the cultural rhetorics methodology of story, they describe their experiences with this issue in the academy to make visible this implicit form of discrimination and challenge the norms that make women of color (especially Black women) feel unwelcome. It was published in a special issue on Dress Practices as Embodied Multimodal Rhetorics, guest edited by Katie Manthey.

---

1. *The Journal of Multimodal Rhetorics*, vol. 3, no. 1, 2019. © 2019 by Brittany Hull, Cecilia D. Shelton, and Temptaous Mckoy.

Dressed but Not Tryin' to Impress: Black Women Deconstructing "Professional" Dress

Brittany Hull, Cecilia D. Shelton, and Temptaous Mckoy

A brief note re: language in this piece—As part of our work as Black women compositionists and scholars, we opt to utilize non-standard English in our writing as a way to reaffirm our various identities, and as a way to speak back against white supremacist standards of language in academia. We pull a page from a legacy of Black women scholars who refuse to capitulate their language for standardized language praxis. With this in mind, dis us and we cussin, reflectin, and telling it how it is—the way we see fit.

Early career scholars spend a significant portion of their doctoral study and junior careers thinking critically and deeply about how to synthesize the various aspects of academic work. Managing research, teaching, and service is difficult. These concerns are amplified for persons from historically marginalized communities, whose identities, epistemologies, and even their very bodies are called into question. Because minority bodies are always, already under scrutiny and subject to explanation and qualification, they are often conditioned to be aware of and responsive to the presumed standards of professionalism just to survive. bell hooks (1989) declares, "While assimilation is seen as an approach that ensures the successful entry of [B]lack people into the mainstream, at its very core it is dehumanizing" (p. 67). Black women embody dual identities and the pressure to conform to spaces where they were not welcome historically must be negotiated almost every day. Consequently, studies show that the varying identities Black women embody while navigating academia, can cause attention to dress to be a problematic focus resulting in sexualization and dismissal by students and colleagues alike (Moses,1997, p.29). Although contemporary, progressive thinking rejects respectability politics and encourages the embrace of difference, the tension between marginalization and inclusion still permeates the daily lives of scholars on the margins.

As three scholars entering new phases of our careers, we see dress practices as a critically symbolic metaphor for the challenges of thriving as Black women in academia. The difficulty of negotiating "Black", "scholar", "woman", and "professional" alongside a myriad of other labels manifests in how we choose, or cannot choose, to compose our bodies for public interpretation through dress practices. Choices about not only clothes, but also hairstyles, demeanor, language, and tone allude very clearly to the "texture, shape, color, consistency, movement, and function" of the body, that comprise embodiment as defined by Johnson et al. We argue that Black female bodies make themselves meaningful in response to a variety of audiences, contexts, and purposes. This article takes up an autoethnographic methodology to reflect on the ever-present task of asserting the meaningful perspectives, contributions, and critiques of black bodies. Our readers will gain insight into the way Blackness can manifest through 'professional' attire; but we will also challenge readers to rethink definitions of *professional attire* vis-a-vis Black bodies and reconsider the implications and assumptions that their pre-conceived notions have on our transfer of knowledge/instruction, both formal and informal.

The central thread in our discussion draws on the notion that the academy is a space fraught with the push and pull of teaching and learning, expert and novice, informed and ignorant. We explore this tension in three critical spaces with important audiences for academics—the classroom, where students are watching, academic and professional conferences where colleagues are watching, and the public where everybody is watching. Each section is framed by a critical reflection of an experience with dress and embodiment in that space, highlighting larger themes, insights, and critiques of the academy.

WHAT I'M GON' WEAR TODAY?—BRITTANY HULL

Prior to startin' my doctoral program, I considered it vital that I presented myself as *professional* in my workplaces. This meant wearing a pantsuit, suit separates, and some sort of relatively comfortable flats (Image 1). The unpredictable weather in my area (eastern Pennsylvania) also meant that I was sometimes lugging a bag with a change of clothes or shoes in addition to my work bag and taking the stairs up just three flights put a strain on me. I followed this routine for four semesters because I was once told by a tenured white woman faculty member that I "needed to wear a suit" to all my classes because I "looked like a student." I understood where this suggestion came from because I was fresh outta my masters' program, and I was strugglin' with feelin' like I didn't "fit" due to my language, my identity as a Black woman, and because white faulty kept implying I didn't deserve to be there; I agreed because I didn't know *how* to disagree (yet). As a result, I wore pant suits and suit separates daily in the classroom. However, after realizing that my suits and blouses ain't prevent microaggressions from students and colleagues, I opted to dress as I was comfortable. And that meant not wearing a pant suit and blouse every damn day.

Image 1. Me in St. Louis after presenting at my first CCCC. It was about 80 degrees and I was stuck in this suit and long sleeve NY & Company shirt because I thought it was "professional". I was burnin up though.

When I got ready to go into another semester, I was a combination of nervous and excited at the same damn time, but I was ready to do what I loved; teach first-year composition. I was ready as far as logistics were concerned. Syllabi approved and printed. Check. Desire2Learn course page set up. Check. Textbook selection sent to the bookstore on time. Check. Pre-semester lunch with cohort members to kick off the semester. Check. I was prepared even, to not allow these emotions to prevent me from goin to bed on time so I could make it to campus to get a good parking spot. The only thought that consumed my mind the night before this first day back in the classroom was: *What I'm gon' wear?*

My hair was already done, as I had just recently gotten a wash and re-twist of my long locs a few days prior. The issue was the clothes. Whatever I chose to wear had to be a combination of comfy *and* cute, period. I searched my closet and found some cropped pants with a light blue diamond shaped pattern that I got from Targeè.[1] Boom, I had bottoms; now, I needed a top. I was back on the hunt; after movin various tops around, I found a white cotton scoop-neck t-shirt. Finally, I grabbed some black flats and a khaki suit jacket I got from H&M way before the bullshit where the popular retail store

---

1. Target (the big retail chain). According to urbandictionary.com this pronunciation is "Fancy way of saying Target." I ain't sure when this trend started, but this pronunciation ain't limited to the Black community. I've seen individuals from a variety of racial backgrounds who are familiar with it.

posted a picture of a Black lil boy[2] wearin a hoodie with the phrase "Coolest Monkey in the Jungle" on they website.[3] Nonetheless, after deciding on each item, I strategically placed the pants, white cotton scoop-neck shirt, khaki suit jacket, and black flats on my bed like I was solvin a puzzle. I liked what I saw and it definitely fit the comfy *and* cute vibe I was goin for. I was ready for my first day back in the classroom; now I could take my ass to sleep.

The next morning, I was greeted by smiling faces and echoes of "Good morning" from colleagues when I got to "my" office space. I responded with my signature "Hey Y'all" and soaked up the positive vibes; everyone was excited to be back. As I moved through the office, I ran into a colleague, one of the other folks of color in my department. When I asked him if he was ready for the first day, he said, "Yes, but I feel under-dressed." I was confused; he looked comfortable, so what was the problem? He explained, "Everyone looks so professional." I looked around the room and saw my peers dressed in business casual or *professional* attire—below the knee-length dresses, blazers, blouses, jeans, button-up dress shirts, cardigans, dress shoes, traditional, cultural, and religious attire.[4] At the same time, I saw jeans, sandals, sneakers, vintage t-shirts, stuff that wouldn't be considered *professional* for the college classroom.

I turned back to my friend and said with a smile, "If I ain't throw this together and it wasn't comfortable, I wouldn't be wearin it. If you comfortable, you good." This topic of *professional* dress would come up again and again during my time in this department. Today, I was confused, but eventually, I would get pissed off.

On the first day of class, I always tell my students to read over the syllabus and jot down any questions they have as we get started. As the students read, I always see some confused facial expressions and some smirks, as if what they was readin was a joke. I know why they're confused. See, I write my syl-

---

2. Liam Mango is the child in the now viral H&M pic. A native of Sweden and the son of Kenyan parents, his mama, Terry, wasn't bothered by the pic; however, she felt the backlash for H&M's "mistake" (Wang, 2019). Check Connie Wang's "The Real Story Behind H&M's Racist Monkey Sweatshirt" for a more extensive run down.

3. While many Black consumers of H&M was pissed, there was just as many who wasn't surprised, as discussed in this joint by by Danielle A. Scruggs', "H&M's 'Coolest Monkey' Hoodie and How Racism Wastes Our Precious Time", in which we are provided one of several responses from the Black prospective. Now, given the racist history of Black people being compared to monkeys and apes, consumers called for a boycott, to which they responded by removing the pic and allegedly hiring a diversity manager (Brennan & Feldman, 2018).

4. A number of my female colleagues practiced Islam; thus, they wore hijabs.

labus introduction in my own speech, my mother tongue, and students (and some of my colleagues, for that matter) ain't used to seein that in the classroom. Students see my "what's up y'all?!" and my talkin through my class in my own words, and while I see a lot of smiles, some of these ain't kind.

On this particular day, as I watched their reactions, I knew someone would ask the obvious question: Why did you write the syllabus like this? As I facilitated our icebreaker, I'm walkin around and I feel my feet start to ache in pain. This was my second time wearin these flats and at this point, I couldn't wait to take them off and switch into my sneakers. As we concluded the activity, my thoughts on my aching feet was interrupted by the inevitable question. One of my new students, a Black man with short locs, raised his hand and asked, "Why you write that part of the syllabus like that? You was usin slang and stuff, can *we* do that?" I was happy that someone opened the conversation about this part of the syllabus, and explained that this was the only part where I could be *me*, (everything else was required to be copy and pasted to follow the standards of the department) and that I felt it necessary to be myself and introduce myself on the page just as I had in class. Furthermore, I told him that there *would* be assignments where they would be able to write usin the language or variety they were comfortable with, depending on their intended audience and the rhetorical situation, and that we would learn all about it this semester. This response acted as an unofficial introduction to our lesson on the rhetorical situation. All in all, class was a success and I was free to go back to my desk and change outta these flats, my feet was hurtin somethin terrible; I knew this would be my last time wearin these damn shoes.

A few weeks later, we was working on literacy narratives, and except for a few who was strugglin, everyone was doing fine. On my way outta the class one day, a student stayed behind and asked me if she could discuss her literacy narrative topic, and I invited her up to my office to talk. As we waited for the elevator, I noticed my "underdressed" colleague from the first day, and I almost didn't recognize him—he had donned a full suit, tie, and dress shoes. He looked dressed to impress, and I thought maybe he had an interview later that day. After I finished with my student, I figured I'd ask 'bout his outfit and wish him positive vibes for a successful interview. Much to my surprise and frustration, he did *not* have an interview, but he'd been told by a white faculty member that he ain't look *professional* enough without it. He was promised that students would "take him more seriously" if he wore a suit and tie in his classroom. *Now* I was pissed.

My experience with my colleague pissed me off, both for me and for him. Why was we tied up in all this uncomfortable shit if it ain't *really* help us? I decided that day that I would start wearing more comfortable clothes in my classroom, and I maintained my casual attire and ain't wear the pant suit, suit separates, or them uncomfortable ass black flats anymore. I began to wear my favorite tees with images or quotes from Black women historical figures, such as Rosa Parks and Assata Shakur; tees that shared my love for Marvel comics or my favorite sports teams. I wore jeans, cardigans, hoodies, and sneakers. Additionally, I kept my hair pulled back in a ponytail unless I got it styled in an up-do.

Even though my attire was supposed to take away from my teaching, it often made my students feel more open to genuine and authentic conversations with me. I had many conversations with students of all colors and creeds, who could connect with Marvel and my favorite sports teams. Yet, most importantly, I believe my approach made students of color feel welcome and safe in my classroom. I constantly remember the brother with the locs askin if he could write like I talked in my syllabus and in class. My clothes opened up impromptu conversations with Black students who was in the beginning stages of they loc process. They'd asked about products I used in my locs, as well as who re-twisted them in the predominantly white area of the campus. I even held, a conversation on the history of AAL after a student asked about the names on a tee I rocked to class. The shirt was worn during my participation in the Digital Black Lit/Literacies and Composition (DBLAC) panel at the 2018 Conference on College Composition and Communication (CCCC) presentation. Me and my co-presenters (Khirsten L. Scott, Sherita Roundtree, and Louis Maraj) wore custom shirts with the names of Black language and literacy scholars from various generations in the field of composition, whose work has impacted our own as Black early career scholars. Specifically, my shirt featured Lorenzo Turner, Geneva Smitherman, Richard Barksdale, and Jaqueline Jones Royster to name a few.[5] Learning more about my students was a direct result of my shift from professional clothes to those clothes that represented me, and I was comfortable as fuck.

As a Black woman scholar and teacher of English, I know I stand out when I walk into spaces that wasn't developed with *me* in mind. When I walk into spaces where white men and women have traditionally been in the role of teacher or professor, I disrupt the status quo. My very *being* is resistance to, not only a field, but a society that privileges whiteness. These various criticisms are a way to articulate a problem that students bring into the classroom

---

5. As earlier mentioned, alongside with my panelist, we wore our own shirts to shout out our fam. Roundtree and Scott wore tees including the names of Beverly Moss, Elaine Richardson, Gwendolyn Pough, Carmen Kynard, Keith Gilyard, Adam Banks and Eric Darnell Pritchard among others. Lastly, Maraj's shirt brought it all togetha wit "DBLAC WE GOT NEXT…" which symbolized the space for budding Black scholars of language and literacy to contribute to the field of composition.

with them - that I am not "white enough" to teach this class. A suit don't shield me from racism or sexism, but it also don't elevate the knowledge I had before I put the damn thing on. My credentials *are* my suit; they suit me to this position. What I wear don't change what I know, as shown in Image 2. This is a conscious choice not to accommodate the sexist and racist feelings of students and faculty who are *looking for reasons to think I'm under/unqualified*, and I am perfectly comfortable filling that role.

Image 2. A pic in my custom tee. The shirt reads "Cook, Smitherman, Royster, Logan, Barksdale, Turner...Our past and living elders of generation 1.0."

I Am My Brand—Temptaous McKoy

The email said, "Congratulations, you've been accepted to present at xyz conference!" or something like that. I was in the first year of my doctoral studies and I didn't really know what "presenting at a conference" was, but my mentor told me I should respond to the call for papers. This was one of the biggest conferences in my field and it would def work in my favor if I got accepted. I got accepted. I was provided the opportunity to give a poster talk. Very low stakes, but also very good for a newbie like myself. It would provide the opportunity for me to chat with some of the big names in my field and get to introduce some of those same people to my love for HBCUs. Showcasing my love for HBCUs was one of the various ways I planned to establish my brand within the field.

What some call their reputation, I prefer to call my brand. I say this because I am a firm believer that we are all walking talking billboards in some form or fashion. And for some, our bodies can become prime real estate to showcase and exemplify other branding initiatives, goals, and outcomes. For example, if a Predominately White Institution wishes to diversify their student body, and I am a part of the current student body, I am a part of that department's branding initiatives as a program for diverse scholars. In addition, I've situated my own personal brand as a Black student, doing Black work, at a white school. Not too far-fetched or different from other Black graduate students. What I believed separated myself? At the time, I was a Black graduate student focusing on an area that was severely under researched, overlooked, and devalued—the Technical and Professional Communication (TPC) knowledge made present at HBCUs. So again, my brand became very important to me early on. Fast forward from the time I got accepted until it was time to head out, I remember looking at my suitcase and thinking, "What should I wear?" And this my friends, is where it all begins.

As previously stated, the conference I was preparing to attend was one of the biggest in my field. Now in case you ain't know, TPC is still a pretty white male dominated field. Not to mention the field brings on some founding principles of what TPC really is. In other words, it can be chopped to professional writing—for some. Professional is typically coded for whiteness and on white folks' terms. This goes from the writing in Standard English all the way to wearing clothing that is a representative of a professional within various fields, hell even in the National Basketball Association (McDonald & Togila, 2010). Suits, blouses, stockings, cute lil heel…all dat are some of the various pieces of clothing that are attributed to professional attire. And like most Black people, I have been socialized fairly early to understand what professional looks like on Black bodies; pressed hair or smooth fade and two steps over regular professional. Business casual?? What's that. Either we business or we casual, we ain't mixin em too much (But when we do, we slay). As in a matter of fact, my Historically Black College/University (HBCU) Elizabeth City State University was adamant to teach us how to "dress for success" or professional. Yet, I would have never guessed such molding would one day lead to my present-day resistance to professional dress.

Back to the conference. So, I sat down and looked in my closet trying to figure out what was I about to wear to this conference. I decided to go with a tan/khaki colored suit that I purchased from Lane Bryant. I then paired it with a black and white speckled shirt, and a slight pump (Image 3). I knew this was the outfit that was it. Now this is a two-day conference, however, I was only able to be there for one of the two days. So that meant I had to look good and mean it. I traveled to the conference certain that my suit would be a hit. It would show that I was serious. It would show I meant business. It would show that a sister was trying to simply match the standards of what she has been taught professional meant.

Image 3. So this is the actual outfit at the actual conference I'm talking 'bout.

light bet, I head on to the conference. I walk into the hotel with confidence. I pull up on the registration table and I then realized I may be a lil' overdressed. However, THIS (my attire) is what I have been taught professional looks like, so I look the part—it's just that everyone else don't know the rules. I get compliments on my attire and I'm so excited to present my poster. As I prepared for all of the great people to come in the room, I began to feel like I just wasn't myself in my suit. Don't get me wrong, I looked damn good and that suit was fitting me just right. Yet, given the circumstance I simply felt overdressed, so I took off my blazer. And then, people make their way in. "Game on Temptaous," I start to think. As everyone begins to come around and I so anxiously wait to answer their questions, I still didn't feel like myself. People came to my poster. I described my work with confidence. I smiled and was so very pleasant. Then I realized something, I was not being myself. I was putting on a front. I wanted to appear like I was supposed to be in that space, and I knew it was my job to do that through my speech and my dress. So, I untuck my shirt. I drop my hair. I get comfortable. I loosen my speech. I begin to talk to everyone like we were family. All while this embodied shift is occurring, I am still articulating my work to all those that came by and were interested in my research. I went back to my room and had an epiphany; my clothes influenced my performance. While I tried to put on that front, I was straight up exhausted. I had to switch to bein' my unapologetic self, in order to preserve my energy for the duration of the poster hour. And it wasn't until I got back to my room, took off that damn suit and realized the power it had at that conference.

From that day forward, I decided I was going to wear what made me comfortable. What made me comfortable? Tee-shirts and sneakers made me comfortable. Yet, I still had a thought in the back of my head that reminded me it was not going to fly because I didn't want to disrupt my brand as a member of my field that belonged. I didn't want to appear as if I had not received any formal training. So, I decided to meet somewhere in the middle. Tee-shirt up top, slacks down bottom. Not only would this look show me as a professional, it would also show who I was an individual and a member of my field. I mean don't get me wrong, I love a bad suit and dress like the next gal, I just know I can be flexible in my choice of dress.[6] But even one step further, I placed a message on all of my tee-shirt so allude to what I was presenting on and so people could easily identify who I was on the program, without having to formally introduce myself. As much as I love networking, I am simply not a fan of going through the "What is your name?" motions. That's another article for another day. Any who, I found a way to establish my brand through my tee-shirts. The shirts started out as just regular tees I found online, and then I went to making custom shirts. And as time went on, I started to notice the pattern happening at other conferences by other participants.

I will not dare say I spearheaded the movement to wear tee-shirts to conferences. What I would say however is that I assisted in having other conference members rethink how our attire could be used in rhetorical ways at conferences, instead as simply our uniforms. Conferences are perfect spaces to showcase your brand. These spaces can help you get a job, publications, network for your life, and learn from fellow scholars. The attire we choose to wear in the conference/ professional space is just as important. Our attire can serve as an outward declaration of resistance and a reflection of who you are as an individual—as I exemplify in Image 4. Even though I do not see an official dress code for the attire worn at conferences in my field, there certainly is a space where I see an assumed dress code, in addition to what that is privileged to certain bodies. As a Black woman, I don't have the option to

---

6. If Imma pull up in the sneakers, ain't nobody gonna check me…trust I wore them to my job talks too.

look like who done it and why. I represent a community that is far greater than myself. Black people must always be extra aware of their Black body in professional white spaces, including conferences. These are spaces that can make or break our careers and the last thing we need is to be denied an opportunity because we were underdressed. But we can take on what it means to be underdressed. And turn it on its head for all conference members to see, understand, and learn from. Learn to not only pick and choose your battles when it comes to dress, but be sure to actually fight your battles, and fight them strategically and unapologetically.

Image 4. Me pictured at CCCC 2018 with my awards and rocking my "Y'all Feel Safe?" shirt in response to the conference and its location choice (see NAACP Travel Advisory Warnings in 2018 and CCCC 2018 Conference location).

I Am My Hair—Cecilia Shelton

People have lots of reactions to discovering that I teach college writing for a living. Surprise is the predominant one.

"Oh, wow, really...where do you teach?" I mention a local college or university.

"Wow. That's impressive. Gee, I'd better watch my grammar around you. Don't judge me."

Cue nervous laughter on both parts. This kind of exchange is somewhat universal. People expect "English teachers" to be strict grammarians out to rid the world of pronouns without antecedents and dangling modifiers.

What people do not expect, though they cannot say so, is for an "English teacher" to look like me. I don't know this because people tell me so directly. But more than 10 years of experience with reactions to my profession has revealed a number of patterns—surprise and exaggerated compliments are common themes; another one is some kind of comment or reaction to my hair.

When I reflect on my time as an instructor of college writing and how my embodiment has most often intersected with my choice to work in the academy, my hair stands out as a point of contention. I am a Black woman and have worn my hair in its natural, kinky state for the duration of the time I've been teaching. While the styles themselves have varied, they have always reflected the texture of my hair and aligned with the hair care choices that are safest and most convenient for my lifestyle. Three casual but memorable interactions illustrate the various ways for which my hair was a point of departure for people to indicate that my body was not the typical English teacher body.

There is a long-standing inside joke in the Black natural hair community—we wear our hair straightened to the interview and then when we get hired, we show up with the afro! Black women have been conditioned to do as much as possible to meet white beauty standards in professional environments; however, the natural hair renaissance of the last twenty years has encouraged a new generation of Black women to choose not to chemically straighten their hair. Many Black women now enjoy the flexibility of naturally curly or kinky hair which can be worn in any number of styles (Image 5).

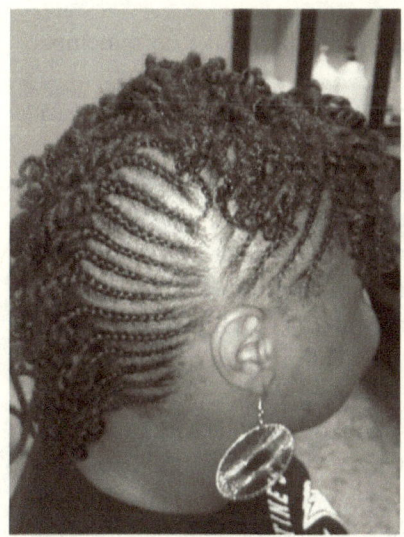

Image 5. Profile of C. Shelton with a braided and twisted natural hairstyle.

I planned to get my hair styled in preparation for my interview for my first full-time academic job just after completing my master's degree. As is common in Black hair salons, my stylist was interested in more than my hair. When she learned that the purpose for my visit was to prepare for an interview, we followed the script outlined above. She was shocked but proud of my accomplishment. After learning that I'd be working as a college writing instructor, she quickly deduced, "Oh, so we must be straightening your hair then" and she quickly set about the task of identifying which heat protectants and flat irons she planned to use. I stopped her.

"I'm not so sure'" I said. "It's an HBCU, so…" my voice trailed off.

She knew what a Historically Black College or University was. But she was not convinced that I could escape the inside joke about Black women and straight hair for interviews. Because we both knew it wasn't really a joke. Black women do get judged more harshly for the presentation of our bodies in professional spaces. Everything about that presentation needed to be strategic, including my hair. But how did the cultural context of a historically Black institution impact my decision? The deciding factor in the conversation was what specifically I was being hired to do—teach students to write by leading the University Writing Center and teaching writing courses. People, even Black people, have been socialized to associate standard English with whiteness—not because Black people don't have a rich language tradition associated with our culture; and not because white people all speak without the influence of dialect and slang—because English teachers are associated with policing language correctness and that policing is a function of whiteness.

As my hair stylist quipped, "They ain't askin you to teach Black history, baby!"

Honestly, I don't remember which hairstyle I chose. But I do remember the conversation and

my persistent efforts to convince my stylist that I'd studied language variation and dialect

during my master's degree and that the way we speak has rules like every other language and that it was perfectly beautiful and valid and I wanted to share that with my would be students. But my stylist, positioning herself as an auntie figure, there to guide and protect me, would not yield. She strongly suggested a straightened style at least for the interview. This experience solidified the ways that professionalism not only colors the academy, but also shapes disciplinary standards in raced and gendered ways.

I got that job at the HBCU and I wore my hair in a wide variety of natural styles over the course of the 7 years I worked there. In all that time, my presence as a Black woman was affirming for many Black students. But the fact remained that my body, for them, was a symbol of whiteness because the subject I taught had been a tool of white oppression for their entire educational careers, dampening and discounting their own linguistic resources. Even with my affirmation of their right to their own language (SRTOL), and my code-meshing pedagogical stance (Shelton & Howson, 2014), my position as an authority figure in the writing classroom aligned me with whiteness and I had to hold that reality in tension with my embodiment. Though I've described it differently here than my stylist did, she was telling me the same thing. And as she predicted, my hair would continue to be a focal point, calling me back to the significance of my embodiment for what I chose to do for work.

Changing hairstyles was interesting and fun but was also time consuming and expensive. I began to search for a hairstyle that would fit my busy lifestyle and keep my commitment to a natural hair care regimen. I chose sisterlocs. Just a year and a half before I began my PhD program, I got my sisterlocs installed and when I was accepted, I knew that they would save me time and energy. They became an instant identifier for my new colleagues. Curious white people with questions about hair are also very familiar to Black women. For the most part, my doctoral community was inquisitive out of curiosity and admiration and everyone was well informed enough to avoid the mistake of touching my hair without permission (and pulling back a nub). Even my students were interested in my hairstyle. I sometimes referred to my hair as an identity marker as I scaffolded into an assignment about critical reflection. A handful of times, I got follow-up questions asking more about my hair and complimenting its beauty. Again, a little zoo-like, but mostly harmless.

Image 6. C. Shelton enjoying the Dreamville festival & rockin sisterlocs.

One day, I was out to meet a friend for a lunch and writing date somewhere close to (but decidedly off) campus. We were in an area that students and faculty frequented, so it was not uncommon to see students who might say hello. We had lunch and wrote, and it was lovely. The next day in class, a student asked if I'd had Mexican for lunch the day before. I said I had and asked if she'd been there too. She confirmed that she had and told me that she'd seen me walk in and sit with my friend, the only other Black woman graduate student who was instructing writing in the department at the time. As she chattered on about the food and about seeing me there and wanting to speak but being unsure, she commented casually,

"I thought it was you, but I really couldn't tell even after I saw your face. It was your hair that convinced me. No other teachers have your hair."

She meant this as a compliment. I didn't think much of it at the time. But in retrospect, it reminds me of the ways that my hair, even when it is admired, marks me as other in my community of scholars. It reminds me that my students and even my colleagues probably, use my body to mark and distinguish me from other Black people—not my research interests, or my teaching style, or my (too) big smile, or my affinity for cardigans. Though her technique for recognizing me worked for her, it was clearly based in a social system that doesn't require her to distinguish between multiple Black bodies in her everyday life and one that has taught her that teachers don't typically, "have hair like" mine. Funny that she'd made this conclusion likely before she'd even worked in a professional environment herself. Another hair-work related experience I had just a year ago demonstrated just how common her sense-making of the world actually is.

Keeping with the theme here, my hair is often a point of conversation when I meet new people—kids included. I am a parent, which involves all kinds of kid related activities. The first time I met one of my daughter's classmates, she was especially excited and full of questions. Some of her questions had specifically to do with my daughter's hair: Why is it always braided? How long does it take? How do you take it down? Her mom stopped her daughter's questions, sensing that they were bordering inappropriate and visibly grateful for my patience. She introduced herself to me and we had the typical, our friends are kids but do we like each other talk. Eventually my attention turned back to the girl. She had already learned all about me from her friend, my kid. She was now standing facing me, while I sat. We were at eye level. She looked at me carefully, asking:

"You're a teacher, right?"

"Yes, I am. I'll be heading to teach college students when I leave here."

Now her gaze drifted away from eye contact. She was looking around my face. She glanced at my daughter. Then back at me. Then at my daughter and back again. She was not looking at my face...she was looking at my hair. She tilted her head slightly and squinted her eyes (this is true—it is not for literary effect).

"You're nothing like I imagined".

We both stared momentarily. I realized that she was trying to make sense of what a teacher was to her and how little I fit the description. Despite my "teacher clothes" casual slacks, a simple shirt, a cardigan, and flats, she seemed to be grappling with how much my body—specifically the hair that she was fascinated with—didn't fit the description of a teacher that she'd come to expect. Her own teacher, a petite and friendly white woman (and a really great teacher, I might add) was not unlike her expectations as I was. And while I'm hopeful that her concept of a teacher expanded that day, what stands out to me is how early her concept of a teacher had solidified—these were 10 year olds.

These three experiences are small, almost insignificant recollections; they are things I might have forgotten if I hadn't been prompted to interrogate my embodiment and its relationship to my professionalism. But the truth is that these kinds of interactions remind me that I am the "other" and that my explicit commitment to my natural, racial features emphasizes and highlights that otherness. None of the people with whom I spoke likely saw themselves as microaggressors—my stylist was being "helpful"; my student was being "complimentary"; my daughter's friend was being "curious." But their ideas about who a professor can be don't include me at first glance. Our argument is that "first glance", the one that our students, and colleagues, and neighbors take when we reveal our professional qualification, is imbued with white, hetero-patriarchy and it harms us.

Conclusion

We understand the risks we take by sharing these experiences, connecting them to our bodies, and attributing them to race and racism. We risk not being believed. We risk our experiences being rationalized, explained away by the possibility of what the various interlocutors we recount could have meant. We risk that they will be given the benefit of the doubt and that we will be doubted. This is not uncommon for Black women.

But we also recognize that our testimony and our ability to make sense of that testimony in relationship to embodiment and professionalism has the potential to be enlightening and persuasive; not sharing and making sense of these narratives is risky too when we consider the potential to change how people think about professionalism on Black women's bodies and the benefit of identifying with the complexity of our experiences for other Black women and women of color in the academy.

This in-between position, one where neither sharing what you know and nor withholding what you know seems like a viable option, has been described as one of the indicators of epistemic oppression by Black feminist epistemologist Kristie Dotson (podcast citation). Dotson (2014) formally defines epistemic oppression as "persistent epistemic exclusion that hinders one's contribution to knowledge production" (pg. 115). One way that this oppression can occur is through silencing, a form of epistemic violence and related concept, which happens when "members of oppressed groups are silenced with respect to giving testimony" (Dotson, 2011 p. 237). This silencing occurs in two forms—testimonial quieting, wherein "an audience fails to identify a speaker as a knower" and testimonial smothering, wherein one's own testimony is truncated "order to insure that the testimony contains only content for which one's audience demonstrates testimonial competence" (Dotson, p. 244).

A white, Western, hetero-normative epistemology governs the controlling narratives in each of the environments where our reflections take place—the classroom, conferences, and public space. When the people with whom we work, interact, teach, and learn all subscribe to this epistemology, it can be difficult to disrupt the norms that determine what is and isn't acceptable. We have each experienced silencing of the kind Dotson references; the kind that either assumes that we don't know what we are talking about or that grows out of the hearer's incapacity to know what we testify to based on their ignorance (for example, a three year old cannot be expected to "know" the voting rules in Michigan, as Dotson explains). We persist in giving testimony because "it is by locating the forms of epistemic violence in silencing that we can begin to delineate, with contextual detail, practices of silencing on the ground" (Dotson, 2011, p. 327). The meaning of "professional" in the academy is the ground upon which we hope to make space for bodies like ours.

Sharing accounts of the intentional ways that we compose our bodies as raced, gendered, *and* professional might help our academic colleagues, our students, our administrators, and the publics with whom we interface to understand professionalism as a construction that can be stifling for Black women and gender non-conforming people. Tracing the ways that we've been silenced and the ways that we subvert those silences offers insight to bridge the gap in knowledge that our white colleagues likely have around our clothing, adornment, hairstyling, and other presentation practices. Even if not, our testimony stands as a beacon to other Black women in the academy: wear that t-shirt, sis; rock them big door knocker earrings; let them locs cascade over your shoulders; speak in your vernacular; be you! We need you!

REFERENCES

Brennan, C., & Feldman, K. (2018, January 8). H&M slammed for racism after showing black boy in 'coolest monkey in the jungle' hoodie. Retrieved from https://www.nydailynews.com/news/world/h-m-slammed-racism-coolest-monkey-jungle-hoodie-article-1.3744160

Dotson, K. (2011). Tracking epistemic violence, tracking practices of silencing. *Hypatia, 26*(2), 236-257. doi:10.1111/j.1527-2001.2011.01177.x

Dotson, K. (2014). Conceptualizing epistemic oppression. *Social Epistemology, 28*(2), 115-138. doi:10.1080/02691728.2013.782585

Dotson, K. (Guest). (2017, January 13). *Elucidations* [Audio Podcast]. Retrieved from https://shows.pippa.io/elucidations/episodes/587a2e9988d80d2d4a1f77e9

Greibel, H.B. (n.d.). The African American woman's headwrap: Unwinding the symbols. Retrieved from http://char.txa.cornell.edu/griebel.htm

Giannoulakis, C., & Drayer, J. (2009). "Thugs" versus "Good Guys": The impact of NBA cares on player image. *European Sport Management Quarterly, 9*(4), 453-468.

hooks, b. (1989). *Talking back: Thinking feminist, thinking black.* Cambridge, MA: South End Press.

McDonald, M. G., & Toglia, J. (2010). Dressed for success? The NBA's dress code, the workings of whiteness and corporate culture. *Sport in Society, 13*(6), 970-983.

Motsemme, N. (2003). Distinguishing beauty, creating distinctions: The politics and poetics of dress among young Black women. *Agenda, 17*(57), 12-19.

Scruggs, D. (2018, January 8). H&M's 'coolest monkey' hoodie and how racism wastes our precious time As Toni Morrison taught us, the ongoing cycle of ignorance keeps us from our work. Retrieved from https://theundefeated.com/whhw/hms-coolest-monkey-hoodie-and-how-racism-wastes-our-precious-time/

Shelton, C & Howson, E. (2014). Disrupting authority: Writing mentors and code-meshing pedagogy. *Praxis, 12*(1), Web. 10 June 2019. Retrieved from http://www.praxisuwc.com/shelton-howson-121

Wang, C. (2019, July 11). The real story behind H&M's racist monkey sweatshirt. Retrieved from https://www.refinery29.com/en-us/2019/07/237347/h-m-racist-hoodie-controversy-diversity-problem

Supplemental Material

Dressed But Not Tryin' To Impress: Black Women Deconstructing 'Professional' Dress

Brittany Hull, Cecilia D. Shelton, and Temptaous Mckoy

Part I: Reflection on the Origins of the Article

This piece is a result of a conversation (a venting session, really) where we each discussed instances where we felt like we had to alter a part of ourselves to appease the predominantly white spaces we inhabit daily as Black women teacher-scholars. Upon seeing the call for papers (CFP), we figured we would reflect on some of these experiences and interrogate how we opted to dismantle white hegemonic ideals of what it means to look, sound, and ultimately *be professional*. As we note in the introduction, "As three scholars entering new phases of our careers, we see dress practices as a critically symbolic metaphor for the challenges of thriving as Black women in academia. The difficulty of negotiating "Black", "scholar", "woman", and "professional" alongside a myriad of other labels manifests in how we choose, or cannot choose, to compose our bodies for public interpretation through dress practices." We hoped to turn our venting session into scholarship that might help other scholars navigate these challenges successfully.

Part II: Description of Research Methods, Findings, and/or Pedagogical Impact

In this piece we opted for an autoethnographic approach. We believe that our personal lived experiences serve as data for how to interrogate the ideological expectations academia has for people of color, with emphasis on Black women. This approach to scholarship has been taken on by various other Black woman scholars (April Baker-Bell, Elaine Richardson, Geneva Smitherman, Carmen Kynard, Gwendolyn Pough, Ersula Ore, and others). Critical self-reflection is vital to unlearning survival tactics (i.e. altering our dress, way of speaking, and physical appearance to name a few) in an effort to be *taken seriously* as teacher-scholars within the predominantly white space of academia.

We also thought it was important to preserve our own voices in keeping with our emphasis on personal lived experiences. We chose the organization and structure that appears in the article so that we could engage in a coherent discussion without flattening our distinctive voices. This choice resonates with a common thread in each of our pedagogical practices—we each value our students' authentic voices. All of us design learning environments and assignments that work to amplify marginalized voices and give space to various kinds of cultural, rhetorical, and linguistic practices.

Part III: Discussion Questions

1. Think about aspects of your identity. Has there ever been a time when you felt like you had to alter yourself in an effort to be accepted by those around you? How did this shift make you feel? Explain.

2. Examine the norms for dress, demeanor, mannerism, hairstyle, etc. that exist in a particular space that you frequently inhabit (i.e. your workplace, your academic department, your place of worship). Who might have a hard time adhering to those norms to navigate that space? How can you work to include those people?

3. Identify some of the racist, classist, ableist, homo/trans phobic, and sexist assumptions we make about marginalized bodies (fat=lazy, unhealthy; non-standard English=unintelligent; gender fluid=confused, attention-seeking). How do these ideas become encoded in the language of professionalism—can you think of examples? How might we respond to these microaggressions?

4. In what ways do you see this type of scholarship as beneficial to supporting students from multiple communities?

WRITING CENTER JOURNAL

Writing Center Journal is one the web at http://www.writingcenterjournal.org/

The Writing Center Journal was launched in 1980 by Lil Brannon and Steven North and remains the primary research journal in the field of writing centers. *WCJ* is the official journal of the International Writing Centers Association, an Assembly of the National Council of Teachers of English. *WCJ* is committed to publishing strong empirical research and theoretical scholarship relevant to writing centers. The journal represents a thriving, diverse, and interactive group that includes researchers and scholars representing a variety of backgrounds.

A Page from Our Book: Social Justice Lessons from the HBCU Writing Center[1]

This joint keynote address to the 2018 International Writing Centers Association conference, adapted for the print medium in WCJ, reflects on the lessons rhetoric and composition scholars can learn from HBCU writing centers. Mitchell and Randolph offer a call to the field's largely white audience of writing center scholars and administrators that if they truly want to embrace the virtues of "citizenship," they should collaborate with HBCU writing center practitioners. They make clear that the work of the HBCU writing center is inherently engaged in social justice and social activism, pushing back against the idea of a single narrative, in Chiminanda Adichie's words. They ask their audience to reflect on who has been missing in their conversations and to recenter their gaze on the experiences of institutions like HBCUs, HSIs, and tribal colleges who have always worked with students from "marginalized races."

---

1. *Writing Center Journal*, vol. 37, no. 2, 2019, pp. 21–42. © 2017 by the International Writing Centers Association.

A Page from Our Book: Social Justice Lessons from the HBCU Writing Center

Kendra L. Mitchell and Robert E. Randolph, Jr.

Ignoring race is understood to be a graceful, even generous, liberal gesture. To notice is to recognize an already discredited difference. To enforce its invisibility through silence is to allow the black body a shadowless participation in the dominant cultural body.

—Morrison, *Playing in the Dark*

Kendra L. Mitchell

A Recentering of Our Gaze: The Occasion

I begin this talk with a poem, "Manual for Hunting White-Tailed Deer: A Found Poem for Trayvon Martin," by my friend and colleague Yolanda J. Franklin, from her first book of poems, *Blood Vinyls* (see the appendix for the full text of this poem).[1] It captures the essence of what it means to be Black, southern, and defiantly oneself—even at the risk of losing one-

---

1. *Editors' Note*: A version of this keynote was delivered at the International Writing Centers Association conference in Atlanta, Georgia, on October 11, 2018. The IWCA call for papers characterized the 2018 conference theme, "The Citizen Center," in the following way: "Thus, we invite you to join us in Atlanta, Georgia, a city with a rich civil rights history, to reflect on how writing center professionals can engage in active citizenship and social justice work and to wonder with us: how might writing center professionals reframe our work through a lens of active *center*ship? How might we actively engage the calls to action that Grimm and others have placed before us? What are we doing in our tutoring sessions, our mission statements, our tutor education, and our campus impact work that demonstrates our active citizenship? What is the role of writing centers regarding social justice work? Our 2018 conference is a timely opportunity to come together to critically examine what we are already doing well and how we can do better."

Authors' Note: The authors wish to present this keynote as a conversation, one that represents our numerous conversations via phone and email. Thus, we preserved the polyvocality of our address and leaned into our shared folk tradition of call and response.

self. Well, at least that is my interpretation of the poem written in honor of Trayvon's life. Dr. Franklin wrote this poem at the height of the collective mourning of the loss of Trayvon as a fellow Floridian who took this murder personally. Though she is my friend, I did not ask her if she knew Trayvon for fear of the likelihood that she had taught him or his brother during her career as a secondary educator. If I really think about it, though, we teach Trayvons. Black young men striding through society carefree during hunting seasons. Earlier this year, some of our Black students at Florida Agricultural and Mechanical University, affectionately known as FAMU (pronounced fam-you) in Tallahassee were threatened by a white man with a gun in a student-housing facility he did not own. They were invited. He was hunting. Fortunately, these Black students lived to tell the story of how their bodies were an act of defiance to this older white male's entitlement to public space. To life. Their vocalizing this injustice was an act of involuntary social justice. You see, black skin places a demand of social justice on Black people at a high price. For us, it becomes more than a curriculum: it is a matter of life and death.

I am careful not to homogenize Black colleges because they are no more monolithic than Black people, or any people for that matter. Although they are similar to predominantly white institutions in many ways, their historical traditions and their levels and types of support make them distinct. Michelle J. Nealy (2009) uses this metaphor to compare HBCUs and historically white institutions: "When traditionally white institutions catch a cold, HBCUs catch pneumonia" (p. 18). Antoine Garibaldi argued that, like many other institutions of higher learning, "Black colleges reflect the diversity that is so characteristic of the United States' postsecondary education system" (as cited in Brown and Freeman, 2004, p. xii). This constant comparison of HBCUs to traditionally white institutions, the latter representing the superior model, reinforces stereotypes of inadequacy in the former.

Given this context, I recognize the exigence of this IWCA conference's theme and its intersection with writing center studies since my dissertation redresses the social injustices embedded in the many ways Black people do language. As we planned, we both recognized the sincerity of the call, and yet we both shared a common response: Haven't we said this before? What have we done about it? This is not a critique of the coordinators or the team because no one group of people could do what needs to be done, but we aim to interrogate the blind spots of theory where we are able to comfortably say we don't do social justice while knowing there is not equal representation in our field of writing studies.

At once I recognize the exigence of this conference and its intersections with the work we do, not just in the classroom but also in the writing center when I reflect on my dissertation research, *Language in the Center*; a closer examination of those interstices leads me to ask: Do you know where your closest HBCU is in your respective cities? And if you do, do you know who directs the writing center there? And if you do, when was the last time you collaborated with that person? These are the questions that help us critique what we mean when we say *social justice*. Said differently, for HBCUs, social justice has always meant social activism, and it requires our moving our gaze beyond those who uphold our comfortable narratives because as Chiminanda Adichie (2009) has told us, we must challenge the notion of a single narrative. Our responses prove the ineffectiveness of sincere queries of social justice without systemic changes in the way we practice ethical writing center studies in our institutions. Social justice, then, requires social action, and we encourage you to use the awkward conversations as a mobilizing tool. Take notes. Whom have you been omitting from your conversations? Recentering the gaze of writing center studies from predominantly white institutions—and by extension, whiteness—towards HBCUs, tribal colleges, and Hispanic-serving institutions is one solution. In other words, issues concerning diversity in writing center scholarship have and continue to be explored in university settings where the demographic has shifted to include more marginalized races, but none of them include historically Black colleges or universities. And while we cannot speak for all these groups—we dare not suggest we speak for all HBCUs—we will point us towards the agentic power of learning from marginalized institutions such as HBCUs.

We offer you a sense from our experiences in these spaces to be coupled with our good intentions in hopes to move the field closer to being the sustainable change agent we hope it will be. Now I turn the page to Robert.

Robert E. Randolph Jr.

WHAT, THEN, IS A CITIZEN?: AN INVITATION

What is a citizen? For me, this is an inherited question, one that echoes within, between, and beyond the interpolating words of Phillis Wheatley and Lucy Terry, or the fiery jeremiads of James Baldwin, or even the magnanimous speeches of Barack Obama. I wish to begin with this simple, yet generous, question because I want to establish a common ground, a center from which to begin. And your answer to my question (what or who is a citizen?), depends upon your vantage point; it depends on the particular democratic vista on which you stand. Perhaps it even depends upon your orientation, your social mobility (or lack thereof), the continuation of a bloodline, or even intergenerational privilege. When I read the call for this year's conference,

I was immediately struck by the word "citizen." As I encountered the word again and again, it began to reverberate in several directions.

I begin with the etymology of the word (etymology is one of my favorite pastimes—I'm a nerd, I know). *Citizen* comes from an Anglo-French word *denizen* and means a person who dwells within a country, as opposed to *foreigners* who dwell outside its limits (Citizen, 1989). Thus, *citizen* connotes a type of freedom in a space or place. But what happens when you wonder beyond the limits of the city or country, or rather you are born just beyond the limits—on the margins? By definition, a citizen occupies the center, the mainstream as it were. For the moment, let us bracket this supposition about the center and the margin, or that *citizen* approximates a type of corporeal and spatial schema.

I also thought about how we bandy that word around without any consideration of privilege and about bell hooks (2003), who talks about how a citizen might operate within our "culture of imperialist white-supremacist capitalist patriarchy" and its attending gaze (p. ix). Whom we identify as belonging to our society and who gets to decide haunt the pages of Claudia Rankine's (2014) genre-bending collection *Citizen: An American Lyric.* Specifically, there is a prose poem that takes up the national obsession with the limitations and ethics of connoting a citizen. The poem is rife with possibility, inheritance, and kinship. On one page, it reads, "In Memory of Jordan Russell Davis/In Memory of Eric Garner/In Memory John Crawford/In Memory Michael Brown/In Memory . . ." On the opposite page, Rankine writes, "Because white men can't/police their imagination/black men are dying" (pp. 134–135). Through the typography and form of the poem, Rankine performs a type of labor we often valorize in the academy, the labor of theory. Many of us would be hard pressed to think about any poem, let alone this poem, as theory. But it is.

Understanding Claudia Rankine and Toni Morrison's theory has framed my scholarship. Poems like Rankine's are, as Toni Morrison has said of *Beloved*, "about remembrance, an act imbued with as much memory as disavowal. That is to say, people are often compelled to paradoxically commemorate trauma even as they are desperately trying to forget it" (Randolph, 2012, p. 105). And perhaps this is what Rankine is doing, a theory of remembrance (and disposability). Elsewhere, I have written that "poetry promises a sense of possibility and existence without binary modalities or the totalizing effects of modern life, society, and culture" (Randolph, 2017, p. 294). Poems like Rankine's work on "so many levels because it does not—in form or as genre—insist on fatalist ways of reading or knowing. Poetry threatens both individualistic and collective epistemic ruptures. Literature has the capacity to alter how teachers and students see the world. And this insight is invaluable to sustain social justice projects" (Randolph, 2017, p. 294).

The poem consists of a list of names of Black people, adults and children alike, who have died at the hands of police officers. What is notable to me, as teacher and as a Black man who is equally subject to the violence of the State, is that with each reprinting of this collection, additional names are added (Waldman, 2015). The effect is one of powerlessness and fungibility: an endless litany of Black names, in black script, cast against a white backdrop, the impossibility of white pages that we, as writers, traffic in day in and day out. It would be foolish of us to think this legacy—its bite and recoil—does not stalk and haunt the students of our institutions. This is a legacy of white supremacy in America. At my institution, the legacy of this racism and white supremacy casts a long shadow. And yet, our students are expected to succeed despite it, in spite of it. With the specter of death painfully present at every quotidian turn, we must ask: And how exactly do we quantify or qualify student success under such strains? And how does the writing center or studio facilitate that success?

To help me think through the meaning of success and labor of survival in such precarious times, I turn to the ancestors, real and imagined. I turn to the performative and sympathetic magic of Black writers. Writing center studies is a trans- and interdisciplinary field, utilizing a plethora of methodologies and theories to flesh out what we do, why, and how. A cursory review of literature reveals how much white critical theorists are centered and privileged. But for my efforts, I have begun to push against the boundaries of writing center studies, to venture beyond the center of the discipline, to examine and utilize Black critical theory. I ask these questions constantly and consistently: What would writing center studies look like if we centered the theories, ideologies, perspectives, and praxes of Black folk who are doing the antiracist and anti-oppression work we purport to do? What would happen if we engaged the critical theory and philosophies of Black women: Morrison's (1993) "rememory," Evelyn Higginbotham's (1993) "politics of respectability," Kristie Dotson's (2012) "epistemic oppression," Sylvia Wynter's (cited in McKittrick, 2015) "being human as praxis," or Christina Sharpe's (2016) "wake work"?

The need, indeed the desire, to assemble unique theories that are intentionally inclusive is important because some of the circumstances in which African Americans learned to read and write were and are not valorized by mainstream, dominant culture, including the academy, even at HBCUs. In order for me to examine the agenda and work of HBCU writing centers, I cannot rely on traditional (read: hegemonic and patriarchal) epistemologies or methodologies. Consequently, my address broaches thematics of (il)legibility, perception, and normativity. As the Black feminist Barbara Christian (1988) tells us,

> People of color have always theorized—but in forms quite different from the Western form of abstract logic. And I am inclined to say that our theorizing (and I intentionally use the verb rather than the noun) is often in narrative forms, in the stories we create, in riddles and proverbs, in the play with language, because dynamic rather than fixed ideas seem more to our liking. How else have we managed to survive with such spiritedness the assault on our bodies, social institutions, countries, and our very humanity? (p. 68)

And this assault, as Christian terms it, is violence, in and of itself, an undertheorized aspect of African American educational and literacy discourses; this talk, project, and inquiry seeks to begin a dialogue about ways we can begin to address inclusion in accessible and tangible ways.

Kendra L. Mitchell

A Black Woman with a Story

I, too, am a Black woman with a few stories of my own. (This story, an excerpt from my research, provides a snapshot of student writers' and writing center staff's embodied experience of many HBCU writing center practices beyond the existing writing center gaze.)

Student J entered the Writing Resource Center, hereafter Center, eager to tackle the revisions suggested by his professor. As the invested educator she was, she had walked him down the flight of stairs to the Center's small room with its accordion-styled dividers. We greeted the student-professor pair with optimism and presented the standard folder with the contract that strongly encourages writers to improve their craft with concentrated assistance with perfecting their writing. His smile reached across his narrow, caramel face as he straddled the chair across the oblong table we shared and initiated the conference. After skimming the instructor's brief comments, I agreed that Student J approached the assignment with a nuanced and fresh perspective, which he demonstrated amply in the first few moments of the session, but some of his word choices, sentence structure, and organization did not follow Edited American English, or academic writing, as expected by the teacher—and probably most writing center practitioners (including myself at the time). Much like many of my former clients and staff in the Center, he was fluent in AAL, defined as an Africanized version of American English, or African American Language (Smitherman, 2006, p. 3) but less proficient in Edited

American English organizational logic. So while Student J used complex sentence structures, these complexities at times resulted in a mixed construction or the occasional run-on sentence. Additionally, he occasionally provided more detail than his professor perceived necessary, and he created new verbs or nouns to suit his purposes. To his credit, he had a knack for using figurative language and rhythmic language: his words rolled off the tongue and into the soul. But he struggled with the required Edited American English. Drawing on our Center's procedures for working with a client's essay, I had Student J read his essay aloud, while I asked questions like, "What did you mean when you said____?" and "This part of your essay is a little unclear to me; can you tell me what you meant without reading the essay to me?" My goal was to help him retain the virtues of his essay while moving the draft closer to tightly organized Edited American English revision.

As we worked together, he hesitantly acknowledged his tendency to write how he spoke, offering this as if he were at confessional sharing a sin. But, instead of becoming excited about the essay's growing clarity, Student J gradually lost his initial enthusiasm. He became increasingly irritable when I queried him about his linguistic choices. He protested that delaying his point to the end of his sentence or the end of the paragraph was a deliberate writing choice of which he was proud. And he objected to what he called "revising his voice out of his essay." Then, as his body slumped to the right of the chair, his right hand propping his drooping face, defeated, he asked in despair and with agitation, "Ain't that what I said?" Fearing I was losing him, I changed tactics. Instead of continuing to use Edited American English, I responded to his question in kind: "But that ain't what you wrote." With that simple gesture of linguistic camaraderie, I showed my respect for the nuances of his expressions and reengaged him in our joint task, never realizing that, in the process of crafting what I thought was a successful session, I was reinforcing what sociolinguist Geneva Smitherman calls the "linguistic push-pull" of language so many African American students experience in the classroom and in the writing center (Mitchell, 2015, pp. 2–3).

In essence, he was toiling with his love for what he wrote alongside the institutionalized disdain for how he writes. This exchange is not unique to me and my HBCU: many others notice this in their writing centers and classrooms. For Student J, it was a kind of intervention. For me, it was an act of social justice that lends itself to the theory of HBCU writing centers as potential third spaces. If we consider Elizabeth Coughlin, Jennifer Finstrom, Elizabeth Kerper, Kevin Lyon, and Sowmya Sastri's (2012) definition of third space in a writing center context as "the location or ideology that is negotiated and/or created when different identities or spaces come into discussion with one another" (p. 4), we can see how HBCU writing centers are always in the process of becoming through cocreation via shared cultural values. When we follow our students' lead and transform marginality into third spaces, we are able to help our students and ourselves shift our gaze towards a theory just beyond our normalized rules and into a more curious space.

Robert E. Randolph Jr.

ON WRITING CENTERS AND CRITICAL MARGINALITY: THE DEAN'S ASSIGNMENT

Earlier this semester, my chair informed me the new dean wanted us to go on a "tour of writing centers." She wanted us to gather information about how other writing centers worked and their "best practices." My chair punctuated "best practices" with a long, dramatic pause. I had been here before; she was my second dean since becoming director. A new dean with cursory "interest" in the writing center and very little strategy for its longevity. For so many deans, perhaps even yours, the writing center operates mysteriously within the nebulous ecology of higher education, an academic unit charged with "student success" and all that means. The dean's assignment further vexed me because I had not met her or submitted a report about our writing center. How did she know my center was not employing "best practices"? I was additionally perplexed by the schools she chose for us to visit: Elon University, North Carolina State University, and the University of North Carolina at Chapel Hill. These are mighty fine institutions, but they don't look or feel like mine, which happens to be the largest HBCU in the country. I began to ask myself: Had my dean come into her new role as leader of the college with preconceived notions about what a writing center was or should be? Had she seen our writing center as inadequate or insufficient? And did these notions have anything to do with deeply entrenched ideas about race and whiteness? The latter question was the one that lingered in my mind as the chair and I embarked on our mythopoetic journey down Interstate 40.

Here, I generously extend grace to my new dean. I will not speculate further about her motives or even her choices of schools. However, for me, her request for this "fact-finding mission" was nevertheless dubiously and tangentially linked to certain sentiments about the worth and value of HBCUs. When some of my colleagues heard about this mission, they encouraged me to speak to the dean. I did not. I had a desire to inform her how the trip to the "premier" institutions in our state trafficked in internalized racial and elitist politics. Instead, I kept that opinion to myself. Since HBCUs are fixed firmly at the margins in the minds of some educators, let us take up the corporeal and spatial nature of the margin in earnest.

The most common definition of margin refers to a border or edge, a space that often marks the furthest limit of an entity. As a spatial concept, it demarcates the space beyond what is deemed necessary or a limit where something ceases to be utilized or desired. Then too, the margin also marks the limit of possibility—of existence, examination, or exploration. However, these definitions connote a hidden symbiotic relationship: the margin does not exist without the center, and this powerful binary reifies power relations and social hierarchies. Though my understanding of the margin/center paradigm is informed by those hierarchical considerations, I do not rely on them. The margin/center paradigm is a social construct with arbitrary meanings and real-life consequences. In *Feminist Theory: From Margin to Center*, bell hooks (1984) asserts that marginality provides a "special vantage point" from which to critique and dismantle social ills such as racism, sexism, and heterosexism (p. 16). The counterhegemonic praxis of critiquing from the margins remains a time-honored tradition with Black public intellectuals. Additionally, Edward Soja (2010) reflects on the possibility of the transdisciplinarity of the "spatial turn," an affective praxis that examines how our social dimensions transform our environmental and geographical realities. This perspective, he argues, utilizes a "socio-spatial dialectic" that moves beyond traditional spatial considerations and emphasizes the processes of class formation.

And so, in my writing center studies inquiries, I take up both hooks's and Soja's theorizing about (and around) the margins. I situate spatial thinking to critically approach how and why the margin (and by extension the center, perhaps) should be important to my work and research. In other words, which writing centers move at the margins of our discourse, and more importantly, why? What discourses reveal themselves when we assume the material conditions of the margins as educative, instructive, and pragmatic? How do the margins and marginal conditions activate and constitute new, inventive knowledges and methods of inquiry? I have had to seriously take up the theorizing of Black folk because "normative modes of inquiry and containment often are incapable of assessing . . . value" (Manning, 2016, p. 27) beyond neoliberal and capitalistic ways.

To write about and for the margin and marginalized people, both within and outside the academy, is to write about an intense predicament. The burden (or reward) of doing so is inextricably linked with seemingly intractable machinations of visibility. And to do this work is to see oneself as the disenfranchised from a vantage point that produces a type of (radical) agency and knowledge—which is to say, inclusion/exclusion has material effects. The margins represent a place where "cultural imaginings, affective experiences, animated objects, marginal voices, narrative densities, and eccentric traces of power's presence" (Gordon, 2008, p. 25) are allowed to illuminate a sensuous knowledge. This knowledge makes one radically available to oneself, operating at the level of impulse, ability, and intimacy. As I have prepared for today's talk, I have vacillated between belief and mania, self-doubt and confidence, between the personal and the social. To make peace with myself as a scholar, researcher, student, teacher, and writing center director, I had to truly take up the margins as a serious inquiry and unequivocal concern. I had to acknowledge and get comfortable with uncertainty, the penultimate condition of the margin.

Again, centering spaces/places has social capital, theoretical or otherwise. The classroom, the archive, fields of study, indeed, the writing center, inculcate their occupants with dimensions of both restriction and promise. The center/margin paradigm is also such a place. This critical project ruminates about how language either confines or regulates people to the margins of our society and how language developed at the margin imbues those inhabitants with certain potentialities. These potentialities are pedagogical and bound to a certain futurity that retheorizes what the purposes of education may become. Additionally, if the margin and the center enter discourses together and can never be separated, we must begin thinking through new ideologies and epistemologies coupled with that association. And while scholars traditionally understand the center as the demarcation of privilege and the margin as a demarcation of disadvantage, the social statuses of these spaces often give way to material realities that cannot be subsumed or understood by the other. That is, to be at the center is not always privilege, and to be on the margin is not always disadvantage. Depending on positionalities, circumstances, and contexts, these spaces represent more, in excess of normative narratives. And this is the lived experience of my writing center. Because we operate on the margins of traditional discourse about writing centers, our methodologies, theories, and praxes are excluded from full consideration. HBCUs and writing centers alike are sociopolitical spaces conceived for exclusion (or for the excluded). Both are often read as spaces of undesirability, illegibility, disposability, and neglect. Again, were these the ideologies that circulated in my dean's mind? Was our visit to these predominantly white institutions informed by these notions of deficit?

What I've laid out thus far represents a counternarrative. It is my perspective on what it means to labor institutionally, racially, disciplinarily at the margins. Herein lies the importance of this address: the insistence to look rigorously at the tendencies, autonomy, and operational pulse contained within a marginal status or marginal spaces. My argument, perhaps, is not so much about the intervention of language to describe these marginal discourses within educational and writing center studies but about activating a continuity of difference, celebrating survival (as only the marginalized truly can), and circumstantiating the prininsence on our radical presence in institutions, disciplines, and discourses. In other words, what life and learning moves at the margins, at the border, at the limit of what is recognized as imperative and generative? Then too, a concomitant aim of this address is to consider how textual gaps, absences, and silences at the margins operate pedagogically and rhetorically. Here, I will ask you: Who are the prominent Black and Brown voices of writing center studies? Can you name them? And how do you account for so few Black and Brown conference participants in this room today?

Kendra L. Mitchell

On Being Curious: A Black Woman with a Theory

In the spirit of using Black women scholars to frame our theory and practice, I stand here as a Black woman with a theory about why we struggle as a field to really move beyond conversations around dismantling the power structures Nancy Grimm (1999) addressed 20 years ago in *Good Intentions* towards sustainable and progressive equitable laws in our society and writing centers that benefit those who have historically been strategically excluded from basic human rights. I believe we lack curiosity about the margins. Specifically, we lack a genuine interest in what we can learn from the margins. Anne Geller, Michele Eodice, Frankie Condon, Meg Caroll, & Beth Boquet (2007 also acknowledge that "our profession has done little to date to complicate tutors' or our own understanding of racism in relation to our individual and professional identities, our teaching and tutoring work, or our institutions" (p. 96). In a similar vein, considering the call addressed in Grimm's 1999 work and juxtaposing it with the line of questioning by my colleague, we also must think about why we are circling back to the same conversations despite the books that have been written by Staci Perryman-Clark (2013), Smitherman (2003), and Elaine Richardson (2003)—to name just a few—that privilege Black and brown voices. We have works in the field. I have referenced Jackie Grutsch McKinney in my own talk and scholarship, and yet we still must ask the same questions at this conference. So we must also ask ourselves: What's missing from our theories? Is theory enough? I reiterate the need for the kind of curiosity that moves beyond theories and the instinct to "Columbus" [here we mean the verb] other people's lived experiences. It can only thrive in that third space that exists outside our comforts—HBCUs are not exempt. In fact, they are in themselves counterspaces that must create new spaces where we can metaphorically hold space for new perspectives.

I am reminded of my nine-month tenure as a Fulbright guest lecturer in South Africa in 2016 during the peak of their nationwide, student-led protests. I challenged my 150 students in my diversity-in-higher-education module to choose to become curious about their colleagues' plight and pair that curiosity with empathy. I had to figure out how I would convince students whose families have been at war for decades to level with one another for an hour: stand in your ideas, turn your heads, and your feet may follow. I invite you to join those brave students in swiveling your heads, hold space for the conversations the margins might lead to—the questions: let them not fall here and onto a dead tree—in print only. Let it be manifested in your writing center spaces. In your communities. In our roles where we are given opportunities to call action to the fore, right? To actually move our fingers to write. To dirty our hands. To move outside of our positions that we've held so dear. We must use curiosity though it is tenuously productive because it is only then that our gaze will follow.

With that, I transition to our closing . . .

Robert E. Randolph Jr.

More Names, More Names, More Names: Why This Wake Work Matters

When I was a new writing center director, one of the highlights of my nascent directorship was attending the 2014 IWCA Summer Institute in Lexington, Kentucky. My chair informed me the institute would be an excellent opportunity to learn more and network. I applied for and was generously awarded a scholarship. I was eager to attend because the theme that year was about diversity and inclusion. Vershawn Young gave a brilliant keynote address. While I was welcomed by some participants at the institute, I also dealt with microaggressions. And I felt isolated in this academic and professional space. The day before the we left, I went walking downtown for our lunch break. That walk culminated in what Morrison calls "rememory" when I encountered a historical marker that read "Cheapside Auction Block." The marker described the ground I was standing on: "African Americans were sold as slaves at Cheapside Auction Block on the public square in the 19th century. Lexington was the center of slave trading in Ky. by the late 1840s and served as a market for selling slaves farther south. Thousands of slaves were sold at Cheapside, including children who were separated from their parents." Those of us who study and lecture about the institution of slavery understand what it means to be sold "further South" to places like Mississippi and Louisiana. Those of us who lecture about the institution of slavery understand the visceral horror of children separated from their parents, never to have sight or sound of loved ones again. That marker reminded me of a lineage of inherited pain and resilience. As all thoroughly ensconced 21st-century citizens do, I posted about the incident to Facebook. But before I did that, I instinctually googled the auction block and its significance. I was interested in why it was call "Cheapside," though intuitively I knew why. It was called Cheapside because at one side of the courthouse, healthy slaves were sold. On the cheap side were sold slaves who were elderly, or disabled, or undesirable.

Beyond rememory, I was embodying Christina Sharpe's (2016) theories about *wakefulness*. In many ways, Sharpe eschews the clichéd millennial idiom of being "woke." Instead, through word magic, she re-orients the "paradox of blackness" around the incompleteness of becoming and being "in the wake" (p. 14). What she's really theorizing is how we (all Americans) are inundated with anti-Blackness, white supremacy, and the aftermath of chattel slavery, even when we aren't consciously thinking about it. When I returned to the institute that day, I must have been visibly shaken because several of the participants asked me how I was doing and what was wrong. I recounted my experience with the historical marker. Some expressed concern and remorse for my having this experience. Some were unconcerned. That indifference left me bereft, and I never intended to participate in another IWCA event. And yet, here I am today.

As I consider my current job as a writing center director at North Carolina A&T State University, I am thinking through the critical commitments and missions of HBCUs in the 21st century. About how a large number of them came into being amid the scraps of postreconstruction, a time when some Black folk desperately wanted to move into the mainstream society, to realize their full citizenship in this country. In many ways, those missions and expectations have changed. The writing center is expected by faculty, students, and administrators to "fix" papers, focusing on grammar and mechanics. But to what end? Writing center theorists and compositionists know the crux of writing does not reside in grammar and mechanics alone. Robert McRuer (2006) asserts, "Composition in the corporate university remains a practice that is focused on a fetishized final product, whether it is the final paper, the final grade, or the student body with measurable skills" (p. 151). This assumption also applies to writing centers. At my school, my tutors must strike a unique balance between allaying fears and anxieties about using vernacular and home languages and educating for the world beyond the college, a world with defiant and embodied consequences of nonstandard language usage, a world rife with difficult and discombobulating moral enactments on the Black mind and body. In other words, my tutors are preparing my students for living "in the wake." And while some university administrators think about student success as landing a good job and the writing center as integral to preparation of career-placement documents, I am also thinking about my responsibility to my students' understanding of the racial world they are entering and inhabiting.

I believe in Asao Inoue's (2016) call for "writing centers to be revolutionary change-agents in the institutions and communities in which they are situated . . . [to] facilitate structural changes in society, disciplines, and the institution itself" (p. 94). And I vehemently agree with his pronouncement that "writing centers are more than centers of writing, but centers for revolutions, for social justice work" (p. 94). Perhaps, if we think through what it means to have a "citizen center" we would first critique the notion of "citizen" and all it implies. My ancestors, for instance, were only "granted citizenship" by virtue of political maneuvering, arm twisting, and the ratification of the 14th Amendment to the U.S. Constitution. But we know legal distinction is a far cry from social acceptance (and we shall not legislate this further). The litany of names in *Citizen: American Lyric* (Rankine 2014), those subjected to extrajudicial killing and violence, bears this out:

> Trayvon Martin. 17 years old. Returning home after purchasing Skittles and iced tea from a corner store. Followed, accosted, and shot to death by a so-called "neighborhood" watch coordinator.
>
> Michael Brown. 18 years old. Stopped by police. Shot 12 times while surrendering with his hands in the air. His body lies in the street for 5 hours.
>
> Miram Carey. 34 years old. Innocent mother with a baby in tow, made a wrong turn near the White House. Shot 5 times from behind.
>
> John Crawford III. 22 years old. Shot by police without warning while shopping at Walmart. Holding a toy BB gun and talking on his phone. At no point did he aim the toy gun.
>
> Eric Garner. 43 years old. Harassed by the NYPD. Died after being held in a chokehold. NYPD policy prohibits the use of chokeholds.
>
> Tamir Rice. 12 years old. Shot by police within 2 seconds of arrival after playing with an airsoft gun. He did not aim the gun at the police.

Aiyana Stanley-Jones. 7 years old. Shot and killed in a police raid while sleeping on her grandmother's couch.

Rumain Brisbon. 34 years old. Unarmed father of four, shot to death when a police officer mistook his bottle of pills for a gun.

Some of the names are familiar; others are not. Perhaps the particulars of their deaths are irrelevant; or, perhaps, the particulars collapse under loss itself. Some of these cases have been adjudicated. Others have not. The results of these adjudications, in any case, are irrelevant. This litany of names is paltry, at best. More names, more names, more names will be added to Rankine's list. As we begin this conference in Atlanta, the social and financial hub of the New South, let us move forward with the understanding of this reality—the imminent and immanent death of folks who are called *citizens* but who lack the "coin of the realm" to confirm that status. As we leave this conference and return to our respective campuses, let us understand the psychic condition we all toil under. Thank you.

Acknowledgments

We'd like to thank our colleagues, mentors, WRC FAMUly, and the IWCA committee for all you have done and continue to do to hold and make space.

References

Adiche, C. (2009). The danger of a single story. TED video, 18:34. https://www.ted.com/talks/chimamanda_adichie_the_danger_of_a_single_story?language=en

Brown, M. C. II, & Freeman, K. (Eds.). (2004). The state of research on black colleges: An introduction. In M. C Brown II & K. Freeman (Eds.), *Black colleges: New perspectives on policy and practice* (pp. xi–xiv). West Port, CT: Praeger.

Christian, B. (1988). The race for theory. *Feminist studies, 14*(1), 67–79.

Citizen. (1989). In *Oxford English dictionary*. Retrieved from https://www-oed-com.er./view/Entry/33513?rskey=hrrKmz&result=1&isAdvanced=false#eid

Coughlin, E., Finstrom, J., Kerper, E., Lyon, K., & Sastri, S. (2012). Outreach: Expanding writing center third space. *East Central Writing Centers Association, 1*, 3–9.

Dotson, K. (2012). A cautionary tale: On limiting epistemic oppression. *Frontiers: A Journal of Women Studies, 33* (1), 22–47.

Franklin, Y. (2018). "Manual for still hunting white-tailed deer in a gated community *found poem for Trayvon Martin*." In *Blood vinyls: Poems*. Tallahassee, FL: Anhinga.

Geller, A. E., Eodice, M., Condon, F., Caroll, M., & Boquet, E. H. (2007). *The everyday writing center: A community practice.* Logan: Utah State University Press.

Gordon, A. (2008). *Ghostly matters: Haunting and the sociological imagination.* Minneapolis: University of Minnesota Press.

Grimm, N. (1999). *Good intentions: Writing center work for postmodern times.* Portsmouth, NH: Heinemann.

Higginbotham, E. B. (1993). *Righteous discontent: The women's movement in the black Baptist church, 1880–1920.* Cambridge, MA: Harvard University Press.

hooks, b. (1984). *Feminist theory: From margin to center.* Boston: Sound End.

hooks, b. (2003). *We real cool.* New York: Routledge.

Inoue, A. B. (2016). Afterword: Narratives that determine writers and social justice writing center work. *Praxis: A Writing Center Journal, 14*(1), 94–99.

Manning, E. (2016). *The minor gesture.* Durham, NC: Duke University Press.

Mitchell, K. L. (2015). *Language in the center: A case study of multilingualism in an historically Black university writing center* (Unpublished doctoral dissertation). Florida State University, Tallahassee. Retrieved from http://purl.flvc.org/fsu/fd/FSU_2016SP_Mitchell_fsu_0071E_13018

McKinney, J. G. (2013) *Peripheral visions for writing centers.* Logan: Utah State University Press.

K. McKittrick. (2015). Axis, bold as love: On Sylvia Wynter, Jimi Hendrix, and the promise of science. In K. McKittrick (Ed.), *Sylvia Wynter: On being human as praxis* (pp. 142–63). Durham, NC: Duke University Press.

McRuer, R. (2006). *Crip theory: Cultural signs of queerness and disability.* New York: New York University Press.

Morrison, T. (1993). *Playing in the dark: Whiteness and the literary imagination.* New York: Vintage.

Nealy, M. J. (2009). Pride and peril: Historically black colleges and universities. In *Diverse: Issues in higher education 26*(14), pp. 18–19.

Perryman-Clark, S. (2013). *Afrocentric teacher-research: Rethinking appropriateness and inclusion.* New York: Lang.

Randolph. R. Jr. (2012). Wanderlust, hysteria and insurrection: (Re)presenting the "Beloved" sweet home men. In T. T. Green (Ed.), *Presenting Oprah Winfrey, her films, and African American literature* (pp. 105–126). New York: Palgrave Macmillan.

—. (2017). The queer poetics of social justice: Literacy, affect(ion), and the democratic rigors of writing. In C. P. Gause (Ed.), *Leadership, equity, and social justice in American higher education: A reader* (pp. 287–295). New York: Peter Lang.

Rankine, C. (2014). *Citizen: An American lyric.* Minneapolis, MN: Graywolf.

Richardson, E. (2003). *African American literacies.* New York: Routledge.

Sharpe, C. (2016). *In the wake: On Blackness and being.* Durham, NC: Duke University Press.

Soja, E. (2010). *Seeking spatial justice.* Minneapolis: University of Minnesota Press.

Smitherman, G. (2006). *Word from the Mother: Language and African Americans.* New York: Routledge.

Waldman, K. (2015). The new printing of *Citizen* adds a haunting message about police brutality. Slate. Retrieved from https://slate.com/culture/2015/01/claudia-rankines-citizen-new-printing-mourns-michael-brown-eric-garner-black-victims-of-police-brutality.html.

APPENDIX[2]

Manual for Still Hunting White-tailed Deer in a Gated Community

found poem for Trayvon Martin, by Yolanda J. Franklin
Deer hunting in Florida is as old as recorded history.
Actions delineated here are designed to ensure public desires
for recreation. As deer populations grow, so does popularity
of hunting for recreation. The exploitation of deer increases
during this period. "Still Hunting" is characterized by stalking
or concealing oneself and waiting for quarry. The practice
of hunting at feeding stations was legalized, enhancing
opportunities for still hunters to locate and harvest.
In vehicles while coordinating movements with cell phones,
hunters hunt larger blocks, sit next to trees or hide in bushes.
The newly formed Florida Fish & Wildlife Conservation
Commission recognizes the need for public hunting
lands, so Florida's acres are open to public hunting, the vast
majority open to deer hunting. To provide landowners with tools
and flexibility to control deer numbers, the Commission
implemented a deer depredation program. Overpopulation
is the most pressing challenge. Deer in Florida are considerably smaller.
In Florida, whitetails are known to have various types of trauma,
and are a species of wildlife whose over-abundance degrades
its own habitat as well as the habitats of others. Delaying
harvest of bucks until maturity carries rewards: more bucks
in subsequent years and seeing bucks is a key component
of hunter satisfaction. Seminole County is infested
with white-tailed deer, so legislation approved deer eradication
throughout south Florida. Managing hunter satisfaction
enhances overall recreational experiences. The Commission began
the comprehensive surveillance program to occur at two levels:
passive and active. Passive involves observation and culling

---

2. The editors gratefully acknowledge Anhinga Press for permission to reprint this poem in full.

of free-ranging deer that demonstrate abnormal behavior
(suspect or target animals). Active includes random investigating
of hunter-harvested deer. The challenge will be to provide
an array of opportunities that deer harvest will continue
as a necessary and desirable practice for many years. Whether
a hunter prefers to harvest only mature bucks, or chooses
to harvest any deer within range is a value judgment.
It is considered the most popular game in Florida.

Kendra L. Mitchell, PhD, is assistant professor of English at Florida A&M University, where she teaches composition, literature, and historical linguistics. Some of her current research interests and pursuits include cosplay in Toni Morrison's *The bluest eye* and codifying registers of culturally situated silences in HBCU writing centers.

Robert E. Randolph, Jr., PhD, is Assistant Director of the Writing Center at American University. Most recently, he is the author of "The queer poetics of social justice: Literacy, affect(ion), and the democratic rigors of writing," in *Leadership, Equity, and Social Justice in American Higher Education: A Reader* (2017).

Supplemental Material

A Page from Our Book: Social Justice Lessons from the HBCU Writing Center

Kendra L. Mitchell and Robert E. Randolph, Jr.

PART I: REFLECTION ON THE ORIGINS OF THE ARTICLE

In summer 2018, we received an email inviting us to deliver the keynote for the International Writing Center Association conference. We were both honored and surprised by the invitation for various reasons. We were junior HBCU faculty members at the beginning of our careers, and had often labored at the margins of our fields and professional organizations. HBCU faculty are expected to participate in these organizations, to show up and take notes from hegemonic culture, to understand and replicate their best practices. We are unaccustomed to being centered, which paradoxically was the theme for the 2018 conference. The gravity of delivering this keynote to one of the leading organizations in our field was apparent. But we took the necessary time to craft our message, to fine tune the language to a fever pitch. Over many emails and phone conversations, we worked through the agenda of our keynote: how would we represent our fellow HBCU colleagues without the shadow of tokenism or elitism? Indeed, how would we bear witness? (These are concerns our white colleagues don't often have to contend with.)

We recognized that we were not arriving in Atlanta that fall as individual scholars, and we accepted that we were not acting out of some sense of individualistic career advancement. In other words, we embodied Maya Angelou's assertion: "I come as one, but I stand as 10,000." Thus it was imperative to show up and tell the truth, to witness. We don't just use the vernacular. We are the vernacular. We understood the assignment. And, in many ways, we are still on assignment. The work is not done. We (still) resist becoming a pithy anecdote or 'diversity, equity, & inclusion' moment. We (still) refuse to allow the conversation to reside in that moment. In short, we refuse to be commodified (The organizers honored their commitment to social justice in their care for us during Hurricane Michael that eventually vanquished parts of the Florida panhandle days after the conference. I [Kendra Mitchell] was able to focus on my presentation in peace while my mother and I nestled in the hotel room a day prior to the previously arranged arrival time at the suggestion of the organizers.).

Privileging individualistic scholarly approaches anchors white mainstream culture and upholds white supremacy. We deliberately wanted to disrupt that. Most keynote addresses are the product of a single person. But the benefit of hearing a collaborative keynote, actually seeing it done, necessitates a kind of scholarly dialogue that we have most often in our offices or in the corridors of conference halls but not on the diaus (We will note that collaborative keynotes are becoming more acceptable). We wanted our audience to be immersed in two different points-of-view, from scholars at two different institutions, with the same concern about the field and the trajectory of research and praxis. Specifically, we had a lot of uniqueness to land at this moment. We asked ourselves: how many keynotes have we seen that center Blackness, polyvocality, gender, and poetics? Beyond novelty, beyond spectacle, beyond cultural awakening at the margins, we seized the moment. Thus, our keynote became a performative critique of the genre, the space, and the organization.

Part II: Description of Research Methods, Findings, and/or Pedagogical Impact

We know that epistemologies, methodologies, and pedagogies are never objective. So we decided early in the writing process to lean into our subjectivities, to let them inform our purpose, our content, and our delivery. As a genre, the collaborative keynote provided space for us to embody the polyvocality of the occasion; more particularly, we wanted to amplify the vernacularity of call and response. This felt not only useful but comfortable. And that comfort eased us into a rhythm of collaboration that proved to be rewarding for us and the audience.

Centering ourselves also meant decentering dominant literacies and theories. We sought to ground our content and message of our keynote in Black womanist approaches, namely storytelling as a valid source of knowledge creation and countering white supremacist culture embedded in our practices. As a preemptive strategy against social injustice, we also explored critical curiosity, employing multiple literacies to foster institutional change through individual action. In short, "swiveling your head and letting your feet follow" allows for curiosity to be coupled with empathy, moving toward the application of social justice practices.

As a research method, witnessing and testifying afforded us the opportunity to use our cultural experiences in conversation with and resistance towards white hegemonic norms in our discipline as a means of collecting data for justifying not only the shifting of our gaze but the admonishing for the field to shift with us. Our individual traumas and triumphs became the evidence-based research to affirm our collective stance. Additionally, critical spatial theory served as an impetus for the keynote, as well. Specifically, the address was a moment to embody a critical spatial critique, a rare opportunity to challenge the organization and their thoughts around what it means to occupy and operate within the language of the center, to challenge the very language of writing center studies itself. The forefront of my [Kendra Mitchell] pedagogical approach attended to how and why I advocated for my students' rights to their own language as well as their right to feel accepted in the classroom. This keynote has challenged me to center Black rhetorical traditions in my assignment design, carefully aligning those assignments with a philosophy of linguistic care to employ polyvocality that made space for my students to create sounds, visuals, and discourse that reflected the genius in all of the languages they speak, compose, and embody.

PART III: DISCUSSION QUESTIONS

1. How might Black poetics move writing center studies towards a praxis of social justice?
2. How might you partner (i.e. training, grants, projects,etc.) with neighboring writing center directors from HBCUs, tribal colleges, HSIs, community colleges, etc.)?
3. How can you leverage your privilege and resources (institutional or otherwise) to level the playing field for other marginalized writing center professionals and colleagues?
4. When pursuing publications, have you considered, collaborated, or made space in the conversation for a scholar whose work is marginalized or not widely circulated (i.e. graduate students, etc.)?
5. When was the last time you positioned yourself to learn from HBCUs, tribal colleges, HSIs, community colleges, etc. without the intent to profit, monopolize, or promote your center or self?

ADDITIONAL ACTIVITIES:

1. Identify a theory from the reading (and create a small reading list). From what social, cultural, linguistic phenomenons does this theory arise? And how do these phenomenons inform your writing center praxis or studies?
2. Explicate Yolanda J. Franklin's "Manual for Still Hunting White-tailed Deer in a Gated Community, found poem for Trayvon Martin." What connections or associations can you relate to the article, particularly notions of citizenship, space, and social justice.

PEDAGOGY

Pedagogy is on the Web at
http://pedagogy.dukejournals.org/

Pedagogy: Critical Approaches to Teaching Literature, Language, Composition, and Culture is an innovative journal that aims to build and sustain a vibrant discourse around teaching in English studies. In spite of the large role that teaching plays in the lives of most English studies scholars, no other mainstream journal in English devotes itself exclusively to pedagogical issues spanning the entire discipline. By contrast, *Pedagogy* covers all areas of English studies from literature and literary criticism to composition and cultural studies. It seeks to reverse the long history of the marginalization of teaching and of the scholarship produced around it. Fusing theoretical approaches and practical realities, *Pedagogy* is an essential resource for teachers.

Rhetorical and Pedagogical Interventions for Countering Microaggressions[1]

This article names microaggressions *as a rhetorical and pedagogical phenomenon*. To make the case for rhetorical and pedagogical intervention, Rasha Diab and Beth Godbee (1) define and trace microaggressions in literature from rhetoric, composition, and literacy studies; (2) share cross-disciplinary understandings of microaggressions; and (3) offer illustrations from sites of research, teaching, and service.

---

1. *Pedagogy: Critical Approaches to Teaching Literature, Language, Composition, and Culture*, vol. 19, no. 3, doi 10.1215/15314200-7615417 © 2019 by Duke University Press

Rhetorical and Pedagogical Interventions for Countering Microaggressions

Rasha Diab and Beth Godbee
With contributions by Cedric Burrows and Thomas Ferrel

In bringing critical attention to dynamic relationships, we open new pathways by which to gain rhetorical knowledge and understanding in more fully textured ways.

—Jacqueline Jones Royster

If the field views rhetoric and literacy as a means to social change, how do our choices—how we sponsor students and community members, participate in relevant rhetorics, and provide resources—position our discipline to address the most fundamental abuses of power?

—Ben Kuebrich

Responding to these calls for action, we write at a time of increased urgency to bring attention to dynamic relationships toward addressing the most fundamental abuses of power. Both relationships and power abuses are essential rhetorical and pedagogical matters that call on all of us, as communicators and educators, to respond. These abuses are enacted in everyday, seemingly small, yet cumulative and consequential acts, so responses must be, too.[1] Cross-disciplinary literature on micro-inequities (Rowe 1990) and microaggressions (e.g., Solórzano, Ceja, and Yosso 2000; Sue et al. 2007; Young 2010; Sue 2010; Kohli and Solórzano 2012; Nadal 2013) shows that everyday ways of being and interacting cumulate over time such that inequities compound like interest in a bank. This literature calls on us to address microaggressions, or "everyday exchanges that send denigrating messages to certain individuals because of their group membership" (Sue 2010: xvi). In such exchanges, we see great stakes. The damage exceeds individual harm when microaggressions "assail the self-esteem of recipients, produce anger and frustration, deplete psychic energy, lower feelings of subjective well-being and worthiness, produce physical health problems, [and] shorten life expectancy" (Sue 2010: 6). Cumulative impact is more insidious still, for microaggressions deny access, constrain agency, and tend to be subtle and unrecognized, undermining possibilities for equity and justice.

Pedagogical spaces inside and outside the classroom abound with microaggressions, and we are haunted by their impact. This article names microaggressions as a rhetorical and pedagogical phenomenon that is conspicuous in many pedagogical spaces. To make the case for rhetorical and pedagogical intervention, we begin by defining and tracing microaggressions (though not named as such) in the literature from rhetoric, composition, and literacy studies. From there, we share cross-disciplinary understandings of microaggressions, discussing three forms: microinsult, microassault, and microinvalidation. We apply this deeper understanding of microaggressions to three instantiations or illustrations of microaggressions in academic contexts. In the first illustration, we describe how epistemic injustice, or harm to persons as knowers (Fricker 2007), impacts undergraduate and graduate student writers as well as marginalized scholars. Educators can counter the various invalidations associated with epistemic injustice by affirming and upholding epistemic rights, or the rights to know, experience, and share with others (Godbee 2017). In the second illustration, we unpack damaging cultural scripts that not only naturalize and recycle microaggressions but also underwrite many of our encounters. These scripts appear in composition textbooks and underline the need to rewrite both the textbooks and the broader stories we tell about rhetoric and rhetors (Burrows 2016). In the third illustration, we identify microaggressions that educators face in their service activities, such as being discounted in meetings, and propose the intervention of a "critical pedagogy of service" (Ferrel 2017), which engages faculty in interrupting business as usual.

Together, these illustrations ask us to (re)consider microaggressions in our everyday lives. We focus on higher education as the space in which we spend much of our time in research, teaching, and service. To focus on these activities is not to say that microaggressions happen only within educational institutions but to say that we must look at all aspects of our lives, especially those that become familiar and second nature.

As coauthors, we are differently positioned in the world: two of us identify as women, two as men, all of us as cisgender; two of us as white, two as racialized in the United States (as black and brown); three of us with US nationality and one as an international scholar; and all of us as able-bodied, though in different body types and with different visible markers of identity. Together, these and other positionalities allow us to recognize, witness, experience, and perpetuate microaggressions differently. In addition to other positionalities (e.g., class, religion, ethnicity, and linguistic background), these locations in the world provide insights into and, conversely, limit recognition of varied microaggressions. And recognition is further constrained by the additional layer of western-centric (Euro-American) disciplinary training.

Certainly in an article of this length we can attend neither to all types of microaggression nor to the many intersectional identities. Instead, we affirm that our theoretical and analytical endeavors address how varied forms of oppression underwrite microaggressions, which hurt individuals and communities. Collectively, we can learn to better understand and respond with increasing awareness to the many microaggressions on and off campus. Toward this goal, we attend to cases that address sexism and racism while recognizing and affirming that additional attention and further research are needed into microaggressions related to many interlocking systems of oppression. With the hope of inspiring additional rhetorical and pedagogical investment in countering microaggressions, we turn next to discussions in writing studies to show the sometimes subtle, sometimes explicit, and always insidious nature of microaggressions.

Microaggressions and Rhetoric

Scholars in rhetoric, composition, and literacy studies have long invested in understanding violence and injustice, holding the space for thinking about what's now understood as everyday microaggressions. For example, the relation between violence and rhetoric is long and complicated, as evidenced in a recent forum on the violence of rhetoric (Engels 2013). For centuries, learned leaders, rhetoric scholars, and philosophers alike have grappled with rhetoric's potential to counter or retrench deceit, glibness, and power abuse in its varied forms. We think, for example, of Plato in the western rhetorical tradition, Confucius in the Chinese (Ding 2007), and Ptahhotep's wisdom literature in the ancient Egyptian tradition (Fox 1983). To illustrate, scholars of argumentation define rhetoric as an "other to violence" (e.g., Crosswhite 2013) and highlight the "duty to dialogue" as a prerequisite to countering the potential abuses of rhetoric (e.g., Perelman and Olbrechts-Tyteca 1969). Their work seeks to counter a recurring and consequential rhetorical phenomenon: rhetors have used language to manipulate others; to cause physical, symbolic, and other types of harm; and even to build armies and launch wars. As another example, Kenneth Burke (2006) describes how discourse has been used to conscript soldiers and reconstitute citizens to fight for the nation even when this meant turning against their compatriots. Similarly, scholars explicate how rhetorical misrepresentations have been used systematically to rally people behind policies that bar disenfranchised groups from access to education (e.g., Canagarajah 1999; Prendergast 2003) and health care (e.g., Scott 2003), among other matters. These works critique large-scale violence while helping us understand rhetoric's role in injustice.

A different and complementary line of scholarship looks at more immediate and interpersonal forms of violence while linking violence to institutional, cultural, and disciplinary dynamics. This line of scholarship is the most relevant to our exploration of microaggressions and helps us see why many scholars, especially scholars of color and scholars from marginalized groups, keep shedding light on *rhetorical violence*, which remains ever present. For example, in her 2012 Conference on College Composition and Communication (CCCC) chair's address, Malea Powell and other invited scholars offered reflective, testimonial accounts of what we would analyze as acts of microaggression in pedagogical spaces.[2]

As a case in point, Leon Kendall recounted:

> I remember once, during a job interview [the typical entry point for being a teacher], the well-meaning scholar who used me as a teachable moment, letting me know that while I studied Chicanas, using Chicana theory, that some of what these Chicanas were saying had been said by this theorist named Foucault. As if I was not using Foucault because I had not read any of his work and hadn't ever heard of him. (qtd. in Powell 2012: 395)

In this brief reference, Kendall reports how her choices as a scholar were invalidated. Assuming her ignorance and that Chicana theory is not of the same caliber, the interviewer, in a corrective (and we'd argue shaming) measure, references Foucault. Though Kendall does not name this as a microaggression, she explains that "what was lost on this scholar was the intentionality of my practice, the intentionality in citation, in making a lineage worth building upon," especially since this lineage "comes from a place that, as Cherrie Moraga writes, is emergent from the "physical realities of our lives" (395). What Kendall recounts here dovetails neatly with the crossdisciplinary scholarship on microaggressions, which shows that similar moments arise from such problematic assumptions.

A multitude of documented microaggressions, even if not named as such, abound in scholarship in rhetoric, composition, and literacy studies. Across studies informed by feminist, Indigenous, critical race, postcolonial, transnational, and queer scholarship, we see attention to documenting and explicating moments when someone's knowledge, expertise, voice, and intellectual pursuits are flattened if not totally erased. For example, in "When the First Voice You Hear Is Not Your Own," Jacqueline Jones Royster (1996: 30–31) layers three scenes that showcase how her voice and knowledge (and many others'), as well as the African American creative and intellectual histories, are absented—literally and symbolically:

> I have been compelled on too many occasions to count to sit as a well mannered Other, silently, in a state of tolerance that requires me to be as expressionless as I can manage, while colleagues who occupy a place of entitlement different from my own talk about the history and achievements of people from my ethnic group, or even about their perceptions of our struggles. I have been compelled to listen as they have comfortably claimed the authority to engage in the construction of knowledge and meaning about me and mine, without paying even a passing nod to the fact that sometimes a substantive version of that knowledge might already exist, or to how it might have already been constructed, or to the meanings that might have already been assigned that might make me quite impatient with gaps in their understanding of my community, or to the fact that I, or somebody within my ethnic group, might have an opinion about what they are doing. I have been compelled to listen to speakers, well-meaning though they may think they are, who signal to me rather clearly that subject position is everything. I have come to recognize, however, that when the subject matter is me and the voice is not mine, my sense of order and rightness is disrupted. In metaphoric fashion, these "authorities" let me know, once again, that Columbus has discovered America and claims it now, claims it still for a European crown.

Once again, the voices and interpretations of "these 'authorities'" are centered, earning them credit, while the voices, experiences, and expertise of Royster and others are invalidated, denying credit.

Such invalidating happens repeatedly. Like Royster, Victor Villanueva (2006) presents numerous representative moments of microaggressions in educational settings. These include interactions with his daughter'steacher, who responds to a disrespectful action by saying, "That might be okay in your culture but not in mine" (13), and a writing center consultation in which the tutor fails to address the author's writing off or excusal of racism in the movie *Crash*. Articulations of how rhetoric and rhetorical education recycle and entrench sexist, racist, classist, homophobic, and other microaggressions can be seen also in the work of Mike Rose (1989), Vershawn Ashanti Young (2010), Eric Pritchard (2013), Elaine Richardson (2013), and Aja Y. Martinez (2016), among others. These scholars recount moments when microaggressions undermined their and others' literacies, learning potential, humanity, and worth. Such moments happen all too frequently in educational settings and in related disciplinary spaces. Though many of these studies (like Kendall's case) foreground moments of microaggressions, those moments cumulate and take larger, systemic turns.

Presentation by presentation, article by article, book by book, microaggressions add up to an exclusionary and inequitable disciplinary landscape (Royster 2003). Royster describes how rhetorical landscapes have typically centered white, male, and elite rhetors and rhetoricians and the rhetorical traditions and practices they represent. Similarly, in *Bootstraps: From an American Academic of Color*, Villanueva (1993) traces how rhetorical education and histories deflect attention from nonwestern rhetorical traditions. This deflection, in turn, excludes peoples, traditions, regions, and centuries from rigorous exploration and results in a very limited view of what we see and count as rhetoric. Within this vicious circle, interpersonal acts of microaggression are informed by and result in macro-level acts of invalidation, which demand disciplinary intervention. The consequences of multilayered invalidations and absenting are addressed in numerous edited collections (e.g., Lipson and Binkley 2004, 2009; Richardson and Jackson 2004; Stromberg 2006; Mao and Young 2008; Baca and Villanueva 2009), anthologies (e.g., Logan 1995; Ritchie and Ronald 2001), and monographs (e.g., Royster 2000; Cushman 2012; Lathan 2015; Ramírez 2015; Carey 2016; Diab 2016; Pritchard 2016; Pandey forthcoming).

Across these works, microaggressions and their consequences are rhetorical phenomena. Microaggressions are mediated by rhetorical acts, assume many forms, are complex, evoke historical discourses, silence their recipients, and mandate a rhetorical response. Yet, this response is challenging for a variety of reasons. When considering an instance of microaggression as a rhetorical situation, it becomes incumbent on us to know its recurring features, how it demands responsivity (Sheridan 2014), and why interlocutors often feel that they have missed the communicative moment. We turn next, therefore, to defining and explaining microaggressions, believing that this cross-disciplinary (and primarily social science) research provides insights for rhetoricians and educators, while rhetoricians and educators have insights to share across disciplines as well.

Understanding Microaggressions

In *Microaggressions in Everyday Life*, psychologist Derald Wing Sue (2010: 5) defines microaggressions as "the brief and commonplace daily verbal, behavioral, and environmental indignities, whether intentional or unintentional, that communicate hostile, derogatory, or negative racial, gender, sexualorientation, and religious slights and insults to a target person or group."[3]

These indignities are acts of aggression that are often dismissed as small (i.e., microand everyday) and therefore inconsequential. What Sue's definition underlines is the complexity of microaggressions: they assume many forms, target people whose identities are marginalized or Othered, and manifest deep, structural, and societal problems like systemic racism and sexism. As we attempted to show in the literature reviewed above, microaggressions send hurtful, denigrating messages. Figure 1 provides the taxonomy that Sue and colleagues developed for racial microaggressions, which includes three forms: microinsult, microassault, and microinvalidation.

This taxonomy has since been used to explain relationships among forms of microaggressions as well as microaggressions faced by people based on other identities and group memberships. Examples include Kevin L. Nadal's (2013) research focused on gender and sexuality, as well as Mary Louise Gomez et al.'s (2011) work on student status. Across studies, microaggressions both reflect and further ingrain deeper cultural logics, those represented, for example, in the treatment of people as second-class citizens and in the perpetuation of the myth of meritocracy.

To illustrate, our text and talk can evidence assumed incompetence, criminality, or even objectification, resulting in microinsults, microassaults, or microinvalidations. Consider, for example, the statement: "You cannot have written this paper yourself. Who helped you?" Assumed incompetence is a form of microaggression that informs these assertions and makes them insulting, hurtful, accusatory, and pernicious, even when held unconsciously. The implied accusation operates on the basis of assumptions that Sue and colleagues label as "ascription of intelligence" and "pathologizing cultural values/communication styles" (see fig. 1). Such assumptions similarly show up in "compliments" or "positive" articulations for being "articulate," "eloquent," or "a good speaker." Consider statements like "You are a credit to your race" and "You sound well educated" (Sue 2010: 32). These surface compliments are made possible because the opposite is assumed typical and true (i.e., people who look like me aren't typically articulate or intelligent, so I stand out as exceptional and praiseworthy). Regardless of packaging (e.g., praise or doubt, compliment or criticism, overt hindrance or on-the-surface helping), microaggressions do violence. And they do this violence in the form of language, as rhetoric, and within pedagogical settings. Especially when they are unnamed or un(der)recognized as violence (as is typically the case), microaggressions are perniciously impactful to individuals and communities alike. Sociologist Joe R. Feagin (1992: 549) alerts us to "cumulative discrimination" as cumulative violence.[4] Cumulative violence is debilitating. Microaggressions have been shown to have far-reaching negative outcomes, from lowered self-confidence to depleted energy, heightening harm not only to individuals' physical or psychological well-being but also to the economy, local/national communities, and international relations. Such negative outcomes impact all of us as communicators, as they entrench wider injustice and inequities.

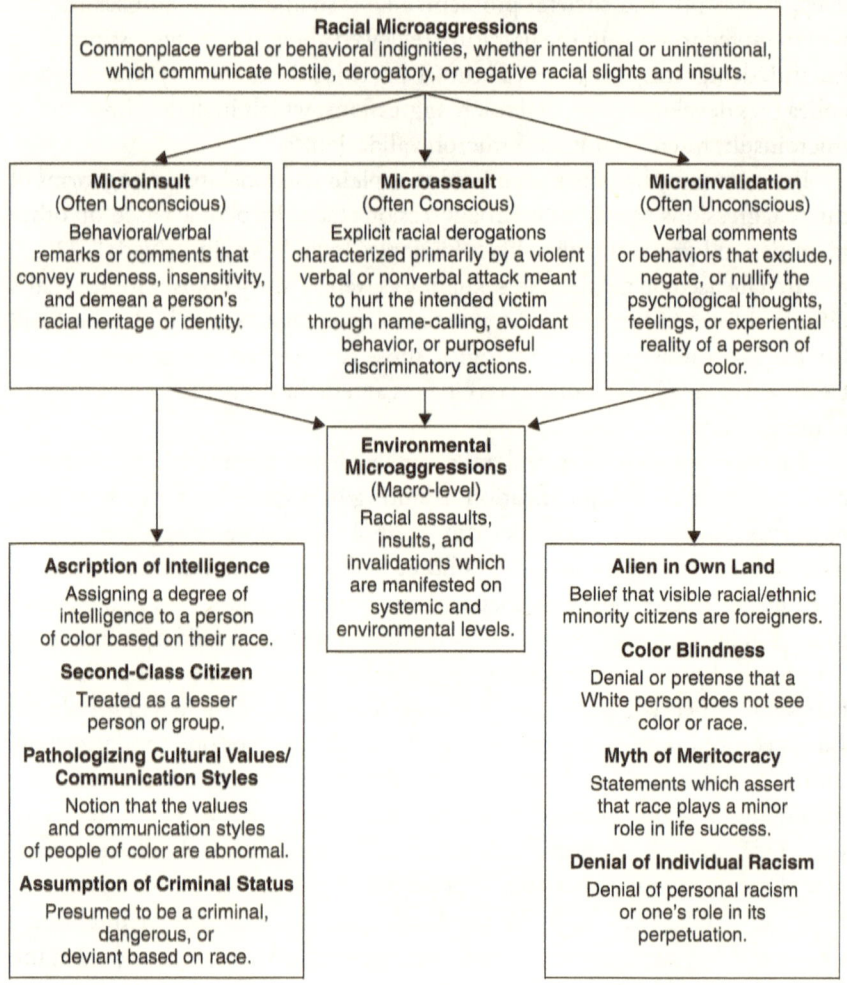

Figure 1. Categories and relationships among microaggressions. Adapted from Derald Wing Sue, Christina M. Capodilupo, Gina C. Torino, Jennifer M. Bucceri, Aisha M. B. Holder, Kevin L. Nadal, and Marta Esquilin, "Racial Microaggressions in Everyday Life: Implications for Clinical Practice," American Psychologist 62, no. 4 (2007): 278. APA is not responsible for the accuracy of this reproduction.

Certainly, all three forms of microaggressions have negative outcomes, but in this article we focus on just two: microinsults and microinvalidations. These two forms are typically implicit, invisible to perpetrators, and interwoven into everyday patterns of life, leaving us unsure or unable to act.[5] Because microaggressions are subtle, they are often difficult to document: "The subtle nature of microaggressions makes it easy to doubt their existence or to dismiss them as innocuous, which contributes to their power" (McCabe 2009: 142). Documenting microaggressions has become a public political project, as we see through the Tumblr/Twitter project @microaggressive (n.d.) and recent news stories (see, e.g., De Witte 2016; Ganote, Cheung, and Souza n.d.; Garcia and Crandall 2016). Without a record to cite as evidence, response to individual microaggressions can feel pointless. These records help make the case that microaggressions—particularly microinsults and microinvalidations—impact graduate students and faculty of color. These records ask those of us in academic spaces to consider whether we recognize violence when we see it, especially when it's packaged as a microinsult or microinvalidation.

We believe that rhetoricians are especially well positioned to name and explain the rhetorical dynamics of microaggressions—to explicate the rhetorical literacies needed to break dysfunctional lack of response. Rhetoricians are particularly well suited to explain what happens in communicative moments—in interactions, utterances, and texts—in which microaggressions occur. Rhetoricians are also trained to read scenes and to imagine (even propose) alternative responses toward alternative ends. Thus, rhetorical education can—should—take up the work of understanding and intervening into microaggressions. We perceive this education to exceed single moments or classroom spaces and to include our disciplinary knowledge, identities, and passing interactions as relevant areas of the reflection-theory-practice cycle. Because we draw on an expanded definition of *pedagogy*, we also imagine expansive interventions that include relations, identities, activities, programs, and other matters that directly and indirectly impact, shape, support, or undermine pedagogical praxis. Though we can't illustrate the many expansive interventions, we spend the remainder of this article with three cases, illustrating where and how we can begin to intervene as educators.

Illustration 1: Countering Microinvalidations by Affirming Epistemic Rights

Given the pervasiveness of microaggressions in everyday life, it is no surprise that they similarly shape writing activities, especially complicating one's rights to speak, write, conduct research, and share expertise. In particular, microinvalidations can undercut people as knowers—a type of wrongdoing that philosopher Miranda Fricker (2007) describes as "epistemic injustice." In

Fricker's words, epistemic injustice hurts "someone specifically in their capacity as a knower" (1). When microinvalidations undermine people as knowers, they also undermine full personhood, which includes having one's experiences acknowledged by others, being able to construct new knowledge, and being able to contribute as a knowledgeable agent within one's community.

Acts of Microaggression: Epistemic Injustice

In academic settings, microinvalidations and microinsults can manifest when someone is assumed less intelligent (ascription of intelligence) or their communicative practices are assumed abnormal (pathologizing cultural values/ communication styles) (see fig. 1). As such, microaggressions undermine or discredit writers (undergraduate and graduate students and faculty) as well as limit what is known and knowable—that is, what questions can be asked, what experiences are deemed worth knowing, and what knowledge counts as intellectual currency. The edited collection *Presumed Incompetent* (Gutiérrez y Muhs, Neimann, González, and Harris 2012) shows that widespread epistemic injustice occurs within higher education, especially for women of color, who are frequently, even typically, presumed incompetent by colleagues, students, administrators, and others. This presumption arises in interactions and often around writing and other communication, resulting in the invisibility of one's presence, perspectives, and lived experience. Presumed incompetence impacts one's entire career: in academic contexts, as Angela P. Harris and Carmen G. González (2012: 4) note, "reputation is the coin of the realm, and reputations are built not only by objective accomplishments but through images and sometimes outright fantasies—individual or collective— that cling to the nature of the work and the person being evaluated." As Harris and González and other authors in *Presumed Incompetent* illustrate, judgments about research need, value, and contributions "are especially susceptible to unconscious bias" (4), and because of bias, microinvalidations happen commonly (not exceptionally) within higher education.

Take this example of epistemic injustice—the experience of being "presumed incompetent"—that we recorded from years of documenting (collaboratively sharing and writing with colleagues) microaggressive moments in writing centers:

> A PhD student in education is "sent" to the writing center by her faculty adviser after failing her first attempt at comprehensive exams. She has been told that her writing is not "graduate level" and not "academic" enough. She comes in devastated. She says that her 20+ years of teaching in a major metropolitan city school system and her intimate knowledge of culturally relevant curriculum are worth

nothing in her department, and she feels acutely isolated and misunderstood (if not worse) as the only woman and only person of color in her program. She has also been accused of plagiarizing a complicated diagram in one of her exam papers. After the faculty member who refused to pass her exam learned that she created the diagram herself by integrating several commonly used diagrams into one, he wants to use her work in a textbook he's writing.

In this example, we see ascription of intelligence. Deficit thinking results in significant material consequences when the only student of color in this graduate program fails her prelim exam because she is assumed not capable of creating high-quality work. Not only is the writer tokenized and assumed inferior within her program, but she also undergoes excessive scrutiny, has to work harder than peers to gain professional recognition and respect, and lacks the professional support of her faculty adviser. Adding insult to injury, the faculty member wants to reproduce her diagram—that is, to earn credit and the related academic currency for publishing her work. This scenario exemplifies the typical move of microinvalidation caused by presumed deficit: the writer (and their intellectual capacities) is diminished, while the adviser, who arbitrates the value of the work and can use it for their own personal gain, benefits.

Microinvalidations like these occur far too often when graduate students negotiate projects with advisers, candidates face hiring committees, faculty are reviewed for tenure and promotion, and researchers submit their work for publication. How often do microinvalidations impact professional possibilities or have professional consequences like those Kendall faced during her job search? How often are authors asked to cite Foucault rather than Anzaldúa or other Chicana scholars for the lineage of their knowledge claims? Judgments about the worthiness of a project reflect/are shaped by the larger disciplinary landscaping (Royster 2003), which we know to be exclusionary and marginalizing. At the same time, these judgments add up to disciplinary norms, constructing the larger landscape. Facing an assumed epistemic deficit, therefore, has far-reaching consequences not only for individual scholars but also for the perpetuation of institutions, disciplines, and higher education as white, male, and elite endeavors.

Rhetorical Intervention: Affirming Epistemic Rights

To counter this sort of epistemic injustice, we must name and unpack the relationships among microinvalidations and linguistic and other forms of prejudice. Within rhetoric, composition, and literacy studies, we have an ever-growing body of literature that advocates for writers' linguistic and cultural rights and, in doing so, addresses the microinvalidation of pathologizing cultural values/communication styles. Such scholarship has led to numerous position statements, including the CCCC's "Students' Right to Their Own Language (SRTOL)" ([1974] 2006) and "Statement on Ebonics" ([1998] 2016). These statements and the policies and practices they advocate for are important starting points for rhetorical intervention.

Building on this language of rights, we can do more to develop an understanding of epistemic rights, or rights to knowledge, experience, and earned expertise (Godbee 2017). During interactions and as a counter to epistemic injustice, educators can affirm marginalized writers' rights to speak from/about experience, to contribute new knowledge, and to share expertise. Rather than undercut and invalidate marginalized writers, we must invest in affirming writers' many rights. Ongoing, persistent validation may be the best antidote to microinvalidation, if/when marginalized colleagues and our/their scholarship are advocated for, read widely, and responded to with mindful reflexivity.

Illustration 2: Recognizing and Rewriting Microaggressions in First-Year Composition—Textbooks

Microaggressions manifest not only through interactions around and judgments made about students' and colleagues' writing but also through the writing we bring into classrooms and ask students to read. We have unpacked deficit thinking and presumed incompetence facing writers and their writing, and we turn now to an analysis of textbooks to show how they enact microaggressions through coded, racially charged language that treats marginalized writers' works as oddities. We show how authors of color and other marginalized writers are limited in the issues they are allowed to address and must defend their views on race and racism, even though they are recipients of direct, cultural, and institutional racism. Looking at the selection, placement, and editorial framing of works by authors of color, we trace microaggressions across four composition textbooks: *Rereading America* (Colombo, Cullen, and Lisle 2007), *The Conscious Reader* (Shrodes et al. 2009), *The Bedford Reader* (Kennedy, Kennedy, and Aaron 2010), and *A World of Ideas* (Jacobus 2010). Reading textbooks as rhetorical documents that are responsive to culture and condition us for particular uptakes, we revisit these four examples, which are not exceptional but rather representative of pervasive cultural scripts replicated across textbooks in our field (Burrows 2016). Textbooks shape countless interactions in classrooms, teacher-student conferences, and student conversational space. Through reading, discussing, sharing, and other activities that take place around textbooks, microaggressions further compound into wide-reaching pedagogical implications.

Acts of Microaggression: Selection, Placement, and Editorial Framing

Read as rhetorical documents, textbooks can be analyzed for the placement of racially coded language as well as the arrangement of selected texts. To begin, arrangement creates a series of microaggressions when all authors of color are lumped into one theme or category, such as in *The Bedford Reader*'s section on "the minority experience" (Kennedy, Kennedy, and Aaron 2010: xxxiii). The phrase and category "minority experience" is microaggressive: it creates a binary of whites versus every racialized group of color and perpetuates a narrative of the white experience as "majority," even when factually inaccurate (i.e., already in some states, including Texas and California, the population of people of color has surpassed the white population). Additionally, grouping every racialized group under "minority experience" fails to recognize diversity. More important, *minority* is a problematic term because it connotes that people of color are a minor part of US culture: the white male author continues to hold the "universal" voice that is tacitly understood as the authoritative figure, while the author of color is considered minor or insignificant. As the "majority" (i.e., white) experience is centered, all others are invalidated and pushed aside.

This compartmentalization of marginalized groups extends to how the editors define "good writing" through coded language. According to its editor, *A World of Ideas* (Jacobus 2010: v) includes selections of "highest quality" because they clarify "important ideas" while "sustaining[ing] discussion and stimulat[ing] good writing," meaning that students should generate good writing from reading "the great works." Among the forty-seven selections are works by Niccolo Machiavelli, Virginia Woolf, Plato, Karl Marx, Henry David Thoreau, and Carl Jung—thinkers who, the editor believes, created "ideas that shaped generations." The selections seem to be informed by a tacit script: because Plato and Thoreau are "serious and important," students will take the writing course more seriously and will learn to "read more attentively, think more critically, and write more effectively" (vi). This script undermines writers of color, including Martin Luther King Jr. and Frederick Douglass, who are tacitly deemed not "serious." The textbook reinforces deeply problematic ideas about white, male, western, elite authors as "the greats" (see Royster 2003), writing into the textbook a multitude of microaggressions that invalidate writings by people of color and other marginalized writers.

Similarly, *The Conscious Reader* (Shrodes et al. 2009) encourages students to develop self-awareness and broaden worldviews; accordingly, the editors caution students not to dismiss a worldview different from their own, especially one that is considered "weird" or "offensive" (23). Words like *weird* and *offensive* indicate that writings by scholars of color and other marginalized people are exotic and entertaining, if not wrong. The implication is that their voices and insights are relevant only for members of their own racial group. In short, the editors' comments undercut the few selections of writers of color, leading readers to dismiss or at least downplay their work. Again, editorial coded language highlights the textbooks' focus on making the white male's voice universal (i.e., normative, not weird; compelling, not offensive). In short, the editors' comments undercut the few selections of writers of color, leading readers to dismiss or at least downplay their work.

Representations of the white, male, elite voice as universal are additionally apparent through microaggressive language that limits how and what marginalized writers can discuss. To illustrate, the textbooks reviewed tended to ghettoize marginalized groups (e.g., women, people of color, Indigenous peoples, nonwestern peoples, LGBTQ folks, poor people) according to specific topics, such as racism and sexism, matters that could be considered "special interest," whereas others are treated as "universal." African American authors in *The Bedford Reader* (e.g., Maya Angelou, Brent Staples, Alice Walker, Gloria Naylor) focus on racism; Latin@ authors (e.g., Sandra Cisneros and Richard Rodriguez) speak to immigration issues; and the majority of Asian and/or Asian American writers (e.g., Maxine Hong Kingston and Yiyun Li) address assimilation. While there is nothing wrong with including writings that reflect an author's background, the trouble occurs when marginalized authors speak about only a few focused topics, while white male writers discuss a wide range of topics from world affairs, finance, and politics to questions of philosophy, human existence, and happiness. To illustrate further, in a section like "Cultural Diversity, Communication, and Community," authors of color are the majority, while in "Childhood and Family," the majority of the writers are women. This compartmentalization conditions students to believe that white men can speak about anything, while marginalized authors are further marginalized to singularly write their experiences with oppression.

Microaggressions appear also in the texts selected from marginalized writers. For African Americans, the most anthologized authors are Martin Luther King Jr., Malcolm X, and Frederick Douglass. King is usually represented by "Letter from Birmingham Jail" and "I Have a Dream." Malcolm X is represented by the stories of when he reads in prison or straightens his hair. Frederick Douglass is represented by his narrative of learning to read with help from his mistress and later his white playmates. The effect is that all of these selections relate personal encounters with racism while backgrounding the cultural and institutional racism that is at the heart of the narratives. Selected texts could highlight the importance of marginalized communities reclaiming voice and speaking out against oppression; instead, the ones selected are framed to illustrate only personal narratives and are devoid of any mention of how institutional racism is a factor in their writings. To illustrate, textbook editors commonly retitle Malcolm X's "Saved" as "Learning to Read," invalidating and stripping away the deeply political and spiritual meanings of the text and treating it as a simple literacy narrative. Further, by anthologizing the same three authors as spokespersons for their race, textbooks reduce the diversity of authors, leaving students to imagine that only a few people of color have successfully written, and they did so in the past (at pivotal historical moments). As a result, these textbooks perpetuate narratives of exceptionalism and tokenism. What is more pernicious is that white audiences can easily believe that racism has been conquered, and there is no need for contemporary voices that call for equity and justice.

These microaggressions continue with the discussion questions. Across composition textbooks, discussion questions put the onus of racism or discrimination on the marginalized group, treating racism as an individual (not systemic) problem and thus excusing people with privilege from complicity. To illustrate, *Rereading America* (Colombo, Cullen, and Lisle 2007) reiterates the trope of the angry black man while not investigating how whiteness contributed to his anger and therefore obfuscates the question of racial justice. For instance, the textbook does not ask students to think about how whiteness constructed Malcolm X's language; instead, it makes Malcolm X the victim whose views have to be justified or defended: "Some readers are offended by the strength of Malcolm X's accusations and by his grouping of all members of a given race into 'collectives.' Given the history of racial injustice he recounts here, do you feel he is justified in taking such a position?" (251). Malcolm X's words are the ones critiqued instead of the "invisible" whiteness and injustices targeting African Americans. As a result, students risk seeing racialized bodies as unnecessary, angry critics of racism while never having to research how institutions that uphold whiteness make racialized bodies critical of those institutions. Taken together with the deeply problematic selection, placement, and editorial framing of marginalized writers, these discussion questions perpetuate microaggressions, further entrenching larger injustices.

Rhetorical Intervention: Recognizing and Rewriting Damaging Cultural Scripts

Analysis of composition textbooks (the surface of which is barely scratched here) necessitates an immediate and strong response if we are to counter the harms that so casually enter the classroom along with these textbooks. Educators, students, editors, and publishers alike need first to recognize educational materials as rhetorical texts that can convey damaging cultural scripts. These scripts authorize racial coding and other microaggressive acts that move outward, beyond the pages of textbooks, and therefore mandate interrogation. Next, educators, students, editors, and publishers alike need to rewrite these damaging scripts—both in the textbooks and beyond. In doing so, we challenge how society writes about and writes off (i.e., invalidates) people of color and other marginalized peoples. We must all be involved in questioning and revising notions of who is allowed to speak in the public sphere—and about what, when, and to what ends. For example, we can position more diverse voices from marginalized groups throughout textbooks, highlighting intersectional identities and recognizing the diversity of voices within communities of color. These voices would show that conversations about race are grounded in both historical and current cultural moments and are still ongoing and evolving. We need, too, to include writings by women, people of color, LGBTQ+ folks, and other marginalized peoples, not as marked but as part of multiple traditions, so that there is no default standard of who is allowed to address particular issues.

The rhetorical work of rewriting composition textbooks highlights the need for and urgency of ongoing rhetorical interventions to counter microaggressions in/through teaching. This work calls on all of us to create accountability systems that truly embrace this critique of damaging cultural scripts and to recognize the humanity of all people. Such rewriting could bring publishers and editors into dialogue with people from marginalized communities about how their peoples are portrayed in textbooks. And it necessitates conversations in and out of classrooms, among teachers and students to reflect critically on any texts or textbooks in use. Certainly, this work connects with other sorts of rewriting, revising, and re-seeing needed across our disciplinary practices and lives, as we show next by zooming in on faculty service.

ILLUSTRATION 3: INTERVENING THROUGH A CRITICAL PEDAGOGY OF SERVICE

In this section, we expand *pedagogy* to go beyond teacher-student interactions and educational materials to consider service. Typically, service is seen as an "amorphous category" that entails "an almost endless number of campus activities—sitting on committees, advising student clubs, or performing departmental chores" (Boyer 1990: 22). As "departmental chores," these and other service activities are undervalued and even viewed as getting in the way of more important work. Yet, service encompasses numerous rhetorical interactions with far-reaching consequences, shaping not only pedagogical decisions but also larger institutional cultures and cultural scripts. Some of the most obvious involve the allocation of faculty and staff time, the contours of the curriculum, and the reach of student support services. Think about the ramifications of hiring, promotion, budgeting, policy making, program review, community engagement, and many other types of leadership. Service has the potential to build or tear down, to inspire or frustrate, to alleviate or cause pain in the pedagogical spaces where we work inside and outside classrooms. Like the production and reception of writing and the use of composition textbooks illustrated above, service is a site of everyday microaggressions, which arise repeatedly: from disembodied online exchanges through listservs and email threads to decision making in committee meetings and behind closed doors. It mandates, therefore, a savvy rhetorical response.

Acts of Microaggression: Service Contexts

To find evidence of microaggressions in service, we can look at our published literature, which includes varied testimonial narratives. In *Bootstraps*, Villanueva (1993) does not just document a personal story of microaggressions involving epistemic injustice, presumed incompetence, and damaging cultural scripts. Villanueva also shows how microaggressions have larger programmatic and curricular ramifications, including an entire curriculum being undermined and written off. The following excerpt comes from a larger story in which Villanueva describes multiyear work on trying to save and make meaningful a basic-writing program:

> Victor convinces the higher administration that the basic-writing program is a cultural education, not remediation. The program survives, eventually acquiring a regular, permanent administrator.
>
> But while Victor was still there, there was still the disgruntled and the irate to contend with. He prepares a memo that quotes Louis Faraq'an, a naive move.
>
> The memo notes that Faraq'an defines black power as the ability for black people to come to the table with their own food. The point is to have teachers stop proffering academic charity, no matter how well intentioned. Victor knows the pain of charity.

> He returns to find a memo announcing his replacement for the coming academic year. He had not been consulted. The rationale was that he would surely get a job.
>
> But he remembered the teachers' argument in that television show. He had gone too far. (94)

This narrative shows how microaggressions arise from closed-door decision making, from people being invalidated and seen as expendable, and from efforts to keep the status quo. When microaggressions arise within service contexts, careers are sidetracked if not railroaded; people's contributions are diminished if not destroyed; institutions are made inhospitable if not outright hostile to research and pedagogical initiatives like basic writing, multi- and translingual writing, and cultural studies.

We see in this example that a personnel decision (one that could be read as simply im2lso broader disciplinary landscapes:

> The chair of a national organization on composition studies, an African American woman that year, gives Dr. V a call. She calls to warn him that his candidacy for a committee position has been questioned—to her—on the grounds that the sevenseat committee already has three minorities on it. The committee threatened to have representation rather than tokenism. The committee's charge is to review and comment on manuscripts submitted for publication. He reads like never before, more careful than ever before, at pains to demonstrate his thorough understanding of rhetoric, composition, literacy, philosophy—his competence despite his color. (119)

Here again, microaggressions are much more than micro, much more than a personal story or a single occurrence. Instead, we see how the rhetoric of invalidation creates narratives that reverberate outward: from one comment to inequitable work patterns when the work of disproving invalidation demands never-ending thoroughness to prove "competence despite . . . color." The rhetoric used to question one's candidacy and then the subsequent time and energy that goes into disproving that rhetoric show how microaggressions represent "the everyday reality of slights, insults, invalidations, and indignities" (Sue 2010: xv) in academic spaces. By documenting his experience, Villanueva underlines not only how microaggressive rhetoric perpetuates inequitable work patterns but also how those patterns result in different (differently consequential) conditions in the lives of educators. This microaggressive rhetoric has rippling impact not only on potential, current, and future committee members but also on larger disciplinary participation and leadership.

The examples from Villanueva's *Bootstraps* illuminate how research, teaching, and service collectively and similarly support or constrain pedagogical spaces, as we continue to see in our own service activities. For example, we see diversity initiatives implemented as token gestures (e.g., Milem, Chang, and Antonio 2005), scholarship by faculty of color being overlooked/invisible despite our recognition of the politics of citation (e.g., hooks 2003; Gutiérrez y Muhs, Neimann, González, and Harris 2012), and faculty of color being asked/expected to perform more than their fair share of service (e.g., Gloria 1998; Harris and González 2012). Such microaggressions become normalized because they are so casual, so common, so everyday, all the while seemingly unconnected. Yet, as we've tried to establish throughout this article, they are consequential. How will we respond, as rhetoricians and educators, who are also committee members, program administrators, and professional leaders?

Rhetorical Intervention: Adopting a Critical Pedagogy of Service

To intervene into microaggressions, we must ask when, where, how, why, to whom, and for whose benefit they occur. Such rhetorical inquiry reminds us of the goals of critical pedagogy, which include developing critical consciousness and using critical literacy skills to transform institutions (e.g., Horton 1990; Freire [1970] 2000). Just as critical pedagogy aims to address oppression and enact justice, so too might we conceive of a critical pedagogy of service that works for change within programs, departments, colleges, universities, professional organizations, community settings, and other local and (inter)national networks (Ferrel 2017). A critical pedagogy of service aligns with a rhetoric of responsivity, which asks us to develop and use our response-abilities (e.g., Sheridan 2014). To enact a critical pedagogy of service, we need to build consciousness that reveals how universities and other institutions work: how they oppress marginalized peoples, deny agency and personhood for some, and entrench power and privileges for others.

We have opportunities to rhetorically intervene into inequitable conditions whenever we lead programs, revise curriculum, amend departmental policies, allocate funds, construct strategic plans, and do countless other activities identified as service. To intervene, we must remember that institutions and individuals are not separate but one and the same. James Porter et al. (2000: 611) address the interconnectedness of individuals and institutions, locating the feasibility of institutional change in people: "Though institutions are certainly powerful, they are not monoliths; they are rhetorically constructed human designs (whose power is reinforced by buildings, laws, traditions, and knowledge-making practices) and so are changeable. In other words, we made 'em, we can fix 'em. Institutions R Us." Truly acting as though "Institutions R Us" invites a different sort of agency, ownership, participation, and leadership in service: all can help us rethink praxis in terms of creating and sustaining pedagogical initiatives and teachers/leaders committed to justice. This differently agentive rhetorical stance, we hope, allows us all to see and intervene into everyday microaggressions, as we actualize a critical pedagogy of service.

A Call for Rhetorical Intervention

Returning to the opening epigraphs, we find calls to address abuses of power, and we respond by calling attention to microaggressions—an all-too-frequent occurrence that necessitates response. We see public recognition of microaggressions daily, as we open news feeds to read about the latest swastika drawn on a school building, the latest incident of bullying or hate speech at one of our campuses, the latest institutional response that falls flat, calling for "unity" without addressing deep hurts. As we hope the three illustrations show, microaggressions run deep, impacting multiple pedagogical spaces and all facets of our teaching/learning lives. The three illustrations underline the need for rhetorical intervention, for an approach to invest rhetorically in lifegiving rather than life-denying speech and writing. In the first illustration, such an intervention invites us to rethink what Rochelle Harris (2004: 409) refers to as "pedagogy of response." Truly, our pedagogies must consider how we respond to writers, doing more to give feedback that affirms writers' rights and counters epistemic injustice. In the second illustration, we see the need for critical reading and rewriting of textbooks to reverse the racially coded language embedded in pedagogical materials. In the third illustration, a call emerges for educators to enact a critical pedagogy of service, an intentional approach to institutional leadership. Reminding us that "Institutions R Us," Porter et al. (2000) invite us to reconsider our rhetorical agency in spaces seemingly unrelated to our pedagogical practices. Together, these interventions add up to the need for rhetorical interventions to countering microaggressions.

As rhetoricians and educators, we spend much of our lives devoted to the activities of research, teaching, and service, which inform the learning environments we cocreate. Within these activities, we have daily the potential to enact or, alternatively, to resist microaggressions. We have daily the potential to keep things as they are or, alternatively, to disrupt the status quo and create a different set of relations. We have daily the choice of whether to acknowledge microaggressions as a problem to be reckoned with. Will we choose to invest our energies toward creating a more just world? Will we choose to consider the *micro*(microaggressions) alongside the macro-logics that generate and fuel aggression or its inverse: affiliation, solidarity, collective action, and social justice?

Returning to the opening epigraphs, we find disciplinary mandates that call on all of us to reflect on how our disciplinary choices position us to sponsor particular narratives, recognize particular rhetorics, provide particular resources, and so on. Taking up Ben Kuebrich's (2015: 568–69) question, we ask: "How do our choices . . . position our discipline to address the most fundamental abuses of power" in the macro as well as the micro? As rhetoricians and educators, we value creative invention as a path to intervention, believing that we must "be adventurous enough in our thinking to take a different path, to find a different viewpoint, and to critique the terms of engagement" (Royster 2003: 161). In resetting terms of engagement, we are guided by Kuebrich's and Royster's powerful critiques and by the many rhetoricians mapping rhetorical literacies that counter violence and strive for justice. May our call for rhetorical intervention contribute to this work, and may we commit to the ongoing, everyday work of countering microaggressions.

Notes

We'd like to thank the editors, anonymous reviewers, and participants in our studies as well as Jacqueline Jones Royster, who encouraged us and offered insightful feedback as we shared several drafts. We also acknowledge Marquette University's Center for Peacemaking for providing financial support and for holding the space for us to share early versions of this work.

1. We attempt here to take a "self-reflexive look at our roles as rhetoricians," as Ellen Cushman (1996: 8) attempted to do and modeled for us. For Cushman, a self-reflexive look involves "turn[ing] our work as scholars inside out, upside down, and back in upon itself" (8) toward necessary re-seeing of what's often unseen. We similarly hope to call attention to what's normalized in our everyday lives. In doing so, we rethink our roles and responsibilities to intervene into everyday violence, injustice, and microaggressions, rhetorically and pedagogically.

2. We find microaggression after microaggression recounted in Powell's collaborative address, so we offer this text as a starting point for readers interested in seeing the range and impact of everyday violence. Powell frames these microaggressions within and speaks to the long reach of colonial legacies as related to national memory/ forgetting; sovereignty and political subjecthood; and the meaning and significance of land, belonging, and self to Indigenous communities.

3. Certainly people also face microaggressions through other group memberships (e.g., socioeconomic class, nationality, and language background). It is equally

important to recognize intersectionality (Crenshaw 1991)—that is, multiple and interlocking identities that, at the same time, influence social interactions and through which microaggressions and other forms of violence may compound, resulting in double or triple jeopardy.

4. Feagin (1992) studies how manifestations of racism morph, sheds light on a continuum of hostile acts, and explicates how hostile acts cumulate and exceed the negative impact of any one instance. Hostile acts comprise "(a) aggression, verbal and physical; (b) exclusion, including social ostracism; (c) dismissal of subculture, including values, dress, and groups; (d) type-casting, including assuming Blacks are all alike" (574). Feagin explains cumulative discrimination as not "just the occasional or isolated discriminatory act in one of the enumerated categories . . . but rather a college career or lifetime series of blatant and subtle acts of differential treatment by Whites, which often cumulates to a severely oppressive impact" (575).

5. Among other scholars, Julie Minikel-Lacocque (2013: 454) has questioned whether microassaults should be considered part of the microaggressions taxonomy, as they are the most overt, explicit, and often intentional. Even Sue et al. (2007: 274) describe microassaults as the most like "old-fashioned racism," referencing highly visible acts like intimidation, racial slurs, and physical violence. Similarly, Gina A. Garcia and Marc P. Johnston-Guerrero (2015) found in their study of racially biased campus incidents that microassaults are intentional and therefore unlike microinsults and microinvalidations. All of this led Gina A. Garcia and Jennifer R. Crandall (2016) to focus on just the two forms of microinsults and microinvalidations. Similarly, we focus on these forms of microaggressions, as they illustrate the everyday, communicative, rhetorical work of enacting or, alternatively, countering microaggressions.

Works Cited

Baca, Damián, and Victor Villanueva, eds. 2009. *Rhetorics of the Americas: 3114 BCE to 2012 CE*. New York: Palgrave Macmillan.

Boyer, Ernest L. 1990. *Scholarship Reconsidered: Priorities of the Professoriate*. Princeton, NJ: Carnegie Foundation for the Advancement of Teaching.

Burke, Kenneth. 2006. "The Rhetoric of Hitler's Battle." In *Readings in Propaganda and Persuasion: New and Classic Essays*, edited by Garth S. Jowett and Victoria O'Donnell, 149–68. Thousand Oaks, CA: Sage.

Burrows, Cedric. 2016. "The Yardstick of Whiteness in Composition Textbooks." *WPA: Writing Program Administration* 39, no. 2: 42–46.

Canagarajah, A. Suresh. 1999. *Resisting Linguistic Imperialism in English Teaching*. New York: Oxford University Press.

Carey, Tamika L. 2016. *Rhetorical Healing: The Reeducation of Contemporary Black Womanhood*. Albany: State University of New York Press.

Colombo, Gary, Robert Cullen, and Bonnie Lisle, eds. 2007. *Rereading America: Cultural Context for Critical Thinking and Writing*. 7th ed. Boston: Bedford/St. Martin's.

Conference on College Composition and Composition. (1974) 2006. "Students' Right to Their Own Language (SRTOL)." www2.ncte.org/statement/affirmingstudents/.

Conference on College Composition and Composition. (1998) 2016. "Statement on Ebonics." www.ncte.org/cccc/resources/positions/ebonics.

Crenshaw, Kimberlé W. 1991. "Mapping the Margins: Intersectionality, Identity Politics, and Violence against Women of Color." *Stanford Law Review* 43, no. 6: 1241–99.

Crosswhite, James. 2013. *Deep Rhetoric: Philosophy, Reason, Violence, Justice, Wisdom*. Chicago: University of Chicago Press.

Cushman, Ellen. 1996. "The Rhetorician as an Agent of Social Change." *College Composition and Communication* 47, no. 1: 7–28.

Cushman, Ellen. 2012. *The Cherokee Syllabary: Writing the People's Perseverance*. Norman: University of Oklahoma Press.

De Witte, Melissa. 2016. "Initial Findings to Be Released in Study of Microaggressions on Campus." University of California, Santa Cruz's NewsCenter, 24 October. news.ucsc.edu/2016/10/byrd-microaggressions.html.

Diab, Rasha. 2016. *Shades of Sulh: The Rhetorics of Arab-Islamic Reconciliation*. Pittsburgh: Pittsburgh University Press.

Ding, Huiling. 2007. "Confucius's Virtue-Centered Rhetoric: A Case Study of Mixed Research Methods in Comparative Rhetoric." *Rhetoric Review* 26, no. 2: 142–59.

Engels, Jeremy D., ed. 2013. "Forum on the Violence of Rhetoric." Special issue of the *Quarterly Journal of Speech* 99, no. 2: 180–232.

Feagin, Joe R. 1992. "The Continuing Significance of Racism: Discrimination against Black Students in White Colleges." *Journal of Black Studies* 22, no. 4: 546–78.

Ferrel, Thomas Robert. 2017. "Possibility and Process in Post Secondary Service Work: Constructing a Critical Pedagogy of Service." PhD diss., University of Missouri–Kansas City.

Fox, Michael V. 1983. "Ancient Egyptian Rhetoric." *Rhetorica* 1, no. 1: 9–22. Freire, Paulo. (1970) 2000. *Pedagogy of the Oppressed*. New York: Continuum.

Fricker, Miranda. 2007. *Epistemic Injustice: Power and the Ethics of Knowing*. New York: Oxford University Press.

Ganote, Cynthia, Floyd Cheung, and Tasha Souza. n.d. "Micro-aggressions, Microresistances, and Ally Development in the Academy." Recorded webinar, National Center for Faculty Development and Diversity. www.facultydiversity.org/support (accessed 21 May 2019).

Garcia, Gina A., and Jennifer R. Crandall. 2016. "'Am I Overreacting?' Understanding and Combatting Microaggressions." *Higher Education Today*, 27 July. higheredtoday. org/2016/07/27/understanding-and-combatting-microaggressions-in-postsecondary-education/.

Garcia, Gina A., and Marc P. Johnston-Guerrero. 2015. "Challenging the Utility of a Racial Microaggressions Framework through a Systematic Review of Racially

Biased Incidents on Campus." *Journal of Critical Scholarship on Higher Education and Student Affairs* 2, no. 1: 48–66.

Gloria, Alberta M. 1998. "Searching for Congruity: Reflections on an Untenured Woman of Color." In *Career Strategies for Women in Academe: Arming Athena*, edited by Lynn H. Collins, Joan C. Chrisler, and Kathryn Quina, 36–39. Thousand Oaks, CA: Sage.

Godbee, Beth. 2017. "Writing Up: How Assertions of Epistemic Rights Counter Epistemic Injustice." *College English* 29, no. 6: 593–618.

Gomez, Mary Louise, Ayesha Khurshid, Mel B. Freitag, and Amy Johnson Lachuk. 2011. "Microaggressions in Graduate Students' Lives: How They Are Encountered and Their Consequences." *Teaching and Teacher Education* 27, no. 8: 1189–99.

Gutiérrez y Muhs, Gabriella, Yolanda Flores Niemann, Carmen G. González, and Angela P. Harris, eds. 2012. *Presumed Incompetent: The Intersections of Race and Class for Women in Academia*. Logan: Utah State University Press.

Harris, Angela P., and Carmen G. González. 2012. Introduction to Gutiérrez y Muhs et al. 2012: 1–14.

Harris, Rochelle. 2004. "Encouraging Emergent Moments: The Personal, Critical, and Rhetorical in the Writing Classroom." *Pedagogy* 4, no. 3: 401–18.

hooks, bell. 2003. *Teaching Community: A Pedagogy of Hope*. New York: Routledge.

Horton, Myles. 1990. *The Long Haul: An Autobiography*. With Judith Kohl and Herbert Kohl. New York: Doubleday.

Jacobus, Lee A., ed. 2010. *A World of Ideas: Essential Readings for College Writers*. 8th ed. Boston: Bedford/St. Martin's.

Kennedy, X. J., Dorothy M. Kennedy, and Jane E. Aaron, eds. 2010. *The Bedford Reader*. 10th ed. Boston: Bedford/St. Martin's.

Kohli, Rita, and Daniel G. Solórzano. 2012. "Teachers, Please Learn Our Names! Racial Microaggressions and the K-12 Classroom." *Race Ethnicity and Education* 15, no. 4: 1–12.

Kuebrich, Ben. 2015. "'White Guys Who Send My Uncle to Prison': Going Public within Asymmetrical Power." *College Composition and Communication* 66, no. 4: 566–90.

Lathan, Rhea Estelle. 2015. *Freedom Writing: African American Civil Rights Literacy Activism, 1955–1967*. Urbana, IL: National Council of Teachers of English.

Lipson, Carol S., and Roberta A. Binkley, eds. 2004. *Rhetoric before and beyond the Greeks*. Albany: State University of New York Press.

Lipson, Carol S., and Roberta A. Binkley, eds. 2009. *Ancient Non-Greek Rhetorics*. Anderson, SC: Parlor Press.

Logan, Shirley Wilson. 1995. *With Pen and Voice: A Critical Anthology of Nineteenth-Century African-American Women*. Carbondale: Southern Illinois University Press.

Mao, LuMing, and Morris Young. 2008. *Representations: Doing Asian American Rhetoric*. Logan: Utah State University Press.

Martinez, Aja Y. 2016. "A Plea for Critical Race Theory Counterstory: Stock Story vs. Counterstory Dialogues Concerning Alejandra's 'Fit' in the Academy." In

Performing Antiracist Pedagogy in Rhetoric, Writing, and Communication, edited by Frankie Condon and Vershawn Young, 65–85. Boulder: Across the Disciplines Books and University Press of Colorado.

McCabe, Janice. 2009. "Racial and Gender Microaggressions on a Predominantly-White Campus: Experiences of Black, Latina/o and White Undergraduates." *Race, Gender, and Class* 16, no. 1–2: 133–51.

@microaggressive. n.d. "Microaggressions: Power, Privilege, and Everyday Life." Public blog project. www.microaggressions.com (accessed 21 August 2017).

Milem, Jeffrey F., Mitchell J. Chang, and Anthony Lising Antonio. 2005. "Making Diversity Work on Campus: A Research-Based Perspective." Association of American Colleges and Universities. www.aacu.org/sites/default/files/files/mei/milem_et_al.pdf.

Minikel-Lacocque, Julie. 2013. "Racism, College, and the Power of Words: Racial Microaggressions Reconsidered." *American Educational Research Journal* 50, no. 3: 432–65.

Nadal, Kevin L. 2013. *That's So Gay! Microaggressions and the Lesbian, Gay, Bisexual, and Transgender Community*. Washington, DC: American Psychological Association.

Pandey, Iswari. Forthcoming. *Global English, Remedial English: Caste, Class, Nation*. New York: Routledge Research in Education.

Perelman, Chaim, and Lucie Olbrechts-Tyteca. 1969. *The New Rhetoric: A Treatise on Argumentation*, translated by J. W. P. Weaver. Notre Dame, IN: University of Notre Dame.

Porter, James E., Patricia Sullivan, Stuart Blythe, Jeffrey T. Grabill, and Libby Miles. 2000. "Institutional Critique: A Rhetorical Methodology for Change." *College Composition and Communication* 51, no. 4: 610–42.

Powell, Malea. 2012. "2012 CCCC Chair's Address: Stories Take Place: A Performance in One Act." *College Composition and Communication* 64, no. 2: 383–406.

Prendergast, Catherine. 2003. *Literacy and Racial Justice: The Politics of Learning after Brown v. Board of Education*. Carbondale: Southern Illinois University Press.

Pritchard, Eric. 2013. "For Colored Kids Who Committed Suicide, Our Outrage Isn't Enough: Queer Youth of Color, Bullying, and the Discursive Limits of Identity and Safety." *Harvard Educational Review* 83, no. 2: 320–45.

Pritchard, Eric. 2016. *Fashioning Lives: Black Queers and the Politics of Literacy*. Carbondale: Southern Illinois University Press.

Ramírez, Cristina Devereaux. 2015. *Occupying Our Space: The Mestiza Rhetorics of Mexican Women Journalists and Activists, 1875–1942*. Tucson: University of Arizona Press.

Richardson, Elaine. 2013. *PHD to Ph.D.: How Education Saved My Life*. West Lafayette, IN: Parlor Press.

Richardson, Elaine B., and Ronald L. Jackson III, eds. 2004. *African American Rhetoric(s): Interdisciplinary Perspectives*. Carbondale: Southern Illinois University Press.

Ritchie, Joy, and Kate Ronald, eds. 2001. *Available Means: An Anthology of Women's Rhetoric(s)*. Pittsburgh: University of Pittsburgh Press.

Rose, Mike. 1989. *Lives on the Boundary.* New York: Penguin.
Rowe, Mary P. 1990. "Barriers to Equality: The Power of Subtle Discrimination to Maintain Unequal Opportunity." *Employee Responsibilities and Rights Journal* 3, no. 2: 153–63. Royster, Jacqueline Jones. 1996. "When the First Voice You Hear Is Not Your Own." *College Composition and Communication* 47, no. 1: 29–40.
Royster, Jacqueline Jones. 2000. *Traces of a Stream: Literacy and Social Change among African American Women.* Pittsburgh, PA: University of Pittsburgh Press.
Royster, Jacqueline Jones. 2003. "Disciplinary Landscaping, or Contemporary Challenges in the History of Rhetoric." *Philosophy and Rhetoric* 36, no. 2: 148–67.
Scott, Blake. 2003. *Risky Rhetoric: AIDS and the Cultural Practices of HIV Testing.* Carbondale: Southern Illinois University Press.
Sheridan, Mary P. 2014. "Responsivity: Defining, Cultivating, Enacting" *Journal of Advanced Composition* 34, no. 1–2: 11–24.
Shrodes, Caroline, Michael Shugrue, Marc F. Di Paolo, and Christine Matuschek, eds. 2009. *The Conscious Reader.* 11th ed. New York: Pearson/Longman.
Solórzano, Daniel, Miguel Ceja, and Tara Yosso. 2000. "Critical Race Theory, Racial Microaggressions, and Campus Racial Climate: The Experiences of African American College Students." *Journal of Negro Education* 69, nos. 1–2: 60–73.
Stromberg, Ernest, ed. 2006. *American Indian Rhetorics of Survivance: Word Medicine, Word Magic.* Pittsburgh: University of Pittsburgh Press.
Sue, Derald Wing. 2010. *Microaggressions in Everyday Life: Race, Gender, and Sexual Orientation.* Hoboken, NJ: Wiley.
Sue, Derald Wing, Christina M. Capodilupo, Gina C. Torino, Jennifer M. Bucceri, Aisha M. B. Holder, Kevin L. Nadal, and Marta Esquilin. 2007. "Racial Microaggressions in Everyday Life: Implications for Clinical Practice." *American Psychologist* 62, no. 4: 271–86.
Villanueva, Victor. 1993. *Bootstraps: From an American Academic of Color.* Urbana, IL: National Council of Teachers of English.
Villanueva, Victor. 2006. "Blind: Talking about the New Racism." *Writing Center Journal* 26, no. 1: 3–19.
Young, Vershawn Ashanti. 2010. "Momma's Memories and the New Equality." *Present Tense: A Journal of Rhetoric and Society* 1, no. 1: 1–6. www.presenttensejournal.org/vol1/momma%E2%80%99s-memories-and-the-new-equality/.

Supplemental Material

Rhetorical and Pedagogical Interventions for Countering Microaggressions

Rasha Diab and Beth Godbee

PART I: REFLECTION ON THE ORIGINS OF THE ARTICLE

For years, together and separately and with other collaborators, including Cedric and Thomas, we (Beth and Rasha) have been researching, teaching, and writing about power and power abuses. Repeatedly, we have witnessed and experienced violent power dynamics ignored and denied when named as such. And repeatedly, we have sought ways to learn more, to show up and act on commitments to justice. This work is deeply humbling, requires a lot of reflective self-work, and asks more of us everyday and for the long haul.

Over time, the study of microaggressions has emerged as an important part of this work, particularly for naming *how* violence happens *everyday*. To be clear, there's nothing *micro* about microaggressions, as so many other activists/educators/scholars are reiterating time after time (see, for example, Lindsay Pérez Huber and Daniel G. Solorzano's "Racial Microaggressions as a Tool for Critical Race Research" in *Race Ethnicity and Education*, 2015; Kejhonti Neloms's "What Exactly Is 'Micro' about Microaggressions?" in *Race Baitr*, 2019; and Asali Solomon's "Conversations with Microaggressions and the Spirit World" in *How We Fight White Supremacy*, 2019). All types of aggression cause harm and have cumulative and far-reaching impacts. The "micro" in microaggression is *not* an indication of small or lesser-than aggression. Instead, the "micro" refers to the unit of analysis, the moment of interaction.

Because microaggressions manifest in moments of interaction, we continue to believe that they demand particular attention from those of us in writing, rhetoric, and literacy studies. Whether personal (e.g., among two or more clearly identified people) or impersonal (e.g., a writer/group of writers writing to and about distant others), these interactions are communicative acts that do harm. When we study microaggressions, therefore, we're asking not only when, where, how, why, and by/to/for whom they happen, but also and significantly when, where, how, why, and by/to/for whom we must intervene. In other words: How do we respond to microaggressions, or those everyday and commonplace communicative actions that enact bias, invalidate people, and reinforce structural oppression?

Our key investment in this article is to highlight such daily interactions in academic spaces (research, teaching, and service). Each interaction is a window to understanding and countering practices of aggression and power abuse. As educators invested in the liberatory potential of education, we need to recognize, name, describe, and interrupt these power dynamics. The stakes are real and high. Educators and learners cannot thrive in environments when microaggressions are neither identified nor addressed.

Part II: Description of Research Methods, Findings, and/or Pedagogical Impact

This work continues to be important, yet fraught with challenges. Over the years, generations of scholars—particularly Black, Indigenous, and people of color (BIPOC), feminist and womanist scholars—have written about the moral imperatives of educators. And generations of scholars have been advocating for the rights and needs of learners. Similarly, generations of scholars have testified to microaggressions faced in higher education. And generations of scholars have called for direct action. The calls are numerous, so when they aren't taken up, when they aren't listened to, when they aren't acted on, the hurt deepens. The harms from ongoing white supremacy, heteropatriarchy, settler colonialism, and interlocking systems of oppression add up, culminating and cutting ever-deeper in the ways that scholarship on microaggressions highlights for us.

To illustrate, April Baker-Bell, Bonnie J. Williams-Farrier, Davena Jackson, Lamar Johnson, Carmen Kynard, and Teaira McMurtry alert us to the rippling effect of what happens in "these academic streets" in the CCCC Statement on Anti-Black Racism and Black Linguistic Justice, Or, Why We Cain't Breathe!: "This Ain't Another Statement! This is a DEMAND for Black Linguistic Justice!" Together, they ask: "How has Black Lives Mattered in the context of language education? How has Black Lives Mattered in our research, scholarship, teaching, disciplinary discourses, graduate programs, professional organizations, and publications? How have our commitments and activism as a discipline contributed to the political freedom of Black peoples?"

These questions point to where we must resist denial of ongoing harms and instead recognize normalized violence and its wide-reaching consequences. As a discipline and as people within the discipline, we must divest from whiteness and interrupt "business as usual." And as scholars in composition and rhetoric, we must trace the rhetorical logics, the fundamental grammars, of injustice, aggression, and violence. This work includes recognizing where we have perpetuated and are complicit with microaggressions. It is work, therefore, that disrupts the narrative that our discipline is/does "good."

Perhaps because it disrupts this sense of "goodness," this work is hard to do and hard to publish. This piece had a long journey before its publication. Beth, Rasha, and Thomas wrote "Expanded Perspectives on Power" in 2015, during that year's RSA Summer Institute, which the four of us attended together. The following year, in 2016, the four of us presented "Countering Microaggressions and Enacting Change: Frameworks for Rhetorical Intervention" at the RSA Conference, and we then revised and submitted the first version of this article in fall 2016—just days after Trump's election. The article was rejected by the editor (a white senior scholar) that same week because they didn't see it as relevant to humanities scholars, though conceded that it might be of use to older white, male scientists. The rejection letter asserted: "Perhaps I am too optimistic about our field, but I don't think there are many readers to whom this essay would bring new insights." So, the article's publication in *Pedagogy* and this reprinting are enactments of sponsorship, holding the space for this work to matter in the discipline.

Whether invalidating, excluding, type-casting, gaslighting, dismissing, insulting, or otherwise enacting hostility, microaggressions do more than communicate harm. They limit what we can know, name, describe, and organize around. They dehumanize, undercut, and undermine possibilities for equity and justice. And they demand a range of responses. Embracing both/and, we need *both* immediate and long-term, practiced and improvised, personal and institutional ways of responding to microaggressions. We need responses now. Is it surprising that April Baker-Bell, Bonnie J. Williams-Farrier, Davena Jackson, Lamar Johnson, Carmen Kynard, and Teaira McMurtry's provocation is "Why We Cain't Breathe!"?

Committed and striving with humility and diligence, we resolve to stay in this work: to keep learning and unlearning: to know better and do better. To us, this piece is a response to the courageous scholars who have offered daring insights, asking us to witness, to intervene, and to be in the struggle. We listen, invest in unlearning, and join many others—hoping you will, too—in this work for the long haul.

Part III: Discussion Questions

To be clear: microaggressions aren't about being small or "micro." Instead, the "micro" refers to the aggression happening in a moment of interaction.

So, spend some time noticing:

1. How does aggression happen in interaction (personal and impersonal)?
2. When are you inclined to minimize interactions or deny aggression?
3. When have aggressive interactions had a big impact in your life? And where/how do you receive support for processing those interactions?
4. How are you resourced (or need to build the resourcing) to take accountability for and/or navigate through (survive and still thrive within) oppression, which includes everyday microaggressions?

Spend some time *contextualizing*:

1. For a few microaggressions you've witnessed, perpetrated, or experienced, consider what each communicates and to whom. What rippling impacts might each have?
2. Was each microaggression addressed/denied/ignored? How and why?
3. Do you see the connection between microaggressions and macro-logics, macro-systems, macro-injustices? If not, why? Explore reasons for these connections being obscured or obfuscated *by design*.
4. What conditions support these microaggressions and their continuation? What needs to change to change the conditions?

Spend some time *intervening/reflecting on possibilities for intervention*:

1. Based on your *noticing* and *contextualizing*, what needs intervention?
2. What would a meaningful intervention feel like?
3. How might you intervene into microaggressions before, during, and after the moment of interaction, particularly by changing institutional structures and culture?
4. What might scholars and educators in rhetoric, writing, and literacy studies contribute to this conversation? Or, what needs to be illuminated about how aggression works in communicative acts and interactions?
5. There's much to learn by studying not only the ongoing enactment of microaggressions but also a range of meaningful, relational responses. How can you engage with this everyday, ongoing learning and unlearning?

ENCULTURATION

enculturation was launched in 1996 by two graduate students. In twenty years it has never been affiliated with a press or organization and has only had minimal institutional support by one university. Currently it is hosted on an individual's server and supported with one RA through the University of South Carolina. Almost all of the managerial, editorial, and production work continues to be done by young faculty and graduate students in the field of rhetoric and composition. The mission of the journal has generally been to publish broader ranging interdisciplinary work related to rhetoric and composition that is more theoretical or media-oriented.

Enculturation is on the Web at http://enculturation.net/

Signs of Disability, Disclosing[1]

Kerschbaum's article makes a significant contribution to addressing the ways disabilities are materially disclosed. Following Susan Hekman, she argues that "Deaf Person in Area" street signs participate in the emergence of reality: "As people move with and around the signs, new disclosures emerge and with them, new perspectives, theories, and concepts." These disclosures happen in and through cultural practices and movements based on positionality. She writes, "In this article, I turn to the Deaf Person in Area sign (and others like it) to understand how interactions around and with the sign disclose orientations to disability, as people and their material surround constellate in dynamic relationships. In asking about the signs of disability that we attend to in the world around us, I suggest we can build a sense of how and when disability is noticed, cued, and engaged. Such noticing will help us build a collective understanding of what meanings are associated with disability and thus contribute to our noticing (or erasures) of it."

---

1. *enculturation*, vol. 30, 2019. https://enculturation.net/signs-of-disability-disclosing. © 2019 by Stephanie L. Kerschbaum.

Signs of Disability, Disclosing

Stephanie L. Kerschbaum

(Published November 12, 2019)

> *Disclosure entails that perspectives/concepts/theories matter—that they are our means of accessing reality. But disclosure also entails that we do not constitute that reality with our concepts, but rather portray it in varying ways. An important aspect of this understanding is that the reality, like the object in the photograph or the subject of the scientist's experiment, is agentic. It pushes back, it effects the result.*
>
> —Susan Hekman, *The Material of Knowledge: Feminist Disclosures*

Figure 1: Image description: A yellow diamond-shaped road sign that reads "Deaf Person in Area" along a well-trafficked road. In the background are large trees with many leaves on them, telephone poles and wires, and a squat brick community center. Newark, DE. (Photo by author.) [2]

Six years ago, this yellow diamond-shaped sign appeared on a busy street that I drive down on my way to work every day (along with a second, identical, sign facing the other direction that I passed on my way home).[1] I say "appeared" because I don't know exactly when it showed up and whether or how often I might have passed it without even noticing it was there. Not long after that, I wrote a conference presentation about disability disclosure. In that talk, I argued that the sign was a metaphor for how most people think disability disclosure works: you announce, loudly, "Deaf Person in Area!" and, well, that's about it. Only nobody knows what to do when they are told "Deaf Person in Area." Do they drive faster? Drive slower? Honk their horn? Avoid honking their horn? Stick their hand out the window? Wave vigorously? Flash their lights? Or nothing at all?

Over the last few years, this sign has worked on and through me in numerous ways: I've talked about this sign in a lot of places with a lot of people. I've taken pictures of more yellow diamond-shaped signs. I've asked others to share pictures of signs. I discovered two additional "Deaf Person in Area" signs near the first ones: one off a side street and another directly in front of a neatly-trimmed suburban house. I used the picture at the start of this article as the background for my computer's desktop, as the cover image for a Facebook group, and as a recurring image on my academic website. Not only was I moving past the original Deaf Person in Area sign on a regular basis, but its images were circulating in numerous spheres of my life.

Figure 2: Image description: A yellow diamond-shaped sign reading "Deaf Person in Area" planted on the grassy median between sidewalk and street on a relatively quiet suburban street. A large pine tree takes up much of the right side of the image, and a single-family home is in the distance. Newark, DE. (Photo by author.)

As these images might suggest, the sign disclosed to me, again and again, as I encountered—and kept encountering—it in numerous forms and in different contexts. My use of "disclosed" follows Susan Hekman as she urges a new feminist ontology to address the problems of over-emphasizing epistemology and orienting to reality as (almost entirely) discursively constructed. She writes, "We must be able to account for the material reality of our social existence without losing sight of the discursive dimension of that reality" (90). Hekman's response to this challenge is disclosure. Her understanding of disclosure is one that "presupposes an external reality that is the object of discursive practices. But the external reality presupposed is not fixed. Rather, it is a product of agents' interaction in a shared environment with a world that emerges through that interaction" (91). The Deaf Person in Area sign, through its influence on the ways that people move, notice, interact, and engage, enacts disclosures that emerge through our perceptions of and responses to it. For instance, drivers who notice the sign might adjust their driving behavior. Or they might think to themselves, "I should request a similar sign for my own neighborhood." They could also, as I do here, wonder about the sign and what it conveys. Each of these reactions is a form of disclosure enacted by the sign as it participates in the emergence of reality.

Figure 3: Image description: A yellow diamond-shaped sign reading "Deaf Person in Area" planted on the grassy median between sidewalk and street directly in front of a well-manicured single-family Cape Cod-style home. Does the Deaf Person in Area live here? (Photo by author.)

In this article's epigraph, Hekman explains that humans access reality through "perspectives/theories/concepts" (92) but those concepts are *portrayals* of reality, not constitutive of it. Thus, as people move with and around the Deaf Person in Area sign, new disclosures emerge and with them, new perspectives, theories, and concepts. In concert with Hekman's concept of disclosure, I take up cultural rhetorics scholarship that emphasizes "the making of cultures and the practices that call them into being as *relational* and *constellated*" (Riley-Mukavetz in Powell et al.), highlighting the ways that cultural practices are created by people moving in relation with one another. The metaphor of a constellation, Powell et al. write, explicitly acknowledges and honors "different meaning-making practices and their relationships" and "allows for different ways of seeing any single configuration within that constellation, based on positionality and culture." In this article, I turn to the Deaf Person in Area sign (and others like it) to understand how interactions around and with the sign disclose orientations to disability, as people and their material surround constellate in dynamic relationships. In asking about the signs of disability that we attend to in the world around us, I suggest we can build a sense of how and when disability is noticed, cued, and engaged. Such noticing will help us build a collective understanding of what meanings are associated with disability and thus contribute to our noticing (or erasures) of it.

Figure 4: Image description: My laptop on a table in my university's library, showing a closely cropped image of the Deaf Person in Area sign being used as my laptop's background. A styrofoam coffee cup and the corner of a notebook are on the right side of the image. Newark, DE. (Photo by author.)

SIGNS OF DISABILITY

Before moving further, it is important to define some key terms, beginning with *signs* and *disability*. The yellow diamond-shaped "Deaf Person in Area" sign may be the exemplar I offer here of the concept of signs of disability, but my use of the word *sign* is not limited to the paper, metal, and wood signs that populate the environments we move through on a daily basis. Here, I draw on the definition of sign offered by Ron Scollon and Suzie Wong Scollon in their work on geosemiotics. They write that "[i]n geosemiotics, as in all branches of semiotics, the word 'sign' means any material object that indicates or refers to something other than itself" (3), although I do not limit signs of disability to material objects. Thus, signs of disability can be understood as perceptual cues that point to disability in some way, shape, or form. My definition of disability takes as a central tenet that disability is an indeterminate and messy category, and is strongly influenced by Elizabeth Barnes's suggestion that we might define disability in terms of "whatever the disability rights movement is promoting justice for" (43). Such a definition is necessarily shifting, contingent on circumstances, contexts, and particular experiences, relationships, and bodily configurations. While Barnes carefully limits her definition to physical disability, my own thinking about signs of disability takes a capacious orientation to disability, attending to the ways that disabilities of all kinds are signaled and taken up by others. The framework of activism and justice that Barnes identifies is important for the way it points to disability as shaped by people, material artifacts, and environments that make claims about access, about the presence (or absence) of disability within an interaction or a space, and about the ways that all kinds of beings can or should move.

Despite its messiness as a category, disability makes itself perceptible and is made perceptible through all kinds of cues. With perceptual cues, I intend the many forms of embodied perception that people perform, using the full range of their sensory capabilities. Thus, signs of disability can be embodied, behavioral, affective, material, and/or discursive, and their perceptibility is intimately tied to the constellations (Powell et al.) between environments, beings, and artifacts. Perception is a carefully-chosen word here, one that I began using in *Toward a New Rhetoric of Difference* (Kerschbaum) to describe the sorts of things people might notice as they interacted with others: seeing lips moving, hearing voices, smelling scents (soap or shampoo, someone's lunch, cigarette smoke), feeling textures of clothing or skin, tasting food or beverages—and more. These perceptions influence interactions even when they are not explicitly raised in conversation, and as rhetoric scholars, we need to cultivate ways of engaging such elements in our data generation and analysis processes.

Signs of disability as a concept gradually emerged as I worked to build on theorizing markers of difference. In *Toward*, I defined markers of difference as dynamic, emergent, and relational rhetorical cues deployed by interlocutors to point to or engage difference between themselves. Paying attention to markers of difference meant focusing on the interactional choices that people make as they interact with others. These choices involve recursive feedback loops whereby what is salient and/or significant to call attention to, what is assumed and/or can go without saying, as well as differences in how people interpret and orient to rhetorical cues *emerge* over the course of an interaction and inform later interactions. And yet, one challenge that markers of difference present for analysts is their emphasis on discursive means of marking. For instance, in *Toward*, which showcased analyses of students performing small-group peer review, I could only attend to material artifacts or forms of embodied presence as markers of difference if students directly remarked or commented upon them. In other words, unless a student explicitly named or described their own or another person's race/ethnic or gender identification, I had to be exceptionally careful in pointing to what that student might be perceiving from or about their peer review partners. In a similar vein, while I recognize that clothing and other material accoutrements play significant roles in identity performances and social negotiations, the articulation of markers of difference and the data available within the book—taken from one semester in a writing classroom—made it difficult for my analyses to engage students' uptake of those elements of a scene unless they did so discursively.

Signs of disability help us better engage a broader range of the perceptual work happening within interactional encounters by enabling attention to the ways that material artifacts as well as forms of behavior, embodiment and presence can be included in analytic scenes alongside discursive elements. My approach to signs of disability builds on work in semiotics—especially Scollon and Scollon's geosemiotics as well as Gunther Kress's work on multimodality—but is distinguished from semiotics in that I incorporate greater attention to narrative constructions of reality in my methodological and analytic approach. My attention to narrative coalesces through my articulation of disclosure, which draws from scholarship in feminist materiality. I understand narratives as one form of what physicist and feminist materialist scholar Karen Barad in *Meeting the Universe Halfway* terms an "agential cut." As Barad explains, an observational apparatus intra-acts with objects being perceived. The result is the materialization of perceived phenomena. Such phenomena do not themselves constitute reality but are the emergent result of an intra-action between perceptual apparatus and material reality. To tell a story, then, is to make an agential cut, to materialize phenomena through intra-action, to enact disclosures.

Disclosing

To study signs of disability and how they matter (literally and figuratively), I take up Hekman's concept of disclosure to generate data and move analytically with that data. More specifically, I understand disclosure in terms of an orientation to particular perceptions and meanings that constellate at a specific time and in a specific space, in different ways for different objects and beings. This definition should be distinguished from what is perhaps a more conventional understanding of disclosure as an act of making perceptible something that might not be immediately apparent to another person, as when someone reveals a disability diagnosis or a need for accommodation. As I use it, disclosure is intended to represent the emergence of a perception (and perhaps, but not always, an interpretation) as a result of intra-actions (Barad) in the world. That is, signs and other material objects intra-act with perceiving beings to participate in acts of disclosure. These acts of disclosure contribute to emerging and dynamic cultural orientations to disability.

To identify some of these cultural orientations, disability studies scholars have studied how people attend to and behave toward disability in public space. Bodies in public are relentlessly surveilled, followed, and watched, and some bodies receive much more scrutiny than others. Critical disability scholar Aimi Hamraie illustrates this by highlighting what they call a post-ADA narrative. They offer the example of a Google-sponsored mural that was painted on the steps around the National Mall in celebration of the 25th anniversary of the signing of the ADA, noting that such post-ADA narratives suggest that now that the ADA has been passed, the problem of accessibility has been solved. However, they note, placing the mural on the built form of a staircase meant that "the murals hid in plain sight (and without a hint of irony) the persistent architectural, attitudinal, and economic barriers that disabled people continue to face in the post-ADA world" (3). Indeed, as disability historian Susan Schweik documents in *The Ugly Laws*, disabled people have a long history of violent mistreatment in public. Such mistreatment has long been documented by disability justice activists tracing what happens when disabled, queer, trans, indigenous people of color encounter police officers (see, e.g., Abdelhadi; Elman; Moore et al.; Sanchez; Vest). Disability justice activists, Abla Abdelhadi explains, explicitly center intersectional experiences in order to "understand violence against and criminalization of disabled people in more critical ways." In turn, strategies for moving in response and in resistance to these forms of oppression must attend to the specificities of as well as patterns in experience across and within groups of disabled people.

Experiences of disability in public are entwined with and reinforced by everyday rhetorical practices that frame disability as a threatening or dangerous difference, presumed threats that are often amplified when disability intersects with other forms of discrimination, oppression, and violence against minoritized bodies. Such identities are both material and discursive: histories of discrimination create real effects on people and influence how they move, interact, and are engaged by others. What people perceive off of one another's embodied and enminded presence—what Scollon and Scollon might describe as the "social actor" and the "interaction order" (14-17)—impacts how they move interactionally. Too, material artifacts and environments—what Scollon and Scollon might orient to in terms of visual semiotics and place semiotics (17-20)—actively participate in these interactions. In all of this, discursive histories, language practices, framing, self-presentation and self- and other-construction play key roles. This article follows the Deaf Person in Area sign disclosing to bring together the material and discursive elements of identity construction and negotiation around disability.

In closely attending to this sign, my goal is twofold. First, I forward a theory of signs of disability that enables attention to both the material and discursive aspects of interactions, and which might usefully be extended to other forms of identity construction. Second, I suggest that signs of disability are necessary to understand because of how they shape everyday perceptions of disability. Such efforts are urgently needed at a time when being disabled in public is often dangerous, particularly for multiply minoritized disabled people, as documented through the Disability Justice movement launched by Leroy Moore and Patty Berne (Sins Invalid). Moore and Berne's work underscores the exigence of probing how the everyday spaces that we move through contribute to the persistent dehumanization and violence performed upon queer, trans, and indigenous disabled people of color. While I draw particularly on encounters in public spaces given my focus on the yellow diamond-shaped Deaf Person in Area road sign, these perceptions also matter to our own classrooms and everyday institutional spaces as beings and material objects constellate within these environments. Studying such constellations help us understand how people are enculturated towards disability in public, revealing how interactions within various environments teach, through mundane, everyday lived experiences, what disability means and how to orient to it. This might also be understood as cultivating a geosemiotics of disability, in a sense. This geosemiotics of disability and the constellations that emerge disclose how links are built (as well as frayed or reinforced) between disability and cultural narratives taking shape through various forms of attention to disability. Ultimately, I hope this work will enable us to better-attend to the constellations always in flux (Edbauer) around us and the meanings for disability that we are continually absorbing, responding to, and (re)shaping in our daily lives.

The Deaf Person in Area Sign Disclosing

When I first encountered the Deaf Person in Area sign, it revealed itself to me as funny. I thought things like, "It's a good thing I live in the neighborhood, so that there actually is a Deaf Person in Area!" Other deaf people have reported similar reactions: in a blog post about a "Deaf Pedestrians" sign complete with flashing lights near Gallaudet University, Tonya Stremlau writes, "When I drive by, I do sometimes irrationally feel like I should get out and walk by the sign, just to give it a raison d'etre." Similarly, in "How Not to be a Dick to a Deaf Person," Kelly Dougher captions a photo of a "Deaf Child in Area" sign with: "This sign is still on my street even though I turned 18 ages ago. This is the first time it has made itself useful." But as I engaged more widely with the sign, it disclosed to me in quite different ways. Most people I talked to didn't experience the sign as funny or ridiculous. These were occasionally difficult conversations. Sometimes I would feel a bit indignant: "Really? Do you think I should have a Deaf Person in Area sign in front of my house? Should I have one at the door to my office? Should I carry one everywhere I go so that everyone always knows that there's a Deaf Person in Area?" "No, no, no," people would respond, "*You* don't need a sign, but there are lots of *other* deaf people who do. You're not like them. You're different."

I don't know that I'm all that different from other deaf people in the ways that these comments presume, but there are lots of ways I already carry Deaf Person in Area signs wherever I go. I wear large behind-the-ear hearing aids. The sound of my voice can reveal me as a deaf person. I often sign with others. I stare intently at people's faces while they are speaking, and if they move around a room, I sometimes stand and move too in order to maintain line of sight. Each of these features of my physical presence and of my behavior within social spaces are forms of disability disclosure. And yet, there is a great deal of ambiguity behind the signs of disability I've just named.

Sociologist and disability theorist Tanya Titchkosky defines disability as "a way of perceiving and orienting to the world" (4) which entails "knowing that we are a part of and apart from—that we are made by and we make—the space where we find ourselves" (21). The emergence of disability within an environment is, of course, no one single thing: our relationships to and experiences with disability, as well as the cultures and spaces in which we live and move, all lead us to notice differently, in ways that are singular to us as individuals with particular life trajectories, lived knowledges, and ways of moving in the world. How a "Deaf Person in Area!" sign discloses—whether it is a yellow diamond-shaped sign, hearing aids, the sound of a voice, hands flying in communication, or particularities of gaze and eye contact—can be deeply idiosyncratic, even when immersed within specific cultural beliefs and attitudes. And yet, as Titchkosky and others have repeatedly shown, perception and attention are highly culturally motivated (Friedman *Blind*; "Cultural"; Zerubavel, *Hidden; Taken*; Citton). We learn what to pay attention to through the relationships we build, the encounters we have, the messages that environments reveal about who belongs and who doesn't, the types of encounters we are likely or unlikely to have, what needs to be said and what is or can be left unsaid. These are forms of collective attention.

Collective attention is a sociological concept that excavates how people learn to build perceptual apparatuses that enable them to navigate their world and move through and within material and discursive environments. Perceptual apparatuses built through forms of collective attention enable attending to some things while ignoring or obscuring others. Sometimes collective attention means disability is highly visible and marked, while other times disability may be erased or unrecognized in conjunction with other identifications. For instance, disability scholars Nirmala Erevelles and Andrea Minear have suggested that "individuals located perilously at the interstices of race, class, gender, *and* disability are constituted as non-citizens and (no)bodies" (p. 129) and Eunjung Kim has analyzed how persistent narratives around sexuality and disability erase possibilities for disabled people to affirmatively claim asexual identities. Such erasures are enacted in many ways through the perceptual filters and forms of attention paid to particular kinds of bodies and minds, and they often reinforce institutional and structural violences. As such, we need to critically examine forms of collective attention as well as develop attentional practices that push back against damaging forces.

One place to launch such an inquiry is to attend to the signs of disability around us and the stories we tell about those signs, including signage and iconography in public spaces. There is rich scholarship in disability studies on how icons and symbols disclose and enculturate. Unsurprisingly, the nearly-ubiquitous wheelchair logo/International Symbol of Access (ISA) has received the greatest attention. In her book *Designing Disability*, Elizabeth Guffey performs an extended historical analysis of the ISA, and others have probed the various functions performed by this icon (Ben-Moshe and Powell), including how it conveys messages about mobility (Hendren), affective valences of disability (Fritsch), and attitudes towards access (Titchkosky). The ISA is not the only public sign to receive significant attention: Alison Kafer and Eli Clare each uncover problematic subtexts behind seemingly innocuous motivational messages featured on billboards across the United

States, and Najma al Zidjaly shows how the use of a universal access symbol effectively erases representations of individual disabled people in Oman. Many less-explicit signs of disability are embedded within built environments, as Hamraie writes in *Building Access*: "From a doorframe's negative space to the height of shelves and cabinets, inhabitants' bodies are simultaneously imagined, hidden, and produced by the design of built worlds" (19). Taken together, these analyses underscore various forms of meaning-making that coalesce around physical signs, and they frequently take the methodological approach of telling and analyzing stories.

It is through stories that we learn how signs disclose. These disclosures are not static; they are made and remade as we move within rhetorical ecologies (Edbauer). Attending to the ways that disability manifests in daily experience means recognizing that that our perceptual terrain is always shifting depending on identities, forms of embodiment and enmindment, past experiences, relationships emerging within particular spaces, affective modalities and reactions, and material artifacts that surround and shape movement. What we are noticing—and what the signs are disclosing to us through our encounters with them—emerges in our storying and is not always, or even often, at the forefront of our awareness or consciousness. One way to build an understanding of what and how we notice is through sociologist Asia Friedman's work with perceptual filters (*Blind*). Friedman uses the concept of a filter to explain how different cues are deemed important or relevant to the perception of male and female bodies. For instance, hairstyles or the presence/absence of facial hair tend to be actively noticed and thus pass through a gender filter while other information, such as the size and shape of someone's shins or their elbow, may be deemed irrelevant and thus filtered out.

Friedman describes gender as a foundational filter, pointing to the fact that, for most people living in the United States, it is (almost) impossible to *not notice* gender. Put another way, because of the binary perception of gender into which they are culturally socialized, Americans are taught that sorting people into male and female is highly relevant information (see also Ridgeway on gender). With regard to disability, however, cultural expectations around noticing others in the United States generally do not compel Americans to seek out information about disability status or relationships to disability, perhaps at least in part because of the messiness of disability as a category. In asking about the signs of disability that we attend to in the world around us, I suggest we can build a sense of how and when disability is noticed, cued, and engaged. Such noticing will help us build a collective understanding of what meanings are associated with disability and thus contribute to our noticing (or erasures) of it. This emphasis on storying is perhaps the biggest departure in my approach to signs of disability from other semiotic approaches to signs (Scollon and Scollon; Kress): I spend less time unpacking the signs' emplacement and signaling and more time zeroing in on the signs' disclosure through stories. The sections that follow unpack some of the stories that have emerged as I've moved with and around the Deaf Person in Area sign in my neighborhood, showing how these stories reinforce problematic orientations to disability.

Yellow Diamond Shaped Road Signs and Their Disclosures

While the Deaf Person in Area sign disappeared from my neighborhood about three years ago, it maintains an active presence in my academic and personal life. To convey a broader sense of the genre of yellow road signs of disability, let me share some of the various terms, images, and phrasings on the signs that I've collected thus far. Many of the signs are diamond-shaped, some are rectangular, and sometimes there is both a diamond and a rectangle.

Figure 5: Image description: A yellow diamond-shaped sign that reads "Blind Pedestrian Xing" sprouts from a gravel berm alongside a street winding through Haverford College's campus. A tan car is parked behind the sign. Haverford, PA. (Photo credit: Kristin Lindgren.)

Signs of Disability, Disclosing 225

Figure 6: Image description: A yellow rectangle with the words "Autistic Child" is situated on a telephone pole just below a white "No Stopping Standing or Parking" sign on a city street. Single family houses, cars parked on the side of the road, a large pine tree, and trees without leaves are in the background, while two trash cans ready for curbside pick up are in the front foreground. Wilmington, DE. (Photo Credit: Kaitlyn Delaney.)

On the nearly fifty signs that I have images of appear the following phrases, many multiple times: "Deaf Person in Area," "Deaf Child Area," "Deaf Child," "Caution Deaf Child in Area," "Deaf Pedestrians" with flashing yellow lights above and below the sign, "Watch for Deaf Child," "Autistic Child," "Autistic Child Area," "Autistic Child in Area," "Blind Pedestrian X-ing," "Blind Ped X-ing," "Blind Pedestrian," "Vision Impaired Person," "Blind," "Blind Child," "Blind Persons Crossing," "Deaf Blind Children X-ing," "Caution Deaf Blind Child in Area," "Handicap Child," "Handicap Child Area," and a wheelchair icon.[3] This collection includes a relatively short list of disabilities: deafness, deaf-blindness, blindness, mobility impairments, and autism. Too, in my sample, the words "Autistic", "Handicap", and "Deaf Blind" always co-occur with "Child" or "Children. Most of the images of signs I have are from suburban residential developments or along winding rural roads, with only a small handful from densely populated and highly trafficked urban settings.

Figure 7:Image description: A yellow diamond-shaped sign with a wheelchair icon on it as well as a rectangular sign with the word "Ahead" just below it are planted on a grassy median alongside a rural road in Connecticut. Large green leafy trees and bushes fill the side of the road. Ellington, CT. (Photo by author.)

The signs are placed by local municipalities, often by specific request from residents with final implementation and decision-making performed by city or state Department of Transportation employees. A Google search turns up many examples of online forms, downloadable PDFs and other means by which residents can put in a request for a sign in a specific location.[4] These forms are themselves a genre worthy of further analysis, although they fall outside the scope of this particular article. The behind-the-scenes maneuvers and structures that lead to the placement of a Deaf Person in Area sign certainly rely on many of the cultural orientations to disability that I detail in this article, but my attention here is fixed on intra-actions (Barad) once a sign is placed, particularly the stories that emerge as people make sense of the signs.[5]

The Deaf Person in Area Might Not Hear Cars Coming

Perhaps the most common rationale given for the sign is *"It's good that there's a sign because the Deaf Person in Area might not be able to hear cars coming."* It is commonsense, unquestioned, that this caution is needed because a Deaf Person in Area who (presumably) can't hear an approaching car might step into the road unexpectedly. As a consequence, motorists need to be vigilant, need to be warned. The sign discloses as valuable and important for protecting the Deaf Person in Area. I sometimes respond to this by pointing out that as a Deaf Person, I never assume that I can cross the street without looking. "In fact," I say, "*because* I know that I won't hear a car coming, I always look." My interlocutor may then say that while *I* might look, lots of other deaf people might not. Sometimes they add to this comment the mention of another (real or imagined) Deaf Person who would definitely need this sign. They might also/instead say, "you can't always see a car coming," challenging my (over)reliance on sight to determine when it is appropriate to cross a street. Underneath these comments lurks a sort of disability exceptionalism (Dunn) that casts successful disabled people as exceptions and positions an (often-imagined) other group as those for whom the signs need to exist.

Now, of course, my own embodied experiences as a deaf person are not representative of how all deaf people move through the world. And certainly, some of my non-deaf interlocutors have significant experiences interacting with deaf people. But there's something very telling about people who are not deaf assuming that they know what deaf people need in order to move safely through an environment. As the sign discloses these beliefs about the need to hear in order to walk safely around a neighborhood or to follow traffic signals, it also exposes some of the limits of hearing people's ability to understand what it means to not assume that they will hear cars approaching or what it means to always be vigilant with one's eyes or other kinds of sensory input. It also discloses the presumption that the only safety risk is disability, ignoring the fact that presumptions of safety are largely reserved for the bodies that are already expected within a space.

Indeed, notions about what constitutes safety vary not only according to individuals' disability identification, but also their perceptible race/ethnic identification, their gender and sexual identity, their relationships in and around an environment, and more. For example, recent events in the United States have highlighted stark differences in how different bodies are treated in public, as a pattern of White people calling the police to report on people of color doing everyday actions that would ordinarily attract no scrutiny (napping in a common area, barbecuing in a park, election canvassing, working as a real-estate agent, or taking a college tour) has been given national prominence (Molina). Thus, we can ask who is likely to believe or assume that a yellow diamond-shaped sign calling attention to a Deaf Person in Area will enhance the safety of said Deaf Person, particularly if the Deaf Person is not read as White. The recent case of Magdiel Sanchez, a deaf Latino man who was shot and killed by Oklahoma City police responding to a call about a hit-and-run (Doubek; Sanchez), makes such questions deeply pertinent to any exploration of the Deaf Person in Area sign. It is through such questions that the signs disclose presumptions of perceptible embodied privilege.

Not only do my interlocutors generally presume embodied privilege for the Deaf Person in Area, they also draw stark contrasts between hearing *ability* and deaf *inability*. When I point out that in my college town people regularly walk around with earbuds or large headphones over their ears, I am presented with a generous belief in the ability of those people to perfectly apprehend their surroundings. These defenses of hearing ability co-occur with presumptions of deaf inability to move safely through a neighborhood, necessitating the sign. Here again, the sign discloses a persistent cultural orientation to disability as a threat, in this case, to the presumed wholeness of a hearing identity.

Drivers Need to Know about the Deaf Person in Area So That They Will Drive More Carefully

A second common explanation for the Deaf Person in Area sign is that *"Drivers need to know there is a Deaf Person in Area so that they will drive more carefully."* Instead of centering the Deaf Person in Area's presumed inability to hear, this rationale centers on assumptions that drivers may make. If drivers assume that all the pedestrians or bicyclists and people in their vicinity can hear, they may then expect those pedestrians to stay out of the car's way. Conversely, if those drivers are reminded of a Deaf Person in Area, they may drive more carefully, now expecting that those in the vicinity may not hear a car. In fact, getting drivers to drive more carefully is the focus of many (if not all) road signs, especially those that feature children (e.g., "Children Playing"; "Keep Kids Alive, Drive 25"). However, this comment once again assumes that deaf people are not using any other sensory input to try and determine the presence of a car, and it ignores the fact that in the absence of specific guidance, most drivers do nothing at all to change their behavior.[6] Indeed, a 2007 Wisconsin Department of Transportation review of existing research indicates that "Children at Play" and other warning signs do not change drivers' behavior. The report specifically calls out the intractability of people's belief in the signs' efficacy: "A common theme is the ongoing struggle to explain to members of the public that their requests for these types of signs are based on faulty assumptions about their effectiveness."

One such faulty assumption might be that such signs would not exist without Good Reasons. But Department of Transportation employees, who ultimately construct and place the signs, do not necessarily have expertise around disability. Yellow diamond-shaped road signs that warn about dangerous curves or road conditions may fall squarely within their skillset, but the danger posed by (or to) a Deaf Person in Area is less clearly a topic about which DOT staff can (or should) claim professional expertise. And even when DOT employees may resist placing warning signs, as advocated in the Wisconsin DOT report, residents can and do draw on their own personal experiences to challenge the authority conveyed by the DOT (e.g., Brownlee). These residents may fear that a driver might not see the Deaf Person in Area or might not drive carefully enough through their neighborhood. Regardless of the process or the human agents involved in the signs' placement, the general perception of the signs' efficacy largely relies on non-disabled people's orientations to disability and its significance for moving in public space. These orientations often solely emphasize disability and tend to ignore intersections between disability, gender, sexuality, race and ethnicity, and other forms of oppression and/or privilege.

A Deaf Person in Area Might Not Follow Traffic Rules

Finally, a third common rationale is that *"A Deaf Person in Area (especially if they are a Deaf Child) might not follow traffic rules."* Fears of an accident may be amplified for many parents of disabled children because their children can take longer to learn expected traffic rules and behaviors. As typically framed, the problem is that because of their disabilities, these children may have an especially hard time following traffic rules. This final logic requires some additional parsing. To do that work, we need to zoom out a bit and consider the broader genre of yellow road signs.

The things on yellow diamond-shaped road signs are quite varied and include road hazards (e.g., "Slippery When Wet," "Bridge Ices Before Road"); various areas or spaces (e.g., bus stop; "Rock Slide Area," "Correctional Facility Area"); upcoming road shapes or conditions (e.g., "Lane Ends Merge Left," traffic signal, intersection, sharp curve); vehicles (e.g., fire engine, tractor, bicycle, horse and buggy, school bus); and animals (e.g., deer, alligator, bear, cougar, moose, bison, armadillo, rattlesnake, cow, duck[7]). The yellow color and (usually) diamond shape associate these signs with warning or caution. Within the broader ecology of yellow road signs, people are not typically indicated. In fact, disabled people, children, and pedestrians, including an immigration pedestrian sign, are the only people I have encountered on yellow diamond-shaped caution signs.[8] What does this disclosure reveal to us?

One way to answer this question is to parallel the common responses to the "Deaf Person in Area" sign with rationales for other things on yellow diamond-shaped signs. For example, one reason we have yellow diamond-shaped signs with different kinds of vehicles on them is because those vehicles move differently than do cars. As a consequence, drivers need to behave differently when one of these vehicles—a fire engine, a bicycle, a horse and buggy, a school bus, a tractor—is in the road. Similarly, being warned of an upcoming change in the road (a sharp turn or an intersection), a road hazard, or an environmental condition can enable motorists to take appropriate driving measures. All of these things involve caution, encouraging drivers to be attentive to things that they might not otherwise anticipate. These logics overlap significantly with rationales for the Deaf Person in Area sign.

But then we come to what is, arguably, the most varied—and for our purposes, interesting—sub-category of "things that are on yellow diamond-shaped signs": animals. The logics that explain why we have yellow diamond-shaped signs featuring an armadillo, deer, duck, moose, kangaroo, alligator, bison, big cats, cow, or rattlesnake in many ways are the same logics that explain why disabled people need to be on the signs. First, there is a presumption that *animals won't follow the rules of the road,* whether this is because they are not cast as intelligent enough, or because they are unreliable and unpredictable, or because they fall outside the boundaries of human rules of behavior. As a consequence, it is drivers who need to be responsible for watching out: they cannot assume that an armadillo (deer, duck, moose etc., etc.) in the vicinity will stay out of the way of their vehicle. There's also the argument that *drivers need to know an animal is in the vicinity so they will proceed more carefully.* This argument presents the sign as there for both drivers and animals: drivers will take in the information on the sign—the knowledge that a specific animal is (likely to be) in the area—and adjust accordingly. As a consequence, the sign helps support ecosystems that have been disrupted by a thick winding ribbon of black asphalt in their midst: if motorists take more care, then the road, the cars, the people, and the animals may be able to co-exist.

A third cultural logic also explains why animals appear on yellow diamond-shaped signs. That is: *a threatening animal is in the area and drivers should exercise caution.* All of the animals on yellow diamond-shaped signs can be interpreted in terms of threat—whether the threat is to the animals (by a car hitting or running into them), or to a car (a large animal like a deer or moose can damage a vehicle), or to people in the car (an accident can cause injury, some animals can harm humans). This threat also calls into being other types of threats presented by yellow diamond-shaped signs. This is the flip side to the paternalistic narrative of disability centered in the earlier discussion of responses to the "Deaf Person in Area" sign. While we can read the yellow diamond-shaped sign as an invitation to take extra care, perhaps in the spirit of "it takes a village," the choice to convey this need for additional care on a yellow diamond-shaped sign (and not, say, on another color or shape of sign [9]) communicate that these are intended as warnings.

What does it mean to connect disabled people with these other concepts on yellow diamond-shaped signs? One answer comes through Mel Y. Chen's theorizing of animacy. Chen notes the linguistic definition of animacy as the "quality of liveness, sentience, or human-ness of a noun or noun phrase that has grammatical, often syntactic, consequences" (24) and then uses this concept to show how "the 'animal' is relentlessly recruited as the presumed field of rejection of and for the 'human'" (23-34). Chen identifies the stickiness of animal-like properties to some categories of humans through animacy, a move that ultimately separates them from having full humanity while preserving humanity for those who are not-disabled, not-queer, not-female, not-children, not racial and/or ethnic minorities, and so on.

Thus, it is no coincidence that the logics used to explain why we need animals on yellow diamond-shaped signs overlap with the logics used to explain why disabled people and disabled children need to be on the signs. Because (some kinds of) disabled people as well as (deaf, blind, and autistic) children are not presumed to have appropriate cognition or behavior or understanding, they need to be warned about. Others around these (disabled) people and (deaf, blind, and/or autistic) children need to be reminded of the presence of disability in order to avoid harm to themselves or to others. This dehumanization is achieved by comparing (some kinds of) disabled people and children with non-human animals. Chen writes, "The sentience of a noun phrase has linguistic and grammatical consequences, and these consequences are never merely grammatical and linguistic, but also deeply political" (55). The political nature of these yellow diamond-shaped signs comes into focus when considering the sorts of animacy—that is, the liveliness, movement, and activity—of groups identified on the signs.

I have numerous examples (and variations) of "Blind Child," "Deaf Child," and "Autistic Child." I have numerous examples of "Blind Pedestrian" and "Deaf Pedestrian" as well as blind and deaf "students." I do not have any examples of an "Autistic Pedestrian" sign or an "Autistic Student" or "Autistic Person in Area" sign. Autism, at least within the genre of yellow diamond-shaped signs that I have collected, is only and always attached to children. The question of disabled personhood and subjecthood, then, is limned through the grammar and genre of yellow diamond-shaped signs.

Again and again, these yellow diamond-shaped signs confirm Chen's observation that vivid links, whether live or long-standing, continue to be drawn between immigrants, people of color, laborers and working-class subjects, colonial subjects, women, queer subjects, disabled people, and *animals*, meaning, not the class of creatures that includes humans but quite the converse, the class against which the (often rational) human with inviolate and full subjectivity is defined. (95)

Let me return to the common responses I get when I raise the topic of the yellow diamond-shaped "Deaf Person in Area" sign. The sticky links between disability and animals that I have been discussing are underscored in the observation that people wearing headphones or earbuds may not hear everything in their surroundings. The (surprisingly fierce) defenses I experience of these pedestrians' ability to hear cars coming, paired with justifications for a Deaf Person in Area to have a sign announcing their presence resonates with the adherence of animacy to Deaf Persons. The de-humanized "Deaf Person" (etc., etc.) is not *presumed* to have competency and agency in the way that the *presumed* perfectly-intact, fully-human hearing person with headphones does. The fully-human person is often akin to the normate (Garland-Thomson), a mythical figure that nobody actually lives up to but which is imagined as embodying and enminding every form of privilege: white, male, cisgendered, able-bodied, heteronormative, wealthy, and so on. When a real figure is revealed, that figure's departure from or relationship to each of these forms of privilege can then become material for dehumanization, for asserting that anything that happens to them is an individual occurrence rather than squarely set within a nexus of intersecting discriminations and patterns of exclusion and violence aimed directly at particular kinds of bodies and minds.

The signs thus operate according to an animate hierarchy that places adult humans with full sensory capacity at the top, while children, disabled people, and disabled children fall lower down the scale, simultaneously de-subjectifying and objectifying them (Chen 40). Being understood as something that would be placed on a yellow diamond-shaped caution sign is effectively to have a comparison made between you and other road hazards, between you and other animals that either don't know or won't follow the rules of the road, or between you and things that are dangerous to drivers. We also can identify a hierarchy whereby autism would arguably be placed below deaf and blind because of its consistent association with childhood and its lack of association with the identities of "Pedestrian" or "Student."[10]

These associations do not emerge out of thin air. We must also ask after the background—what environments or support systems make these dehumanizations so sticky, so persistent in our cultural attention (Chen). For example, as I noted earlier, many of the images of yellow diamond-shaped signs that I've collected are from suburban locations, largely featuring neatly trimmed yards and single-family homes. This might seem to suggest that disability is an unusual presence within such environs, as well as reinforcing links between (presumed) whiteness and assumptions around safety and risk and disability. The logic of yellow diamond-shaped signs discloses assumptions about disability as inability, disability as threat, and disability as requiring protection. The signs, through dehumanization and objectification of disability, disclose ableist logics of humanity that deny full agency and subjecthood to disabled people. By revealing the operations of animacy that play out on yellow diamond-shaped signs, then, rhetoricians and community-members can intervene in these structures of meaning-making by challenging and addressing the oppressive logics that perpetuate these cultural narratives of disability, race, gender, class, and more.

Signs of Disability Disclosing Differently

In this article, I've explored how yellow diamond-shaped signs disclose disability within public spaces. Attention to such disclosures can help rhetoric scholars understand what people perceive and pay attention to as they negotiate everyday environments and encounters. In the course of such encounters, the material world and environment discloses meanings and possibilities and orientations. The rhetorical analyses performed in this article aim to deepen our understanding of the meanings of disability that emerge as people move among material artifacts and environments. The disclosures effected through these movements significantly shape the orientations people take towards disability and in turn, their engagement with cultural logics that shape perceptions of and interactions with disability.

These cultural logics are not unique to the yellow diamond-shaped signs that I've focused on in this article, of course. Yellow diamond-shaped signs that index (some kinds of) disability owe to their very existence already-circulating cultural logics of disability that enable such signs to "make sense." Titchkosky calls attention to the separation between disability and humanity observed within the yellow diamond-shaped signs as she muses on justifications for person-first language. These justifications, she argues, suggest that "[w]e should cautiously move disability to the rear and move personhood to the front with the hope of removing, or at least minimizing, the danger that disability is" (54). While her focus is not yellow diamond-shaped caution signs, she presciently uses the word "caution" to indicate the relationship formed with disability through person-first language. In this way, the yellow diamond-shaped signs come into contact and interact with other linguistic moves around naming and pointing to disability, creating amplifications and resonances that seep into and shore up collective orientations to disability-as-threat that have material and discursive consequences for disabled people.

My intention with this critique is for rhetoricians of everyday life to analyze and surface cultural logics that stigmatize and diminish disability by making them more perceptible and thus available for critique. When cultural logics operate at the level of common sense or assumption, they erase the range and variation of lived experiences and can subsume disabled people into paternalistic narratives that presume their inability and incompetence—or deny their humanity and perpetuate violence upon them. This article has shown how rhetoricians can access these signs' disclosures through the stories people tell about interactions with the signs.

Signs of disability enable close, patterned attention across interactions for what perceptual cues different kinds of signs make available for examination. The framing of disclosure in this article contributes to new materialist rhetorical scholarship by demonstrating how rhetoricians can gather data about and analyze people's interactions with their material surround generally and with signs of disability specifically. Hekman reminds us that "[t]o disclose is not to reveal the true objective reality of an object. Rather, it is to engage in a complex practice in which multiple elements interact, or intra-act, to produce an understanding of the reality that we share" (93). This broader awareness of and attention to signs of disability can help rhetoric scholars unpack disability as it is disclosed and takes shape interactionally. Rhetorical analysis will then be better-poised to intervene in discourses that amplify violences against disabled people, particularly those who experience multiple forms of marginalization and oppression. Through such work, the signs of disability around us can disclose differently.

Notes

1. I'm deeply grateful to Laurie Gries and two anonymous reviewers for their thoughtful and generous feedback on this piece as it moved through the publication process. I thank Jessica Edwards, Asia Friedman, Annika Konrad, Melanie Yergeau, and especially Sean Zdenek for their thoughts and comments as the project developed. And last but not least, I owe a tremendous debt of gratitude to the academic writing space created by Jacquie and Nadine Mattis at Easton's Nook, where this project unfolded over multiple deep dives into the material and writing.

2. I include image descriptions of each photograph for accessibility purposes and because these descriptions serve an analytic function within the article. Throughout, I follow guidelines for image descriptions offered by accessibility resources such as WebAIM and AbilityNet. This means I focus on "describe[ing] the information, not the picture" (Rule 2, Sollinger) and because my descriptions

are longer than generally desirable for hidden alt-attribute information, I prefer to include the image descriptions immediately below the image, set aside and marked as image descriptions. This move also helps all readers—not simply those who rely on image descriptions—follow my argument and notice key aspects of the image. In this way, the descriptions are not intended to serve as a "neutral" recounting of what is in the image (indeed, neutrality in image descriptions is impossible, as what we notice, and consequently describe, is always influenced by what we are poised to notice, a key point I develop throughout this essay).

3. Relatedly, I have a few examples of signs that are not yellow, such as a white rectangular sign with red lettering that says "Caution Disabled Pedestrians in Area" photographed in Newark, DE).

4. Some require certification of disability, others simply ask a set of questions about desired sign placement. Some indicate an age cap and most stipulate that if the person for whom the sign is being placed moves away, residents should request that the sign be taken down. Some offer some guidelines for when a sign would be considered. Language for the signs varies from community to community as well, reflecting the variety in the signs that I've collected photographs of.

5. Some additional discussion may be important on this point, simply because of the sheer number of times this question has come up as I've presented and shared this work in different contexts. Perhaps the most common questions I get when I share my work with these signs are: "Tell me more about how these signs even get placed in this environment? How did that sign get there? Who was responsible?" The truth is that I don't have access to the interactions that lead these signs to be placed in communities, although I have engaged with some of the texts that support the signs' emergence: news articles, blog posts, online forms for requesting a sign's placement. And yet, even though I *am* intensely interested in social interaction, which has been the focus of a great deal of my earlier work, my current project, of which this article is one small part, does not rely on recorded interactions of disclosure (for several complex methodological reasons). Thus, in order to understand the meanings for disability that matter to the world that humans move within, I've turned my attention to materiality, disclosure, and narrative to (even partially) build an understanding of how disclosures work. My focus on storying, then, means that I am less concerned with how a sign got there and more concerned with what sense people make—through narrative—of a sign that is in place.

6. Towner (2019) acknowledges the difference in experience between navigating warning signs in a familiar environment versus experiencing signs in an unfamiliar environment (e.g., a vacation locale). Research on perception, routine, ritual, and cognitive processing has shown that as people build familiarity in their environment and in their daily practices, they attend less carefully to individual steps and moments along the way. The same goes for warning signs: perhaps when the signs are new, they are carefully attended. After a period of time, they become part of the background and are not actively perceived and attended to.

7. I have examples of each of these signs.

8. We could, arguably, include a "Correctional Facility Area" that I photographed on NY-273 just outside of Fishkill as an indirect reference to people, on the

basis that the caution sign is not about the facility itself per se, but likely warning against picking up hitchhikers or people who might be walking along the highway in this area.

9. For instance, many "Keep Kids Alive, Drive 25" signs are white rectangles with black and red text and images, rather than yellow diamond-shaped caution signs.

10. The persistence of rhetorics that dehumanize autism are powerfully documented in Melanie Yergeau's *Authoring Autism*.

Works Cited

Abdelhadi, Abla. "Addressing the Criminalization of Disability from a Disability Justice Perspective: Centring the Experiences of Disabled Queer Trans Indigenous and People of Colour." *Feminist Wire*, 21 Nov. 2013, https://thefeministwire.com/2013/11/addressing-the-criminalization-of-disability-from-a-disability-justice-framework-centring-the-experiences-of-disabled-queer-trans-indigenous-and-people-of-colour.

Al Zidjaly, Najma. *Disability, Discourse and Technology: Agency and Inclusion in (Inter)action*. Palgrave Macmillan, 2015.

Barad, Karen. *Meeting the Universe Halfway: Quantum Physics and the Entanglement of Matter and Meaning*. Duke UP, 2007.

Barnes, Elizabeth. *The Minority Body: A Theory of Disability*. Oxford UP, 2016.

Ben-Moshe, Liat and Justin Powell. "Sign of our Times? Revis(it)ing the International Symbol of Access." *Disability and Society*, vol. 22, no. 5, 2007, pp. 489-505.

Brownlee, Mike. "City Reverses Stance on 'Deaf Child' Signage." *The Daily Nonpareil*, 28 Feb. 2010, https://www.nonpareilonline.com/archive/city-reverses-stance-on-deaf-child-signage/article_a90ca15a-bed8-5bfd-b3a7-0f7f629aefdd.html

Chen, Mel Y. *Animacies: Biopolitics, Racial Mattering, and Queer Affect*. Duke UP, 2012.

Citton, Yves. *The Ecology of Attention*. Translated by Barnaby Norman, Polity Press, 2017.

Clare, Eli. *Brilliant Imperfection: Grappling with Cure*. Duke UP, 2017.

Doubek, James. "Oklahoma City Police Fatally Shoot Deaf Man Despite Yells Of 'He Can't Hear.'" *National Public Radio*, 21 Sep. 2017, https://www.npr.org/sections/thetwo-way/2017/09/21/552527929/oklahoma-city-police-fatally-shoot-deaf-man-despite-yells-of-he-cant-hear-you.

Dougher, Kelly. "How Not to be a Dick to a Deaf Person." *xoJane*, 29 May 2013, https://web.archive.org/web/20170207010832/http://www.xojane.com/issues/how-not-to-be-a-dick-to-your-deaf-friend.

Dunn, Dana S. *The Social Psychology of Disability*. Oxford UP, 2015.

Edbauer, Jenny. "Unframing Models of Public Distribution: From Rhetorical Situation to Rhetorical Ecologies." *Rhetoric Society Quarterly*, vol. 35, no. 4, 2005, pp. 5-24.

Elman, Julie Passanante. "Policing at the Synapse: Ferguson, Race, and the Disability Politics of the Teen Brain." *Somatosphere: Science, Medicine, and Anthropology.* 4 May 2015, http://somatosphere.net/2015/05/policing-at-the-synapse-ferguson-race-and-the-disability-politics-of-the-teen-brain.html.

Erevelles, Nirmala and Andrea Minear. "Unspeakable Offenses: Untangling Race and Disability in Discourses of Intersectionality." *Journal of Literary and Cultural Disability Studies*, vol. 4, no. 2, 2010, pp. 127-145.

Friedman, Asia. *Blind to Sameness: Sexpectations and the Social Construction of Male and Female Bodies.* U of Chicago P, 2013.

—. "Cultural Blind Spots and Blind Fields: Collective Forms of Unawareness." Forthcoming in *The Oxford Handbook of Cognitive Sociology*, Oxford UP.

Fritsch, Kelly. "The Neoliberal Circulation of Affects: Happiness, Accessibility, and the Capacitation of Disability as Wheelchair." *Health, Culture and Society*, vol. 5, no. 1, 2013, pp. 135-149.

Garland-Thomson, Rosemarie. *Extraordinary Bodies: Figuring Physical Disability in American Culture and Literature.* Columbia UP, 1997.

Guffey, Elizabeth. *Designing Disability: Symbols, Space, and Society.* Bloomsbury, 2018.

Hamraie, Aimi. *Building Access: Universal Design and the Politics of Disability.* U of Minnesota P, 2017.

Hekman, Susan. *The Material of Knowledge: Feminist Disclosures.* Indiana UP, 2010.

Hendren, Sara. "An Icon is a Verb: About the Project." *The Accessible Icon Project*, Feb. 2016, http://accessibleicon.org/#an-icon-is-a-verb.

Kafer, Alison. *Feminist, Queer, Crip.* Indiana UP, 2013.

Kerschbaum, Stephanie L. *Toward a New Rhetoric of Difference.* National Council of Teachers of English, 2014.

Kim, Eunjung. "Asexuality in Disability Narratives." *Sexualities*, vol. 14, no. 4, 2011, pp. 479-93.

Kress, Gunther. *Multimodality: A Social Semiotic Approach to Contemporary Communication.* Routledge, 2010.

Molina, Brett. "Cashing Checks, Napping, More Activities Leading to Police Calls on Black People in 2018." *USA Today.* 20 Dec. 2018, https://www.usatoday.com/story/news/nation/2018/12/20/black-people-doing-normal-things-who-had-police-called-them-2018/2374750002/.

Moore, Leroy F. Jr., Talila A. Lewis, and Lydia X. Z. Brown, et al. "Accountable Reporting on Disability, Race, and Police Violence: A Community Response to the 'Ruderman White Paper on Media Coverage on Use of Force and Disability.'" *Tumblr*, https://harriettubmancollective.tumblr.com/post/174479075753/accountable-reporting-on-disability-race-and.

Powell, Malea, Daisy Levy, Andrea Riley-Mukavetz, Marilee Brooks-Gillies, Maria Novotny, Jennifer Fisch-Ferguson, and the Cultural Rhetorics Theory Lab. "Our Story Begins Here: Constellating Cultural Rhetorics." *enculturation*, no. 18, 2014, enculturation.net/our-story-begins-here.

Ridgeway, Cecilia L. *Framed by Gender: How Gender Inequality Persists in the Modern World.* Oxford UP, 2011.

Sanchez, Rebecca. "Linguistic Othering." The Paradox of the Other Conference, Brooklyn College, Brooklyn, NY. 5 May 2018. Conference presentation.

Scollon, Ron and Suzie Wong Scollon. *Discourses in Place: Language in the Material World*. Routledge, 2003.

Schweik, Susan M. *The Ugly Laws: Disability in Public*. New York UP, 2010.

Sins Invalid. "10 Principles of Disability Justice." *Sins Invalid*, http://sinsinvalid.org/blog/10-principles-of-disability-justice.

Sollinger, Stefan. *AbilityNet*. 1 Feb. 2014, https://www.abilitynet.org.uk/blog/five-golden-rules-compliant-alt-text.

Stremlau, Tonya. "Deaf Pedestrians." *241 Mom*. 9 Apr. 2013, https://241mom.wordpress.com/2013/04/09/deaf-pedestrians/.

Titchkosky, Tanya. *The Question of Access: Disability, Space, Meaning*. U of Toronto P, 2011.

Towner, Emil B. "Danger in Public Spaces: Strengths and Limitations of Image- and Text-Based Warning Signs." *Business and Professional Communication Quarterly*, vol. 82, no. 1, 2019, pp. 53-73.

Vest, Jennifer Lisa. "What Doesn't Kill You: Existential Luck, Postracial Racism, and the Subtle and Not So Subtle Ways the Academy Keeps Women of Color Out." *Seattle Journal for Social Justice*, vol. 12, no. 2, 2013, pp. 471-518.

WisDOT Research & Library Unit. "Effectiveness of 'Children at Play' Warning Signs." Wisconsin Department of Transportation. 25 Sep. 2007, 54.172.27.91/transportation/signs/ChildrenWarningSigns_TSR_2007.pdf.

Yergeau, Melanie. *Authoring Autism: On Rhetoric and Neurological Queerness*. Duke UP, 2017.

Zerubavel, Eviatar. *Hidden in Plain Sight: The Social Structure of Irrelevance*. Oxford UP, 2015.

—. *Taken for Granted: The Remarkable Power of the Unremarkable*. Princeton UP, 2018.

Supplemental Material

Signs of Disability, Disclosing

Stephanie L. Kerschbaum

Part I: Reflection on the Origins of the Article

The Deaf Person in Area sign that is at the heart of the article first appeared in my neighborhood in the early 2010s, but it was a long process of carrying that sign with me in various ways that led to it becoming an article. Looking for signs that named or pointed to disability led to me also paying attention to what types of signs pointed to disability. That in turn led me to begin sorting into categories the kinds of things that are on yellow diamond-shaped signs.

At one point while these ideas were still germinating, I was driving through a wooded area and thinking about yellow diamond-shaped signs with deer on them and thinking about where such signs were likely to appear. This, along with the work on disability and animality by scholars such as Mel Chen and Sunaura Taylor helped me to link the signs to strategies and practices of dehumanization that often relied upon animal figures.

This is a piece that very much grew from lived experience of navigating everyday spaces—a form of theorizing that many cultural rhetoric scholars and critical race scholars have long recognized as significant for building scholarly knowledge. In this, the piece also developed through the opportunities and generosity shared by many people—on social media and through text messages and email—who sent me signs that they observed in their neighborhoods and communities or on their travels as well as their thoughts and observations about these signs. The methodology of story that undergirds this article was thus deeply supported by regular opportunities to talk about, notice, and interact with other people performing their own noticing as well as offering me some access to signs beyond those I personally encountered. In this way, this work reflects an outgrowth of tremendous generosity, emerging and shaped by practices of daily noticing and shifting attunement(s).

Part II: Description of Research Methods, Findings, and/or Pedagogical Impact

Thinking about the Deaf Person in Area sign opened up a lot of questions for me about how disability comes to be recognized in all kinds of spaces and environments and interactions. I spent time thinking about, for instance, my own (relational) embodiment as manifesting signs of disability, building on the concept of markers of difference that I forwarded in *Toward a New Rhetoric of Difference*. Markers of difference were defined in that book as dynamic, emergent, and relational rhetorical cues that pointed to difference between two or more interlocutors, but the yellow diamond-shaped Deaf Person in Area sign required me to ask some different questions. In particular, it invited a turn to considering the mattering of material artifacts and environments that are at work in interactions but are not always openly named, pointed to, or described. This led to thinking about signs of disability as enabling attention to cues that point to disability but not limiting those cues to linguistic and interactional means of signaling. This article was my attempt to write through all that I was learning about various approaches to the material in rhetorical studies and related disciplines, including feminist studies, cultural rhetorics, and disability studies.

Part III: Discussion Questions

1. This article uses a story-driven methodology to understand how the Deaf Person in Area sign is doing rhetorical work. What are the affordances and challenges associated with this approach? What approaches might complement or offer other possibilities for interpretation / analysis?

2. Consider where you are as you read and discuss this article. How is your body arranged in space and/or in relation to other entities? Notice the sensory input you are processing. What signs of disability are available to you? What about signs that might indicate disability's absence or erasure?

3. What (types of) signs of disability are you already attentive to, and which ones might you need to challenge yourself to recognize? What interrelationships among race, gender, sexuality, geographic region, socioeconomic class, religion, and more influence the signs of disability that you recognize or don't recognize / are learning to recognize?

COLLEGE COMPOSITION AND COMMUNICATION

College Composition and Communication is on the web at https://cccc.ncte.org/cccc/ccc

The Conference on College Composition and Communication (CCCC) is committed to supporting the agency, power, and potential of diverse communicators inside and outside of postsecondary classrooms. CCCC advocates for broad and evolving definitions of literacy, communication, rhetoric, and writing (including multimodal discourse, digital communication, and diverse language practices) that emphasize the value of these activities to empower individuals and communities. CCCC promotes intellectual and pedagogical freedom and ethical scholarship and communication.

Developing a Relational Scholarly Practice: Snakes, Dreams, and Grandmothers[1]

Andrea Riley Mukavetz weaves stories on her relationships with the land, ancestral knowledge, and her experiences in doing research to theorize a relational scholarly practice. She invites readers to contemplate and grapple with her on what land-based knowledges, indigenous intellect, and relationality can offer rhetoric and composition studies.

---

1. *College Composition and Communication*, vol. 71, no. 4., 2020. © 2020 by NCTE.

Developing a Relational Scholarly Practice: Snakes, Dreams, and Grandmothers

Andrea Riley Mukavetz

"For all of us, becoming indigenous to a place means living as if your children's future mattered, to take care of the land as if our lives, both material and spiritual, depended on it" (Kimmerer 9)

I come to you with a good heart.

   I have been afraid of snakes since I was around seven years old. As a child, my boy cousins used to chase me around the neighborhood with water snakes and garter snakes. Thirty years later and I still haven't forgiven them. I've always defined my relationship with nature and the land by my fear of snakes. Whether I am fishing, swimming, strolling on the trail behind my house, or gardening, I often wonder if there is a slithery friend close by. My body is full of adrenaline and my experience outside is often a mix of fear and tranquility. Whenever I see a slithery friend greet me, I shriek, jump, and run in the other direction. I retreat indoors.

   Relatives, I am going to tell you some stories about my relationship with snakes. These stories are snake stories *and* used to theorize a relational scholarly practice that draws from the decolonial option in cultural and indigenous rhetorics. By reflecting on the complicated and somewhat obsessive relationship to snakes, I articulate a relationship to land-based practices and land-based methodologies in my writing. It is easy to write joyfully about the practices that are easy and uncomplicated (are there practices that are easy and uncomplicated?) but what about the practices that scare us, challenge us, leave us with few answers or unarticulated meanings? Like my relationship with snakes, I am, in fact, somewhat obsessed with the concept of relationality--a core practice and worldview that guides and frames my orientation to knowledge making. In *Research is Ceremony* (2008), Shawn Wilson describes an indigenous research paradigm as one built on relationships--on accountability. He writes that "relationships do not merely shape reality, they are reality (7)." To orient to the world--to knowledge making through relational accountability is to develop a series of respectful and reciprocal practices to other agents and beings where we (re: human actors) are not at the center of this constellated network but just one aspect of the web.

I want to share that I've been writing this article, in some variation, for a long time. Some of these stories were written from 2008-2012 when I conducted two oral history projects with a group of Odawa women. A few stories came from the B-sides of my dissertation--the scraps that I saved and tucked into my back pocket for later always carrying them with me like a tobacco pouch. The rest of these stories have arisen as I've carried and returned to the B-sides while completing other projects, living that tenure-track life, and having babies. I share this because it further exemplifies my understanding of relationality: relationships are ever changing and always in negotiation. My relationship to this knowledge has changed as my relationship to time, space, and my own body have changed. As relationality guides my framework and worldview, I am encouraged to make knowledge and pay attention to how the meaning and the knowledge itself changes as the relationships do.

I am invested in theorizing and enacting a relational scholarly practice because I hope it contributes to the sub-field of cultural rhetorics and the overall discipline of Rhetoric and Composition as another option for making and sharing knowledge. I see my work as a part of an ongoing discussion on understanding how to write from and about a rhetorical tradition that disrupts a post-Enlightenment narrative of rhetoric--one that prioritizes a Greco-Roman tradition as the referent for rhetorical knowledge (CR Theory Lab, 2014). This constelled discussion takes place as critical rhetorics (Kynard 2018, Martinez 2014), disability rhetorics (Yergeau 2017, Price 2011), feminist rhetorics (Royster and Kirsch 2012), critical pedagogy (Haas 2012, Cedillo 2017, Inoue 2015), administration and higher education (Perryman-Clark and Craig, 2019), and trans and queer rhetorics (Hsu 2018, Patterson 2016). Here, I offer a web of relations who might orient to rhetoric or knowledge differently and speak to additional audiences than I do. Yet, they all acknowledge an investment in disrupting this preference for a Greco-Roman canon for the pain it has caused and how it has furthered imperialistic and heteronormative beliefs and practices in our professional spaces, classrooms, and research. These scholarly conversations do not end with deconstruction or disruption. As The Cultural Rhetorics Theory Lab acknowledges: cultural rhetorics is a "temporarily, hopeful intervention" designed to make space for another generation of scholars to write and research in their language, on their terms, and for and with and alongside the communities they value. All of these scholars and so many more are invested in making space for another generation and kind of scholarship. Typically, there would be a literature review here that traces the scholarship that has shaped my understanding of land-based methods, snake semiotics, or relationality. Some of that will come much later when I am ready to situate my own snake stories into larger conversations by Indigenous women. Before telling any snake stories, I want to begin my dwelling on the land with you where I will share more about myself and how I understand my relationship to the world. My hope is that this intimate offering of story and experience will create an opening for you to land-story with me. After all, being a good storyteller means creating an intimate and participatory relationship with the audience.

A relational scholarly practice is about developing a relationship with indigenous intellect. I am going to encourage you, dear reader, to develop a rich, deep, and reciprocal relationship to the land you dwell on and the indigenous people of that land—to carry those histories, cultures, and teachings with you in your writing, research, teaching, and every day practice. In tribal nations communities, it is a common practice to extend a land-recognition before a meeting or ceremony occurs. These recognitions or acknowledgements are intentional statements of relational accountability: to the land and the people. It's a way to announce that one will be a good visitor and practice right relations. Now we will practice it together, I will go first.

> Aaniin,[1] Andrea Riley Mukavetz nindizhinikaaz. Deshkan Ziibiing Anishinaabeg. Ahjijawk nindoodem. Waawiyaataanong Nindonjibaa. My mother's people, the Bakkals and Mansours, come from Baghdad, Iraq. Currently, I live in Gaaginwaajiwanaang, at the place of the long rapids. Michigan is the recognized territory of the People of the Three Fires: Ojibwe, Odawa and Bodowadomie (Potawatomie). In Gaaginwaajiwanaang, there are several recognized nations such as the Match-E-Be-Nash-She-Wish Band (Gun Lake Nation), the Grand Traverse Band of Ottawa and Chippewa Indians, Little Traverse Bay Band of Odawa Indians, the Saginaw Chippewa Indians, and Grand River Band of Ottawa Indians.

In *As We've Always Done: Indigenous Freedom through Radical Resistance* (2017), Leanne Betamosake Simpson begins with the importance of land-recognitions as a form of community and communal memory. She shares a story about how she witnessed community elders take the time to share what the land was like before settlement--before contact. For Simpson, the insistence of sharing these stories become a teaching to remember how colonialism impacted the actual land--that industrialization and other narratives of progress, innovation, and improvement have consequences to impact generations to come. Simpson argues that these teachings are necessary for

---

1. Miigwetch to my cousin, Ashley Riley for helping me with the language and sharing her teachings. Miigwetch to Belinda Bardwell, Steven Naganashe Perry, Rob Yob, Hunter Genia, Simone Jonatis, Becky Wilson Matthews, Samantha Gaan, Brooklynn Lipponen, and Natasha Stewart for sharing their stories, teachings, and language with me.

indigenous resurgence. Like Simpson, I understand land recognitions as a land-based method that is embodied, ancestral, and necessary for indigenous visibility and want to share additional details about Grand Rapids, Michigan where I am currently living and working.

> In Gaaginwaajiwanaang (the place of long rapids), the city is separated by the Grand River. Before settlement, the Odawa lived along the shores. As I learned from community member Lin Bardwell, on one side of the river, it was swampy and the other side was much higher. On the higher side, is where the Odawa set up their camps and retrieved the materials needed to build these camps. Sometimes, when I am at the Eberhert Center, I take some time to stand and visit with the river. I put tobacco down. I try to erase the bright blue steel bridge and the buildings owned by Amway and DeVoss. I imagine the black walnut trees, the gardens created by the families who lived there, the smell of the wild strawberries and blueberry bushes, and the multiple fires set up. I wonder about the way grass looked before settlement--about how it felt, the length, how it was mixed with clover and daisy, and native plants we might never even know of.

To remember and acknowledge the land is to engage in bloody memory and felt theory[2]. All our histories and relationships are different. When I story the Grand River, I cannot help but mourn. I feel encouragement to keep remembering and to continue learning my traditions and histories. Where I am encouraging an emphasis on recognizing indigenous histories and territories, this is not where settlers should end especially if they are interested in settler harm reduction and decoloniality. Performing a land recognition during a conference or meeting is an important gesture of acknowledging indigenous visibility but it is nowhere near enough. In other words, I am encouraging you to acknowledge whose land you are settled on because I believe it is a crucial step to land-based methods and it will, hopefully, impact how you understand your relationship to land and those multiple, constellated histories should impact your orientation to research and writing. Yet, I am also saying that you should not and cannot end with a land recognition.

As I've tried to show, the landscape and understanding of indigenous nations has changed due to settler colonialism. In an effort to better make visible settler privilege, the change of landscape, and to be in relation to all the histories of this land, it's necessary to also know settler histories. I consider all those who intended to stay and lay claim to a space that is not their ancestral

---

2. For more information on felt theory and blood memory, please look to Dian Million's work.

territory as settlers. Of course, this becomes complicated when considering those stolen, those who had to leave, and those who may call another country home. Not all settlers carry the same privileges yet they might be complicit in the occupation of indigenous land. There are multiple settler histories in West Michigan from the Latinx and Xicanx populations who understand Grandville Avenue as an important cultural marker, the Dutch community who mainly arrived during and after WWII and have a strong connection to the rural and farming communities, or the Black population mainly around Burton Heights and Garfield Park. These settler histories, which do not include the refugee experiences from Bosnia and the Sudan or the large yet often invisible Korean and Vietnamese communities, narrate and map Grand Rapids--they inform my work, orientation, and ways of being. Now, it's your turn. Take the time to learn about the indigenous people of your land. Begin with an internet search. Locate the local tribal nations (recognized and unrecognized), find the friendship center, the American Indian lodge, the American Indian Health clinic, or who puts on the powwow. When you go to the powwow, listen to the MC perform the land recognition, tell some jokes, and then get real serious sharing his knowledge. Take some time to read poetry, fiction, or non-fiction by tribal nations people from the same territory. Pay attention to how they describe the land[3]. Then, take some time to do some research on settlers in your area. What stories do settlers tell about the land and settlement? What kind of visibility is apparent? What businesses and store fronts make their existence tangible? How do you make sense of all of these histories together?

I know that I am asking a lot of you, dear readers. Or, when considering the current political climate including the lack of consultation and listening to indigenous perspectives when dealing with global climate justice, tribal nations voting rights, the kidnapping of indigenous children, and murdered and missing Indigenous women, maybe I am not asking enough. I share this because I want to emphasize that indigenous survival and self-determination is deeply tied to the land. I hope that this activity gives you some access to contemplating the role of settler history and settler visibility in your area. Theorizing through relationality is a long, snakey process. I don't always know where it ends and where it begins. It slinks through, above, and within the land--exposing while hiding.

---

3. In all my classes, I ask my students to do this activity to locate themselves in West Michigan.

Snake-Grandma Stories

In my family, sharing stories about our dreams and trying to understand the meaning of our dreams is a common practice--a way we spend time together. I can still remember spending mornings at the kitchen table with my parents drinking chai or coffee and sharing dream stories. There were so many times when my mother woke us with her screaming. At the old oak table, we would find out that she thought she lost us or our father—that someone was trying to hurt her. She referred to them as stress dreams from working too many hours at Montgomery Wards. When I started graduate school, snakes, rats, hybrid rat-snakes or snake-rats taunted and haunted me in my dreams. I would feel them in my bed, wrapping themselves around my legs. Sometimes, they would slither around my desk or poke their small heads out while I worked. At one point, I would pull the covers back before going to bed or check the drawers of my desk before sitting down to write. I admit, it was a little neurotic but rat-snakes are pretty fucking scary.

Everyone thinks that my nightmares are the funniest: my sisters are unsympathetic when I tell them that I had another dream about snakes. They laugh and laugh, slapping their hands to their thighs. But, I'll call my mom for our morning chat, when we both are having our first cup of tea--bitter from steeping too long. It's how the Bakkal women like their tea. My mom understands. She's always asking me, "What does it mean, Andrea?" I don't really have an answer and tend to shrug it off. The dreams that get the most attention are when our family members visit. These are the dreams that our family considers blessings; moments when we can remember our deceased family member, reflect on our relationship to that person, and think about the significance of the family member coming to us; to take the time to speak to us, guide us, and teach us. When I talk about these dreams, even my sisters look up from their phones waiting for the story. The Riley/Bakkal stories are often positioned between a sense of loss for the deceased loved one while negotiating the joy of being presented with another opportunity to revisit our relationship to the family member, to fellow family members, to the old ways and the old world. I understand my dreams similarly to how I understand my writing. The making of writing is the work of grief and joy: always intertwined, inseparable—in constant loss and renewal. I have always been a writer and a dreamer just like academia has been and will always be an indigenous space.

For a long time, I carried one specific dream with me telling it to anyone who will listen. Through re-telling, I created an embodied re-experiencing of the story to engage in understanding and critical reflection[4]. In my dream,

---

4. In *Asegi Stories* (2014), Qwo-li Driskill theorizes "restorying as a retelling and

my maternal grandmother, Najiba tells me to go and visit my paternal grandmother, Helena, at her house on Waverly Road. For a long time, that is all I remembered. Instead, I was stuck on wondering why one grandmother encouraged me to visit another grandmother in a different space/time. These women rarely spoke to each other when they were alive. There isn't one photo of them together. In both of my large families, there were few who were happy when my Iraqi-born mother married my Ojibwe-Lebanese father. It wasn't because of the thirteen-year age difference or that my mother hadn't finished high school yet. At the time, my mother was the first person in the family to marry outside of her village, nonetheless her ethnicity. For years, my maternal side rarely, if ever, spoke to my mother and my paternal side continues to make comments about how my mother is "too old world." Even though my parents have been married for over 38 years, my Chaldean family continues to refer to my father as "The American." My family considers my siblings and I to be white—not mixed. To be American, according to my maternal side, is to be raced white—to be without culture[5]. Of course, now I know that to be American or white is not homogenous or culture-less. But, for the longest time, I didn't have a language to talk about how I understand my identity as something extraordinary textured, material, and interconnected. What I've learned from the experience of re-telling this dream is an understanding of the complexity of relationships, accountability, and responsibility. Relationships are never in balance--they are always uneven[6]. Najiba's encouragement to visit Grandma Helena became a prompting to pay attention to the interconnected indigenous histories and relationships between land from all my backgrounds.

As a graduate student, I lived just a few miles away from Helena's house on Waverly Road. Recently, my father told me that this house was a resting place for relatives who were in trouble or just needed a place to stay. As a little girl, the Waverly house was always my grandma's and auntie's home. Helena kicked Harold out long before I was born and lived there with her sister. As a young girl, I would stay with them during the summer. It was one of my very favorite places: two large gardens, a sizable backyard that hung laundry, a basement with an extensive collection of jarred vegetables and fruit, boxes with thousands of kept memories, a back porch where I would sit and snap

---

imagining of stories that restores and continues cultural memories" (3).

5. I find Frankie Condon's book, *I Hope I Join the Band* extremely useful in understanding whiteness and the constructs of whiteness as without culture.

6. Daisy Levy's work on embodied rhetorics has impacted how I understand balance. In "Calling for Balance: Looking for Bodies in Cultural Rhetorics" Levy argues, balance is a colonial fantasy. Levy argues that "balance is something we look for, and when we find it, we are especially aware of how easy it is to move out of it again."

peas and listen to the old women talk. They would give me fifty cents and I would walk to Quality Dairy for a sherbet cone. Even though I loved that house, I still carried my fear of snakes with me. While picking tomatoes for the old women, I would stay on my tippy toes between the plants flinching as something grazed my ankle. As a city girl, this piece of land meant so much to me; time with the old women and their stories shaped me. These women, like all the women in my family, are my first teachers. After the Farhat side moved from Lebanon, they settled in Detroit and owned a bar/restaurant on Cass Avenue in Detroit named after my great aunt. It was where my Ojibwe grandfather met my Lebanese grandmother.

Although the visits with my paternal relatives are a cherished memory, I spent the majority of my life being raised and cared for by my mother's family. We lived within two miles of each other. Like most tribal or immigrant families, it was common to stay close to family and have a strong, support network where everyone pitched in, shared resources, and cared for each other's children. Even though we lived in the city, we still found a way to imitate this ancient, ongoing practice. I spent the end of my summers foraging and harvesting wild grape leaves in urban areas with the women of my family. In some ways, I think that this is what my parents, who came from very different indigenous backgrounds and generations saw in each other, this belief in traditional, extended familial support. I spent a lot of time at my Aunt Karima's house in Madison Heights, right behind Simon's Elementary with her three children and all the cousins. Karima's house was the place where all the working parents dropped their kids off before working a full-day at one of our family-owned party stores. It's through the party store and the church that one can trace the immigrant experience of Chaldeans and their future generations[7] . It was during this time when the boy cousins would play in the little bit of wooded area by the house catching frogs and snakes. They would chase me with snakes--sometimes hiding them behind their backs and putting the poor snake in my face at the last second. I kind of hated my boy cousins back then even if they let me listen to their rap collection when my mom wasn't around or would always make sure I had a ride to the lake for a cookout and fishing. Thirty years later, my relationship to my cousins have changed greatly. We only see each other a few times a year and find ourselves huddled around the coffee machine catching up. Our wild children are in the next room plotting and causing trouble like we used to. Our parents are getting older, sicker, or passing on. It's our responsibility to keep traditions going.

---

7. There have been some recent publications that explore Chaldean experiences in Michigan. *Chaldeans in Michigan* by Mary C. Sengstock is a useful resource.

I won't understand my dream until I sit at the old, oak table with my parents, sisters, and husband and tell them about the prompting, my introspection, and remembering the touch of the tomato leaves. This prompting of returning to a land/space where I received teachings was an encouragement to bring story, relatives, and memory into my writing—into my scholarly practice. The next day, I sat down to write this passage for my dissertation:

> In a few days, it will be April and in Michigan, there will be no signs of a permanent thaw for a few more weeks. I'm waiting for the snow to melt and for the grass to re-grow before I drive to that old, yellow three-bedroom house on Waverly Road. My grandfather and Uncle Mack built that house. I am waiting to put my feet to that ground—to feel the cold, damp land. I will (try to) wait for the snakes.

Snakes had been on my mind because that year a family of garter snakes chose to nest in the bushes near my front door. Sometimes, I wondered if they returned to that spot in the same way I return to Lake Michigan--for sustenance, re-memory, community, and nourishment. Occasionally, my husband would relocate the snakes to a nice meadowed area a few feet away, but the snakes always came back—sunbathing on our steps and lawn. Before the snakes came, I spent so much time outside with the baby frogs singing with them. In bed, I would hear their stories before falling asleep. It was easy for me to identify the frogs as relatives. Then the snakes came--hungry. Sometimes, I would sit outside the window and talk to the snakes. I would put tobacco down and gently ask them to leave. Sometimes, I watched the cat watch the snakes. She was not afraid of them. She too, sat by the window talking to them. I have never been able to approach a relationship to snakes the way I could to bats, frogs, deer, or rabbits. While on the land, I am often obsessed in my thoughts about snakes and my writing. Will I step on one? Is it too cold or warm for the snakes to be out? How can I revise that story to do what I need it to? These snake-grandma stories remind me what I've always known: when I learn from and with the land, I am presented with a teaching on the tangledness of knowledge making and relationships. I feel prompted to bridge the precolonial, the colonial past, and the paracolonial present. I am okay with the tangledness as it allows me to demonstrate a deep respect and accountability for my first teachers: the land, grandmas, and snakes. Instead of seeking to separate the personal and professional or the teachings from my paternal and material sides, I consider them relational and reconstruct myself as a whole being in the world.

SNAKE-SEMIOTICS: A TALKING CIRCLE

Here's the thing, a lot of indigenous women contemplate their relationships to snakes. Gloria Anzaldúa, Joy Harjo, and Mabel McKay are just a few writers who tell snake stories. Their stories offer further insight into the tangledness of knowledge making, relationships, land, and memory. When I put MacKay, Harjo, and Anzaldua in a talking circle with the Riley-Bakkal snake and dream stories, I weave a relational scholarly practice that is ancestral and a form of survivance[8]. As Shawn Wilson observes, it's totally possible to have a ceremony in literature review and I want to invite you, dear reader, into that talking circle now. In *Borderlands/La Frontera*, Gloria Anzaldúa writes that after being bitten by a rattlesnake, she believes the snake to be her animal counterpart, coiling the Earth, Indigenous—woven (in)to land:

> Since that day, I've sought and shunned them. Always when they cross my path, fear and elation flood my body...She—that's how I think of *la Vibora,* Snake Woman...I know Earth is a coiled Serpent. Forty years it's taken me to enter into the Serpent, to acknowledge that I have a body, that I am a body and to assimilate the animal body, the animal soul (48).

I am drawn to how Anzaldua offers a relational approach to land, embodiment, and the world. Through this approach, she is critically reflective of her own identity and its formation. When Anzaldúa talks about seeking and shunning, I feel a connection to how I seek (obsess over) and shun snakes. These practices (to seek and to shun) are land-based practices--knowledge making practices that impact how we orient to knowledge and to the land.

In *Weaving the Dream*, Pomo basket weaver Mabel McKay tells the story of how she became a dreamer. She was given the gift of the rattlesnake song. She sang that song as she dreamed and when she awoke, she noticed rattlesnakes everywhere; they came to visit her. For the Pomo, rattlesnakes are good friends and helpers. "On hot days they came into the house and rested in the cool bathtub. They curled up in her shoes. She found them in her purse and coat pockets (81-82)." Mabel honored these visits. In fact, she

---

8. Here, I am referring directly to Dian Million's work in *Therapeutic Nations*. Her chapter (previously an article) on felt theory connects ancestral memory to gendered violence. Ancestral memory or blood dna is the idea that one is able to know or carry their ancestors' stories, histories, teachings, and traumas. Additionally, I connect Million's idea on felt theory, ancestral memory, to Gerald Vizenor and Malea Powell's work on survivance (survival + resistance). For me, to make visible and learn from ancestral memory is a relational practice that allows us to survive as well as resist paracolonial influences.

asked the spirits to take the rattlesnake song away from her because she was worried that euro-immigrants would kill the snakes; that they would misunderstand them. It is through this sacrifice and demonstration of relational accountability that McKay encourages me to reevaluate my relationship to snakes. In this story, I dwell, a bit, over how McKay gives up the rattlesnake song because she knows how euro-immigrants perceive rattlers as dangerous--a threat. Here, McKay encourages me to reevaluate my relationship to colonial rhetorical practices and decoloniality. I can talk big decolonial talk in my writing, in my classroom, over drinks with friends, but maybe these snakes are trying to call me in on how I have yet to form accountable and reciprocal relationships to and with the land. Although the song left McKay's body, a scar remained for her to remember and be reminded. Like Anzaldua, McKay emphasizes the body as central to developing a relationship with the land. Mabel still noticed the snakes and the snakes still made them known to her, but not as much as before. These snakes helped Mabel gather materials to weave and heal and to dream. McKay teaches me to pay attention and listen to the stories, memories, and histories our bodies hold. Our bodies carry these stories. We need to develop strategies to listen, reevaluate, and reciprocate.

In "The Flood," Joy Harjo, Muscogee/Creek poet and musician, uses the (hi)story of the watersnake to trace how the Muscogee/Creek people formed relationships to it during different stages of colonial contact and colonization. She writes, "Embedded in Muscogee tribal memory is the creature the tie snake, a huge snake of a monster who lives in waterways and will do what he can to take us to him" (14). The Anishinaabek (my people) also tell stories about Mishibizhii, the underwater panther or snake. In both stories, the creature is what it seems and something unexpected and dangerous. These snake monsters are protective of our sacred resources, dangerous to settlers, and can cause destruction. Anzaldúa, McKay, and Harjo make visible that sometimes a snake is just a snake. And, sometimes it's a teaching on locating oneself in the ongoing paracolonial landscape. The teaching here, is learning to take the time to find out and not expect the answers to come immediately or easily. As academics, this can be a hard teaching to take. We want the knowledge to come quickly. We want to show our expertise and ability to grasp and control the material. We want a familiar narrative writing style where the signposts in writing are easy to follow and spot. We want to see the change within our discipline or university to happen soon and if it doesn't then it's evidence that decoloniality isn't possible. We want to finish the research because we have deadlines to meet. This is one of the best tricks of the colonial project: time is a settler construct used to obviate any moments to pause, breath, and put our feet on the land. Even as I write this literature review, I find myself holding my breath. I just need to exhale and slow down. As Naijba used to say "Slow down Andrew[9]--you talk too fast. I can't understand you when you talk so fast." I return to these three writers often and how they grapple with their relationships to snakes. For me, they serve as reminders that it's okay to have a complicated relationship to the land and that I still have a lot to learn. It's okay to admit when I just don't know and when I'm scared to dwell deep.

I am still trying to figure out my own relationship to snakes. Occasionally, I fantasize about that moment when I am hiking and a serpent will cross my path. I like to think I will have learned from previous experiences and be calm. But this isn't the case. The other day, I was putting my garden in. My oldest, Turtle, and my youngest, Otter, were with me, their feet and hands in the dirt giggling and talking sweetly to the tomato plants when I saw a baby garter snake--all green taking some time to enjoy the sun--the first sun of May in Michigan. In Michigan, that first day of actual warm sun is a gift that any being should be able to enjoy. I screamed and ran away. The girls were watching and very worried for me. Turtle, the maternal one asks, "mama, what's wrong?" I tell her that I saw a baby snake.

Oh, is that all? Mama, it's just a baby. She's your friend and won't hurt you.

I called for my husband, he doesn't like snakes either. I asked him to gently lead the girls to visit with the snake. I stayed very calm and distant as I watched them hunch down and say hello. This is what the next generation teaches me: a snake is a visitor that should be greeted. I promise myself that it is my responsibility to listen to them and take their advice. This baby green snake was just the first visitor this year. Since then, I've seen much bigger snakes on my campus. I don't run away but stop and step aside. I say to the snake, *can you leave please so I can keep going?* The snake always listens, slithering away under a hosta while I hurry past them. I say *miigwetch* and move on. What makes this even more remarkable is that twice, the snake has gifted me with people from my past life--old loves or members of my tribal nation who appear right near the spot where the snake was. We stop and chat shocked to see each other in this new space. I tell them about the snake I saw earlier. We revisit our relationships to each other and I thank the snakes for this gift.

Reader, as I trace my relationship to snakes, I am also tracing a relationship to indigenous women intellectuals, to my daughters, the women in my family, and the land that I am dwelling on to better understand how to engage in a relational scholarly practice that prioritizes a land-based approach.

---

9. Her nickname for me was "Andrew" because she wanted my mother's first born to be a boy. Sometimes, grandmas can be pretty mean.

By listening relationally to Anzaldúa, McKay, Harjo, and my daughters, this is what snakes teach me so far:

How to care for the land like it's a relative

That when I make something it's important to be careful, a little scared, always honest, and attentive

This fear that I feel is a reminder that the stakes are high when it comes to land-based methods--that it is something to do not because it's trendy but because it will heal us from colonial impact

BODY-SNAKE STORIES

By listening relationally to Anzaldúa, McKay, Harjo, and my daughters, I find myself deliberately asking: How can I do scholarship that remembers and honors the land? How do I misunderstand the land? What do I do with teachings presented to me again and again that I ignore because I'm afraid? How does the struggle to form relationships with the land appear in my writing and research? When I attempt to answer these questions, I draw from the snake-semiotic stories but I also look to my own body to clue me in to the answers I may already know yet struggle to articulate. In "Embodiment: Embodying Feminist Rhetorics," Johnson, Levy, Manthey, and Novotny write, "To think about rhetoric, we must think about bodies. To do this means also to articulate how scholars' own bodies have intimately informed our disciplinary understanding of rhetoric (39)." To develop a relational scholarly practice is to understand how bodies are a part of knowledge and power--that bodies make meaning and that we have been convinced, again and again, to not listen to our bodies and instincts, and instead commit to the work of academe. I dwell here because I have a long history of not listening to my body while composing--of ignoring every sign. It's taken years for me to declare that my body matters, that I should take up space, and that my body carries the stories and teachings of my ancestors. I dwell here, with you, dear reader on the interconnectedness of embodiment, composing, and practice because I am aware of how colonial rhetorical practices impact *our* orientation to knowledge and reality in higher education.

While I was dreaming about snakes and my grandmothers, I was also taking comprehensive exams, finishing core courses, and trying to complete an oral history project with an Odawa elder. I was managing a lot. Every day, I felt ill. It was hard for me to be sick, not because of the pain, but because I didn't want to stop working. Almost every morning, I would eat half a grapefruit, walk to the bus stop, and immediately throw up. I hated going to the doctor for the same reason I dreaded institutional milestones. I have to face a reflective moment on whether or not I know my body, my subject of expertise, or the language of the institution. In the doctor's office, I must defend my body and explain how I make my body move through spaces and places. Often, the doctor doesn't believe me. When the doctor at the student clinic told me that my vomiting, fatigue, and nausea was actually "just a little acid-reflux," I just believed her. I didn't want to be bothered. I wanted to go home and write. She told me to just stop eating all of the foods that made me sick, which were primarily heritage foods. Due to my body size and ethnicity/race, she assumed I was eating too much fried food. But it meant, no longer eating any of the Chaldean and Lebanese foods that my grandmothers, aunts, and mother raised me on. It would also mean my relationship to knowledge would change as these practices taught me how to be on the land. Giving up these foods, in a way, was also giving up these histories and knowledge making practices.

Almost a year later, I was on a liquid diet. Like the exams and then the prospectus, I just had to get through it, push through the pain and keep working. I didn't like the answer I got when I asked for help and so I decided to not ask someone else. Once I became ABD and with my advisor's urging, I was ready to listen to my body. I went to see another doctor. I was diagnosed within minutes. "Yep, it's your gallbladder." My doctor told me that a gallbladder is supposed to contract, almost like how lungs inhale and exhale. My sad little organ barely fluttered. As Anzaldua reflected on her relationship to snakes, she also explored the way her body informed her writing and process. She writes,

> When I don't write the images down for several days or weeks or months, I get physically ill. Because writing invokes images from my unconscious, and because some of the images are residues of trauma which I then have to reconstruct, I sometimes get sick when I *do* write. I can't stomach it, become nauseous, or burn with fever, worsen. But, in reconstruction the traumas behind the images, I make "sense" of them, and once they have "meaning" they are changed, transformed. It is then that writing heals me, brings me joy (53).

As Anzaldua describes both the desire to write with managing her trauma and illness, I hear a connection to how she described her relationship to snakes as seeking and shunning. For me, Anzaldua reminds me of the responsibility that women of color and indigenous women carry: that we must make and share our knowledge to instruct and care for ourselves and the next generations. For me, to discuss my body is an admittance that the work I do is not just for academia but for myself, my communities, the ancestors I've never met, and the relatives after me. As Anzaldúa theorizes the relationship to the practice of making to the body, I think back to Mabel McKay and how she understands herself--a dreamer--a basket weaver--a medicine woman as intellectual practices where acknowledging one's body is crucial. Both women theorize how they negotiate the perceptions of dominant discourses and their desires to make meaning in their language, on their terms, and through their intellectual genealogy. These body-snake stories instruct me: I am a writer and dreamer and it is my responsibility to continue for the next generation. I am reminded that knowledge making is difficult, regardless of the spaces we live in. Yet, we need to learn how to listen to our bodies while we are making—while we are dwelling. Sometimes, it's okay to let your body do what it needs to do even if it means puking by the bus stop on Hagadorn Road for six months. We might feel better if we do.

Maybe, dear reader, you are thinking that this feels extremely obvious and if so, that is okay. Yet, in these pretty mundane statements, from my positionality as an Ojibwe, Chaldean, and Lebanese woman, my body has never been my own. Indigenous women are murdered and go missing every day. Every indigenous woman and two-spirit person I know has experienced gender violence, and every year, I endure the Pocahotties around October and November. As a form of survival, I have been trained to pass, blend in, tuck away. If no one can see me or know me then I might survive and not be found wrapped in a garbage bag by the river. This impacts my reality. It impacts how I orient to writing. To reorient myself to listen to my body, to acknowledge its existence, and to ask you to see it and learn from it is to refuse the survival practices my relatives had to endure during the Termination Era of the 20th century.

On my way to the surgical consult, I found myself drive past that yellow house on Waverly Road. The same house that I promised Najiba I would return to, put my feet to the land, and wait for snakes. I didn't even notice where I was going until I saw the intersection with the Big Lots and the Quality Dairy. It was the same QD that I would walk to for a sherbert cone. After the consult, I drive to the house and park across the street. The owners are working in the garden and I'm too afraid to be like "My grandmother told me in a dream to visit my childhood home, can you let me in the backyard for a minute?" For awhile, I sit and read *Not Vanishing* by Chrystos because this is the type of book I bring to waiting rooms. I take a walk around the block and try to figure out what I'm doing there without being noticed. I feel Najiba and Helena urging me to return to the writing. I feel good for the first time in months. When I return home, I find myself ready to sit with my research. I'm ready to re-listen and start writing.

This is what the snakes teach me

It's September and I haven't been in my garden in a few days. This pains me. My garden is such a source of pride. I step barefoot into my garden and assess: there are so many tomatoes to harvest, one last muskmelon is ripe and ready to be picked, a caterpillar is full from the brussel sprout seedlings I planted for fall, and there are some weeds to pull. As I kneel down, deep in the dirt, I contemplate what to do about these seedlings. They seem strong enough to keep going and there are plenty for all of us to enjoy. As I pluck the tomatoes and separate them into two baskets: one for the humans and the rest to offer to the animals later, I am thinking about this article. Theorizing through story is such a difficult and yet easy thing for me to do--it is such a vulnerable practice to share stories like these to make arguments about writing, methodology, and knowledge. I am contemplating if it's enough—if I am enough. As I start to talk myself out of publishing this piece, I hear my husband, who is gathering some wood for the evening bonfire, "Oh! Hello there." And immediately, I know a snake friend has come to visit. Turtle jumps off the swing "Baba, who are you talking to?" They kneel down together and talk sweetly to the snake. I ask, "is the snake headed this way?" He replies, "nope." I stand up and watch a tiny brown striped garter snake slither away. I think, *see you soon friend. Thanks for stopping by.* This snake friend has been so helpful this summer to do its part eating the bugs who want to make a home in my garden. Turtle runs to me, "mama, don't worry, I spoke to the snake and told it to come to me instead of you." Turtle, the oldest one who carries so much responsibility--so much empathy. This is what I hope for the next generation: that they may learn from the previous generation, to identify our baggage and trauma, and learn from our lived experiences but do not feel compelled to carry that trauma. May they find ways to heal and to help us heal. In many ways, I have this same hope for the discipline of Rhetoric and Composition as well. May we collectively find ways to make space and imagine new possibilities for what constitutes rhetorical knowledge. It is my hope that developing a relationship to the land through an indigenous orientation may help us further understand how colonial impact and the paracolonial present impact our writing--may these land-based relations give us another option to do the work we love to sustain another generation. Miigwetch.

Acknowledgments

I have been writing this essay, in some form or another, since 2008. I would like to say miigwetch to the *CCC* staff and reviewers for publishing this article. Miigwetch to Phil Bratta, Marilee Brooks-Gillies, Christina Cedillo, Timothy Dougherty, Deidre Evans Garriott, Cael Keegan, Daisy Levy, Wendall Mayo, Maria Novotny, and as always, Malea Powell, for their continuous feedback and support. Chi miigwetch to the women in my family who will always listen to my dream stories.

Works Cited

Anzaldúa, Gloria. *Borderlands/La Frontera: La Mestiza*. Aunt Lute Books, 1999.

Condon, Frankie. *I Hope I Join the Band: Narrative, Affiliation, and Anti-Racist Rhetoric*. University of Colorado Press, 2012.

The Cultural Rhetorics Theory Lab (Malea Powell, Daisy Levy, Andrea Riley Mukavetz, Marilee Brooks-Gillies, Maria Novotny, Jennifer Fisch-Ferguson). "Our Story Begins Here: Constellating Cultural Rhetorics." *enculturation: a journal of writing, rhetoric, and culture*, October 2014.

Driskill, Qwo-Li. *Asegi Stories: Cherokee Queer and Two-Spirit Memory*. U of Arizona P, 2016.

Harjo, Joy. *The Woman Who Fell From the Sky*. W.W. Norton & Company, 1996.

Johnson, Maureen, Daisy Levy, Katie Manthey, and Maria Novotny, "Embodiment: Embodying Feminist Rhetorics," *Peitho* 18.1 (2015): 39-44.

Kimmerer, Robin. *Braiding Sweetgrass: Indigenous Wisdom, Scientific Knowledge, and the Teaching of Plants*. Milkweed Editions, 2013.

Kynard, Carmen. "Stayin Woke: Race Radical Literacies in the Makings of a Higher Education." *College Composition and Communication*. 69.3 (2018). 519-529.

Haas, Angela M. Race, "Rhetoric, and Technology: A Case Study of Decolonial Technical Communication Theory, Methodology, and Pedagogy," *Journal of Business and Technical Communication* 26:3 (June 2012). 277-310.

Hsu, Jo V. "Afterword: Disciplinary (Trans)formations: Queering and Trans-ing Asian American Rhetorics." *enculturation: a journal of rhetoric, writing, and culture*. 2018.

Inoue, Asao. B *Antiracist Writing Assessment Ecologies: Teaching and Assessing Writing for a Socially Just Future*. The WAC Clearinghouse and Parlor Press. 2015.

Levy, Daisy, ""Calling for Imbalance" Looking for Bodies in Cultural Rhetorics." CRCON16. Cultural Rhetorics Consortium, October 2016, East Lansing, Michigan. Conference presentation.

Maracle, Lee, *On Oratory: Coming to Theory*. Gallerie Publications, 1990.

Martinez, Aja Y. "A Plea for Critical Race Theory Counterstory: Dialogues Concerning Alejandra's 'Fit' in the Academy." *Composition Studies*, vol. 42, no. 2, 2014, pp. 33-55.

Million, Dian. *Therapeutic Nations: Healing in an Age of Indigenous Human Rights.* U of Arizona, 2013.

Mignolo, Walter. *The Darker Side of Western Modernity: Global Futures, Decolonial Options.* Duke University Press, 2011.

Patterson, G. "Queering and Transing Quantitative Research." *Sexual Rhetorics: Methods, Identities, Publics,* edited by Jonathan Alexander and Jacqueline Rhodes, Routledge, 2016, pp. 136–46.

Perryman-Clark, Staci and Collin Craig. *Black Perspectives in Writing Program Administration: From the Margins to the Center.* National Council for Teachers in English, 2019.

Price, Margaret. *Mad at School: Rhetorics of Mental Disability and Academic Life.* University of Michigan Press, 2011.

Royster, Jacqueline Jones and Gesa Kirsch. *Feminist Rhetorical Practices: New Horizons for Rhetoric, Composition, and Literacy Studies.* Southern Illinois University Press. 2012.

Sarris, Greg. *Mabel McKay: Weaving the Dream, University of California P,* 1994.

Sengstock, Mary C. *Chaldeans in Michigan.* Michigan State University P, 2005.

Simpson Betasamosake, Leanne. *As We Have Always Done: Indigenous Freedom Through Radical Resistance.* U of Minnesota Press, 2017.

Vizenor, Gerald, *Manifest Manners: Narratives on Postindian Surviviance.* U of Nebraska Press, 1999.

Wilson, Shawn. *Research is Ceremony: Indigenous Research Methods.* Fernwood Press, 2008.

Yergeau, Melanie. *Authoring Autism: On Rhetoric and Neurological Queerness.* Duke University Press, 2017.

Andrea Riley Mukavetz is an Assistant Professor in the Integrative, Religious, and Intercultural Studies Department at Grand Valley State University. She is co-chair of the American Indian Caucus, current board member of the Cultural Rhetorics Consortium, and Editor of the *constellations' Pedagogy Blog.* She is past co-organizer of the Cultural Rhetorics Conference (2016, 2018). Her scholarship has appeared in *Studies in American Indian Literature, Rhetoric, Professional Communication, and Globalization,* and *enculturation: a journal of writing, rhetoric, and culture.* Andrea is passionate about gardening, sewing, spending time with Lake Michigan, and cultural rhetorics and decolonial practices.

Supplemental Material

Developing A Relational Scholarly Practice: Snakes, Dreams, and Grandmothers

Andrea Riley Mukavetz

PART I: REFLECTION ON THE ORIGINS OF THE ARTICLE

I began writing this essay as a graduate student. Instead of writing a traditional methodology chapter for my dissertation, I asked my adviser if I could tell research stories instead. This came about because it felt only appropriate for me to take time to reflect on and understand how the oral history work changed me. It's like what Shawn Wilson says, "if research doesn't change you as a person, you're doing it wrong." For a long time, I didn't know what to do with these stories. I wasn't even sure if it was something that people would want to publish or if I wanted to share as a publication.

When I first started using story as methodology, it was to demonstrate *how* story was a form of theoretical knowledge making. I wrote about how American Indian women used story as theory and invited readers to listen to those theories as teachings. It felt like my writing was not for my community but it was to show that my community existed and to highlight our rhetorical contributions. Where those arguments are sometimes important, I want more for all of us as we expand what constitutes rhetorical knowledge and theory. For me, this essay was a way for me to understand how I, as an Anishinaabekwe, used story as theory--how I make theory. It was to invite readers to practice Indigenous paradigms.

I have always had a deep connection with the practice of writing. It's a complicated relationship that reflects the trauma I experienced in school because I was expected to assimilate and conform to a euro-centered approach to knowledge making. It's also a healing relationship because writing--storying is how I make sense of the world. For me, this essay celebrates my whole self and how I want to be in the world whether it's within my discipline and my professional identity or as just me in all the other spaces I exist in.

PART II: DESCRIPTION OF RESEARCH METHODS, FINDINGS, AND/OR PEDAGOGICAL IMPACT

Story as methodology is an embodied, ancestral, material, and relational approach to knowledge making. As you engage with this piece, I hope it is clear how I try to make it participatory. I hope you find ways to story with and alongside me. My findings are that it is important to listen to our bodies, ancestors, and the stories that haunt us--there are important teachings/theories in these sites of knowledge. This essay is an invitation for readers to take seriously Indigenous intellect and consider how to be accountable to Indigenous communities.

I teach through story and as story. In all my classes, I invite students to draw from their lived experiences and their understanding of space and culture to practice and reflect on their own approaches to theory making. We talk a lot about their own knowledge making experiences and the role of power in the practice of making knowledge. We read Lee Maracle's "On Oratory" to talk about the hierarchy of knowledge and how colonialism created categories for knowledge. For me, this framing is crucial so students can understand that the anxiety, fear, or confusion they experience when writing comes from particular disciplinary and ideological beliefs.

Part III: Discussion Questions

1. What does your approach to a relational scholarly practice look like?

2. Who are your animal and plant relations? What have you learned from them? How do you learn from them?

3. What stories do you continue to carry with you across your communities? What can each community learn from these stories?

Additional Information

Early in the essay, I prompt readers to learn about the Indigenous people of the land they are on. Using my directions in the essay, I would like you to learn about the Indigenous people--their past and present as well as their future goals. Depending on where you live, you might immediately find federally recognized tribes or you might find relocated or unrecognized tribes. These are important details to learn about. I would like you to also learn about the settler history of where you are located. Take some time to map your space and try to make sense of those constellated histories. What did you learn? What did you already know? How does this knowledge impact your own sense of belonging? From there, take some time to think about how you can practice relational accountability to Indigenous communities in your area.

KAIROS

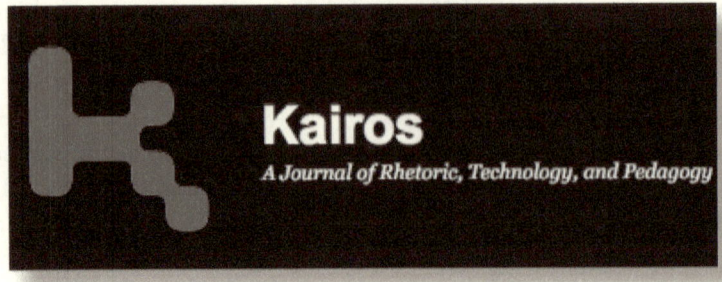

Kairos is on the Web at http://www.kairos.technorhetoric.net/

Kairos is a refereed open-access online journal exploring the intersections of rhetoric, technology, and pedagogy. Since its first issue in January of 1996, the mission of Kairos has been to publish scholarship that examines digital and multimodal composing practices, promoting work that enacts its scholarly argument through rhetorical and innovative uses of new media.

Arranging a Rhetorical Feminist Methodology: The Visualization of Anti-Gentrification Rhetoric on Twitter[1]

This webtext provides a model for collecting, analyzing, and visualizing a large set of data from Twitter. Through her methodological discussion, Desiree Dighton provides feminist interventions in data collection and analysis, using her 2-year data collection of Tweets using the word "gentrification." Dighton's methodological discussion is well-grounded in theories and practices in both writing studies and in data science and visualization beyond the field, providing both models and questions for future research in the field involving the collection, analysis, and visualization of large data sets.

---

1. *Kairos*, vol. 25, no. 1, 2019. https://kairos.technorhetoric.net/25.1/topoi/dighton/index.html © 2019 Desiree Dighton

Arranging a Rhetorical Feminist Methodology: The Visualization of Anti-Gentrification Rhetoric on Twitter

Desiree Dighton

Abstract

In this webtext, I develop an *in situ* approach for the rhetorical study of large-scale social media data. Grounding this in situ methodology in rhetoric and feminist critiques of data and visualization, this webtext models techniques and strategies for collecting, analyzing, and visualizing Twitter data. I utilize a large Twitter data collection, visualization applications, and grounded theory to locate unfolding rhetorical encounters that occur around  shared interests rather than unified and stable hashtags or images. This approach extends rhetorical and interdisciplinary scholarship calling for attention to materiality and infrastructure in digital methodologies, and engages rhetoric's focus on contemporary everyday phenomena and lived experience. I offer a feminist rhetorical framework for data analysis and visualization, and demonstrate this framework with a Twitter data collection of approximately two million tweets and associated metadata gathered through Twitter's Application Programming Interface (API) from February 2016 to 2018 using the keyword "gentrification." Taken together, the visualizations generated through this methodology create a nuanced, polyvocal antenarrative of anti-gentrification rhetorical circulation on Twitter. I conclude by discussing the limitations and future directions of this study and offer recommendations to extend this study's feminist rhetorical methodology through scholarly, institutional, and community collaborations.

You can read the full webtext by following the QR code or this URL: http://kairos.technorhetoric.net/25.1/topoi/dighton/index.html

Supplemental Material

Arranging a Rhetorical Feminist Methodology: The Visualization of Anti-Gentrification Rhetoric on Twitter

Desiree Dighton

PART I: REFLECTION ON THE ORIGINS OF THE ARTICLE

This *Kairos* piece is part of a larger monograph-in-progress project. At the time, I was teaching at Shaw University, watching the city of Raleigh and the exploding real estate gradually chip away at the historically black neighborhood surrounding the school, putting more financial pressure on students and other community members looking for affordable housing. This experience led to thinking rhetorically about housing justice and anti-gentrification activism and connecting to conversations about gentrification happening locally and occurring globally via Twitter.

When I began collecting Twitter data in 2016, I was very much caught up in the enthusiasm about digital methods happening in writing studies and in the digital humanities. I was eager to learn how to use digital methods for text analysis, and I was thinking about applying text analysis to research everyday conversations happening on social media, particularly about social issues like gentrification. By the time I wrote this piece of *Kairos*, my enthusiasm for social media research had turned more skeptical and critical, as our collective attitude towards social media moved from idealistic notions of Twitter as a democratic space to more critical perspectives on social media's power to upend democracy and further oppression. These two perspectives seem quite opposed to each other, but I wanted to find a way to continue to examine social media conversations, but also listen for critiques and apply notions of data ethics and responsibility. I also wanted to find a way to shift the focus from activists/activism, somewhat, to research that focuses on illuminating how oppressive power systems might take shape in contemporary moments and scenes, in my research's case, related to gentrification. This piece is my attempt to find a generative route forward in digital methods for social media research by considering both ethical and rhetorical considerations of that work, and, of course, that understanding and way forward is always evolving for me and for our fields.

Although primarily a Twitter-based study, I wanted to illuminate how this social media data connects with present-day lived experiences and conflicts over space that I saw happening around me and in cities all over the world. With these interests in mind, this webtext gestures towards extending data critiques into a flexible methodology for working with large Twitter data. To do so, this methodology centers rhetorical considerations of the platforms, data collection, and data analysis tools. In addition to the rhetorical considerations of technological influence, the methodology begins to account for the multidimensionality of tweets in aggregate and, in some cases, in the context of the spaces and bodies involved in gentrification and its resistance. The results of this data study point to the value of feminist rhetorical methodologies to expand our engagement with socio-political issues of concern as they surface and circulate in everyday conversations that shape our social and physical realities. At the same time, to achieve something like true participatory work with communities and activists, our higher education institutions and professional associations need to develop ways to support rhetoric and writing studies work with communities and social issues by valuing this engagement.

Part II: Description of Research Methods, Findings, and/or Pedagogical Impact

I've brought this methodology into the classroom in several ways. In upper-level rhetoric courses, I've introduced students to the ethics of social media data collection and analysis and also gave them practice applying those ethics in collecting their own Twitter data research. For instance, in a course based on the rhetoric of protest, we engaged with readings on the rhetoric of social movements and other social-media based rhetorical studies. Students use Hawksey's TAGS to set up an ongoing data collection. Over several weeks, students are guided through analyzing this data with analytical applications like Google Sheets, Voyant, and Tableau, but they also learned about grounded theory and developed their own coding system. We toggle back and forth between working with technology-enhanced data analysis and human coding/analysis, while also engaging readings in critical data/DH studies. Students have really engaged well with D'Agnazio & Klein's *Data Feminism* (2020), and I've found the chapters to be captivating and accessible discussion starters for undergraduates on the power structures at work in data and quantification. Students experience how seemingly neutral concepts like "data" are wrapped up in historical and contemporary social injustices, and paired with hands-on data collection and analysis, they're able to more deeply understand the rhetorical dimensions of data and their own passive and active association with data collection.

Social media data collections are also meaningful contemporary pedagogical tools to introduce students to visual rhetoric and circulation studies research. For instance, we read "Behold the Corpse" (Harold & DeLuca, 2005) and consider Mamie Till's 1955 insistence on the open public viewing of her son's dead and mutilated body, which circulated via print and broadcast media, in connection with contemporary racial violence, image events, and public conversations related to Black Lives Matter. These kinds of hands-on data experiences and structured engagement with undergraduate accessible readings in rhetoric, media studies, and writing studies have helped students approach their own data collections in a variety of ways, including writing rhetorical data analysis essays that address the aggregate results and also examine smaller subset of their data, much like the approach I take in the Kairos piece. Students have also explored creative "remixes" of their data for public audiences, such as one group who created a participatory archive on campus that connects to #metoo. Regardless of the ultimate project's shape, I try to emphasize the importance of narrowing down from their large data collections, usually a few thousand to tens of thousands of tweets, to a smaller data study. These smaller data studies, then, usually involve a closer analysis that reveals more clearly the way that our own choices shape our results. This helps us talk about "bias," which they understand as perhaps related to political views and prejudice, vs. simply the way that a process like categorization, which is involved in most human and computer analysis, can create likeness and difference that has consequences on our understanding of the world and our in interactions with each other. Perhaps most importantly, students begin to more clearly understand how researchers and computers make choices that shape results, often through processes like selection and categorization. Importantly for those of us interested in rhetoric, students see the value in contextualizing data in its technological, physical, and embodied networks, while also being able to articulate smaller data's relationship and divergence from larger aggregate data patterns. Not only do I think this provides a fresh route into traditionally valued rhetoric and writing studies concepts like authorship, audience/publics, multimodality, and context, but it also expands students' critical data literacies, including awareness of the way they shape and are shaped by social media platforms, algorithms, and data collections. I don't think these literacies can be so deeply felt through just reading about them, but through the active learning involved in collecting and researching with social media data, even as we also, inevitably, cannot quite untangle the research from fraught issues of privacy, consent, and representation.

Part III: Discussion Questions

1. What's involved with the rhetorical canon of arrangement? How do different scholars Dighton cites, such as Doug Eyman, theorize arrangement in light of the digital? How has Dighton's study of anti-gentrification practiced enacting rhetorical arrangement in the Twitter data study? What traces can you find of how this rhetorical arrangement has been made through human choices? How about technological mechanisms and/or affordances?

2. How does this engagement with arrangement connect with the feminist data critiques Dighton foregrounds and condenses in the "Framework for Feminist Rhetorical Data Visualization Methodology."

3. Choose another piece of scholarship that utilizes social media and/or your own data research. List several ways in which rhetorical arrangement has played a part in this study and/or the way in which the study could more explicitly connect with rhetorical arrangement to further enhance its results and outcomes.

Part IV: Additional Information

Data Analysis Essay

6-8 pages (not including images and/or graphs)

Halfway through the semester, you will work individually with your growing data collections to analyze your preliminary results. We will devote two class periods to creating a workshop space for you to collect Twitter data and run those files through Tableau (or an alternative coding scheme approved by me). Tableau will generate graphs and tables that will allow you to explore your data through computational methods that quantify the data across time, illuminating peaks and valleys of activity that may have meaningful connections to events occurring outside of social media. Key steps in this project:

- Collect Twitter data around a social movement or protest through a keyword or hashtag by using TAGS.
- Once you have a robust collection that seems interesting to you, which could be anywhere from a few thousand to tens of thousands of tweets, you'll import that data into Tableau.

- Using Tableau, we'll work together to:
- locate patterns and outliers in your data,
- experiment with visualizations, and
- develop an analytical reading of your dataset
- Additionally, you'll identify key aspects of your dataset for a "small data" study. This small data study will involve you human reading and coding a data subset.
- This human reading and coding will be informed by additional research into your data's context and application of a rhetorical theory we've studied in class.

In the 4-6 page essay, I expect you to describe your data set with precision and specificity. Your paper should include the following sections:

Context & Methods (~2 pages)

I. Begin with broad strokes and gradually become more specific:
- Why did you decide to collect this hashtag/keyword? What is the specific related history and exigency we should be aware of to contextualize your analysis?
- Provide specifics that characterize your data and your method. For instance, over what dates did you collect? Quantify your data. How many total tweets did you collect? What else might be relevant for an audience to understand your data? How many unique languages, geographic locations, and/or users were involved in this excerpted conversation?
- Describe the processes of using digital and human-based methods.

II. Results & Discussion (~3 pages)--Choose the Tableau results and visualizations that are most important for understanding your particular dataset.
- Reconstruct the Twitter story you see taking shape over the time, the key users, and the circumstances of your dataset.
- Do not simply include every visualization you've created and explain them. Instead, be selective. What visualizations are most meaningful to how you understand the dataset's connection to your issue? Include those visualizations in the essay and explain why they are illustrative and significant. You might try to answer some of the questions about quantification and pattern finding that we've raised in class. In your data analysis, what rises to the top for you? Do not include these questions and answers like a list in your paper. Instead, use them to generate insights, and structure your essay's paragraphs and visualizations around them.

- Connect to the rhetorical theory and data ethics concepts we've been learning in class. Make sure to attribute and cite the concept(s) that are most relevant for how you understand this flash of data. How does theory, digital methods, and your own choices play a role in illuminating the larger narrative of this movement and its relationship to the mainstream? For ideas of concepts to connect to your data, you might look at the collective glossary of terms we've developed and review the reading list and forum responses we've completed thus far.

III. Conclusions (~2 pages). Ultimately, your essay should illuminate how you understand this conversation and how it's taken its current shape partly through digital and human methods of collection and analysis.
- In terms of thesis, you can adopt a delayed thesis structure. Instead of beginning the paper with an argument, conclude with one. Perhaps in the first paragraph of the conclusion, you'll end that paragraph with an argument. For instance: This Twitter conversation around #sayhername reveals that the movement relies on ....to garner attention and disseminate a message that unites publics by.... ; this message values ...and tries to change the dominant norm by reconfiguring the way we understand.... (That's just an idea of how your thesis might take shape, but feel free to use it as a template if it makes sense to you).
- The rest of your conclusion section would expand and support that statement.
- What new insights do you have into the social movement and/or issue? How have digital means been used to further the goals of activism or to disrupt them. How have the ways you as a researcher and rhetorical critic used digital and human methods to understand and make meaning from this data?
- Include reflectiveness about how you, these tools, and these users are co-producers in the meaning you're making. How have you come to understand the strengths and weaknesses of each approach and the benefits and drawbacks of employing a combined approach?
- We might find another story on a different day, with different methods, through different perspectives--reflect that ethic in your conclusions.

Additionally, make sure to include a Works Cited page with the research you've done on the context of your issue/social movement and at least two course readings that have helped you to think critically through this data study.

RHETORIC OF HEALTH & MEDICINE

Rhetoric of Health & Medicine is on the web at http://journals.upress.ufl.edu/rhm/index

Rhetoric of Health & Medicine (RHM) is a multidisciplinary journal publishing original rhetorical studies (e.g., studies that use theories of rhetoric or persuasion) of health and medical practices involving communication. By rhetorical studies, we mean work that entails more than examining the language or discourse involved in health and medical issues, but that also uses theories of rhetoric to guide inquiry and arrive at nuanced observations about how persuasion works (or could/should work) in discourse and practice. Such studies can combine rhetorical analysis with any number of other humanistic or social scientific methodologies, including critical/cultural analysis, ethnography, qualitative analysis, and quantitative analysis; indeed, *RHM* seeks to encourage scholarly conversations about health and medicine across fields of inquiry and spheres of practice, in part by publishing inter- and trans-disciplinary research.

The Ostomy Multiple: Towards a Theory of Rhetorical Enactments[1]

Molly Margaret Kessler's article is an impressive example of theory building from the bottom up—developing a notion of "rhetorical enactments" from a praxiographic study that draws on various data streams about patients' (including the author's) lived experiences with ostomies. The notion of rhetorical enactments, Kessler argues, can help us attune to "how entities such as mind, body, self, and non-self--typically separated in "perspectival" analyses--are co-enacted "in space and time through practice, and how such enactments are made meaningful." This article provides a new understanding of rhetoric's importance in new materialist frameworks, and illustrates how an understanding of rhetorical enactments of ostomies can guide ameliorative responses to patients' healthcare.

---

1. *Rhetoric of Health & Medicine*, vol. 3, no. 3, pp. 293–319 DOI: 10.5744/rhm.2020.1016 © 2020 by the University of Florida Press.

The Ostomy Multiple: Toward a Theory of Rhetorical Enactments

Molly Margaret Kessler

Recent research in rhetoric of health and medicine (RHM) has called on scholars to find ways to more adequately attend to patients' lived and embodied experiences. At the same time, scholarship within and allied to RHM has long worked to address the problems of perspectivalism and relatedly, Cartesian binaries such as mind/ body or self/nonself. This article aims to build theory that simultaneously addresses these concerns by examining patients' experiences with ostomies. This article develops rhetorical enactments as a theoretical frame that enables RHM scholars to explore lived experiences and account for diverse entities that participate in those experiences. The analysis presented focuses on how entities like "self" and "ostomy" are rhetorically enacted within lived experiences and become meaningfully different. Ultimately, this article advocates rhetorical enactments as a productive way to both understand and intervene in patients' lived experiences.

Keywords: multiple ontologies theory, lived experience, perspectivalism, binaries, intervention

Ostomies keep approximately one million people in the United States alive (United Ostomy Association). A metonymic term, "ostomy" actually refers to 1) the surgery in which all or part of either the gastrointestinal or urinary tracts are either missing or have been surgically removed, 2) the opening on the surface of the body (usually the abdomen) through which digestive or urinary waste is excreted (called a stoma), and 3) the disposable pouch or bag worn over the stoma. As a system, ostomies enable excretion of waste and are key in treating or curing a variety of conditions including chronic diseases such as cancer and inflammatory bowel disease (IBD) as well as congenital conditions, acute illnesses, or injuries resulting in severe damage to the gastrointestinal or urinary tracts. In the case of gastrointestinal ostomies, an end of the intestine is pulled to the surface of the skin through which digestive waste is excreted into an ostomy pouch worn over the opening in the abdomen.

Despite their lifesaving function and the substantial portion of the population living with them, ostomies have been strongly associated with social stigma and adverse quality of life outcomes. Depression, isolation, anxiety—

are but a few of the well-documented outcomes associated with the lived experience of having an ostomy. Furthermore, research into these negative effects and experiences regarding ostomies repeatedly ties negative ostomy outcomes to the psychological, specifically perspectives, attitudes, and experiences that folks with ostomies have about their ostomy (see, for example, Smith et al., 2007). While the mind (i.e. attitudes, perspectives, opinions) no doubt informs the experience of having an ostomy, this discrete focus on solving negative experience and quality of life with ostomies through psychological and perspectival intervention may fall short in actually improving patients' lives, especially considering that, despite the wealth of research in this area, negative outcomes remain pervasive.

Thus, in this article, I explore how rhetoric of health and medicine (RHM) can help. If negative ostomy experiences aren't being solved through perspectival understanding and intervention, can RHM help surface alternative understandings of negative ostomy experience and alternative pathways to improving these lived experiences? To answer this question, I work to build theory that enables RHM scholars to move beyond perspectival approaches toward a theoretical lens that illuminates other interventional pathways in lived experiences. Specifically, I examine why and how the meaning-making experiences for folks with ostomies come to be negative or otherwise, *and how we might use this rhetorical understanding to push intervention in patients' lived experiences with ostomies away from the long-standing focus on patient perspective into new, more productive domains.

In what follows, I ground this project in current conversations within RHM and allied disciplines regarding perspectivalism, then I calibrate Annemarie Mol's (2002) theory of multiple ontologies and Karen Barad's (2003; 2007) agential realism to build *rhetorical enactments*, an alternative theoretical frame to perspectivalism. I then use rhetorical enactments to argue that these lived experiences with ostomies, rather than perspectives about ostomies, result in *different ostomies*. That is, for people who have had ostomy surgery, the boundaries and ontologies of self, body, or ostomy can be dramatically different across people. This article, therefore, aims to understand how these different ostomies emerge and what rhetorical significance this might have in patients' lives and experiences. My analysis draws upon a multi-year study designed to examine chronic illness and patient experience. This study combines research from a three-year praxiographic study, including interviews, observations, and analysis of digitally and publicly available data such as tweets, blog posts, and web pages.[1] Taking these cases together,

---

1. This study was approved by and conducted in accordance with the University of Wisconsin-Milwaukee Institutional Review Board. Interviews were conducted using convenience sampling (n=9) and digitally and publicly available data

I advance rhetorical enactments as a framework for examining patients' lived experiences with ostomies—negative, positive, or otherwise—with the hope of building valuable theory, while advancing RHM's ameliorative and interventional goals in the context of ostomies.

Problematic Perspectivalism

To begin, I'd like to clarify just what I mean when I say perspectivalism. In previous RHM scholarship, perspectivalism has most often been used to describe "the belief that representation ensures effective and adequate inclusion" (Melonçon & Scott, 2018, p. vii), most often in terms of including patients' perspectives in health policy and deliberation spaces. However, perspectivalism, more broadly construed, describes the privileging of perspective itself, specifically perspectives about an entity or object. Perspectivalism engages interpretations or representations of an object or experience. It is a theory of seeing and knowing (Mol, 2002). Indeed, perspectivalism productively emerged as part of a reaction to modernist paradigms (wherein perspectives and representations were ignored in service of discovering *the* truth),[2] yet perspectivalism nonetheless risks significant problems.[3]

One such problem is that perspectivalism is deeply entangled with a host of Cartesian binaries. As others have argued, when the object of study is perspectives or interpretations, other entities such as nature, disease, ostomy, or bodies are ignored or rendered less or inaccessible. In other words: perspective can become privileged over so-called reality, representations over matter, minds over bodies, and through this privileging binaries are reified. This is what S. Scott Graham (2015) refers to as the "two-world problem" or "the series of bifurcations" (p. 17) that are grounded in postmodern perspectivalism that is "shot through with visual metaphors that serve to (re) establish the profound modernist separation between a subject and an object, culture and nature, a view and the world" (p. 28). Put another way, perspectivalism encourages us to focus on the perspectives, interpretations, even descriptions of some other entity—but never the entity itself, as that remains beyond our epistemological and ontological reach. Mol explained (2002):

---

were collected using a theoretical sampling protocol. See Amy Koerber and Lonie McMichael (2008, p. 465) for more on these data collection strategies.

2. In addition to the postmodern project of perspectivalism, feminist standpoint theory emerged in response to problematic dualisms and the marginalization of perspectives and experiences. Importantly, perspectivalism and standpoint theory have significant differences and I do not mean to conflate the two here. For more on distinctions between standpoint and perspective, see Harding, 2009.

3. For more on the problems and critiques of perspectivalism, see Pender, 2018, and Graham, 2015.

> It may seem that studying 'perspectives' is a way of finally attending to 'disease itself'—but it isn't. For by entering the realm of meaning, the body's physical reality is left out . . . in a world of meaning, nobody is in touch with the reality of diseases, everybody 'merely' interprets' them . . . all interpretations, whatever their number, are interpretations *of.* Of what? Of some matter that is projected somewhere. Of some nature that allows culture to attribute all these shapes to it. This is built into the very metaphor of 'perspectives' itself. This multiplies the observers—but leaves the object observed alone. All alone. Untouched. It is only looked at. (pp. 11–12)

The binary between perspective/reality, in addition to corollary subject/ object, mind/body, language/matter, nature/culture divides, is one of especially pressing concern for RHM. Similar to Mol, philosopher Karen Barad (2007) explained, when we divide perspective, subjects, minds, and language from so-called reality, objects, bodies, and matter, we become ensnared in a "spectator sport of matching linguistics representations to preexisting things" (p. 54). This sort of matching game is especially risky within health and medical contexts because not all perspectives are treated equally. For example, patients' perspectives, to be authorized or validated, often need to be matched with an external biomedical reality considered more objective, such as a physician's perspective, blood tests, or MRI scans. This perspectival logic is especially entangled with the disease/illness dichotomy[4] so prevalent within biomedicine, where disease is the verifiable entity assessed by healthcare providers and biomedical researchers, and illness is the subjective interpretations, feelings, and thoughts.

Therefore, although scholars in RHM have "advocated for and focused on" the importance of patient perspective in domains of healthcare, patientprovider interactions, and health policy (Graham et al., 2018, p. 62), new materialist advocates have begun to push back against this so-called perspectivalism and attendant issues with Cartesian dualisms (Pflugfelder, 2015; Graham et al., 2018; Pender, 2018). Including patient voices, valuing their perspectives, incorporating their feedback—these are all important and valiant goals of much work advocating or operationalizing perspectivalism. However, "perspectivalism may actually serve to replicate the inequitable power structures patient inclusions efforts are designed to correct" by tokenizing patients' perspectives, requiring that patient perspective be authenticated via another supposedly more objective perspective, or simply pro-

---

4. For more on the prevalence and problems with the disease/illness dichotomy see Mol, 2002; Teston et al., 2014; Graham et al., 2018.

viding patients with a seat at the table or a voice in the conversation without actually allowing full, valued participation (Graham et al., 2018, p. 65).

Moreover, while patient narrative has emerged as a primary approach for examining patients' lives and experiences, narrative is frequently treated as textual representation of perspective. Consequently, focusing exclusively on patient narrative as representation risks privileging language and perspectives over embodied experiences and meaningful material forces. In turn, this privileging encourages us to 1) treat these narratives/perspectives as if separate from the lived realities for patients, and 2) elide important nonlinguistic entities and practices that significantly influence how patients make meaning in the world. Perspectivalism in RHM contexts often has the adverse, sometimes unintended, consequence of placing embodied experience, pain, emotions, symptoms, or disease itself "all in the patient's head" as the saying goes. RHM research, according to Lisa Melonçon (2018), should "more concretely and acutely" focus on the embodied experiences of our research participants because for "too long" traditional rhetorical approaches have "put the primary emphasis on texts" (p. 97).

However, many rhetoricians question if, how, and to what extent we should embrace these new materialist calls. That is, how might we overcome this two-world problem without privileging any one entity (language, materiality, or otherwise) in the process, especially as rhetoric has for so long focused on language? With what theories, methods, or approaches might we continue to leverage the unique expertise of rhetoric without assumptively dividing language from materiality, minds from bodies, culture from nature, perspective from reality? Such questions and their answers are especially important for RHM scholars, whose work is often devoted to understanding patients' lives and experiences that do not divide so easily into predetermined binaries and cannot be reduced to perspectives. Accordingly, I suggest rhetorical enactments as a theoretical frame that attunes to how entities such as mind, body, self, and non-self are enacted in space and time through practice, and how such enactments are made meaningful. Rhetorical enactments shift the analytic focus away from perspectives about ostomies toward practices and experiences that rhetorically enact multiple ostomies.

Multiple Ontologies, Agential Realism, and Rhetorical Enactments

Already, some RHM scholars have aimed to overcome binaries, move away from perspectivalism, and/or take a more materially and ontologically focused approach by embracing Mol's (2002) theory of multiple ontologies (Card,

Kessler, & Graham, 2018; Graham, 2015; Graham & Herndl, 2013; Molloy, 2015; Pender, 2018; Teston et al., 2014). Adopted to better understand pain medicine (Graham, 2015; Graham & Herndl, 2013), lived experiences with mental illness (Molloy, 2015), genetic risk (Pender, 2018) and health policy deliberation (Card, Kessler, & Graham, 2018; Teston et al., 2014), Mol's (2002) multiple ontologies theory (MOT) has been particularly useful in helping RHM scholars move toward analyses that study the practices that stage[5] entities, rather than focusing exclusively on the perspectives, language, and knowledge surrounding a particular, stable object, idea, or reality.

Specifically, MOT relies on praxiography, a method similar to ethnography but distinctive in that it requires attentiveness to how entities and realities emerge in practices. As Mol (2002) put it, "ontology is not given in the order of things, but instead, ontologies are brought into being, sustained, and allowed to wither away in common, day-to-day sociomaterial practices" (p. 6). That is, ontology is not an inherent property but a becoming: "objects come into being—and disappear—with the practices in which they are manipulated" (Mol, 2002, p. 5). This move toward practices and ontology, as RHM scholars have illustrated, allows our work to examine "a constellation of diverse practices" (Teston et al., 2014, p. 162) to understand how "differently situated material activities . . . produce different objects" (Graham, 2015, p. 31). Praxiography, Kelly Pender (2018) argued, provides "a much-needed alternative to perspectivalism" because it enables scholars to "[follow] an artifact across time or space to investigate the spaces through which it emerged" (p. 77). Extending Pender's argument here, I would add that the praxiographic approach of MOT guides scholars to investigate the range of entities (language, bodies, technologies, germs, cells, etc.) that come into being and become meaningful within health and medical situations, specifically those entities often divided dualistically. For example, rather than examine how different people perceive or discuss an ostomy, MOT directs us to investigate what practices participate in the emergence and meaningfulness of that ostomy.

In addition to this focus on practice, a commitment to the *multiplicity* of ontologies for entities is key for MOT. As Mol (2002) explained,

> If practices are foregrounded there is no longer a single passive object in the middle, waiting to be seen from the point of view of seemingly endless series of perspectives And since the object of manipulation

---

5. To be clear, I follow Mol (2002) in my use of verbs like "stage," "do," and "enact." Such verbs diffuse the action among entities involved in a given moment. As Mol explains, these verbs suggest "that activities take place—but leaves the actors vague . . . that in the act, and only then and there, something is—being enacted" (2002, p. 32).

tends to differ from one practice to another, reality multiplies. The body, the patient, the disease, the doctor, the technician, the technology: all of these are more than one. More than singular (p. 5).

For instance, Mol (2002) argued that the disease atherosclerosis comes into being in the surgical ward as "something that can be pushed aside by a balloon" (p. 102) or as "the interaction between blood components and the vessel wall" in the hematology lab (p. 109). That is, different practices enact different entities—entities that may fall under a single name like "atherosclerosis." There are not simply several perspectives about atherosclerosis; atherosclerosis is done differently in different (rhetorical) contexts. For Mol (2002), this multiplicity is not just a theoretical insight, but has key ramifications in determining treatment and understanding how multiple medical stakeholders coordinate patient care.

MOT, then, with its focus on practice-based research and intervention, is a rich tool for those in RHM aiming to study embodied experiences with the goal of advocacy, intervention, or amelioration. Accordingly, those within RHM aiming to advance and adapt MOT for rhetorical work have consistently emphasized two important takeaways: 1) a praxiographic focus enables us to account for diverse entities and actions that are involved in rhetorical contexts, including but not limited to language; and 2) through multiple ontologies reality multiplies—in other words, MOT requires a shift from the idea that there is a single object/idea about which people have many perspectives, but rather multiple objects staged differently through different practices which give way to multiple realities. Put simply, MOT and its RHM adaptations provide an important foundation for examining patients' complex lived realities. Too, MOT emphasizes diverse practices rather than focusing on any particular type of practice or artifact (linguistic, material, social, etc.).

However, MOT does not provide specific tools for examining *how particular enacted entities come to have boundaries distinct from other enacted entities*. A methodological shift from capturing perspectives/descriptions/ narratives to doings/practices/enactments is a first critical step in moving beyond perspectivalism, but further consideration to how particular entities have shifting boundaries and thus different ontologies is necessary, especially for a study aiming to understand how ostomy comes to be and become meaningful in different ways for different patients. For example, MOT enables us to study the practices in which the ostomy is enacted but not necessarily how the enacted ostomy comes to be part of the self for some people and distinctly separate from the self for others. "Executing a praxiographic study" Pender (2008) argued, "is not a straightforward matter of replicating Mol's method in a different context" (p. 78). Therefore, I turn to Barad's (2007) theory of agential realism because it productively aligns with MOT, while adding a more specific set of tools to investigate the meaningful boundary-work that emerges simultaneously with enactments.

Much like Mol (2002), Barad (2003) calls for a shift toward "practices/doings/actions" as a way of bringing questions of "ontology, materiality, and agency" to the forefront of analyses (p. 802). Barad is motivated by such framings of enactments, doings, and performances to resist perspectival and constructionist renderings of the world. In particular, Barad (2007) theorizes what she calls "agential realism," which figures the world as ontologically dynamic and "inquires into the very practices" through which entities become determinate (p. 66). Central to agential realism are two additional concepts: intra-activity and agential cuts. First, intra-activity posits that boundaries among entities are not "fixed" (Barad, 2007, p. 155), and that they do not "sit still" (Barad, 2007, p. 171), but instead are always moving and transforming as they emerge in time and space. In this sense, entities cannot be defined in opposition to one another or through some "fixed referent" (Barad, 2007, p. 30), as would be the case with default binaries. Instead, entities become determinate through their intra-action with other entities. Barad (2007) clarified,

> the notion of *intra-action* (in contrast to the usual 'interaction,' which presumes the prior existence of independent entities or relata) represents a profound conceptual shift. It is through specific agential intra-actions that boundaries and properties of components of phenomena become determinate and that particular concepts (that is, particular material articulations of the world) become meaningful (p. 139).

Put another way, entities come into being through mutual entanglement with other entities. There are, therefore, no preexisting entities to be categorized into inherent binaries. Where *interaction* looks for differences between stable entities, defining mind and body, language and matter, self and nonself, human and nonhuman through their opposition to one another, *intra-action* re-orients us to look for what emerges within phenomena. Entities emerge through a "dynamic process" of engagement with other entities, and this dynamic process enables entities to temporarily become determinate from other entities (Barad, 2007, p. 140).

Moreover, Barad contended that as entities intra-act and emerge in practices, they come to have boundaries through "agential cuts" (p 140). In contrast to stable, intrinsic "Cartesian cuts," agential cuts aim to capture the emergent and transient enactment of boundaries (Barad, 2003, p. 815). For instance, entities such as ostomy, self, or atherosclerosis, come to be separate from other entities through specific agential cuts that are enacted within practices. Importantly too, agential cuts are temporary and ever-changing; in one intra-action an agential cut between two entities might be enacted, while in another, a different agential cut that unifies those same entities might be enacted. Accordingly, different practices enact different agential cuts. Enactments of entities previously thought to be bound within binaries are, thus, the result of agential cuts enacted in time and space. As an extension to MOT, agential cuts reveal how phenomena come into being and become distinct from other entities. For instance, self, non-self, mind, disease, body, language, ostomy, etc., are mutable and only become determinate through agential cuts from other entities within practices.

Agential realism also extends MOT to begin accounting for meaning. For Barad (2007), neither matter nor meaning has inherent boundaries or properties. Entities become meaningful through articulations with other entities, through intra-actions. Both *what* entities emerge and *how* they are made meaningful relies on the intra-actions through which they are enacted. As Barad (2007) argues, what comes to matter—have meaning and significance—is also emergent in these entangled relationships. Meaning is not confined to "individual words or groups of words" (Barad, 2007, p. 32) but, like entities, is enacted in space and time as entities entangle. In other words, entities come to matter as they intra-act and agentially separate from other entities.

Through this calibration of multiple ontologies and agential realism, I developed the term rhetorical enactments to describe entities that are agentially cut among other entities and emerge through lived practices and how those enacted entities become meaningful. Specifically, RHM's utility for understanding meaning-making in health and medical contexts infuses theories of enactments. MOT "looks *at* practices that enact" different entities "not *behind* them for hidden forces or agendas" (Pender, 2018, p. 78). Agential realism and intra-activity, however, add a specific focus on both how boundaries are established for entities enacted, and encourage attentiveness to how such entities are made meaningful. As a theoretical lens, rhetorical enactments look at the entities enacted in particular contexts with particular consequences.

In the next section, I deploy rhetorical enactments to demonstrate its potential within RHM to sidestep dualistic and perspectival approaches, study embodied practices, and recognize that boundaries are neither fixed nor stable. In putting this theory into practice, I argue that in the case of ostomies and the people who have them, both the ostomy and self are ontologically multiple with changing boundaries, these different ostomies and selves emerge through the diverse practices in which people are engaged, and these different ostomies and selves come to matter in significant ways for peoples' lived experiences and quality of life with ostomies.

Multiple Ostomy Ontologies

As I mentioned earlier, the data presented are part of a larger project that more broadly attends to patient experience and chronic illness communication. Throughout this project, I used rhetorical enactments to focus on what entities are enacted and become meaningful for these patients in everyday lived experiences with disease, ostomies, and more. As I illustrate, the ostomy emerged as ontologically multiple in the lived practices I studied throughout this project. Specifically, four primary or common ostomy ontologies emerged in the practices I examined, which I call: parasite, companion, cyborg, and self. The cases presented in this section condense the ontological practices and the metaphysics that emerged from those practices into a single name to represent the experiences and practices in ways that patients themselves provided. While I refer to these ontologies enacted by their emergent metaphysics[6] as a sort of shorthand, in each description, I unpack the relationships among patients' practices, enacted ontology, and the emerging metaphysics of ostomy as parasite, companion, cyborg, or self. Importantly, I recognize that these nouns—parasite, companion, cyborg, self—do not, on the surface, indicate practices. In fact, these names may look like metaphorical representations. However, seeing these emergent metaphysics as metaphors slips into a dualistically reliant position that would treat ostomy and parasite, companion, cyborg, or self as *stable* entities under comparison, and critically, as entities that can never fully coalesce. Furthermore, treating these ostomy ontologies as metaphor, rather than multiple ostomies enacted differently, retreats to perspectivalism. That is, recognizing ostomy as parasite under a perspectival logic suggests that "the ostomy" is a single, static object in the world about which patients have different perspectives or attitudes. When analyzed through the lens of rhetorical enactments, however, entities only contextually emerge and are only momentarily stable. The practices and experiences that enact these ontologies and stage the emergent metaphysics are complex, diverse, and at times unwieldy. Therefore, for analytic ease and to not get caught up in a dense theoretical web, I refer to each ontology by the shorthand of "ostomy as . . .". For example, ostomy as parasite as a rhetorical enactment simply serves as a shorthand for an ontologically emergent

---

6. See Graham & Herndl (2013) for a more thorough theoretical discussion of the relationship between ontologies, practices, and emergent metaphysics in a multiple ontologies analysis.

ostomy as an entity with distinct boundaries separate from the wearer and whose boundaries and ontology become meaningfully negative and unwanted. In later sections of this article, I further discuss the role of language and discursive practices within an enactment approach.

Parasite

In many of the experiences I examined during this project, the ostomy emerged as an entity distinctly separate from the self of the person wearing it. I call this enactment of the ostomy the "parasite". Specifically, ostomy as parasite is enacted when the self of the wearer and ostomy intra-act such that the ostomy becomes an entirely separate entity. In other words, a boundary is enacted between self and ostomy. This boundary serves not only to separate the person from the ostomy but also to create meaningful distance between the self and this unwanted technology. With strong negative connotations, such parasitic agential cuts emerge in cases where ostomy and self become distinct from one another, often at least partially due to the ostomy's undesirability and the challenges it presents for a patient. For example, in a commercial sponsored by the Centers for Disease Control and Prevention, Julia, who previously needed an ostomy, described her distinctly negative experiences with her ostomy. She explains:

> You go wherever *it* goes. You have no control. If *it* comes loose, it smells. I had no control. I had to wear *it* for a whole year. I was at home the majority of the time because I was scared that *it* would come loose and *it* would smell, and I didn't want to be around anyone. I was really kind of like stuck at home (Centers for Disease Control and Prevention, 2015, emphasis added).

Here, Julia continually referred to her ostomy as "it," enacting a very distinct separation between herself and the ostomy (Centers for Disease Control and Prevention, 2015). In so doing, Julia's ostomy became a parasitic attachment to her, separate but deeply entangled. Just as atherosclerosis emerged as blood clots in some cases or as the inability to walk in other cases in Mol's (2002) research, ostomy emerges as a parasite—something attached, but not self—in some patient experiences. Furthermore, Julia's words here can be treated praxiographically—that is, I can attune my analysis (as MOT requires) to the practices presented by Julia herself. In this passage, she recalls the practices that were *limited* by the existence of her ostomy, and at the same time emphasizes the potential practices (such as the ostomy smelling or coming lose) that were distinct from her own practices. Julia herself was not the actor or doer in the practices of smelling or coming lose, but rather the ostomy was engaged in those practices. The ostomy, emergent as separate, however directly influenced practices that Julia would have liked to participate in (for example, leaving the house). Cumulatively, these practices (smelling, coming losing, being stuck at home) influence the enactment of the ostomy as not only separate from self but meaningfully negative in the lived experience of Julia. It was not Julia's negative perspective about the ostomy nor simply a bad attitude; instead, the embodied everyday experiences she lived gave way to the ontology of her ostomy as well as how her ostomy came to have meaning in her life.

Additionally, the depersonalizing pronoun "it" Julia uses is a common discursive practice deployed to separate and refer to an ostomy. However, naming an ostomy is also a common practice for many in this community. I noticed naming practices throughout my ethnography, having had the opportunity to "meet" various ostomies—Stella, Gandalf, Stewie, Sophia, and others. What's particularly interesting about the practice of naming is the reason patients often provide for doing so: to distance themselves from their ostomies. As one interview participant explained to me, "I was told to name my ostomy so I had someone to blame, someone to yell at." Moreover, explaining why naming is powerful for patients, another interview participant said, "I know [naming] helps others to detach—to separate their identity." Discursive practices such as calling the ostomy "it" or giving the ostomy a distinct name help to enact the agential separability among the self/identity of the wearer and the device of the ostomy. Put another way, when the self and ostomy intra-act, they become distinct through their entanglement with one other and with the lived experiences (physically wearing an ostomy pouch) and discursive practices (using pronouns, naming) engaged in day-to-day life with an ostomy.

The agential cut separating self and ostomy in each of these cases has interesting resemblances to a parasitic relationship, which is why I call this type of enactment ostomy as parasite. While literal parasites are defined by the fact that their dependency and attachment is at the expense of the host, the inverse is true for some people with ostomies; yet the nature of the relationship bears a resemblance. As parasites rely upon hosts for survival, they become deeply entangled with their hosts yet maintain distinctiveness. Similarly, the people described in this section depended upon their ostomies for survival; yet, practices such as calling the ostomy "it" or naming the ostomy, as well as the experience of not being able to leave the house, enacted a meaningful separation between the ostomy and the self of these individuals. Much like the distinction between parasite and host, a separation between ostomy and the wearer becomes a discrete characteristic of this ostomy ontology.

Even though many of these patients realized that their ostomies are medically necessary, the ostomy's entanglement with the wearer is at the expense of the quality of life and desired everyday experiences of the wearer.

ComPanion

Similar to the parasitic agential cut just described, the enactment of ostomy as companion is staged by a cut that separates patient and ostomy, but as a separation whose meaningfulness is not necessarily negative. I term this agential cut "companion" precisely because the separation enacted frequently presents as accepting, and in some cases even friendly or jovial. For instance, although naming an ostomy often is associated with negative experiences, for some ostomy wearers the practice of naming provides a way to recognize or even highlight the active existence of the ostomy. Through her laughter, an interviewee told me that she has given her ostomy a name so "when [her] ostomy makes noise in public, [she] can just say, 'Oh, Sophia feels like talking to you!'" Additionally, in a blog post in which the "funniest remarks" from patients with ostomies were compiled on The Ostomy Connection—an education and advocacy websites for IBD and ostomy patients—one patient said, "I call my stoma 'Politician' because it's either full of crap or making a lot of noise but not producing[7] a damn thing." Through the agential cuts enacted in such remarks, the ostomy becomes companion-like, a distinctly separate entity, yet one that is closely, often positively, linked to the wearer. Similarly, in a blog on the Ostomy Outdoors page, the founder of the site explained that she named her ostomy Wilbur (after the pig in Charlotte's Web) because it is a "crazy little critter on [her] belly that likes to dance, sing, and spit," so Wilbur "seemed like a perfect name" (Skiba, 2011). As these examples demonstrate, naming the ostomy, while enacting a distinct boundary between the self and the ostomy, does not always mark or result from negative experiences with the ostomy. It seems, at least in these cases, that naming, possibly combined with positive lived experiences, stages a friendship or alliance in which the self and the ostomy are still ontologically discrete.

Other practices are also evidenced in these positive naming practices. For example, instances of ostomies making noise were repeatedly mentioned by those who positively named their ostomies. Just as bellies can gurgle when they are hungry, ostomies make noise as part of the digestive process. When the ostomy is enacted as companion, often a combination of practices are involved: noise-making and naming are two that I commonly noticed in my

---

7. "Producing output" is a phrase used to describe the waste yielded through the stoma into the ostomy.

research. The ostomy making noise and a person naming that ostomy as a way to socially navigate such noises in public contexts combine to enact the ostomy as a companion. These combined practices both establish an agential cut between the self and the ostomy while giving a friendly, positive, or jovial meaning to that relationship and the ostomy itself.

Ostomy as companion is also enacted in cases where the ostomy goes unnamed. For example, in my observations, I observed a long discussion among ostomy pouch wearers in which they described having an ostomy as similar to "having a baby." They explained that an ostomy requires you to carry a changing bag and to adjust to life with a new companion. Here, the lived experiences and practices of carrying a changing bag with supplies and the potentiality of needing to empty or change the ostomy bag, as well as the discursive practice of articulating such experiences as similar to having a baby, highlight the variety of entities and practices that result in the ostomy done as a separate, but not necessarily negative, entity from the self.

Together, these cases show that entities that go by the same name (self and ostomy) when intra-active among different practices and experiences result in different rhetorical enactments of those entities. Self and ostomy maintain ontological separation when ostomy emerges as companion, yet the meaningfulness of the ontologies of self and ostomy are done differently than when ostomy is enacted as parasite. Common across the cases in this section is an ostomy that becomes companion—closely linked and under the responsibility of the wearer, but a distinct object with distinct behaviors and needs. The intra-action of manageable/positive experiences, discursive practices, adaptive behaviors (like preparing a changing bag), the ostomy, and the wearer enact an ostomy separate from the self, but meaningfully tolerable or even positive.

Cyborg

Although there are many life experiences and instances in which the ostomy becomes distinct from self, there are also many cases where the ostomy becomes part of self. For such cases, there are two primary ontologies enacted—the cyborg ontology and the self ontology. In this section and the section that follows, I will unpack how such rhetorical enactments of ostomy as self are staged and made meaningful.

When the ostomy becomes cyborg[8]—that is, a hybrid with the human—the agential cut enacted does not divide the ostomy from the self, but rather a

---

8. The notion of the more-than-human cyborg has been theorized extensively in disability studies under the concept of the "supercrip." See for example, Marie Hardin and Brent Hardin (2004); Amanda Booher (2010); Margaret Gutsell and

cut enacted surrounds the self and ostomy—a cut that unites ostomy and self in a way that changes the status of the human self—specifically, to a "more than self" status. In other words, the cyborg ontology is done in practices and experiences that directly result in a self better than the one before the ostomy. For example, in a tweet featuring a picture of herself lifting her shirt to reveal her ostomy, a woman named Vicky who frequently tweets about life with her ostomy wrote: "#myillnessisnotyourinsult my stoma makes me superwoman, has given me my life back and makes me awesome[.] think before you make a joke" (TheDazzleDoll, 2017).

Mulholland's tweet, as part of the #myillnessisnotyourinsult social media initiative, responded to instances in the media in which ostomies and related conditions are used to insult or stigmatize. As she explained, her life is possible because of her ostomy;[9] further, her ostomy makes her self "awesome." Even through Mulholland's tweet, a particular agential cut is enacted: intra-acting with the ostomy transformed Mulholland into "superwoman," giving her more-than-human cyborg status. Through intra-actions with her ostomy, both Mulholland and her ostomy became cyborg superhuman—both Mulholland and the ostomy transformed ontologically through their intra-action. Though Mulholland did not point to specific practices that enact this ostomy as part of her cyborg self, she did use the practice of displaying her ostomy to embody the positive, celebratory relationship she had with her ostomy. The practice of revealing, particularly in this public way, has become a common practice within the ostomy community to not only make ostomies visible, but also to make normal ostomies as part of the people who have them (see #getyourbellyout for more examples of this).

The superhero theme present in Muholland's tweet is common throughout the IBD and ostomy communities. Sometimes used as a metaphor for expressing the immense challenges patients must overcome to live "normal" lives,[10] the superhuman cyborg ontology is enacted differently in the cases

---

Kathleen Hulgin, 2013. My analysis extends such work into domains of ontology and new materialisms.

9. To be clear, I interpret Mulholland's reference to her stoma here as synonymous with the metonymic use of ostomy that I've used throughout this article for two reasons: stoma and ostomy technology are often referred to together under one of the terms, and secondly, Mulholland's image reveals her stoma covered by ostomy technology. For consistency, I'll continue to use "ostomy" as the operative term.

10. I use normal here not to evoke any particular connotation and or set of practices. A "normal" life is a common discussed in the language practices of patients with IBD and ostomies, but what normal means varies from patient to patient. Typically, it refers to the practices, experiences, and sense of self prior to developing IBD or receiving an ostomy.

I'm discussing. For instance, consider Gut Girl, a self-proclaimed IBD superhero, who, while wearing an ostomy pouch, "fights IBD" and gives others the "tools" to do so too (Ringer, 2012). The intra-action of the ostomy, Gut Girl's descriptions of herself and her superhero status, her personal experiences with IBD, her role with the IBD community, social media, and likely more, entangled such that an agential cut is enacted around her self and the ostomy, resulting in ostomy as part of cyborg self. Like Muholland, Gut Girl wore and displayed her ostomy specifically as part of her superhero armor, and in doing so, celebrated her ostomy. By integrating her ostomy has part of her tools to fight IBD, Gut Girl showcased the ostomy as part of her superhero self, making the ostomy meaningfully positive, even extraordinary. Together, these cases suggest that certain intra-actions and practices, particularly involving positive experiences with the ostomy, enact cyborg ontologies in which ostomy becomes a distinct but important part of self.

Self

The last of the four agential cuts that presented as common in my dataset enacts the ostomy as self. Unlike the other three ostomy enactments, this one has no unique or clever name ascribed to it; it is simply self. If we think about the four ostomy ontologies along a spectrum, ostomy as parasite and ostomy as self might serve as the two poles. Whereas ostomy as parasite is enacted through mostly negative experiences and practices and an agential cut separates ostomy and self, the ostomy becomes self when the agential cut made surrounds the ostomy such that the ostomy becomes fully integrated into the self. For example, during interviews, one participant told me "[the ostomy] is all who I am" and another said her ostomy was "absolutely" part of her. Much the same is Jessica Grossman, co-founder and contributor to Uncover Ostomy, an educational and support-focused website for people with ostomies and related diseases. In several of the blog posts on her site, Grossman explained that her ostomy "is part of [her]" or "part of who [she] is" (Grossman, 2013). Even more, writing of her experiences with her ostomy before she had a takedown surgery to replace her ostomy with an internal pouch, Shawntel Bethea (2016), a contributor to The Mighty, wrote, "My body wasn't weird. I was unique. . . . Sure, I was different. I still am. But I have grown to love myself for that" (Bethea). Here discursive practices (such as a writing a blog depicting her experiences) and the embodied practice of loving herself intra-act to enact ostomy as self for Bethea.

What's interesting about both Bethea and Grossman, whose experiences are presented across several blogs, is how their descriptions shift when they discuss their ostomies. In both cases, the writers began by saying "my ostomy" but seem to seamlessly, perhaps subconsciously, shift to "my body," "me," and "who I am." Consider, Grossman's comments in fuller context:

> I decided right away that I was going to be ok *with myself* as soon as I woke up from surgery. That's not the case for everyone. I have met many people who have suddenly woken up with an ostomy, having no clue what it was until a doctor explained the "thing on their abdomen" and who were more scared and upset more than they've ever been in their lives. I've also met people who knew they were having surgery, but still needed time to adjust. It is ok to take the time you need *to love yourself*. It doesn't always happen overnight, and it's not a race for who can get there first. Don't get down on *yourself* because you're not loving your difference the moment it appears (Grossman, 2013, emphasis added).

Throughout this statement, Grossman switched between "ostomy" and "myself," which staged her ostomy just like other parts of herself such as her hair, mind, or personality, all of which people regularly talk about distinctly while maintaining those elements as part of self. Also, Grossman depicted the embodied experience of waking up from ostomy surgery to a significantly changed body and self. Her body, self, surgical experience, personal mindset, as well as her written description of these experiences intra-acted to enact a new version of herself in which the ostomy is a fully integrated part.

In another post, Grossman elaborated on her life experiences that got her to the point of self-acceptance and self-love that she describes in the above passage. Specifically, she outlined a range of practices and experiences that made her life *before* her ostomy negative, including being isolated when she was hospitalized for the majority of her pre-teen years, being bullied by classmates and peers, and the "unending physical pain" from Crohn's disease that resulted in "nights on the toilet, bleeding internally, constantly battling the feeling of hot knives ripping through [her] abdomen." Then, she explained, "after ostomy surgery" things "actually got better." Her ostomy "saved her life in more ways than one" as she puts it. What's clear in Grossman's case is that her lived experiences before her ostomy were far more negative to her than the ones that her ostomy made possible. Consequently, those positive practices have enacted her ostomy has part of herself and a meaningfully central part of the positive life she leads as a person with an ostomy.

Patient Ethnographers and Enactment as Intervention

In following Mol (2002), Barad (2003; 2007), and rhetoricians who have compellingly argued that ontologies emerge through practices, I argue the enactments of ostomies in the practices described above are not simply different perspectives on ostomies. Instead, the four ostomy ontologies are enacted through specific agential cuts, not inherent binaries. Enacted through two agential cuts, the ostomy becomes non-self—in one case an unwanted non-self and in the other, an acceptable non-self. Conversely, enacted through the two other agential cuts, the ostomy becomes self, either more than self or completely integrated. In focusing on what is done or enacted in diverse practices, as rhetorical enactment theory requires, space for ontological multiplicity opens up. When we examine how practices stage agential cuts in which objects are enacted, the ostomy multiplies, just as disease does in Mol's (2002) analysis. Recall, in describing surgery to treat atherosclerosis, Mol (2002) wrote, "atherosclerosis is enacted as something that can be pushed aside by a balloon" (p. 102). We might say similar things about the cases presented in this article: 1) the ostomy is enacted as something separate and negative from the person wearing it (parasite); 2) the ostomy is enacted as something neutral/positive but still a separate entity from the person wearing it (companion); 3) the ostomy is enacted as something that improves the self (cyborg), 4) the ostomy is enacted as something no different than any other part of the person (self).

Furthermore, I must emphasize that it is not simply that different versions of the ostomy exist or that different people have different perspectives about the ostomy. Rather, by assuming no prescribed ontological differences at the outset of this analysis, it becomes "possible to understand" the ostomy as "manipulated in practices," which as Mol (2002) explained, has the "far-reaching effect" of multiplying reality (p. 5). The ostomy is not a "universal object," but is both emergent and manipulated in its intra-action among other entities (medical histories, personal experience, minds, bodies, selves, surgeries, images, blog posts, tweets, etc.). The ostomy (in whatever ontological form) is enacted and made meaningful through intra-actions with other entities in space and time. But these agential cuts are neither fixed nor permanent, leaving space for the ostomy's multiplicity. Sometimes agential cuts emerge *around* what we might casually consider self and ostomy, and in other instances, agential cuts divide what we call self and ostomy.

Ultimately, in exploring lived experiences with ostomies, my goal in this article is to articulate an approach that foregrounds practices, ontologies, and intra-actions as a way to avoid perspectivalism and Cartesian dualisms, respond to new materialist calls, and better understand patients' lived experiences. I'd like to end, therefore, with a discussion of how rhetorical enactments theory 1) accomplishes this goal by leveraging rhetoric's expertise in language practices, and 2) contributes to RHM's interventional mission. Specifically, I propose that rhetorical enactments can help us attune to the important role language can have within the intra-actions and practices through which entities become determinate. The theory I've presented throughout this article has aimed to engage patients' lived experiences and, in so doing, examine how entities like ostomy and self come into being and become meaningful for patients. In deploying this theory, I have taken care to examine entities as they intra-actively emerged within phenomena and became determinate through their agential separability (cuts) from other entities. While this approach provides a way to make sense of how different ostomy ontologies come into being and are made meaningful, what many rhetoricians might be wondering at this point is how this particular theory is distinctly rhetorical? And, since I looked mostly at patient language practices, how is this approach different than rhetorically examining patient narratives?

Notably, many of the practices presented in this article are discursive. However, those discursive practices are situated among material, embodied, lived experiences of patients, even if such lived experiences are sometimes shared through language. My point here is that within rhetorical enactments language does not solely mediate reality (and the entities within it); rather *practices*, including discursive ones, stage enactments that become meaningful for patients. As Barad (2003) argued, "discursive practice are ongoing agential intra-actions of the world through which local determinacy is enacted" (pp. 820–1). Language need not be understood as reporting perspectives. Rather than reducing all other practices and entities to talk (Graham, 2015, p. 8), which problematically leads to an "ontological gap" between what is represented (objects) and what does the representing (language) (Barad, 2007, p. 47), rhetorical enactments calibrate any and all practices that shape meaning in patients' lives. In doing so, rhetorical enactments theoretically depart from many of solutions and approaches to binaries and ontologies in which the social, linguistic, and cultural become the focus, and other entities and practices that might participate in staging entities and boundaries are downplayed or treated as representational. Rhetorical enactments theory diverges from representational approaches in that representationalism relies on stable entities and privileges a stable ontology of language, and therefore negates the multiplicity of ontologies that could be made possible through an intra-active and ontologically dynamic enactive approach.

As a rhetorician, I of course recognize the power and influence of language. However, I propose rhetorical enactments, grounded in MOT and the aforementioned principles of intra-activity, agential cuts, and ontological dynamism, as a way to understand the rhetorical work at play in patients' lived experiences without consuming all practices and activities into linguistic artifacts. Therefore, keeping in line with the three principles outlined, rhetorical enactments account for the role of linguistic elements as part of intra-actions through which agential cuts are made. As Graham (2015) reminded us, "Language is doing. It has impacts and consequences—social, political, material" (p. 84). Making this shift to treat language as one practice among many through which ontologies are staged helps sidestep the manifest issues with representationalism. In this sense, words do not represent. Words intra-act and enact. Indeed, if language is an act of doing, then, a study of these practices "focuses not so much on what people say or what texts mean but rather on how representational activity circulates and contributes to a deeper ecology of practices in which those acts of representation are embedded" (Graham, 2015, p. 69). This means that language can and often does play a vital role in the intra-actions and agential cuts that stage ontologies. If, at the outset, language is not "presumed to serve a mediating function between independent existing realities," (Barad, 2007, p. 47) but instead "the practices and performances of representing" become the focus, as both Graham and Barad suggested, we can both account for the role language plays in intra-actions without assuming inherent ontological and representational distinctions (Barad, 2007, p. 49).

Understanding language as a practice, rather than a representation, Mol (2002) argued for treating people as ethnographers of their own lives. That is, in contrast to analyses of patient narratives, Mol (2002) advocated that we listen to each person (and their reports) as if the person is their "own ethnographer. Not just an ethnographer of feelings, meanings, or perspectives. But someone who tells how living with an impaired body is *done* in practice" (p. 15). Understanding the cases presented in this article as entangled phenomena of bodies, diseases, and experiences "done in practice" has specific implications: "It is possible to listen to people's stories as if they tell about events. Through such listening an illness takes shape both as material and active . . . This illness is something being done to you, the patient. And that, as a patient you do" (Mol, 2002, p. 20).

Rather than treating the language practices presented in this article (namely blog posts, tweets, and conversations with me as well as with others) as perspectives/representations of ostomies or selves, or as metaphors used to connect to some underlying reality, rhetorical enactments theory makes the shift to examine patients' language practices as ethnographic, as patients telling how living with an ostomy, disease, or other health condition is done in practices.

The theory of rhetorical enactments and its deployment in this article thus treats patients as ethnographers of their own lived experiences, and in so doing, focuses on how discourse participates in the staging of various agential cuts in which ontological differences are enacted. Indeed, language practices play an important role in the ontologies and entities enacted. "Events are made to happen by several people and lots of things," Mol argued, "*Words participate, too.*" (2002, p. 26, emphasis added). That is, words[11] have an important role in enacting the agential cuts in which the ostomy becomes companion, parasite, self, or cyborg. The descriptions, reports, and confessions powerfully participate in the agential cuts that are made. Graham (2015) further reminded, "words are things" (p. 212) and in practices, words calibrate with and among objects (p. 209). Discursive practices (in calibration with other practices) are key to the enactment of separations from or inclusions into the self for those with ostomies.

Importantly though, discursive practices are only one type among many through which these enactments become determinate and meaningful. Language is but one intra-acting entity, and language practices are among a diverse ecology of practices in which ontologies come into being. Words may play a significant role in the agential cuts staged, but such cuts are only possible among all intra-active elements, which may include, as my analysis shows, many diverse entities such as histories, experiences, space, time, other humans, objects, and more. However, we might highlight particular entities (such as words) that emerge as especially influential as a means of understanding how certain enactments are made to be rhetorically influential. For instance, words are often some of the most important entities that participate in the enactments of the ostomy ontologies presented in this article. This may not always be the case. Nonetheless, recognizing the agential separability made possible through intra-active language requires the expertise of rhetoricians. Who better to understand the role of language and language practices in the enactment of ontologies? Who more adequately attuned to how enactments come to matter?

Finally, in recognizing the unique role rhetorical expertise offers in an ontological inquiry guided by rhetorical enactments theory, I'd like to end by pointing toward the ways in which rhetorical enactments might serve RHM's interventional goals. As J. Blake Scott and Catherine C. Gouge (2019) pointed out, theory-building is not only an "inventional" practice, but it can be practice "of caring for our research practices, the phenomena of which they are a part, and the embodied stakeholders that participate

---

11. To be clear, when I refer to "words" I am referring to a nuanced conception of words as embodied movements, metonymic for a suite of discursive practices.

in both" (Scott & Gouge, 2019, p. 191). Indeed, theories "shape what we believe and how we make judgments and otherwise act" (Scott & Gouge, 2019, p. 183). Approaching theory in these ways, I have worked to build rhetorical enactments as both sense-making and interventional—a methodology for understanding lived experiences and improving them. Specifically, rhetorical enactments shift our focus from perspectives and representations toward practices, which potentially has key interventional ramifications for patients. Kelly Pender (2018) aptly pointed out that the "turn to enactment" (a phrase credited to John Law) is interventional itself insofar as focusing on enactments orients us toward practices that "participate in the making, and unmaking, and remaking of realities" with the goal to "intervene . . . rather than describe or tell" (p, 73).

As I mentioned at the beginning of this article, current practices within the treatment and care for folks with ostomies overwhelming focus on attitudes, opinions, and perspectives about ostomies. With approaches that privilege language as representational and objects as ontologically fixed, the primary (if not, the only) interventional pathway is to tell patients to have a better attitude, to think, talk about, and perceive their ostomies differently. If the ostomy is ontologically stable or inaccessible, and representations of ostomies are the only thing that make meaning out of ostomies, then intervention targets how ostomies are represented. For example, to move from ostomy as parasite to ostomy as self becomes a matter of having a more positive perspective. According to this framework, it really is "all in the patient's head"; if patients can just think or talk about their ostomies more optimistically, maybe their relationship with the ostomy, and consequently their quality of life, will improve. Certainly, attitude and perspective play a role, but perhaps this isn't the best or most productive way to help patients move from one entanglement with their ostomy to another.

As an alternative theory, rhetorical enactments point to intervention in patient *practices* rather than patient perspectives, moving the locus of blame and agency away from patients' thoughts and attitudes toward a more diverse constellation of practices. With an attendant focus on practices and the entities that are staged through practice, rhetorical enactments shift the interventional target to the practices themselves. We might ask: How do the practices that stage ostomy as parasite differ from those that stage the ostomy as self? If different practices stage different ostomies, then changing practices (more so than attitudes) might better help patients who wish to wish to transform their lived experiences with their ostomy. Toward this end, rhetorical enactments theory might better equip RHM scholars to understand how patients are engaged with entities like the ostomy and disease and to use the insights of RHM to best contribute to the lives of the patient ethnographers to whom we are fortunate enough to listen.

References

Barad, Karen. (2003). Posthumanist performativity: Toward an understanding of how matter comes to matter. *Signs: Journal of Women in Culture and Society, 28*(3), 801–831.

Barad, Karen. (2007). *Meeting the universe halfway: Quantum physics and the entanglement of matter and meaning.* Duke University Press.

Bethea, Shawntel. (2016, November 18). Why I'm so thankful for my ostomy. https:// themighty.com/2016/11/feeling-thankful-for-my-ostomy-as-a-woman-with-ulcerative-colitis/

Booher, Amanda. K. (2010). Docile bodies, supercrips, and the plays of prosthetics. *IJFAB: International Journal of Feminist Approaches to Bioethics, 3*(2), 63–89.

Card, Daniel, Kessler, Molly, & Graham, S. Scott. (2018). Representing without representation: A feminist new materialist exploration of federal pharmaceutical policy. In Amanda K. Booher & Julie Jung (Eds.), *Feminist rhetorical science studies: Human bodies, posthumanist worlds.* (pp. 183–204). Southern Illinois University Press.

Centers for Disease Control and Prevention (2015, May 15). CDC: Tips from former smokers: Julia's ad. [Video file]. https://www.youtube.com/watch?v=3q80UdOdP7o

Graham, S. Scott, & Herndl, Carl. (2013). Multiple ontologies in pain management: Toward a postplural rhetoric of science. *Technical Communication Quarterly, 22*(2), 103–125.

Graham, S. Scott. (2015). *The politics of pain medicine: A rhetorical-ontological inquiry.* University of Chicago Press.

Graham, S. Scott, Kessler, Molly, Kim, Sang-Yeon, Ahn, Seokhoon, & Card, Daniel. (2018). Assessing perspectivalism in patient participation: An evaluation of FDA patient and consumer representative programs. *Rhetoric of Health & Medicine, 1*(1), 58–89.

Grossman, Jessica. (2013, January 30). 13 years of being different: Bag-Mitzvah edition. http://uncoverostomy/org/2016/01/30/13-years-of-different-bag-mitzvah-edition/

Gutsell, Margaret, & Hulgin, Kathleen. (2013). Supercrips don't fly: Technical communication to support ordinary lives of people with disabilities. In Lisa Melonçon (Ed.), *Rhetorical accessibility: At the intersection of technical communication and disability studies* (pp. 84–94). Baywood.

Hardin, Marie Myers & Hardin, Brent. (2004). The 'supercrip'; in sport media: Wheelchair athletes discuss hegemony's disabled hero. *Sociology of Sport Online-SOSOL, 7*(1).

Harding, Sandra. (2009). Standpoint theories: Productively controversial. *Hypatia, 24*(4), 192–200.

Koerber, Amy, & McMichael, Lonie. (2008). Qualitative sampling methods: A primer for technical communicators. *Journal of Business and Technical Communication, 22*(4), 454–473.

Melonçon, Lisa. (2018). Bringing the body back through performative phenomenology. In Lisa Melonçon & J. Blake Scott (Eds.), *Methodologies for the rhetoric of health and medicine.* (pp. 96–114). Routledge.

Mol, Annemarie. (2002). *The body multiple: Ontology in medical practice.* Duke University Press.

Molloy, Cathryn. (2015). Recuperative ethos and agile epistemologies: Toward a vernacular engagement with mental illness ontologies. *Rhetoric Society Quarterly, 45*(2), 138–163.

Pender, Kelly. (2018). *Being at genetic risk. Toward a rhetoric of care.* Pennsylvania State University Press.

Pflugfelder, Ehren Helmut. (2015). Rhetoric's new materialism: From micro-rhetoric to microbrew. *Rhetoric Society Quarterly, 45*(5), 441–461.

Ringer, Sara. (2012, July 22). Meet Gut Girl, the IBD superhero! http://www.inflamed-and-untamed.com/GutGirl

Scott, S. Blake & Gouge, Catherine (2019). Theory building in the rhetoric of health and medicine. In Andrea Alden, Kendall Gerdes, Judy Holiday, & Ryan Skinnel (Eds.), *Reinventing with theory in rhetoric and writing studies: Essays in honor of Sharon Crowley.* (pp. 181–195). University Press of Colorado, Utah State University Press.

Skiba, Hiedi. (2011, Oct 23). What's in a name? that which we call Wilbur! https://ostomyoutdoors.com/2011/10/23/what's-in-a-name-that-which-we-call-wilbur

Smith, Dylan., Loewenstein, George, Rozin, Paul, Sherriff, Ryan & Ubel, Peter. (2007). Sensitivity to disgust, stigma, and adjustment to life with a colostomy. *Journal of research in personality, 41*(4), 787–803.

Teston, Christa B., Graham, S. Scott, Baldwinson, Raquel, Li, Adria, & Swift, Jessamyn. (2014). Public voices in pharmaceutical deliberations: Negotiating "clinical benefit" in the FDA's Avastin Hearing. *Journal of Medical Humanities, 35*(2), 149–170.

TheDazzleDoll (2017, December 23). #myillnessisnotyourinsult my stoma makes me superwoman, has given me my life back and makes me awesome[.] think before you make a " joke". [Twitter Post]. https://twitter.com/The DazzelDoll/status/812220637703966720

The Ostomy Connection. (2018, January 16). 14 funny remarks from ostomates that will make you LOL. https://ostomyconnection.com/news-and-culture/14-funny-remarks-from-ostomates-that-will-make-you-lol

United Ostomy Association (n.d). Living with an ostomy: FAQs. https://www.ostomy.org/living-with-an-ostomy/

Molly Margaret Kessler is an assistant professor of writing studies at the University of Minnesota, Twin Cities. She specializes in the intersections of rhetoric of health and medicine, lived experiences, medical technologies, and chronic gastrointestinal conditions.

Supplemental Material

The Ostomy Multiple: Towards a Theory of Rhetorical Enactments
Molly Margaret Kessler

PART I: REFLECTION ON THE ORIGINS OF THE ARTICLE

Tis essay stemmed from a several-year project that was focused broadly on the lived experiences of people living with chronic gastrointestinal (GI) conditions, including how they communicate about themselves and their conditions to a variety of audiences and in a variety of contexts. In this research I was driven to see what my rhetorical expertise could bring to GI-related discourses and the people who are most impacted by those discourses (the people who have GI conditions). What shows up in this article is just one slice of this larger project, which included interviews, several hours of observations, and, as this piece discusses, analyses of various public examples and discourses.

This article, specifically, came into being because I kept noticing that entities like "ostomy" and, more intriguingly, "self" were really different (rhetorically and materially) for different people, and those differences seemed to be deeply connected with individuals' lived experiences with their GI conditions and ostomies. At the same time, when I looked for a rhetorical theory that really explained this complexity, nothing seemed to *quite* describe what I was noticing and also center lived experiences. So this article attempts to bridge that gap, which is to say, it attempts to string together theories (e.g. Mol's praxiography and Barad's intra-activity) I found especially helpful in describing my data and helping me make sense of it.

In particular, the article tries to build the theory of rhetorical enactments as one resource that might first help other rhetoricians examine the rhetoricity and materiality of lived experiences, specifically when it comes to the meaning and boundaries of entities like self or ostomy, and then potentially intervene in those experiences. The theoretical dimension responds to ongoing conversations in the field regarding "new materialisms" and what rhetoricians might add or complicate regarding the recent wave of materiality-oriented scholarship in both rhetorical studies and many allied disciplines like anthropology, sociology, and philosophy. The idea of rhetorical enactments is an attempt to find some middle ground between rhetorical approaches that center language and new materialist approaches that argue language has been given too much due. These tensions leave rhetoricians invested in both language and materiality between a rock and a hard place so rhetorical enactments is my suggestion for a workaround that gives space for both language and materiality to be equally powerful meaning-making entities.

At the same time, the interventional piece of "rhetorical enactments" is especially important to me as a patient-researcher. I live with a chronic GI condition, which is how I came to this research in the first place, so a priority for me in building theory was not only to just add to the many insightful theories that currently exist in a rhetorician's toolkit but also to help myself and others in the field find ways to bring our rhetorical insights to the communities we study. Over the course of collecting data for this project and analyzing the cases, I kept thinking about Julia and the CDC, GutGirl, Vicky Mullholland, and others whose stories and discourses I examined. I kept wondering what I would tell them about my research if they asked me, which led me to really grappling with the non-academic "so what?" of this article. My hope is that rhetorical enactments and this article are generative for readers in pursuing interventions or takeaways for community audiences like patients.

Part II: Description of Research Methods, Findings, and/or Pedagogical Impact

While this article is largely a theoretical piece, there is a robust dataset that undergirds the claims I make. At the time of writing, I had conducted nine interviews with people living with ostomies and related chronic gastrointestinal (GI) conditions. I had also conducted over 200 hours of ethnographic observations at an annual event for people with ostomies and GI conditions. And, as the article shows, I also conducted textual analysis on publicly available discourse including tweets, blogs, TV commercials, and news stories. My dataset was diverse in this way because I wanted to get both a broad view (in terms of different kinds of discourses and patient perspectives) and intimate view (in terms of patients' stories and lived experiences) of what it is like to live with an ostomy or GI condition and make meaning of those conditions and related experiences.

Much of this data doesn't show up in a thorough or concrete way in this article, which is certainly a limitation, but it was also a necessary move I had to make in order to keep the article focused on the theory building that I set out to do. The original draft of this article was several thousand words longer because it was trying to be both an empirical article reporting specific findings *and* a theory building piece. I learned through the revision process that I couldn't do both at the same time and do either well. Therefore, the empirical aspects of my research and a more concrete reporting of findings became less explicit in this particular article (though those data and discussions show up in other publications). That said, I see this theory of rhetorical enactments as one of the most significant contributions or findings from my broader research. Thinking through the idea of rhetorical enactments helped me to later rhetorically theorize lived experiences with stigma, which, as this article alludes, is a significant dimension of lived experiences for people with ostomies and GI conditions.

This research and the importance of patients' lived experiences also directly informs my pedagogy. I'm committed to centering my students' lived experiences as central starting places for learning, because as this article shows, our lived experiences influence how we make meaning in the world. Therefore, while the article itself doesn't discuss pedagogy, I think the idea that entities like self are staged *through* lived experience and *with* other entities like language, embodied forces (like an ostomy), and contexts is relevant and applicable to classroom spaces. It's been especially helpful for me to think through my own research with Christina Cedillo's (2018) "critical embodiment pedagogy." This article itself is also one I teach in graduate seminars on the rhetoric of health and medicine and in undergraduate courses on health writing or medical rhetoric. In graduate seminars, I frame this article as part of an ongoing disciplinary conversation regarding materiality and the publicly engaged or interventional capacities that rhetorical theory offers. In undergraduate courses, I focus especially on the analysis presented in this article and invite students to think through how an understanding that lived experiences shape rhetorical situations might influence the ways we write and communicate about health and medicine topics. For example, I might ask students how they would suggest the CDC revise Julia's commercial with the insight of rhetorical enactments in mind or I might invite students to create public awareness materials about ostomies based on the understanding that ostomies might rhetorically show up for different people as self, parasite, cyborg, or companion, which are *very* different audience dimensions that make for a tricky rhetorical situation. I think the theory and analysis in this article present a complicated but rich set of examples and ideas for students to contemplate as they learn about rhetorical theory and its application for writing in health and medical contexts.

Part III: Discussion Questions

1. In what other cases or contexts/for what other conditions or lived experiences might rhetorical enactments be a productive analytic?

How might additional applications of rhetorical enactments expand or complicate this theory?

2. What affordances and constraints emerge when rhetoricians, specifically of health and medicine, treat research participants as their own ethnographers? What method/ological considerations or questions emerge when research participants are engaged in this way?

3. What pedagogical implications might rhetorical enactments have for rhetoric and composition teachers? What lessons, assignments, or discussions might this article be appropriate and for what purpose(s)?

4. How might (if possible) rhetorical enactments be used to advance social justice? Could rhetorical enactments be used for intersectional analyses and/or other rhetorical approaches that take a more effective or explicit critical approach?

www.ingramcontent.com/pod-product-compliance
Lightning Source LLC
Chambersburg PA
CBHW021651230426
43668CB00008B/585